2015年ネパール・ゴルカ地震災害調査報告書

Reconnaissance Report on
the 2015 Nepal Gorkha Earthquake

2016年8月

日本建築学会

Architectural Institute of Japan (AIJ)

ご案内

本書の著作権・出版権は（一社）日本建築学会にあります．本書より著書・論文等への引用・転載にあたっては必ず本会の許諾を得てください．

Ⓡ〈学術著作権協会委託出版物〉

本書の無断複写は，著作権法上での例外を除き禁じられています．本書を複写される場合は，学術著作権協会（03-3475-5618）の許諾を受けてください．

一般社団法人　日本建築学会

© 2016
by Architectural Institute of Japan

All rights reserved. No part of this book may be reproduced in any form or by any means, without permission in writing from the publisher.

AIJ
5-26-20, Shiba, Minato-ku, Tokyo, Japan
Printed in Japan, 2016

序

　今回の震災で亡くなられた方々に深く哀悼の意を表するとともに，被災された方々に衷心よりお見舞い申し上げ，一日も早い被災地の復興を切に望みます．

　現地時間の2015年4月25日午前11時56分頃（現地時刻）に，ネパールの首都カトマンズの北西約77km，震源深さ15kmの地点を中心にマグニチュードMw 7.8の地震が発生した．ネパール政府の発表によれば，この地震により，8,787人が亡くなり，20,000人が被災した．また，500,000棟の建物および4,000棟の官公庁建物，8,200棟の学校建物が被害を受けた．さらに本震の直後に発生した余震（Mw 6.9, Mw 6.7, Mw 7.3）によりネパール中心部の被災者は増大した．多くの建物で甚大な被害が発生し，主に鉄筋コンクリート造建物と組積造建物が被害を受けた．そこで，日本建築学会災害委員会では，現地の被害調査および日本の耐震技術の応用の可能性について調査を実施することを計画した．日本側の調査団は，被害の中心となる鉄筋コンクリート造建物や組積造建物を対象としている構造本委員会・鉄筋コンクリート造運営委員会および壁式構造運営委員会の委員や主として組積造建物および鉄筋コンクリート構造の耐震性に関する研究者を中心にして構成し，トリブバン大学（Tribhuvan University），ネパール計画・公共事業省都市開発住宅建築局（DUDBC）をネパール側のカウンターパートとして，共同調査を実施した．

　本調査の目的は，次の8項目とした．
1) 地震動の概要を把握し，余震観測を実施する
2) 被災地域の地形・地質を把握する
3) ネパールの建築構造・基礎構造の基準と関連規定，施工方法の現状を把握する
4) 首都カトマンズを中心とした建物の被害概要を把握する
5) 世界遺産など歴史都市の被害状況を把握する
6) 人的被害状況に関する情報を収集する
7) 適切な個別被害事例を選択し，被害状況を解析する
8) 被害原因を推定して実務上の教訓あるいは必要な研究項目を整理する

本報告書はこのようにして得られた調査結果を取りまとめたものである．

　現地調査においては，上記カウンターパートの他に，地方行政庁などの多くの機関，建物所有者，建設関係団体，被災者の皆さんの多大なご協力を頂いた．ここに記して感謝の意を表するとともに，ネパールの地震災害軽減の一助となることを切に願うものである．

2016年8月

日本建築学会
2015年ネパール・ゴルカ地震災害調査委員会

Preface

We, first of all, would like to express our heartfelt condolence to all the people who lost their lives during the 2015 Gorkha earthquake in Nepal and would like to extend our deep sympathy to all the affected people during this disaster. We hope, pray and wish to bring them hope of light as well as ease and fast recovery from the pain of loss.

A strong earthquake of Mw 7.8 hit central Nepal on April 25th, 2015 at around 11:56 am according to the Nepal local time. The hypocenter was estimated at 77 km northwest of Kathmandu with the depth of about 15 km. It is reported from the publicity of Nepal Government that this disaster caused 8,787 casualties and 20,000 injured, and damages to around 500,000 buildings, 4,000 government offices and 8,200 school buildings. Also, immediate aftershocks with Mw 6.9, Mw 6.7 and Mw 7.3 further enhanced the damage and casualties at the central areas of Nepal. Most of the affected buildings in this earthquake were reinforced concrete (RC) and masonry buildings. Therefore, the disaster investigation committee of AIJ initiated to send the reconnaissance team to Nepal. The AIJ team members were selected in co-operation with research committee on structure, managing committees on reinforced concrete and box-shaped wall structure to conduct reconnaissance survey and possibility of application of Japanese seismic evaluation methodology giving the priority to researches on RC framed and masonry structures with the purpose to reduce disaster losses in future. The site survey and related further research were conducted in collaboration with the counterparts of Nepal, selected from Tribhuvan University (TU) and Department of Urban Development and Building Construction (DUDBC) with the following research objectives, such as:

1) to identify the characteristics of the earthquake motions and carry out the aftershock observation,
2) to estimate the topographical and geological features of affected areas,
3) to collect information on the building standard, design and construction practice of Nepal,
4) to observe the damages to buildings in Kathmandu valley,
5) to record the damages to the world heritages in the historical areas,
6) to collect information regarding the casualties,
7) to select and analyze the damages to representative buildings,
8) to estimate the causes of the damages and compile the lessons in practice and necessary research items,

The outcome of the collaborative investigation with above objectives has been compiled in this volume.

Last but not the least, we would like to express our deep gratitude to number of institutions such as local government agencies, building owners, construction related organizations and disaster victims in addition to above mentioned counterparts, for their kind cooperation and contributions to the course of our investigation. We, again, pray for faster recovery from the 2015 Gorkha earthquake and also strongly hope that this research report will work as milestone for the reduction of possible disaster due to future earthquakes in Nepal.

August, 2016

Reconnaissance Committee for the 2015 Nepal Gorkha Earthquake
Architectural Institute of Japan

2015年ネパール・ゴルカ地震災害調査報告書
調査委員会委員名簿
― （五十音順・敬称略） ―

災害委員会
委員長　壁谷澤寿海
幹　事　五十田 博　　市古太郎　　川辺秀憲　　北山和宏
委　員　（略）

2015年ネパール・ゴルカ地震災害調査委員会
委員長　楠　浩一
幹　事　真田靖士　　日比野陽
委　員　大西直毅　　河野　進　　大窪健之　　柏　尚稔　　田尻清太郎
　　　　中村聡宏　　中村孝也　　中村友紀子　毎田悠承　　前島彩子
　　　　李　日兵　　Krishna Kumar Bhetwal

調査協力
安藤尚一　　一柳昌義　　笹谷　努　　重藤迪子　　高井伸雄　　多幾山法子
花里利一　　藤田香織　　三宅弘恵　　村上ひとみ　Bijukchhen Subeg
Nagendra Ray Yadav　　Krishna Kumar Bhetwal

Reconnaissance Report on the 2015 Nepal Gorkha Earthquake
Committee Members

Disaster Investigation Committee
Chair	Toshimi Kabeyasawa		
Secretaries	Hiroshi Isoda	Taro Ichiko	Hidenori Kawabe
	Kazuhiro Kitayama		
Members	(omitted)		

Reconnaissance Committee for the 2015 Nepal Gorkha Earthquake
Chair	Koichi Kusunoki		
Secretaries	Yasushi Sanada	Yo Hibino	
Members	Naoki Onishi	Susumu Kono	Takeyuki Okubo
	Hisatoshi Kashiwa	Seitaro Tajiri	Akihiro Nakamura
	Takaya Nakamura	Yusuke Maida	Yukiko Nakamura
	Ayako Maejima	Yuebing Li	Krishna Kumar Bhetwal

Cooperating Individuals
Shoichi Ando	Masayoshi Ichiyanagi	Tsutomu Sasatani
Michiko Shigefuji	Nobuo Takai	Noriko Takiyama
Toshikazu Hanazato	Kaori Fujita	Hiroe Miyake
Hitomi Murakami	Bijukchhen Subeg	Nagendra Ray Yadav
Krishna Kumar Bhetwal		

執筆者 / Authors

1章 はじめに
　　　壁谷澤寿海　　楠　浩一　　真田靖士　　日比野陽
2章 地震の概要
　　　高井伸雄　　重藤迪子　　三宅弘惠　　Bijukchhen Subeg　　一柳昌義
　　　笹谷　努
3章 地形・地質
　　　高井伸雄　　柏　尚稔
4章 基礎構造
　　　柏　尚稔
5章 建物の被害
　　　楠　浩一　　安藤尚一　　Nagendra Ray Yadav　　日比野陽　　中村聡宏
　　　毎田悠承　　大西直毅　　真田靖士　　中村孝也　　中村友紀子
　　　李　日兵　　前島彩子　　田尻清太郎　　楠　浩一　　河野　進　　柏　尚稔
　　　Krishna Kumar Bhetwal
6章 歴史都市の被害状況
　　　真田靖士　　大窪健之　　多幾山法子　　李　日兵　　花里利一　　藤田香織
7章 人的被害
　　　村上ひとみ　　安藤尚一
8章 詳細調査建物の解析
　　　楠　浩一　　毎田悠承
9章 まとめ
　　　楠　浩一　　真田靖士　　日比野陽　　Krishna Kumar Bhetwal
10章 教訓
　　　楠　浩一　　真田靖士　　日比野陽　　Krishna Kumar Bhetwal

Chapter 1　Introductions
　　　Toshimi Kabeyasawa, Koichi Kusunoki, Yasushi Sanada, and Yo Hibino
Chapter 2　Outline of the Earthquake
　　　Nobuo Takai, Michiko Shigefuji, Hiroe Miyake,
　　　Bijukchhen Subeg, Masayoshi Ichiyanagi, and Tsutomu Sasatani
Chapter 3　Characteristics of Surface Layers
　　　Nobuo Takai and Hisatoshi Kashiwa
Chapter 4　Foundation of Buildings in Nepal
　　　Hisatoshi Kashiwa
Chapter 5　Building Damage
　　　Koichi Kusunoki, Shoichi Ando, Nagendra Ray Yadav
　　　Yo hibino, Akihiro Nakamura, Yusuke Maida, Naoki Onishi
　　　Yasushi Sanada, Takaya Nakamura, Yukiko Nakamura, Yuebing Li, Ayako Maejima,
　　　Seitaro Tajiri, Koichi Kusunoki, Susumu Kono,
　　　Hisatoshi Kashiwa and Krishna Kumar Bhetwal

Chapter 6   Damage to Historical Cityies
            Yasushi Sanada, Takeyuki Okubo, Noriko Takiyama, Yuebing Li, Toshikazu
            Hanazato, and Kaori Fujita
Chapter 7   Human Damage
            Hitomi Murakami and Shoichi Ando
Chapter 8   Numerical Analysis
            Koichi Kusunoki and Yusuke Maida
Chapter 9   Concluding Remarks
            Koichi Kusunoki, Yasushi Sanada, Yo Hibino and Krishna Kumar Bhetwal
Chapter 10   Lessons
            Koichi Kusunoki, Yasushi Sanada, Yo Hibino and Krishna Kumar Bhetwal

目 次/ Table of Contents

1 はじめに/ Introductions 1
   1.1 背景/ Background 1
   1.2 調査目的/ Objectives of the Investigation.. 1
   1.3 調査団の構成と調査期間/ Team Members and Duration 2

2 地震の概要/ Outline of the Earthquake 4
   2.1 ネパールとカトマンズの地震環境/ Background 4
   2.2 カトマンズ盆地と盆地内の強震観測/ The Kathmandu Valley and Strong Ground Motion Observation 5
   2.3 強震記録/ Strong Ground Motion Records 8
   2.4 強震観測点の表層の地盤特性/ Shallow Underground Structure 13
   2.5 まとめ/ Summaries 14
   2.6 謝辞/ Acknowledgements 14
   2.7 参考文献/ References 15

3 地形・地質/ Characteristics of Surface Layers 20
   3.1 一般地理の概要/ Outline of Topography in Kathmandu Basin 20
   3.2 表層地盤の特徴/ Chracteristics of Surface Layers 21
   3.3 まとめ/ Summaries 25
   3.4 参考文献/ References 26

4 基礎構造/ Foundation of Buildings in Nepal 27
   4.1 ネパールにおける基礎構造の関係基準/ Nepalese Building Standard about Foundation 27
   4.2 ネパールにおける建物の基礎構造/ Foundation of Buildings in Nepal 27
   4.3 地震後の基礎・地盤の目視踏査結果/ Reconnaissance Results on Soils and Foundations 32
   4.4 まとめ/ Summaries 38
   4.5 参考文献/ References 39

5 建物の被害/ Building Damage 40
   5.1 ネパールの建築基準/ Nepalese Building Standard 40
      5.1.1 はじめに/ Introduction 40

5.1.2 ネパールの建築基準の概要/ Outline of National Building Code in Nepal 40
5.1.3 ネパールの耐震規定/ Nepalese Seismic Codes 45
5.1.4 インドの耐震規定/ Indian Seismic Codes 48
5.2 被害の概要/ Outline of Damage 52
5.2.1 カトマンズ市内の被害/ Damage of Buildings in Kathmandu Valley 52
5.2.2 カトマンズ市外の被害/ Earthquake Damage outside Kathmandu 118
5.2.3 中高層集合住宅/ Mid- to High-rise Apartment Buildings 189

6 歴史都市の被害状況/ Damage to Historical Cities 267

6.1 カトマンズ盆地の世界文化遺産の概要/ Summary of World Heritages in Kathmandu Valley 267
6.2 世界文化遺産の被害/ Damage to World Heritages 268
6.2.1 Kathmandu Durbar Square 269
6.2.2 Patan Durbar Square 274
6.2.3 Bhaktapur Durbar Square 277
6.2.4 Swayambhunath Temple 280
6.2.5 Boudhanath Stupa 284
6.2.6 Pashupatinath Hindu Temple 284
6.2.7 Changunarayan Hindu Temple 287
6.3 世界文化遺産の周辺地域の被害/ Suffered Condition of Residents' Area Surrounding World Heritages 290
6.3.1 Patan Durbar Square の周辺住区の被害/ Suffered Condition of Residents' Area Surrounding Patan Durbar Square 290
6.3.2 Bhaktapur Durbar Square の周辺住区の被害/ Suffered Condition of Residents' Area Surrounding Bhaktapur Durbar Square 304
6.3.3 Dharahara 塔の被害と再建へ向けて想定される課題/ Challenges for the Recontruction of Dharahara Tower 307
6.3.4 謝辞/ Acknowledgements 308
6.3.5 参考文献/ References 308
6.4 歴史都市の被害が示す教訓/ Lessons Learnt from the Damages in Historic Districts 308
6.4.1 7つの世界文化遺産において/ From the Cases of Seven World Curutural Heritage Sites 308
6.4.2 2つの歴史地区において/ From the Cases of Two Histric Districts 309

7 人的被害/ Human Damage 310
7.1 はじめに/ Overall Human Casualty Conditions 310
7.2 人的被害の統計および地理的分布/ Statistics of Human Casualty and Geographical Distribution 311
7.2.1 郡別の人的被害地理的分布/ District-wise Human Casualty Distribution 311
7.2.2 Sindhupalchok 郡の人的被害分布 / Distribution of Human Damage in Sindhupalchok 314
7.2.3 人的被害の年齢性別分布/ Distribution of Human Damage by Age Group and Distinction of Sex 316
7.3 過去の地震との比較/ Comparison with the Past Earthquakes 320
7.3.1 1934 年ネパール・インド国境地震/ 1934 Nepal India Border Earthquake 320
7.3.2 1988 年ネパール・インド国境地震/ 1988 Nepal India Border Earthquake 323
7.4 カトマンズ盆地の都市 （カトマンズ，ラリトプール，バクタプール）/ Municipalities in Kathmandu Valley (Kathmandu, Lalitpur, Bhaktapur) 324
7.5 まとめ/ Summaries 336
7.6 謝辞/ Acknowledgements 337
7.7 参考文献/ References 337

8 詳細調査建物の解析/ Numerical Analysis 339
8.1 解析の概要/ Outline of Analysis 339
8.2 Gongabu 地区の建物 G7/ Building G7 in Gongabu 339
8.2.1 検討建築物/ Target Building 339
8.2.2 解析モデル/ Analysis Model 341
8.2.3 建物性状/ Building Properties 342
8.2.4 検討用入力地震動/ Input Ground Motion 343
8.2.5 解析結果/ Analysis Result 344
8.2.6 まとめ/ Summaries 346
8.3 Building C 346
8.3.1 はじめに/ Introduction 346
8.3.2 材料強度/ Material Properties 363
8.3.3 部材耐力の計算/ Ultimate Strength of Members 364
8.3.4 降伏メカニズム/ Yield Mechanisms 368
8.3.5 外力による仕事量の算定/ Virtual Work Due to External Force 371

  8.3.6 内力による仕事量の算定/ Interior Virtual Work 372

  8.3.7 保有水平耐力計算結果/ Calculated Ultimate Lateral Strength 372

  8.3.8 まとめ/ Summaries 372

 8.4 参考文献/ References 373

9 まとめ/ Concluding Remarks 374

10 教訓/ Lessons 379

2015年ネパール・ゴルカ地震災害調査報告書

Reconnaissance Report on
the 2015 Nepal Gorkha Earthquake

1 はじめに/ Introductions

1.1 背景/ Background

ネパール現地時間の 2015 年 4 月 25 日 11:56 a.m.ごろ，カトマンズ市の北西約 80km，深さ約 10km を震源とする Mw 7.8 (アメリカ地質調査所，以下，USGS という) の地震が発生した．本地震により，カトマンズ市内をはじめ，広範囲において多くの建物に甚大な被害が生じた．度重なる余震も影響し，多くの人が建物外での生活を余儀なくされた．

同年 5 月 12 日 12:51 a.m. (現地時間) 頃には，カトマンズ市から東北東へおよそ 75km，深さ約 15km を震源とする，Mw 7.3 の余震が発生した．これらの地震を原因として，5 月 15 日現在，死者 8,787 人，負傷者 2 万人以上に上っている (ネパール内務省報道官)．余震による二次的な被害を軽減するため，ボランティア組織を中心として，被災建物の被災度区分判定が行われ，数万棟に及ぶ建物が判定された．

この地震を受けて，日本建築学会では，地震発生の翌日の 4 月 26 日より，災害関連メーリングリストを介して，広く本地震に関する情報提供を呼びかけた．その後，5 月 8 日には拡大災害委員会を実施し，災害調査団の派遣の可能性について議論を行い，団長を楠浩一 (東京大学地震研究所) として，災害調査団を現地に派遣することを決定した．

The Gorkha earthquake occurred at 11:56 a.m. (Nepalese Time) having epicenter located around 80 km north-west from Kathmandu City on April 25, 2015 with the magnitude 7.8 Mw (depth: 8.5 km by USGS). Many buildings in its vicinity including Kathmandu city suffered from damages due to the main shock and immediate strong aftershocks. Many people had been forced to evacuate from their houses and stay on streets.

A large aftershock occurred at 12:51 a.m., May 12 having magnitude 7.3 Mw (depth: 15 km by USGS), with epicenter 75km east-north-east from Kathmandu city. The number of casualties and injuries were reported as 8,787 and more than 20,000 by the reporter of the Internal Ministry of Nepal, respectively, as of May 15. Volunteer groups were organized to conduct rapid inspection of damaged buildings to avoid additional human losses due to aftershocks, and thousands of buildings were inspected.

The Architectural Institute of Japan (referred to as AIJ, hereafter) started calling information of the earthquake from April 26 through AIJ mailing list for disaster information. An extended disaster management committee of AIJ was held on April 26 and decide to dispatch an AIJ reconnaissance team to the affected area. Mr. Koichi Kusunoki (Associate Professor, Earthquake Research Institute, The University of Tokyo) was selected as a leader for this reconnaissance survey.

1.2 調査目的/ Objectives of the Investigation

現地災害調査では，1 週間程度の調査期間を想定して，以下をその調査目的として設定した．

- 余震観測による表層地盤特性の把握
    余震観測では，地震発生後比較的早期に被災地を訪れ，地震前から設置していた地震計 4 点に加えて，さらに臨時観測点として 4 点を追加した．
- 中高層鉄筋コンクリート造建物の被害状況の把握と詳細な建物情報の入手
    耐震規定に従って設計された，およそ 10〜18 階建ての鉄筋コンクリート (RC) 造集合住宅のうち，13 団地 38 棟を対象に，被害調査を行うとともに，建物の構造関係資料の収集を行った．また，一部建物では被災度区分判定の適用を試みた．
- カトマンズ市外の被害状況の把握
    低層の組積造，枠組み組積造の学校建物を中心に，その被害状況を調査するとともに，構造図面の入手を試みた．
- カトマンズ市内の被害状況の把握
    Gongabu 地区では，全数調査による被害率の実測を行い，およそ 1,300 棟の建物の被害を分類した．一部建物については，詳細調査を行うとともに，構造図面の入手を試みた．

- 歴史都市の被害状況の把握
    7つの世界遺産では，個別の被害状況を記録するとともに，4つの世界遺産地区でおおよその被害率を実測した．また，立命館大学 GCOE チームが過去に実施した現地での研究成果と被災後の状況比較を行った．
- 人的被害の把握
    人的被害状況に関する情報収集，1934 年に発生したネパール大地震との比較，および被災者へのアンケートに基づく震度調査を実施した．

The objectives of the field investigation with expected duration as one week, were set as follows;
- To investigate the characteristics of the ground surface layers.
- A strong ground motion team visited the affected area soon after the main shock to conduct field measurement with 4 tentative accelerometers in addition to another 4 permanent ones installed before the earthquake.
- To investigate the damage of mid- to high-rise reinforced concrete (referred to as RC, hereafter) buildings and to gather building information.
- The damage of 13 apartment complexes with 38 RC middle- to high-rise apartment buildings, ranges from 10 to 18 stories, were investigated and their building information was gathered. The Japanese damage classification method was applied for some of the buildings.
- To investigate the damage of the buildings outside of Kathmandu city
- Mainly low-rise masonry and infilled brick wall buildings (school) were investigated and their building information was gathered.
- To investigate the damage of the buildings inside of Kathmandu city
- A complete survey of building damage level was conducted in Gongabu district, and then about 1,300 buildings were evaluated. Detailed investigation of some buildings was also carried out.
- To investigate the damage of historical buildings and monuments.
- Damage conditions of 7 world heritages were recorded. The damage ratios of 4 world heritage districts were also measured. The damage condition was also compared with that before the earthquake reported by GCOE team of Ritsumeikan University.
- To investigate the human loss
- A statistic data of human damage was gathered and it was compared with the damage due to 1934 Nepal Earthquake. Seismic intensity was evaluated with questionnaire survey to the affected people.

1.3　調査団の構成と調査期間/ Team Members and Duration

　日本建築学会の主たる調査団は，2015 年 5 月 23 日～30 日をコア調査期間と設定して，現地調査を実施した．それとは別に，地震動チームは 5 月 3 日より，その他 2 グループも現地入りした．調査を実施し，本報告書に調査結果をとりまとめたメンバーを Table 1.3-1 に示す．

Table 1.3-1 Names and durations of reconnaissance team

	氏名 (Name)	所属 (Affiliation)	期間 (Duration)
団長/ Leader	楠　浩一 (Koichi KUSUNOKI)	東京大学地震研究所 (ERI, Univ. of Tokyo)	May 23 – May 30
幹事/ Secretary	真田靖士 (Yasushi SANADA)	大阪大学 (Osaka Univ.)	May 23 – May 31
団員/ AIJ Team Member	日比野陽 (Yo HIBINO)	広島大学 (Hiroshima Univ.)	May 23 – May 30
	河野　進 (Susumu KONO)	東京工業大学 (Tokyo Tech.)	May 23 – June 1
	高井伸雄 (Nobuo TAKAI)	北海道大学 (Hokkaido Univ.)	May 3 – May 9
	田尻清太郎 (Seitaro TAJIRI)	東京大学 (Univ. of Tokyo)	May 23 – May 30
	中村友紀子 (Yukiko NAKAMUAR)	千葉大学 (Chiba Univ.)	May 23 – May 29
	中村聡宏 (Akihiro NAKAMURA)	名古屋大学 (Nagoya Univ.)	May 23 – May 30
	中村孝也 (Takaya NAKAMURA)	千葉大学 (Chiba Univ)	May 23 – May 30
	大西直毅 (Naoki ONISHI)	北海道大学 (Hokkaido Univ.)	May 23 – May 30
	大窪健之 (Takeyuki OKUBO)	立命館大学 (Ritsumeikan Univ.)	May 24 – May 29
	前島彩子 (Ayako MAEJIMA)	明海大学 (Meikai Univ.)	May 28 – May 31
	毎田悠承 (Yusuke MAIDA)	千葉大学 (Chiba Univ.)	May 23 – May 30
	柏　尚稔 (Hisatoshi KASHIWA)	建築研究所 (BRI)	May 23 – May 30
	李　日兵 (Yuebing LI)	大阪大学 (Osaka Univ.)	May 23 – May 31
団員外/ Not AIJ Team Member	村上ひとみ (Hitomi MURAKAMI)	山口大学 (Yamaguchi Univ.)	May 24 – May 30
	安藤尚一(Syoichi ANDO)	政策研究大学院大学 (GRIPS)	May 29 – June 6 June 25 – June 30 July 31 – Aug.12 Oct. 7 – Oct. 20
	多幾山法子 (Noriko TAKIYAMA)	首都大学東京 (Tokyo Metropolitan Univ.)	May 29 – May 31

　5月23〜30日をコア調査期間としたメンバーは，次のようにTeam A〜Team Cの3チームに分かれて，それぞれの調査を実施した．

Team A：中高層鉄筋コンクリート造集合住宅の調査
　　リーダー：楠，メンバー：河野，田尻，柏
Team B：歴史地区，カトマンズ市外の調査
　　リーダー：真田，メンバー：大窪，中村（友），中村（孝），李，前島，Bhetwal
Team C：カトマンズ市内の調査
　　リーダー：日比野，メンバー：中村（聡），大西，毎田

　The main team conducted field investigation between May 23 and May 30. The strong ground motion team visited the site from May 3, and two other teams were conducted field investigations. The member list of AIJ team and this report is on Table 1.3-1. The main team was divided into three sub teams: Team A; Team B; and Team C; as follows;

Team A: for the mid- to high-rise RC apartment buildings
　　Leader: Kusunoki, Members: Kono, Tajiri, and Kashiwa
Team B: for the historical districts and damage outside of Kathmandu city
　　Leader: Sanada, Members: Okubo, Y. Nakamura, T. Nakamura, Lee, Maejima and K. Bhetwal
Team C: for damage in Gongabu district
　　Leader: Hibino, Members: A. Nakamura, Onishi, and Maida

2 地震の概要/ Outline of the Earthquake

(*本章は第43回地盤震動シンポジウムで発表した高井ほか（2015）[2-1]，三宅ほか（2015）[2-2]，および Takai et al. (2016) [2-3]，を基本として再構成したものである．)

(*This section is based on the Takai et al. (2016) [2-3].)

2.1 ネパールとカトマンズの地震環境/ Background

ネパール連邦民主共和国はヒマラヤ山脈の南に沿って位置しており，インド・オーストラリアプレートがユーラシアプレートに衝突を伴いながら低角で陸域に沈み込むことでその造山活動は生じている[2-4]．世界でも有数のプレート衝突速度を有するため，活断層調査[2-5~7]，INDEPTH[2-8]や Hi-CLIMB[2-9]プロジェクト等の構造探査，測地観測[2-10]が行われてきている．この地域では，ヒマラヤ主前縁衝上断層 Main Frontal Thrust: MFT・主境界衝上断層 Main Boundary Thrust: MBT・主中央衝上断層 Main Central Thrust: MCT といったテクトニクスに起因する複数の低角逆断層が形成されており[2-11]，頻発する M7〜8 クラスの地震や Central Seismic Gap と呼ばれる地震の空白域が指摘[2-11,12]されていた中，2015年 Gorkha 地震が Central Seismic Gap の東端で発生した．

2015年4月25日にネパールの首都カトマンズから北西約80 km付近で発生したGorkha地震（Figure 2.1）は，ヒマラヤ衝突帯における陸域のプレート境界地震であり，その規模は，Mw 7.8[2-13]〜7.9[2-14]であった．震源メカニズム解は東西走向・北傾斜の極低角逆断層で，周辺のテクトニクスと整合的である．震源は Gorkha 郡付近の深さ 8.2 km[2-13]であり，断層破壊は東側に約150 km 進行し，首都カトマンズ付近を通過して Sindhupalchok 郡付近まで至ったと推定されている[2-15~21]．また，比較的規模の大きな余震が発生しており，2015年5月12日に Mw 7.3[2-22]の余震が本震震源断層東端で発生した（Figure 2.1）．

首都カトマンズを有するカトマンズ盆地では，これまで近地の地震のみならず，遠地の地震において被害が発生してきた．その要因としては，前述のサイスミシティの高いプレート境界上に位置する都市であることに加えて，メキシコシティーのように湖成堆積盆地[2-23]上に形成されている都市のためである．さらに，近年の爆発的な人口増加に伴う建造物の無秩序な増加により大地震において甚大な被害を及ぼすことが以前より指摘されていた[2-24]．最近では，2011年9月18日にカトマンズから 250 km 以上離れた，インド北東部で発生した Mw 6.9 の地震において，市中心部のレンガ塀が倒壊し，3名の死者が発生している[2-25]．地震防災対策立案の基礎となる強震動評価は，過去の地震被害や地震危険度評価から実施されているものの[2-24,26]，観測記録に基づいた強震動評価はこれまでになされていなかったが，本地震発生時，カトマンズ盆地内には数点の強震観測点が存在していた．本章では，それらにより得られた強震記録を紹介し，その特徴を述べるものであり，震源特性に関しての詳細は三宅ほか(2015)[2-2]を参照されたい．

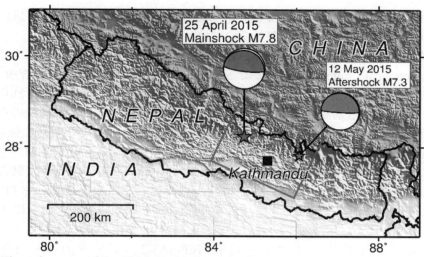

Figure 2.1 The epicenters of the 2015 Gorkha earthquake and Mw 7.3 aftershock are shown by the red star and the blue star respectively. The main shock fault plane shown with the red rectangle and the focal mechanisms are estimated by USGS (2015)[2-13), 2-22)].

The Himalayan mountain range formed by the collision between the Indian and Eurasian plate is regarded as an earthquake prone zone[2-11)]. Therefore many active fault surveys[2-5, 7)], deep underground structure surveys[2-8, 9)] and geodetic survey[2-10)] have been carried out. The Indian Plate under thrusts the Eurasian Plate in this region, and a number of large earthquakes have occurred in the Himalayas[2-11)].

On 25 April 2015, a large Mw 7.8 earthquake occurred along the Himalayan front [2-13)]. This event had a low-angle thrust faulting mechanism and an 8.2 km hypocentral depth [2-13)]. The epicenter was near the Gorkha region (Figure 2.1), 80 km north-west of the Kathmandu Valley, and the rupture propagated eastward from the epicentral region passing through the Kathmandu Valley and reached Sindhupalchok region[2-15 to 21)]. The largest aftershock (Mw 7.3) occurred on 12 May 2015 (Figure 2.1) at Sindhupalchok region.

Kathmandu, the capital city of Nepal is located inside the Kathmandu Valley formed by drying of a paleo-lake similar to Mexico City, and consists of thick soft sediment below the center of city[2-23)]. Hence, the Kathmandu city has been damaged not only by near field earthquakes but also far field earthquakes in the past. In fact, a collapsing of wall killed three people during 18 September 2011 Sikkim earthquake that occurred over 400km away from Kathmandu.

In this section, we will introduce strong ground motion records during the Gorkha earthquake and the largest aftershock.

2.2 カトマンズ盆地と盆地内の強震観測/ The Kathmandu Valley and Strong Ground Motion Observation

カトマンズ盆地はヒマラヤ山間盆地の中でも最も厚く湖成の泥質堆積物が沈積し [2-27)]，ボーリング調査から，泥質層は盆地の中心部に向かって厚くなり，最大厚さ 600 m を超えることが確認されている [2-28)]．重力探査の結果においても，トリブバン国際空港付近に低重力異常が認められ，この重力異常の結果を基に求めた第四紀堆積物の深度分布図（Figure 2.2）[2-29)]からは，厚さ 650 m に達する堆積物の存在が推定されている [2-29)]．これらとボーリングデータに基づいて作成された南北に切る模式地質断面（Figure 2.3）を併せて見ると，盆地中央部の最も堆積層が深い地域に市街地が形成されていることが理解できる [2-27)]．その他，単点微動の移動観測により，H/V スペクトル比のピーク周期の分布を盆地内で求め，堆積層深さを議論した研究においては，重力探査の結果等と整合性が高い [2-30)]としているが，堆積層の S 波速度は明示されていない．このようにい

くつかの堆積層深さ，速度構造に関する検討はなされているものの，強震動評価に用いることが可能な3次元の速度構造は現時点で存在していない．

本地震発生時，カトマンズ盆地には強震観測点として，ネパール産業省鉱山地質局（DMG）の National Seismological Center（NSC）による DMG 観測点[2-31]と米国地質調査所（USGS）による米国大使館内に設置された KATNP 観測点[2-32]が公のものとして存在し，それらで強震記録が得られている．NSC による基盤岩観測点を含めたカトマンズ盆地外の強震記録の有無は確認できていない．上記 2 点のほか，北海道大学は現地トリブバン大学と共同で 4 点の強震観測点（HU-TU 観測点，Kirtipur：KTP，Tribhuvan Univ.：TVU，Patan：PTN，Thimi：THM）を地下構造モデル構築とそれに基づく強震動評価のために設置しており（Figure 2.4），全地点で強震記録が得られている．観測点は盆地内の東西方向のほぼ一直線上に存在し，西端の観測点 KTP は近傍に岩盤露頭が認められる岩盤サイトである[2-33]．全ての観測点は表層地質分布とともに Figure 2.4 に同時に示した．

観測には，加速度強震計：ミツトヨ社製 JEP-6A3-2，データロガー：白山工業社製 DATAMARK LS-8800 を用い，GPS による時刻校正をおこなっている．現地の電源供給は非常に不安定であり，低電力消費を重視して機器選定を行った．使用している加速度強震計は帯域が狭く，長周期側で観測記録を検討する際は特性の補正が必要となる[2-34]．観測点はトリブバン大学および公共施設の低層 RC 建物の 1 階に設置し，全ての強震計はコンクリート床にアンカーボルトで固定している．2011 年 9 月に設置し，現在まで連続観測を行っている．

観測開始から本地震発生以前には，カトマンズから半径約 300 km 以内での M5 クラス以上の地震は数イベントしかないが，その 1 つである 2013 年 6 月 28 日に発生したカトマンズから西に約 300 km の Rukum 郡で発生した地震（Mw 5.0，深さ 10.0 km）等で記録が得られている．この地震の観測記録では，岩盤上に位置する KTP に対し，堆積層上に位置する TVU，PTN，THM において振幅が大きく，そのスペクトルは，地下構造に起因すると考えられる顕著な差異が観測点間に見られ，KTP からわずか約 1 km に位置する TVU で 0.3-2.0 Hz において，その振幅は KTP の 10 倍以上であった[2-35]．

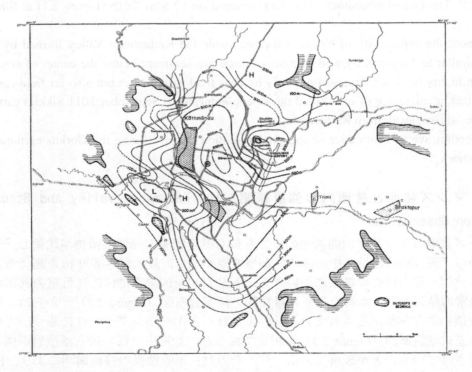

Figure 2.2 Basement contour map in the Kathmandu Valley estimated from the gravity anomaly (after Moribayashi and Maruo (1980)[2-29]).

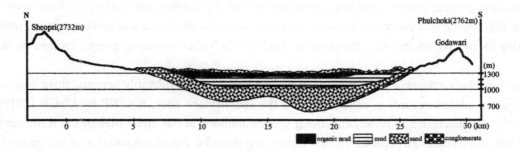

Figure 2.3 Geological cross-section of the Kathmandu Valley based on drilling data (after Sakai *et al.* (2000)[2-27])

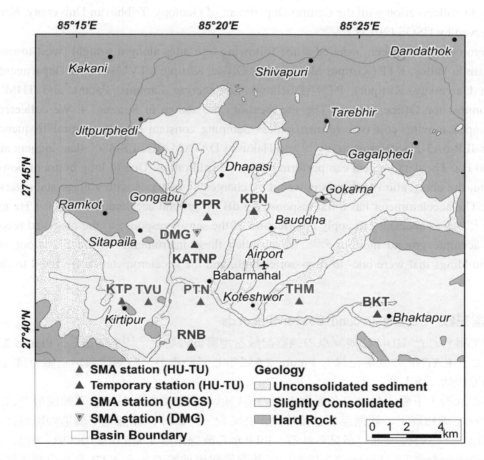

Figure 2.4 Observation sites in the Kathmandu Valley with geological formations (modified from Shrestha *et al.* (1980)[2-36]). Strong motion accelerometer (SMA) stations are divided into HU-TU (Hokkaido University and Tribhuvan University), USGS and DMG sites. Temporary stations of HU-TU are also plotted.

Previous studies indicated an uneven basement topography of the valley with many undulations [2-29, 30]. Figure 2.2 shows the basement contour map[2-29] based on gravity anomaly distribution. The valley is surrounded by mountains on all sides and is filled with soft lake sediments of Plio-Pleistocene origin [2-23]; the thickness of the sediments is more than 650 m in the central part of the valley [2-27, 29] (Figure 2.3). The principal factor associated with the significant damage is considered to have been the responses of soft lake sediments during seismic motion.

Considering these tectonic and site conditions within the Kathmandu Valley, we have established an array of four strong motion observation stations (one rock site and three sedimentary sites; Figure 2.4) in the valley to understand the site effects of the Kathmandu Valley to strong ground motion on September 2011.

Although the earthquake vulnerability of Kathmandu was considerably serious, there were only two official seismometers recording earthquakes on the sedimentary sites; KATNP by USGS (2015)[2-32] and DMG [2-31]. We succeeded in observing strong ground motions at our array sites in the Kathmandu Valley during this devastating earthquake. In this report, we describe the characteristics of the ground motions observed in the Kathmandu Valley and perform a simple examination of the long-period valley response in the frequency domain. Finally, we discuss the velocity response spectra for the horizontal ground motions. Data used in this report include the ground motions observed by the Faculty of Engineering, Hokkaido University in collaboration with the Central Department of Geology, Tribhuvan University, Nepal, and also those observed by USGS (2015)[2-32].

Accelerometers have been installed at the following four sites along a straight (west-to-east) profile in the Kathmandu Valley: KTP (Kirtipur Municipality Office, Kirtipur), TVU (Central Department of Geology, Tribhuvan University, Kirtipur), PTN (Pulchowk Engineering Campus, Patan), and THM (University Grants Commission Office, Thimi). The site locations are shown in Figure 2.4. We collected data using highly damped moving coil type (dimensionless damping constant h ~ 26, natural frequency of 3 Hz) Mitsutoyo JEP-6A3-2 accelerometers [2-34] and Hakusan DATAMARK LS-8800 data loggers at a sampling rate of 100 Hz. The data loggers can perform GPS time calibration. Due to long hours of power outage in Kathmandu, the observation system is powered by chargeable batteries with voltage stabilizers for smooth operation. The accelerometer has a flat response (-3 dB) of ground acceleration from 0.1 Hz to an aliasing frequency [2-34]. It is necessary to apply a correction of the sensor-response to the observed records in order to derive accurate ground motions [2-34]. We installed these instruments on the first floor of reinforced concrete buildings that were one- to four-stories high, and the accelerometers were fixed to the floor with bolts.

2.3 強震記録/ Strong Ground Motion Records

本地震で得られた HU-TU 観測点の強震記録を地震計の特性 [2-34]を補正し，Figure 2.5 に示す．USGS による KATNP の強震記録も Figure 2.5 に示しているが，時刻情報が正確ではない [2-32]ため，適宜初動で併せて示した．

加速度記録の上下動成分は，各観測点での違いはわずかであるが，水平動成分では，岩盤上の KTP に比べて堆積層上の観測点で継続時間が長くなっており，深部地下構造の影響による盆地内での明瞭なサイト特性の違いが見られる．KTP から直線距離 1 km 程度の TVU では，周期約 1 秒程度の後続成分を有し，Figure 2.2 において基盤岩露出地域である KTP から急激に堆積層深度が深くなっていることが影響していると理解できる．また，HU-TU 観測点のうち堆積層深度が最も深い地点と考えられる THM では周期 3〜5 秒の波群を有する．

カトマンズは震央から南東約 80 km[2-13]に位置するが，推定される断層面はカトマンズの真下のプレート境界であり [2-13]，断層最短距離は約 10 km となる．最大加速度は最も大きかった KTP においてベクトル合成値で 250 cm/s^2 であり，既往の距離減衰式 [2-37]を用いた断層最短距離に対する予測値と比較して小さい（Figure 2.6）．本地震による強震記録の短周期成分が地震規模に対して小さいことが堆積層サイトである KATNP で指摘されているが [2-19]，岩盤サイトである KTP における低加速度は，震源特性を知る上で重要である．

得られた記録の水平動の加速度応答スペクトルは，TVU 以外では 1 秒付近の応答値は小さいが，一方で 3〜5 秒程度の応答値が大きく，THM においては 4 秒付近で 500 cm/s^2 に達する

(Figure 2.7). 得られた記録を基に，気象庁震度階相当値を計算すると TVU における震度 6 弱が最大で，日本における被害との相関性が高い 1～2 秒震度：Ip[2-38)]で当地点の Ip=4.87 が最大であり（Table 2.1），現地観測点周辺の被害状況を確認しても 10 %程度の被害率であった．なお，本震の HU-TU 観測点の記録は Takai et al.（2016）[2-3)]とともに公開している．

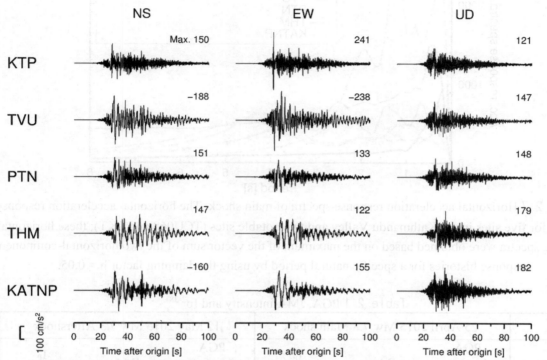

Figure 2.5 Observed ground accelerations at five stations during the 2015-04-25 Gorkha EQ. The HU-TU records have been corrected for the sensor-response; KTP is a rock site and the others are soft sedimentary sites. The waveform records at KATNP were provided by USGS (2015)[2-32)].

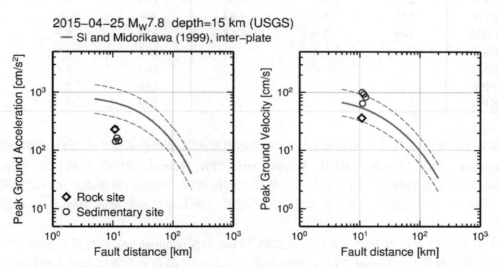

Figure 2.6 Relationships between fault distances and PGAs with GMPE[2-37)].

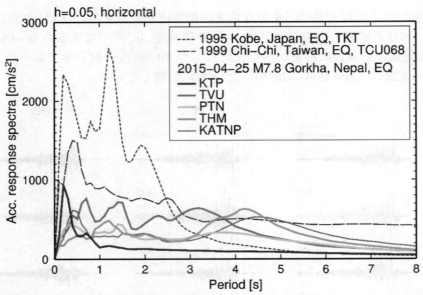

Figure 2.7 Horizontal acceleration response spectra of main shock. The horizontal acceleration response spectra for five sites in the Kathmandu Valley and two notable sites (TCU068 and TKT); these horizontal response spectra were obtained based on the maximum of the vector sum of the two horizontal-component response histories for a specific natural period by using the damping factor h = 0.05.

Table 2.1 PGA, JMA intensity and I_P [2-38)]

Site	25 April 2015 Mw 7.8 Main shock			12 May 2015 Mw 7.3 Aftershock		
	PGA (cm/s^2) (highest in horizontal)	JMA Intensity	I_P Sakai et al. (2004)[2-38)]	PGA (cm/s^2) (highest in horizontal)	JMA Intensity	I_P Sakai et al. (2004)[2-38)]
KTP	241	5 -	4.85	66	4	4.01
TVU	238	6 -	4.87	114	5 -	4.80
PTN	151	5 +	4.83	84	4	4.27
THM	146	5 +	4.65	113	5 +	4.76
BKT	-	-	-	125	5 -	4.79
RNB	-	-	-	189	5 +	5.01
PPR	-	-	-	125	5 -	4.73
KPN	-	-	-	139	5 -	4.85

　本震発生直後の5月2日からカトマンズ盆地内で余震観測を実施するため，臨時観測点を4点（Bhaktapur：BKT, Ranibu：RNB, Panipokhari：PPR, Kapan：KPN）設置した（Figure 2.4）．観測計器は全て定常観測点と同一である．観測点の配置は，既往の観測点が東西に展開されているため，南北へ3点設置し，さらに本震による被害が甚大となった東部Bhaktapurに設置することとした．

　2015年5月12日にカトマンズから東に約70 kmのSindhupalchok郡付近を震央とする，Mw 7.3の最大余震が発生し（Figure 2.1），被害が拡大した．この最大余震による8記録を本震と同様にKATNP観測点の記録とともにFigure 2.8に示す．記録を基に既往の距離減衰式[2-37)]を用いて震源距離と最大加速度・速度の関係を比較すると，予測値にほぼ収まっている（Figure 2.9）．

　加速度応答スペクトルでは，TVU，THMにおいて1秒付近の応答が大きいほか，臨時観測点である南部のRNBにおいて短周期での応答が大きい（Figure 2.10）．一方で，RNBのすぐ北に位置するPTNでの振幅が小さいことは，盆地の断面が模式的はFigure 2.3で単純に示されているも

のの，中央部も含めた盆地内で岩盤が露頭している地点が見られることからも（Figure 2.2），カトマンズ盆地の複雑な構造をうかがい知れる．

最大加速度と気象庁震度相当値，1〜2秒震度：$Ip^{2-38)}$を一覧として，本震と併せて Tabel 2.1 に示した．最大余震では RNB において Ip=5.01 と大きい値となっており，また，THM において Ip は最大余震が本震を上回っており，1秒付近の応答が最大余震で本震より大きいことを反映している．最大余震の震源に最も近い BKT では，本震の記録は無いが，最大余震により建物被害が多く発生しており，THM の記録から見ても，一部破損や半壊の建物がさらに破壊されたことが想像できる．

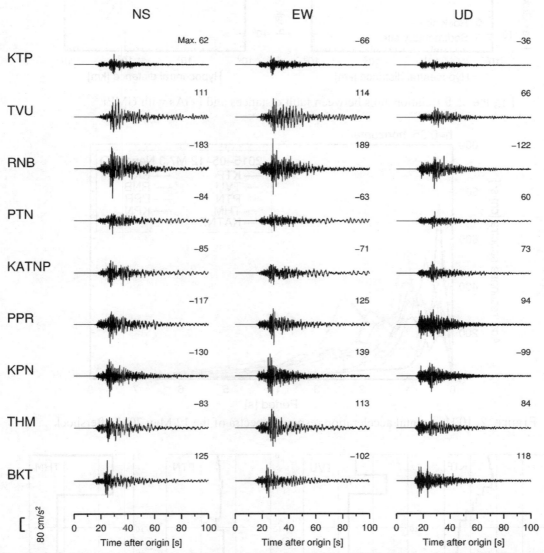

Figure 2.8 Observed ground accelerations during the 12 May 2015 aftershock. The HU-TU records have been corrected for the sensor-response; The waveform records at KATNP were provided by USGS (2015)[2-32].

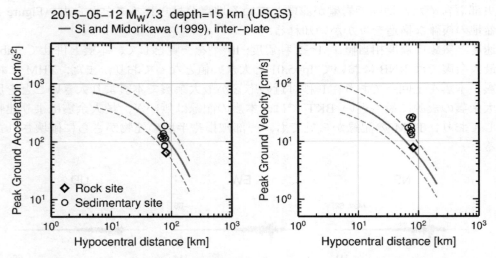

Figure 2.9 Relationships between fault distances and PGAs with GMPE[2-37].

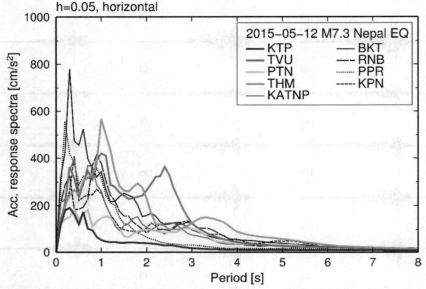

Figure 2.10 Horizontal acceleration response spectra of the 12 May 2015 aftershock

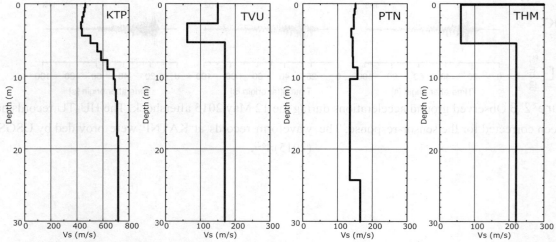

Figure 2.11 Shear wave velocity structure around four stations (after Sawada et al.(2013)[2-33])

— 12 —

The fault size of the 2015 Gorkha earthquake estimated by USGS (2015)[2-13] was about 200 km long and 150 km wide, and it was associated with a large slip area near the Kathmandu Valley. During data processing, we first made a base-line correction by removing the mean determined from a segment of the pre-event part of the original record from the entire original acceleration record. Next, we made the sensor-response correction by using the FFT deconvolution filter. The accelerograms obtained after applying the sensor-response correction are shown in Figure 2.5 along with those from the KATNP (Kanti Path, Kathmandu) station, which is managed by USGS (the records of KATNP lack absolute timing).

The largest peak ground acceleration (PGA: 241 cm/s^2) was recorded on the EW component at the rock site KTP, and the peak amplitude of the horizontal components was 250 cm/s^2 at this station. This large PGA was due to isolated short-period waves at about 30s from the origin time. The horizontal PGA values were compared with those predicted by the ground motion prediction equation (GMPE) for ground accelerations (Figure 2.5). We found that the observed PGA values were smaller than those estimated by the GMPE [2-37]. While the observed PGA values were smaller than the predicted ones, the observed PGV values were slightly larger than the predicted ones (Figure 2.6).

The horizontal accelerograms at the sedimentary sites had long duration with conspicuous long-period oscillations; however, the envelopes of oscillations in waveforms differed from site to site. Conversely, the vertical accelerograms at all the sites were nearly the same and were associated with no long-period oscillations. These observations are characterized by the site effects of the Kathmandu Valley, that is, the valley response.

We calculated horizontal acceleration response spectra (h = 0.05); based on the maximum of the vector sum of the two horizontal-component response histories for a specific natural period. Figure2.7 shows the horizontal acceleration response spectra for the five sites in the Kathmandu Valley. The spectral peaks for the sedimentary sites (TVU, PTN, THM, and KATNP) were considerably larger than that for the rock site KTP in the period range of 3 to 5 s. The strong motion records of the mainshock were made public with Takai et al.(2016) [2-3].

We installed four more stations in the Kathmandu Valley on 2 May 2015 to grasp site condition in the valley (Figure 2.4). On 12 May 2015, Mw 7.3 aftershock occurred at Sindhupalchok region. Figure 2.8 shows the accelerograms of this aftershock. The horizontal PGA and PGV values were compared with those predicted by the GMPE (Figure 2.9). We found that the observed PGA and PGV values were nearly similar to those estimated by the GMPE [2-37]. The horizontal acceleration response spectra (h = 0.05) are shown in Figure 2.10. The observed PGA and JMA Intensity and Ip[2-38] are shown in Table 2.1.

2.4 強震観測点の表層の地盤特性/ Shallow Underground Structure

定常観測点の設置時に表面波探査を実施し，表層の S 波速度構造を得ている．岩盤観測点として設置した KTP では表層に S 波速度が 500 m/s を超える層を有するが，他の観測点では 150 m/s 前後の軟弱な層が分布していることが確認できている [2-33]．澤田ほか [2-33]による各観測点の表層の S 波速度構造を Figure 2.11 に再掲する．これによれば，TVU と THM での最表層は締め固め，コンクリートによる舗装により極めて高速な値が得られているが，その下層では非常に軟弱な層が見られており，本震時に地盤が非線形化して強震記録に影響を与えている可能性が示唆できる．これらの結果と堆積層深度（Figure 2.2）は矛盾していないが，強震動評価を実施するためには，さらに深部の速度構造と 3 次元基盤構造が必要となる．

The shallow subsurface S-wave velocities of the observation sites were investigated by the surface wave method during installation of accelerometers [2-39]. The tested velocity of S-wave at a depth of 10 m was over 700 m/s at the KTP site, but it was less than 200 m/s at the other three sites. These velocities are consistent with the geological formations; KTP is located on a rock and TVU, PTN and THM are located on lake sediments in the valley (Figure 2.4). Figure 2.11 shows shallow S-wave velocity structure detected by Sawada *et al.*(2013)[2-33].

2.5 まとめ/ Summaries

本章では本地震群のカトマンズ盆地における強震記録の特徴を示した．これまでに断層近傍の強震動として取り上げられることの多い既往の強震記録の応答スペクトルを本地震に併せてFigure 2.7 に比較している．比較する記録は，指向性パルスが建物の破壊力として指摘される長周期パルスタイプ[2-40]の 1995 年兵庫県南部地震の JR 鷹取（TKT）の記録と，大変位タイプ[2-40]の1999 年台湾・集集地震の石岡（TCU068）における記録である．本地震の現地観測点周辺の被害状況を確認しても 10 %程度の被害率と低く，1~2 秒における加速度応答値と TKT との比較から見て整合性があると思われるが，3~5 秒における応答では THM と KATNP では TCU068 の応答値を超えている．地表断層の極近傍の TCU068 におけるパルス性地震動では付近の建物の被害率が最大速度に対して非常に小さいこと[2-41, 42]が指摘されている一方で，高層建物が存在すれば被害が発生しているであろうことも指摘されている[2-41]．このカトマンズ盆地内での 3~5 秒における応答は，KATNP の記録を入力地震動として超高層免震建物の応答解析を実施した事例において，甚大な被害の発生を示唆している[2-43]．プレート境界直上の堆積盆地であるカトマンズ盆地での強震記録の特徴を述べたが，構造物によっては非常に深刻な記録も一部含まれ，日本の都市においても考慮すべきか否かはその生成要因の解明が必要であり，それらを明らかにする必要がある．

Since the capital city of Kathmandu in Nepal is located on a sediment-filled valley and was located at a very close distance to the fault plane of the 2015 Gorkha earthquake, a wealth of new information on strong ground motions was captured there. At the rock sites, simple velocity pulses were observed on the three components; these were the result of the tectonic offset. At the sedimentary sites, although velocity pulses were also observed on the vertical component, the horizontal ground velocities showed largely amplified and prolonged long-period oscillations compared with the rock site motions; these resulted from the valley response.

In Figure 2.7, the two notable response spectra TKT (Takatori, Kobe, Japan) and TCU068 (Shigang District, Taichung, Taiwan) are also shown; these were derived from records observed at the near-surface fault. The ground velocity at TKT showed pulse-like motion caused by the directivity effect [2-44] with a large PGV of 161 cm/s during the 1995 Kobe earthquake in Japan. The ground velocity at TCU068 showed a velocity pulse with a large PGV of 400 cm/s and a long pulse width of 8 s during the 1999 Chi-Chi earthquake in Taiwan; the velocity pulse was caused by fling-step motion [2-45]. These records are frequently used for building structure assessments of pulse motion [e.g., 2-46, 47]. The comparison shows that the horizontal long-period oscillations of the Gorkha Earthquake had enough destructive power to damage high-rise buildings.

It will be important for us to understand the factors involved in the long-period valley response observed in the Kathmandu Valley based on the three-dimensional velocity structure of the valley in future studies.

2.6 謝辞/ Acknowledgements

本観測は，トリブバン大学 Megh Raj Dhital 教授，トリブバン大学博士課程学生 Sudhir Rajaure 氏，防災科学技術研究所研究員 Yadab Dhakal 博士，元北海道大学大学院生，澤田耕助・岡島秀樹・宮原有史・青木雅嗣諸氏との協働により設置・実施された．本観測の一部は科研費補助金，平和中島財団，大林財団の助成により実施された．余震記録の収集にあたっては，科学研究費補助金特別研究促進費「2015 年ネパール地震と地震災害に関する総合調査（代表：矢田部龍一）」，JST 国際緊急共同研究・調査支援プログラム（J-RAPID）「余震および微動観測によるカ

トマンズ盆地の地震動被害メカニズムの解明（代表：纐纈一起）」の助成を受けている．強震記録は，KATNP における記録を USGS[2-32]，1999 年台湾・集集地震を台湾交通部中央気象局[2-48]．1995 年兵庫県南部地震を JR 総合技術研究所[2-49]によった．作図の一部は GMT[2-50]による．ここに記して感謝する．

The KATNP record was provided by USGS [2-32]. TCU068 [2-48] and TKT [2-49] records were downloaded from the Center for Engineering Strong Motion Data (CESMD) at http://www.strongmotioncenter.org/ (Accessed 20 October 2015). The KKN4 and NAST data were obtained from the UNAVCO website [2-19]. This study was partly supported by the Grant-in-Aid for Scientific Research (Nos. 23404005 and 15H05793) from the JSPS (Japanese Society for the Promotion of Science) and the MEXT (Ministry of Education, Culture, Sports, Science, and Technology) of Japan, the Heiwa Nakajima Foundation, the Obayashi Foundation, the MEXT program entitled Japan's Earthquake and Volcano Hazards Observation and Research Program, and the Japan Science and Technology (JST) agency's J-RAPID Program. Our grateful thanks to Dr. Y. Dhakal, S. Ghimire, Messrs. K. Sawada, H. Okajima, Y. Miyahara, and M. Aoki for their assistance. We used the Generic Mapping Tools [2-50] for drawing portions of the figures.

2.7　参考文献/ References

2-1) 高井伸雄, 重藤迪子, Bijukchhen, S., 一柳昌義, 笹谷努: 2015 年ネパール Gorkha 地震のカトマンズ盆地における強震動, 第 43 回地盤震動シンポジウム資料, pp.33-38, 2015.

2-2) 三宅弘恵, 小林広明, 纐纈一起, 高井伸雄, 重藤迪子, Bijukchhen, S.: 2015 年ネパール Gorkha 地震の震源破壊過程, 第 43 回地盤震動シンポジウム資料, pp.29-32, 2015.

2-3) Takai, N., Shigefuji, M., Rajaure, S., Bijukchhen, S., Ichiyanagi, M., Dhital, M., Sasatani, T.: Strong ground motion in the Kathmandu Valley during the 2015 Gorkha, Nepal, earthquake, Earth, Planets and Space, 68:10, 2016.

2-4) 在田一則: ヒマラヤのテクトニクス・山脈隆起・気候変動—概論（総特集 ヒマラヤ山脈の構造と上昇過程），月刊地球, 24, pp.227-233, 2002.

2-5) Sapkota, S. N., Bollinger, L., Klinger, Y., Tapponnier, P., Gaudemer, Y., Tiwari, D.: Primary surface ruptures of the great Himalayan earthquakes in 1934 and 1255, Nature Geoscience, 6, pp. 71-76, 2012.

2-6) 熊原康博: ヒマラヤ前縁の活断層運動の地域的差異とその原因, 地理科学, 60, pp.206-212, 2005.

2-7) Tapponnier, P., Zhiqin, X., Roger, F., Meyer, B., Arnaud, N., Wittlinger, G., Jingsui, Y.: Oblique Stepwise Rise and Growth of the Tibet Plateau, Science, 294, pp.1671-1677, 2001.

2-8) Zhao, W., Nelson, K. D., Che, J., Quo, J., Lu, D., Wu, C., Liu, X.: Deep seismic reflection evidence for continental underthrusting beneath southern Tibet, Nature, 366, pp.557-559, 1993.

2-9) Nábělek, J., Hetényi, G., Vergne, J., Sapkota, S., Kafle, B., Jiang, M., Su, H., Chen, J., Huang, B.-S., Team, t. H.-C.: Underplating in the Himalaya-Tibet Collision Zone Revealed by the Hi-CLIMB Experiment, Science, 325, pp.1371-1374, 2009.

2-10) Bilham, R., Larson, K., Freymueller, J.: GPS measurements of present-day convergence across the Nepal Himalaya, Nature, 386, pp.61-64, 1997.

2-11) Avouac, J. P.: Mountain building, erosion, and the seismic cycle in the Nepal Himalaya, Advances in Geophysics, 46, pp.1-80, 2003.

2-12) Bollinger, L., Sapkota, S. N., Tapponnier, P., Klinger, Y., Rizza, M., Van der Woerd, J., Tiwari, D. R., Pandey, R., Bitri, A., Bes de Berc, S.: Estimating the return times of great Himalayan earthquakes in eastern Nepal: Evidence from the Patu and Bardibas strands of the Main Frontal Thrust, Journal of Geophysical Research: Solid Earth, 119(9), pp.7123-7163, 2014.

2-13) USGS: M7.8 - 36km E of Khudi, Nepal, http://earthquake.usgs.gov/earthquakes/eventpage/us20002926#scientific_finitefault:us_us20002926, (2015SEP20 accessed)

2-14) Project, G. C.: http://www.globalcmt.org/, (2015JAN05 accessed)

2-15) Kobayashi, T., Morishita, Y., Yarai, H.: Detailed crustal deformation and fault rupture of the 2015 Gorkha earthquake, Nepal, revealed from ScanSAR-based interferograms of ALOS-2, Earth, Planets and Space, 67:201, 2015.

2-16) Hayes, G. P., Briggs, R. W., Barnhart, W. D., Yeck, W. L., McNamara, D. E., Wald, D. J., Nealy, J. L., Benz, H. M., Gold, R. D., Jaiswal, K. S., Marano, K., Earle, P. S., Hearne, M. G., Smoczyk, G. M.,

Wald, L. A., Samsonov, S. V.: Rapid Characterization of the 2015 Mw 7.8 Gorkha, Nepal, Earthquake Sequence and Its Seismotectonic Context, Seismological Research Letters, 86, pp.1557-1567, 2015.

2-17) Grandin, R., Vallée, M., Satriano, C., Lacassin, R., Klinger, Y., Simoes, M., Bollinger, L.: Rupture process of the Mw = 7.9 2015 Gorkha earthquake (Nepal): Insights into Himalayan megathrust segmentation, Geophysical Research Letters, 42(20), pp.8373-8382, 2015.

2-18) Yagi, Y., Okuwaki, R.: Integrated seismic source model of the 2015 Gorkha, Nepal, earthquake, Geophysical Research Letters, 42(15), pp.6229-6235 , 2015.

2-19) Galetzka, J., Melgar, D., Genrich, J. F., Geng, J., Owen, S., Lindsey, E. O., Xu, X., Bock, Y., Avouac, J. P., Adhikari, L. B., Upreti, B. N., Pratt-Sitaula, B., Bhattarai, T. N., Sitaula, B. P., Moore, A., Hudnut, K. W., Szeliga, W., Normandeau, J., Fend, M., Flouzat, M., Bollinger, L., Shrestha, P., Koirala, B., Gautam, U., Bhatterai, M., Gupta, R., Kandel, T., Timsina, C., Sapkota, S. N., Rajaure, S., Maharjan, N.: Slip pulse and resonance of the Kathmandu basin during the 2015 Gorkha earthquake, Nepal, Science, 349, pp.1091-1095, 2015.

2-20) Fan, W. Y., Shearer, P. M.: Detailed rupture imaging of the 25 April 2015 Nepal earthquake using teleseismic P waves, Geophysical Research Letters, 42(14), pp.5744-5752, 2015.

2-21) Avouac, J. P., Meng, L., Wei, S., Wang, T., Ampuero, J. P.: Lower edge of locked Main Himalayan Thrust unzipped by the 2015 Gorkha earthquake, Nature Geoscience, 8, pp.708-711, 2015.

2-22) USGS: M7.3 - 19km SE of Kodari, Nepal, http://earthquake.usgs.gov/earthquakes/eventpage/us20002ejl#general_summary, (2015JAN10 accessed)

2-23) Dhital, M. R.: : Geology of the Nepal Himalaya, Springer International Publishing 2015.

2-24) 瀬川秀恭, 金子史夫, 大角恒雄, 香川秀郎, 藤谷秀雄: カトマンズ盆地における建物被害想定および耐震性の改善に関する検討, 地域安全学会論文集, pp.183-190, 2002.

2-25) 高井伸雄: 2011年インド北東部地震, 日本建築学会地盤震動小委員会編, 基礎から学ぶ地盤震動, pp.334, 2016.

2-26) 大角恒雄, 金子史夫, 藤谷秀雄: カトマンズ盆地における地震防災のための建築物インベントリ調査と建物分布, 地域安全学会論文集, pp.175-182, 2002.

2-27) 酒井治孝, 藤井理恵, 桑原義博, 野井英明: 古カトマンズ湖の堆積物に記録された気候変動とテクトニックイベント, 地學雜誌, 109, pp.759-769, 2000.

2-28) 名取博夫, 滝沢文教, 本島公司, 永田松三: カトマンズ盆地の天然ガス-その１地質-, 地質ニュース, 312, pp.24-35, 1980.

2-29) 森林成生, 丸尾祐治: ネパール・カトマンズ盆地の基盤地形：重力によるヒマラヤ構造盆地の探査例, 応用地質, 21, pp.80-87, 1980.

2-30) Paudyal, Y. R., Yatabe, R., Bhandary, N. P., Dahal, R. K.: Basement topography of the Kathmandu Basin using microtremor observation, Journal of Asian Earth Sciences, 62, pp.627-637, 2013.

2-31) Bhattarai, M., Adhikari, L. B., Gautam, U. P., Laurendeau, A., Labonne, C., Hoste-Colomer, R., Sèbe, O., Hernandez, B.: Overview of the Large 25 April 2015 Gorkha, Nepal, Earthquake from Accelerometric Perspectives, Seismological Research Letters, 86, pp.1540-1548, 2015.

2-32) USGS: NetQuakes:Station KATNP_NQ_01, 25 April 2015, http://earthquake.usgs.gov/monitoring/netquakes/station/KATNP_NQ_01/20150425061138/, (2015SEP20 accessed)

2-33) 澤田耕助, 岡島秀樹, 高井伸雄, 宮原有史, Dhakal, Y., 重藤迪子, 笹谷努: ネパール国カトマンズ盆地の強震動評価：強震観測点各点の表層地盤のS波速度構造と強震記録, 日本建築学会大会学術講演梗概集, 構造Ⅱpp.239-240, 2013.

2-34) Kudo, K., Kanno, T., Okada, H., Özel, O., Erdik, M., Sasatani, T., Higashi, S., Takahashi, M., Yoshida, K.: Site-specific issues for strong ground motions during the Kocaeli, Turkey, earthquake of 17 August 1999, as inferred from array observations of microtremors and aftershocks, Bulletin of the Seismological Society of America, 92(1), pp.448-465, 2002.

2-35) 重藤迪子, 高井伸雄, 澤田耕助, 青木雅嗣, 一柳昌義, 笹谷努, Dhakal, Y., Dhital, M. R.: ネパール国カトマンズ盆地における強震観測, 日本地震学会講演予稿集秋季大会予稿集, pp.192, 2013.

2-36) Shrestha, O., Koirala, A., Karmacharya, S., Pradhananga, U., Pradhan, P., Karmacharya, R.: Engineering and environmental geological map of the Kathmandu valley, 1998.

2-37) 司宏俊, 翠川三郎: 断層タイプおよび地盤条件を考慮した最大加速度・最大速度の距離減衰式, 日本建築学会構造系論文集, pp.63-70, 1999.

2-38) 境有紀, 神野達夫, 纐纈一起: 震度の高低によって地震動の周期帯を変化させた震度算定法の提案, 日本建築学会構造系論文集, pp.71-76, 2004.

2-39) Takai, N., Sawada, K., Shigefuji, M., Bijukchhen, S., Ichiyanagi, M., Sasatani, T., Dhakal, P., Rajaure, S., Dhital, M. R.: Shallow underground structure of strong ground motion observation sites in the Kathmandu valley, Journal of Nepal Geological Society, 48, pp.50, 2015.

2-40) 久田嘉章: 震源近傍の強震動－改正基準法の設計用入力地震動は妥当か？－, 日本建築学会第29回地盤震動シンポジウム資料, pp.99-109, 2001.

2-41) 林康裕: 台湾・集集地震の活断層近傍における建物被害, 第28回日本建築学会地盤震動シンポジウム資料, pp.53-62, 2000.

2-42) 境有紀, 吉岡伸悟, 纐纈一起, 壁谷澤寿海: 1999年台湾集集地震に基づいた建物被害を予測する地震動の破壊力指標の検討, 日本建築学会構造系論文集, pp.43-50, 2001.

2-43) 林康裕, 杉野未奈: 上町断層帯の地震への対応事例, 日本建築学会大会構造部門PD　大振幅予測地震動を耐震設計にどう取り込むか, pp.27-38, 2015.

2-44) Kamae, K., Irikura, K.: Source model of the 1995 Hyogo-Ken Nanbu earthquake and simulation of near-source ground motion, Bulletin of the Seismological Society of America, 88(2), pp.400-412, 1998.

2-45) Bolt, B., Abrahamson, N.: Estimation of strong seismic ground motions,Lee, W.H.K., Kanamori, H., Jennings, P., Kisslinger, C., International Handbook of Earthquake & Engineering Seismology, pp.983-1001, 2003.

2-46) Hall, J. F., Heaton, T. H., Halling, M. W., Wald, D. J.: Near-source ground motion and its effects on flexible buildings, Earthquake Spectra, 11, pp.569-605, 1995.

2-47) Kalkan, E., Kunnath, S. K.: Effects of fling step and forward directivity on seismic response of buildings, Earthquake Spectra, 22, pp.367-390, 2006.

2-48) Lee, W. H. K., Shin, T. C., Kuo, K. W., Chen, K. C., Wu, C. F.: CWB free-field strong-motion data from the 9-21-1999 Chi-Chi earthquake, digital acceleration files on CD-ROM, Seismology Center, Central Weather Bureau, Taipei, Taiwan, publication version, 9 January 2001, 1, 2001.

2-49) 中村豊, 上半文昭, 井上英司: 1995年兵庫県南部地震の地震動記録波形と分析(II), JR地震情報, 23d, 1996.

2-50) Wessel, P., Smith, W. H. F.: Free software helps map and display data, Eos, Transactions American Geophysical Union, 72, pp.441, 1991.

2-1) Takai, N., Shigefuji, M., Bijukchhen, S., Ichiyanagi, M., Sasatani, T.: Strong Ground Motions in the Kathmandu Basin during the 2015 Gorkha, Nepal, earthquake, The 43th Symposium of Earthquake Ground Motion, 43, pp.33-38, 2015 (in Japanese).

2-2) Miyake, H., Kobayashi, H., Koketsu, K., Takai, N., Shigefuji, M., Bijukchhen, S.: An Orverview of Rupture Processes for the 2015 Gorkha, Nepal, earthquake, The 43th Symposium of Earthquake Ground Motion, 43, pp.29-32, 2015 (in Japanese).

2-3) Takai, N., Shigefuji, M., Rajaure, S., Bijukchhen, S., Ichiyanagi, M., Dhital, M., Sasatani, T.: Strong ground motion in the Kathmandu Valley during the 2015 Gorkha, Nepal, earthquake, Earth, Planets and Space, 68:10, 2016.

2-4) Arita K.: Chikyu Monthly, 24, pp.227-233, 2002 (in Japanese).

2-5) Sapkota, S. N., Bollinger, L., Klinger, Y., Tapponnier, P., Gaudemer, Y., Tiwari, D.: Primary surface ruptures of the great Himalayan earthquakes in 1934 and 1255, Nature Geoscience, 6, pp.71-76, 2012.

2-6) Kumahara, Y.: Regional Difference of Active Faulting along the Himalayan Front and Its Origin, Geographical sciences, 60, pp.206-212, 2005 (in Japanese).

2-7) Tapponnier, P., Zhiqin, X., Roger, F., Meyer, B., Arnaud, N., Wittlinger, G., Jingsui, Y.: Oblique Stepwise Rise and Growth of the Tibet Plateau, Science, 294, pp.1671-1677, 2001.

2-8) Zhao, W., Nelson, K. D., Che, J., Quo, J., Lu, D., Wu, C., Liu, X.: Deep seismic reflection evidence for continental underthrusting beneath southern Tibet, Nature, 366, pp.557-559, 1993.

2-9) Nábělek, J., Hetényi, G., Vergne, J., Sapkota, S., Kafle, B., Jiang, M., Su, H., Chen, J., Huang, B.-S., Team, t. H.-C.: Underplating in the Himalaya-Tibet Collision Zone Revealed by the Hi-CLIMB Experiment, Science, 325, pp.1371-1374, 2009.

2-10) Bilham, R., Larson, K., Freymueller, J.: GPS measurements of present-day convergence across the Nepal Himalaya, Nature, 386, pp.61-64, 1997.

2-11) Avouac, J. P.: Mountain building, erosion, and the seismic cycle in the Nepal Himalaya, Advances in Geophysics, 46, pp.1-80, 2003.

2-12) Bollinger, L., Sapkota, S. N., Tapponnier, P., Klinger, Y., Rizza, M., Van der Woerd, J., Tiwari, D. R., Pandey, R., Bitri, A., Bes de Berc, S.: Estimating the return times of great Himalayan earthquakes in eastern Nepal: Evidence from the Patu and Bardibas strands of the Main Frontal Thrust, Journal of Geophysical Research: Solid Earth, 119(9), pp.7123-7163, 2014.

2-13) USGS: M7.8 - 36km E of Khudi, Nepal, http://earthquake.usgs.gov/earthquakes/eventpage/us20002926#scientific_finitefault:us_us20002926, (2015SEP20 accessed)

2-14) Project, G. C.: http://www.globalcmt.org/, (2015JAN05 accessed)

2-15) Kobayashi, T., Morishita, Y., Yarai, H.: Detailed crustal deformation and fault rupture of the 2015 Gorkha earthquake, Nepal, revealed from ScanSAR-based interferograms of ALOS-2, Earth, Planets and Space, 67:201, 2015.

2-16) Hayes, G. P., Briggs, R. W., Barnhart, W. D., Yeck, W. L., McNamara, D. E., Wald, D. J., Nealy, J. L., Benz, H. M., Gold, R. D., Jaiswal, K. S., Marano, K., Earle, P. S., Hearne, M. G., Smoczyk, G. M., Wald, L. A., Samsonov, S. V.: Rapid Characterization of the 2015 Mw 7.8 Gorkha, Nepal, Earthquake Sequence and Its Seismotectonic Context, Seismological Research Letters, 86, pp.1557-1567, 2015.

2-17) Grandin, R., Vallée, M., Satriano, C., Lacassin, R., Klinger, Y., Simoes, M., Bollinger, L.: Rupture process of the Mw = 7.9 2015 Gorkha earthquake (Nepal): Insights into Himalayan megathrust segmentation, Geophysical Research Letters, 42(20), pp.8373-8382, 2015.

2-18) Yagi, Y., Okuwaki, R.: Integrated seismic source model of the 2015 Gorkha, Nepal, earthquake, Geophysical Research Letters, 42(15), pp.6229-6235, 2015.

2-19) Galetzka, J., Melgar, D., Genrich, J. F., Geng, J., Owen, S., Lindsey, E. O., Xu, X., Bock, Y., Avouac, J. P., Adhikari, L. B., Upreti, B. N., Pratt-Sitaula, B., Bhattarai, T. N., Sitaula, B. P., Moore, A., Hudnut, K. W., Szeliga, W., Normandeau, J., Fend, M., Flouzat, M., Bollinger, L., Shrestha, P., Koirala, B., Gautam, U., Bhatterai, M., Gupta, R., Kandel, T., Timsina, C., Sapkota, S. N., Rajaure, S., Maharjan, N.: Slip pulse and resonance of the Kathmandu basin during the 2015 Gorkha earthquake, Nepal, Science, 349, pp.1091-1095, 2015.

2-20) Fan, W. Y., Shearer, P. M.: Detailed rupture imaging of the 25 April 2015 Nepal earthquake using teleseismic P waves, Geophysical Research Letters, 42(14), pp.5744-5752, 2015.

2-21) Avouac, J. P., Meng, L., Wei, S., Wang, T., Ampuero, J. P.: Lower edge of locked Main Himalayan Thrust unzipped by the 2015 Gorkha earthquake, Nature Geoscience, 8, pp.708-711, 2015.

2-22) USGS: M7.3 - 19km SE of Kodari, Nepal, http://earthquake.usgs.gov/earthquakes/eventpage/us20002ejl#general_summary, (2015JAN10 accessed)

2-23) Dhital, M. R.: Geology of the Nepal Himalaya, Springer International Publishing 2015.

2-24) Segawa, S., Kaneko, F., Ohsumi, T., Kagawa, H., Fujitani, H.: Damage Estimation of Buildings in the Kathmandu Valley and Proposals for Improvement of the Earthquake-Resisting Capacity, Journal of social safety science, pp.183-190, 2002 (in Japanese).

2-25) Takai, N.: Earthquake Ground Motion and Strong Motion Prediction - Key items for learning the basics-, pp.334, 2016 (in Japanese).

2-26) Ohsumi, T., Kaneko, F., Fujitani, H.: A Building Inventory & Building Typology Analysis in the Kathmandu Valley for Earthquake Disaster Assessment, Journal of social safety science, pp.175-182, 2002 (in Japanese).

2-27) Sakai, H., Fujii, R., Kuwahara, Y., Noi, H.: Climatic Changes and Tectonic Events Recorded in the Paleo-Kathmandu Lake Sediments, Journal of Geography, 109, pp.759-769, 2000 (in Japanese).

2-28) Natori, H., Takizawa, F., Motojim, K., Nagata, S.: Chishitsu News, 312, pp.24-35, 1980 (in Japanese).

2-29) Moribayashi, S., Maruo, Y.: Basement topography of the Kathmandu Valley, Nepal : An application of gravitational method to the survey of a tectonic basin in the Himalayas, Journal of the Japan Society of Engineering Geology, 21, pp.80-87, 1980 (in Japanese).

2-30) Paudyal, Y. R., Yatabe, R., Bhandary, N. P., Dahal, R. K.: Basement topography of the Kathmandu Basin using microtremor observation, Journal of Asian Earth Sciences, 62, pp.627-637, 2013.

2-31) Bhattarai, M., Adhikari, L. B., Gautam, U. P., Laurendeau, A., Labonne, C., Hoste-Colomer, R., Sèbe, O., Hernandez, B.: Overview of the Large 25 April 2015 Gorkha, Nepal, Earthquake from Accelerometric Perspectives, Seismological Research Letters, 86, pp.1540-1548, 2015.

2-32) USGS: NetQuakes:Station KATNP_NQ_01, 25 April 2015, http://earthquake.usgs.gov/monitoring/netquakes/station/KATNP_NQ_01/20150425061138/, (2015SEP20 accessed)

2-33) Sawada, K., Okajima, H., Takai, N., Miyahara, Y., Dhakal, Y., Shigefuji, M., Sasatani, T.: Estimation of Strong Ground Motion at Kathmandu basin : Study on Surface Ground Conditions of Strong Motion Stations and Earthquake Record, Summaries of technical papers of annual meeting, pp.239-240, 2013 (in Japanese).

2-34) Kudo, K., Kanno, T., Okada, H., Özel, O., Erdik, M., Sasatani, T., Higashi, S., Takahashi, M., Yoshida, K.: Site-specific issues for strong ground motions during the Kocaeli, Turkey, earthquake of 17 August

2-35) 1999, as inferred from array observations of microtremors and aftershocks, Bulletin of the Seismological Society of America, 92(1), pp.448-465, 2002.
2-35) Shigefuji, M., Takai, N., Sawada, K., Aoki, M., Ichiyanagi, M., Sasatani, T., Dhakal, Y., Dhital, M. R.: Strong motion observation in the Kathmandu basin, Nepal, Programme and Abstracts, the Seismological Society of Japan, Fall Meeting, pp.192, 2013 (in Japanese).
2-36) Shrestha, O., Koirala, A., Karmacharya, S., Pradhananga, U., Pradhan, P., Karmacharya, R.: Engineering and environmental geological map of the Kathmandu valley, 1998.
2-37) Si, H., Midorikawa, S.: New attenuation relationships for peak ground acceleration and velocity considering effects of fault type and site condition, Journal of structural and construction engineering, pp.63-70, 1999 (in Japanese).
2-38) Sakai, Y., Kanno, T., Koketsu, K.: Proposal of Instrumental Seismic Intensity Scale from Response Spectra in Various Period Ranges, Journal of structural and construction engineering, pp.71-76, 2004 (in Japanese).
2-39) Takai, N., Sawada, K., Shigefuji, M., Bijukchhen, S., Ichiyanagi, M., Sasatani, T., Dhakal, P., Rajaure, S., Dhital, M. R.: Shallow underground structure of strong ground motion observation sites in the Kathmandu valley, Journal of Nepal Geological Society, 48, pp.50, 2015.
2-40) Hisada, Y.: Evaluation of the Input Ground Motion of the Revised Seismic Code 2000 Considering the Characteristics of Near-Source Strong Ground Motions, The 29th Symposium of Earthquake Ground Motion, pp.99-109, 2001 (in Japanese).
2-41) Hayashi, Y.: Building Damage near Active Faults in Taiwan, Chi-Chi Earthquake, The 28th Symposium of Earthquake Ground Motion, pp.53-62, 2000 (in Japanese).
2-42) Sakai, Y., Yoshioka, S., Koketsu, K., Kabeyasawa, T.: Investigation on Indices of Representing Destructive Power of Strong Ground Motions to Estimate Damage to Buildings Based on the 1999 Chi-Chi EarthquakeTAIWAN, Journal of structural and construction engineering, pp.43-50, 2001 (in Japanese).
2-43) Hayashi, Y., Sugino, M.: Case study for Uemachi-Fault, AIJ Panel Discussion: Introducing Extreme Predicted Ground Motions to Earthquake Resistant Design, pp.27-38, 2015 (in Japanese).
2-44) Kamae, K., Irikura, K.: Source model of the 1995 Hyogo-Ken Nanbu earthquake and simulation of near-source ground motion, Bulletin of the Seismological Society of America, 88(2), pp.400-412, 1998.
2-45) Bolt, B., Abrahamson, N.: Estimation of strong seismic ground motions,Lee, W.H.K., Kanamori, H., Jennings, P., Kisslinger, C., International Handbook of Earthquake & Engineering Seismology, pp.983-1001, 2003.
2-46) Hall, J. F., Heaton, T. H., Halling, M. W., Wald, D. J.: Near‐source ground motion and its effects on flexible buildings, Earthquake Spectra, 11, pp.569-605, 1995.
2-47) Kalkan, E., Kunnath, S. K.: Effects of fling step and forward directivity on seismic response of buildings, Earthquake Spectra, 22, pp.367-390, 2006.
2-48) Lee, W. H. K., Shin, T. C., Kuo, K. W., Chen, K. C., Wu, C. F.: CWB free-field strong-motion data from the 9-21-1999 Chi-Chi earthquake, digital acceleration files on CD-ROM, Seismology Center, Central Weather Bureau, Taipei, Taiwan, publication version, 9 January 2001, 1, 2001.
2-49) Nakamura, Y., Uehan, F., Inoue, H.: Waveform and its analysis of the 1995 Hyogo-Ken-Nanbu Earthquake (II), JR Earthquake Information, 23d, 1996 (in Japanese).
2-50) Wessel, P., Smith, W. H. F.: Free software helps map and display data, Eos, Transactions American Geophysical Union, 72, pp.441, 1991.

3 地形・地質/ Characteristics of Surface Layers
3.1 一般地理の概要/ Outline of Topography in Kathmandu Basin

　本節では，既往の文献を参照することにより，カトマンズ盆地の表層地盤の特徴を整理する．文献 3-1)によると，カトマンズ盆地は最大で約 500m の深さの粘性土堆積物が蓄積した山間の盆地である．過去に大地震の発生が認められていることから，カトマンズ盆地の地震リスク評価を目的として，世界各国の研究機関によって，カトマンズ盆地の地盤調査および建物調査が実施されている[例えば 3-2)~3-4)]．文献 3-2)では，カトマンズ盆地において高密度の単点微動観測を実施し，微動の卓越周期を読み取ってマッピングしている（Figure 3.1）．これによると，カトマンズ盆地中央部で，1.5~2.0 秒程度の周期の振動が卓越すること，5.2.1 節で調査対象となった Gongabu 地区では，1.0 秒程度の周期の振動が卓越することが読み取れる．文献 3-3)では，カトマンズ盆地内の 5 点でボーリング調査および地質調査が実施され，カトマンズ盆地の地震リスク評価が実施されている．具体的な地質調査の内容は，標準貫入試験，地下水調査，粒度試験，土粒子密度試験，PS 検層となっており，地震動の表層地盤増幅特性の評価および液状化危険度の評価に活用されている．また，シナリオ地震による地震動評価は，せん断波速度 400m/s^2 の工学的基盤を盆地中央で深さ 100m 程度と仮定して実施されている．

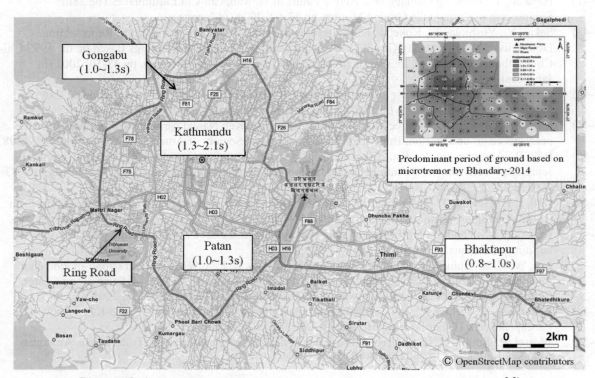

Figure 3.1 Predominant period of representative area in Kathmandu basin[3-2)]

　The characteristics of the surface layer of the Kathmandu basin is described in this section by referring to the previous reports. The basin is filled with thick lacustrine and fluvio-lacustrine sediments, reaching a depth of more than 500m[3-1)]. Due to the major earthquakes occurred in the past, the ground as well as building investigations in the Kathmandu basin have been carried out for the purpose of an earthquake risk assessment by the research organizations of the countries in the world. The study of Ref. 3-2) was conducted a number of single-station microtremor observations in the Kathmandu basin and evaluated the predominant periods distribution of surface layer as shown in Figure 3.1. This map indicates that the central area of the Kathmandu basin has a predominant period of around 1.5 second, and Gongabu area, which is the area investigated by the AIJ reconnaissance team, has around 1.0 second. (Section 5.1.1: reference) The study of Ref. 3-3) was conducted borehole survey and geotechnical investigation with five points in Kathmandu basin and earthquake disaster assessment in the Kathmandu Valley. In this geotechnical investigation, standard penetration tests, groundwater surveys, grain size analyses, density tests of soil particle and PS loggings were conducted to evaluate liquefaction potentiality and surface stratum amplification of seismic amplitude. The engineering bedrock (400m/s) was assumed to exist at the depth of 100m below surface ground.

3.2 表層地盤の特徴/ Chracteristics of Surface Layers

　Figure 3.2-1 に，文献 3-3)に記載されているものと，今回の調査で収集された中高層集合住宅の設計資料に記載された地盤調査データの位置を示す．今回の調査で収集された地盤調査データは，中高層集合住宅の基礎構造の設計および設計用地震荷重の評価を目的としたものである．具体的な地盤調査の内容は，標準貫入試験，地下水調査，粒度試験，土粒子密度試験，圧密試験，液性限界・塑性限界試験，1軸圧縮試験となっている．ネパールの中高層集合住宅の耐震設計はネパールの規定 [3-5]もしくはインドの規定 [3-6]に則って実施されることが多い．どちらの耐震規定でも，設計用地震荷重は表層地盤の特性により，3種類に分類されている．ネパールの規定 (NBC105) では，地盤種別 I：深さ 20m までに基盤（基盤とは1軸圧縮強度が 500kPa 以上の地層と定義）があり，かつ，表層地盤が硬い地盤（粘性土の場合は，非排水せん断強度が 200kPa より大きい地盤，砂質土の場合は N 値が 30 より大きい地盤），地盤種別 II：地盤種別 I および III 以外の地盤，地盤種別 III：基盤が深く表層地盤が厚い地盤，および表層地盤が極めて軟らかい地盤，と定義されている．一方，インドの規定 (IS1893) では，地盤種別 I：N 値が 30 を超える良質な地盤（土質の規定あり），地盤種別 II：N 値が 10～30 の地盤，もしくは，特定の土質で N 値が 15 を超える地盤，地盤種別 III：N 値が 10 より小さな地盤，と定義されている．設計用地震荷重の詳細は 5.1.3「ネパールの耐震規定」および 5.1.4「インドの耐震規定」に示す．

　Figure 3.2-2 に，文献 3-3)に記載されているボーリングデータのうち，カトマンズ盆地内を東西方向に横切るデータの N 値分布およびせん断波速度分布を示す．表層地盤の浅部では砂質の地層が見られるが，深くなるにつれてシルト質の地層が支配的になる．シルト質地層の N 値は 10～20 程度となっており，同地層のせん断波速度は 200m/s 程度となっているものが多く見られる．ただし，日本において杭基礎の支持地盤に用いられる N 値 50 以上の地層は，得られているボーリングデータの深度 30m 以浅にはほとんど認められない．

　Figure 3.2-3 に，文献 3-3)に記載されているもの，および今回の調査で収集された中高層集合住宅設計用のボーリングデータのうち，カトマンズ盆地南部に位置するデータの N 値分布を示す．Figure 3.1-1 によると，この地域での地盤の卓越周期は 1.0 秒程度となっている．該当する中高層集合住宅はいずれも杭基礎となっている．いずれの建物も杭長は 10m 以下となっているが，N 値 50 以上の堅固な地層が認められるものは少ない．

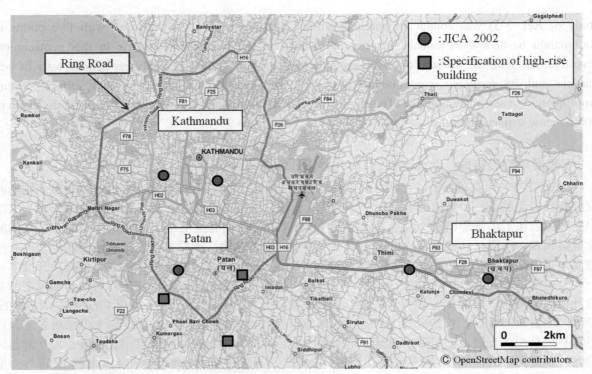

Figure 3.2-1 Locations of borehole survey sites in Kathmandu basin
(JICA-2002[3-3], Specification of high-rise building in Kathmandu)

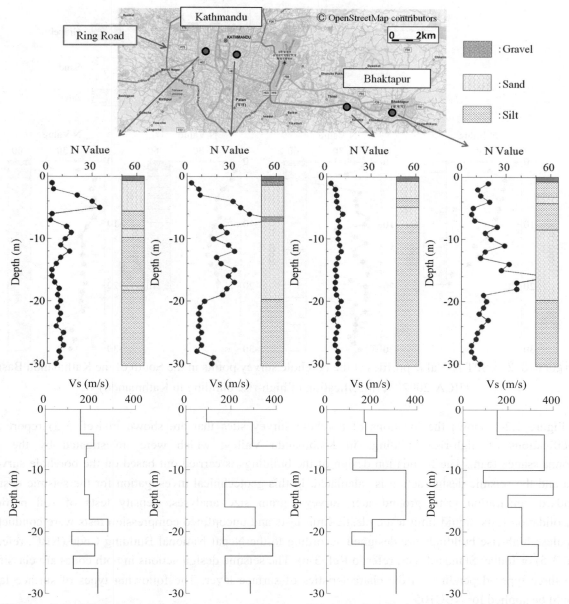

Figure 3.2-2 SPT N-Value and S-wave velocity profiles at the borehole survey points in West-East straight line (JICA-2002[3-3])

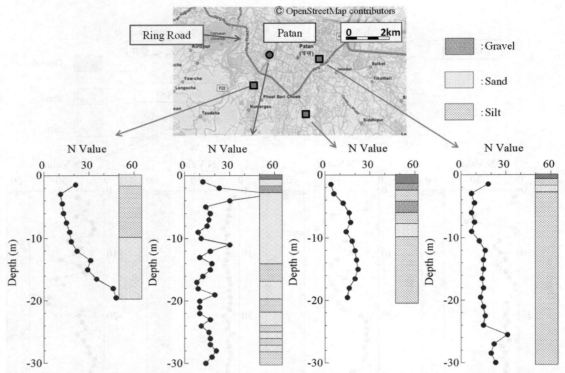

Figure 3.2-3 SPT N-Value profiles at the borehole survey points in the South of the Kathmandu Basin (JICA-2002[3-3], Specification of high-rise building in Kathmandu)

Figure 3.2-1 shows the locations of borehole survey sites that are shown in Ref. 3-3) report and specifications of high-rise buildings in Kathmandu Valley, which were investigated by the AIJ reconnaissance team. The foundation design of the buildings is carried out based on the borehole surveys data and the seismic design action is calculated. In this geotechnical investigation for the seismic design, standard penetration tests, groundwater surveys, grain size analyses, density tests of soil particle, consolidation tests, liquid limit tests, plastic limit tests and unconfined compression tests were conducted. Nepalese high-rise buildings are designed according to the Nepal National Building Code (NBC, refer to Ref. 3-5) or Indian Standards (IS, refer to Ref. 3-6). The seismic design actions in both codes are classified into three types depending on the characteristics of surface layer. The following types of surface layer should be applied for NBC105,

Type I: Rock or Stiff Soil Sites

Sites with bedrock, including weathered rock with an unconfined compression strength greater than 500 kPa, overlain by less than 20 m of (a) very stiff cohesive material with an unconfined compression strength greater than 100 kPa, or (b) very dense cohesionless material with N > 30, where N is the standard penetration (SPT) value.

Type II: Medium Soil Sites

Sites not described as either Type I or Type III

Type III: Soft Soil Sites

Sites where the depth of soil of a particular type exceeds the following values:
(a) Cohesive soil
For $12.5 < c_u \leq 25$: $L_{min} \geq 20$
For $25 < c_u \leq 50$: $L_{min} \geq 25$

For $50 < c_u \leq 100$: $L_{min} \geq 40$

For $100 < c_u \leq 200$: $L_{min} \geq 60$

in which c_u is representative undrained shear strength, L_{min} is minimum depth of soil

(b) Cohesionless soil (sand)

For $4 < N_{spt} \leq 10$: $L_{min} \geq 40$

For $10 < N_{spt} \leq 30$: $L_{min} \geq 45$

For $30 < N_{spt} \leq 50$: $L_{min} \geq 55$

For $50 < N_{spt}$: $L_{min} \geq 60$

in which N_{spt} is representative N value of SPT

(c) Cohesionless soil (gravel)

for $30 < N_{spt}$: $L_{min} \geq 100$

On the other hand, the following types of surface layer should be applied for IS1893,

Type I: Rock or Hard Soil

Well graded gravel and sand gravel mixtures with or without clay binder, and clayey sands poorly graded or sand clay mixtures (GB, CW, SB, SW, and SC which are soil classification according to IS 1498) having $30 < N_{spt}$

Type II: Medium Soil

All soils with $10 < N_{spt} \leq 30$, and poorly graded sands or gravelly sands with little or no fines (SP) with $15 < N_{spt}$

Type III: Soft Soil

All soils other than SP with $N_{spt} < 10$

The details of seismic design action are shown in Section 5.1.3 (NBC) and Section 5.1.4 (IS).

Figure 3.2-2 shows the ground profiles in West-East straight line of the Kathmandu Basin according to Ref. 3-3) reports, which is the SPT N-Value and S-wave velocity. The sandy soil is observed in the shallow part of the surface layer, but the silty strata becomes dominant with increasing deeper. SPT N value of silty stratum is about 10-20, and the shear wave velocity is about 200m/s dominantly. However, the N value above 50 of the strata, which is often the value of supporting layer in Japanese structural design, are observed hardly up to a depth of 30m.

Figure 3.2-3 shows the ground profiles in the South of the Kathmandu Basin according to Ref. 3-3) reports and the specifications, which is the SPT N-Value. The dominant period of the surface layer in this area is about 1.0 second according to Figure 3.1-1. All investigated high-rise building are supported by pile foundation, of which length is less than 10m. However, the N value above 50 of the stratum was not observed.

3.3 まとめ/ Summaries

既往の文献と今回の調査で得られた地盤調査資料に基づいて，カトマンズ盆地の表層地盤の特徴を整理した．カトマンズ盆地内のボーリングデータによると，表層地盤の深い位置になるほど，

シルト質の地層が支配的になり，その N 値は平均で 10〜20 程度であること，GL-30m までに N 値 50 以上の堅固な地盤がほとんど確認できず，表層地盤が厚いことを示した．

The characteristics of the surface layer of the Kathmandu basin is described in this section by referring to the previous reports. The major findings obtained from this study are summarized as follows; the silty strata become dominant with increasing deeper and SPT N value of silty stratum are about 10-20 according to borehole data in the Kathmandu basin, the surface layer is thick and the N value of more than 50 of the stratum is observed hardly.

3.4 参考文献/ References

3-1) Sakai, H, Fujii, R and Kuwahara, Y.: Changes in the depositional system of the Paleo-Kathmandu Lake caused by uplift of the Nepal Lesser Himalayas, J. of Asian Earth Sciences, Vol.20, Issue3, pp.267–276, 2002.

3-2) Bhandary, Netra, P., Yatabe, Ryuichi, Yamamoto, Koji, and Paudyal, Youb, R.: Use of a Sparse Geo-Info Database and Ambient Ground Vibration Survey in Earthquake Disaster Risk Study – A Case of Kathmandu Valley, J. of Civil Eng. Research, Vol.4(3A), pp.20-30, 2014.

3-3) JICA: The Study on Earthquake Disaster Mitigation, Vol.1-5, 2002.

3-4) MoHPP and HMG of Nepal: Seismic Hazard and Risk Assessment for Nepal (liquefaction susceptibility map of the Kathmandu Valley), UNDP/UNCHS (Habitat) Sub-project, NEP/88/054/21.03, 1993.

3-5) Nepal National Building Code (NBC)

3-6) Indian Standards (IS)

4 基礎構造/ Foundation of Buildings in Nepal

4.1 ネパールにおける基礎構造の関係基準/ Nepalese Building Standard about Foundation

　本節では，ネパールにおける基礎構造の関係基準の概略を示す．ネパールの構造規定（NBC108）に基礎構造に関する記述があるが，具体的な規定の記載はなく，インドの構造規定に準じることとなっている．インドの構造規定では，地盤調査－IS:1892, IS:4968 など，土質試験－IS:2720，土質種別－IS:1498，沈下計算－IS:8009，直接基礎－IS:1080, IS:2950，杭基礎－IS:2911，地盤反力係数－IS:9214，が示されており，ネパール建物の基礎はこれらの基準に従って設計されている．

　The structural codes enforced to the foundations of Nepalese buildings are outlined in this section. The guidelines about the foundation structures are described in NBC108, but due to the lack of specific provisions IS code is referred for the detail design. The major structural codes among the Indian Standard (IS) are listed below;

　　　IS:1892, 4968　　　: Ground investigation
　　　IS:2720　　　　　　: Soil test
　　　IS:1498　　　　　　: Soil classification
　　　IS:8009　　　　　　: Settlement calculation of shallow foundation
　　　IS:1080, 2950　　　: Shallow or raft foundation
　　　IS:2911　　　　　　: Pile foundation
　　　IS:9214　　　　　　: Subgrade reaction of soil

The foundation of Nepalese buildings is designed according to these codes.

4.2 ネパールにおける建物の基礎構造/ Foundation of Buildings in Nepal

　ネパール国内の一般住宅には組積造の建物が多いが，そのほとんどは直接基礎と考えられる．文献 4-1)では，直接基礎の施工過程を写真で確認できる（Figure 4.2-1）．また，文献 4-2)のように，Web 上で施工過程が紹介されている事例もある．

　一方，中高層集合住宅には直接基礎のほか，杭基礎も認められる．ただし，杭は摩擦杭となっている場合が多く，杭基礎というよりもパイルド・ラフト基礎にきわめて近い．まず今回の調査で対象とした直接基礎建物の事例を取り上げる．

　Figure 4.2-2 に対象建物の外観と断面図を示す．対象建物は地上 14 階＋塔屋 1 階，地下 1 階（駐車場）の RC 造建物 2 棟からなり，調査結果の詳細は本報告書 5.2.3.13 に示している．建物平面の大きさは東西・南北方向でほぼ同じ長さとなっており，1辺の長さはおおよそ 50m である．Figure 4.2-3 に地下周りの様子を示す．対象建物の地下平面は上部建物躯体よりも大きくなっている．上部建物躯体外側の地下部の天井は人工地盤となっており，その外側に地下外壁を配置している．カトマンズ盆地内の中高層集合住宅の多くは，本対象建物と同様に人工地盤付きの地下階を有しており，そのほとんどが駐車場として利用されている．Figure 4.2-4 に基礎伏図と基礎周りおよび地下外壁周りの詳細断面図を示す．本報告書 5.2.3 にも示すとおり，ネパールの中高層集合住宅の特徴として見られるように，柱が扁平で向きが揃っておらず，平面形状が複雑になっている．対象建物も同様の平面形状となっている．基礎には基礎梁が見当たらず，各フーチングはマットスラブを介して繋がっている．耐圧版の厚さは約 800mm となっている．

　次に，パイルド・ラフト基礎建物の事例を取り上げる．Figure 4.2-5 に対象建物の外観，地下階平面図および柱脚の詳細断面図を示す．対象建物は A 棟，B-I 棟，B-II 棟の 3 棟からなる集合住宅で，Figure 4.2-5 は 3 棟のうち B-II 棟を示している．B-II 棟は地上 15 階，地下 2 階の RC 造建物となっている．調査結果の詳細は本報告書 5.2.3.3 に示している．Figure 4.2-2〜4 の直接基礎建

物と同様に，柱が扁平で向きが揃っていない（Figure 4.2-5(b)参照）ため，平面形状が複雑になっている．また，基礎梁がないことも共通しており，マットスラブの厚さは約 500mm となっている．Figure 4.2-6 に対象建物 B-II 棟の地下階の様子，杭の断面図および杭伏図を示す．対象建物のうち，B-I 棟，B-II 棟のマットスラブ直下に杭が設置されており，多数の杭でマットスラブを支持する基礎形式となっている．杭の合計本数は 318 本と非常に多くなっている．図面上では，対象建物の杭長は約 7m，杭径は 500mm となっており，杭主筋として 16φの鉄筋を 8 本配筋し，8φの鉄筋を 200mm ピッチでフープ筋として配筋している．柱直下の杭の主筋は基礎版内に 850mm の長さで 90°フック付き定着されている．ただし，杭の直上に柱がない場合が多く，実際の杭頭接合部の状態は不明である．本建物における地盤調査は，地表面より深さ 20m 程度まで実施されているが，堅固な地層は確認されておらず，この建物基礎はパイルド・ラフト基礎に該当すると思われる．

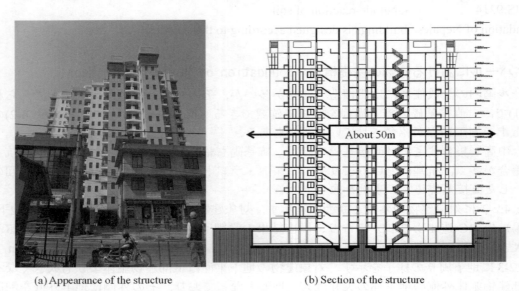

Figure 4.2-1 Foundation work of general house in Nepal (JICA-2002[4-1])

(a) Appearance of the structure　　(b) Section of the structure

Figure 4.2-2 Example of the high-rise building supported by spread foundation

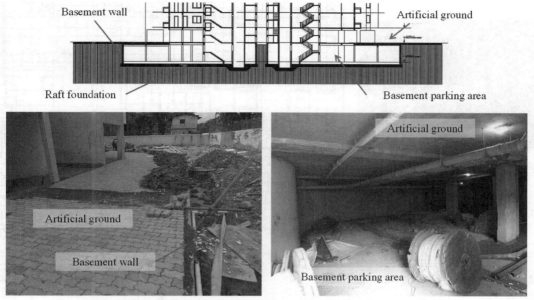

Figure 4.2-3 View of basement and section in Figure 4.2-2

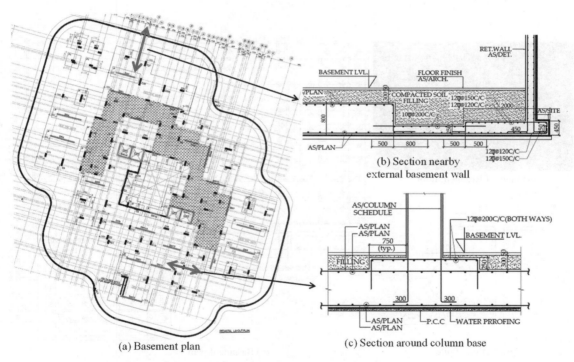

Figure 4.2-4 Detail drawing of basement in Figure 4.2-2

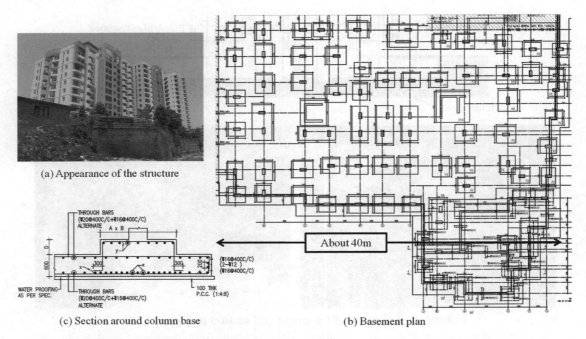

Figure 4.2-5 Example of high-rise building supported by pile foundation

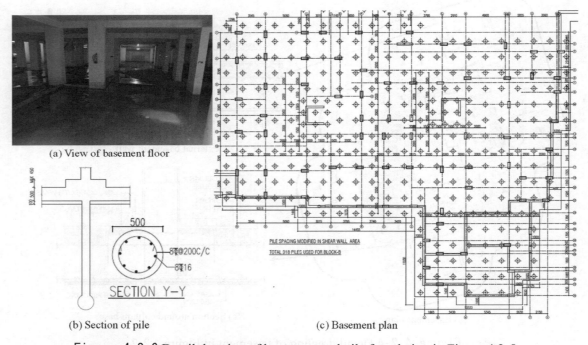

Figure 4.2-6 Detail drawing of basement and pile foundation in Figure 4.2-5

The common low to middle rise buildings in Nepal is masonry buildings generally, and the most of them have spread foundation. A construction process of the spread foundation is confirmed with the photograph in Ref. 4-1) (See Figure 4.2-1). A construction prosess is introduced on Web(refer to Ref. 4-2)).

On the other hand, the pile foundation is accepted other than the spread foundation for high-rise buildings. The piles supported the building by friction, and the foundation type of the structures is almost the piled raft foundation.

At first, the outlines of the spread foundations among the investigated buildings are introduced in this section. The full view and the section of the building is shown in Figure 4.2-2. The complex has two buildings. Both of the buildings have fourteen stories and one basement floor. The basement floor of both buildings are connected and used as a parking space. The details of the investigation are referred to Section 5.2.3.13. The plan of the complex is almost a square shape and the length of a side is about 50m. The view of the basement with the section of the basement floor is shown in Figure 4.2-3. The area of the basement floor is bigger than that of the superstructure. The ceiling of the basement floor at the outside portion of the superstructure is the artificial ground, and the basement walls are arranged at the outside position of the basement floor. The most of the high-rise buildings in Kathmandu basin have the basement floor with the artificial ground, which is used as parking space, similar to this complex. The basement plan, section, and details around basement wall are shown in Figure 4.2-4. The columns are arranged irregularly and the sections of all the columns are narrow. These characteristics are often observed in the high-rise buildings in Nepal, as shown in Section 5.2.3. The footing beam is not observed in the foundation and every footing is connected with the mat slab which has about 800mm thickness.

In the next, the outlines of the piled raft foundations among the investigated building are introduced. The full view, the basement plan and the section around column bases of the basement floor are shown in Figure 4.2-5. The complex has three residential buildings, which are Tower A, B-I and B-II. Figure 4.2-5 shows Tower B-II. Tower B-II is a fifteen stories reinforced concrete building and has two basement floors. The details of the investigation are referred to Section 5.2.3.3. The plan shape is complicated because the columns have narrow shapes and are arranged irregularly (refer to Figure 4.2-5(b)), similar to the building shown in Figure 4.2-2 to 4.2-4. This building has no footing beams and every footing is connected with the mat slab, which has about 500mm thickness. The basement floor plan and section of piles of Tower B-II are shown in Figure 4.2-6. Tower B-I and B-II have piles below the mat slab, and piles support the mat slab. The total number of piles is 318. The Length of piles is about 7m and the diameter of each pile is 500mm. The piles have the longitudinal reinforcements of 8-D16, and hoops of D8@200. The reinforcements of each pile under the column bases are anchored to the mat slab and column by length of 850mm with 90 angle hooks according to the drawings. However, there are many cases without the columns on the piles, and the details of the pile cap connections are not clear. The borehole surveys were carried out at the sites of this complex to the depth of 20m from ground surface, and the strong stratum, which have enough end bearing capacity of pile, is not observed in the survey. It seems that the foundation of this complex corresponds to the piled raft foundation.

4.3 地震後の基礎・地盤の目視踏査結果 / Reconnaissance Results on Soils and Foundations

本節では，今回の調査で対象とした中高層集合住宅において，地震後の基礎周りの状況を目視踏査した結果を示す．

Figure 4.3-1 に，今回の調査で対象となった中高層住宅の位置を示す．中高層集合住宅は，カトマンズ盆地のリングロード周辺に散在している．今回の調査対象とした建物の基礎形式の内訳は，直接基礎の建物が 4 棟，杭基礎の建物が 5 棟，確認できなかったものが 4 棟であった．上部構造を含めた各建物の調査結果の詳細は本報告書 5.2.3 を参照されたい．

Figure 4.3-2 は，本報告書 5.2.3.3 の建物の地下で確認された地下外壁のひび割れおよび地下水の漏水の様子である．この建物は A 棟，B-I 棟，B-II 棟の 3 棟からなる集合住宅で，基礎形式はパイルド・ラフト基礎となっている．写真は B-I 棟の地下駐車場である．敷地は川に隣接しており，地下水位は比較的高いと推察される．地下外壁からの地下水の漏水により，地下の床は水浸しになっていた．Figure 4.3-3 は，同じ建物の盛土に設置された階段で見られたひび割れの様子である．このような盛土の被害は，この建物の敷地内でしばしば見られた．

Figure 4.3-4 は，本報告書 5.2.3.5 の建物における人工地盤表面の様子および地下で確認された人工地盤と柱の接合部の様子である．この建物は地上 11 階建てで，基礎はパイルド・ラフト基礎と思われる．人工地盤表面を見ると，人工地盤と建物の間に段差が生じており，地下の人工地盤と柱の接合部では隙間が生じていることが確認できる．現象として，建物側が下向きに変位したか，人工地盤が上向きに変位したかのいずれかが生じた可能性が考えられる．

Figure 4.3-5 は，本報告書 5.2.3.7 の建物における地下外壁のひび割れの様子である．この建物は地上 18 階，地下 1 階の RC 造建物で，基礎形式はわかっていない．本報告書 5.2.3.5 の建物と同じように，地下外壁から地下水が漏水していた．地下外壁のひび割れが地震前から生じていたかどうかはわかっていない．

Figure 4.3-6 は，本報告書 5.2.3.9 の建物の地下で確認された人工地盤直下の梁のひび割れである．この建物は地上 9 階，地下 2 階（駐車場）の RC 造建物で，基礎形式は直接基礎である．ひび割れは梁の中央付近で生じており，長期荷重によるひび割れと推察される．梁の内法スパンは約 8.0m，スラブ下端から梁下端までは 450mm である．Figure 4.3-7 は，同じ建物の地下駐車場への入口部分で確認された外壁のひび割れの様子である．ひび割れが生じた壁はブロック壁と推察されるが，ブロック壁が擁壁として用いられているのか，観察されたブロック壁の背後に別の擁壁が設置されているのか，詳細はわからない．

Figure 4.3-8 は，本報告書 5.2.3.10 の建物における基礎周りの地盤の様子である．この建物は地上 8〜13 階の RC 造建物 4 棟からなり，基礎形式は直接基礎である．写真は地上 11 階建ての建物周りの様子であり，この建物のみ地下階がある．建物周りの地盤は埋土で，埋土部分が地震後に沈下したと推察される．

Figure 4.3-9 は，本報告書 5.2.3.12 の建物における基礎周りの地盤の様子である．この建物は地上 11〜16 階＋塔屋 1〜2 階，地下 1 階（駐車場）の RC 造建物 4 棟からなり，4 棟は南北に並んでいる．地下の駐車場は 4 棟共通で，地下でつながっている．この建物の基礎はパイルド・ラフト基礎となっており，Figure 4.2-5,6 で示した杭基礎と同様の基礎形式である．写真は最も南側に位置する建物の 1 階柱脚部を撮影したもので，写真手前の柱の直下に地下外壁があり，沈下している地盤は地下外壁外側の埋土と推測される．道路の舗装には変形およびひび割れの形跡が確認できる．地震時の震動によって埋土が沈下したことで，写真のような状況が生じたと推察される．このような埋土の沈下と思われる形跡は，他の集合住宅でもしばしば見られた．

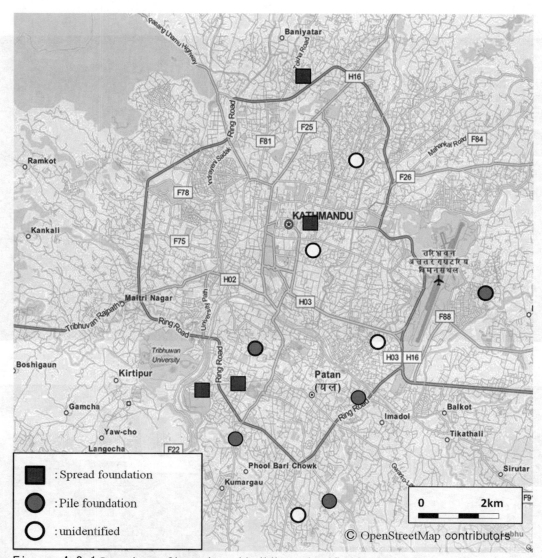

Figure 4.3-1 Locations of investigated buildings classified by foundation type (cf. 5.1.5.1)

Figure 4.3-2 Damage of basement wall and water leakage (cf. 5.2.3.3)

Figure 4.3-3 Damage of embankment (cf. 5.2.3.3)

Figure 4.3-4 Settlement of artificial ground and gap between artificial ground slab and support (cf. 5.2.3.5)

Figure 4.3-5 Damage of a basement wall and water leakage (cf. 5.2.3.7)

Figure 4.3-6 Cracking of a beam of B1 floor caused by long term loading (cf. 5.2.3.9)

Figure 4.3-7 Damage of the basement wall (cf. 5.2.3.9)

Figure 4.3-8 Settlement of the ground around the building (cf. 5.2.3.10)

Figure 4.3-9 Damage of column bases in the 1st floor and deformation of ground around the building (cf. 5.2.3.12)

　　The results of the reconnaissance survey about the foundations of the high-rise residential buildings after the seismic events are outlined in this section.

　　The locations of the surveyed high-rise residential buildings during the reconnaissance are shown in Figure 4.3-1. The high-rise buildings are located around The Ring road in the Kathmandu basin. The number of the buildings with spread foundation is four and the number of buildings with piled raft foundation is five among the surveyed high-rise buildings, respectively. The foundation types of five buildings are uncertain. The details of reconnaissance results of each building are referred to Section 5.2.3.

The shear cracks and groundwater leakage in the basement wall are shown in Figure 4.3-2. This complex (refer to Section 5.2.3.5) has three residential buildings, Tower A, Tower B-I and B-II, and the foundation types of Tower B-I and II are the piled raft foundation. Figure 4.3-2 shows the view of basement floor of Tower B-I. The site of the complex is next to a river and the groundwater table may be high. The basement floor was submerged by the leakage water which leaked from the shear cracks in the basement wall. The damage of the stair, which was constructed at the embankment in the building site, is shown in Figure 4.3-3.

The artificial ground and the connection between the artificial ground and the column support at the basement floor of the complex (refer to Section 5.2.3.5) are shown in Figure 4.3-4. This complex has a 11-story building and the foundation type of the building is the piled raft foundation. The bump between the artificial ground and the structure was observed on the ground surface, and the gap between the artificial ground and the support column was observed in the basement floor. These bump and gap was suggested that either the settlement of the buildings or the uplift of the artificial ground occurred.

The damage of the basement walls of the complex referred to Section 5.2.3.7 is shown in Figure 4.3-5. This complex has two 18-story reinforced concrete buildings and one basement floor. The foundation type of the buildings is uncertain. The groundwater leakage was observed in the basement wall. It is uncertain that the shear cracks of the wall occurred during the earthquake.

The crack on the beam of the artificial ground in the complex (refer to Section 5.2.3.9) is shown in Figure 4.3-6. This building is 9-story reinforced concrete building and has two basement floors used as parking space. The foundation type of this building is the spread foundation. The crack due to the vertical load was observed near the middle portion of the beam. The length of the beam in an inner span is about 8m and the depth is about 450mm. The damage of the basement wall near the entrance to the basement floor is shown in Figure 4.3-7. It seems that the damaged wall is a brick wall. It is uncertain that the brick wall is used as the retaining wall or other concrete wall behind the brick wall is used.

The ground settlement around the foundation of the complex (refer to Section 5.2.3.10) is shown in Figure 4.3-8. This complex has four buildings which are 8-13-story reinforced concrete buildings. The types of the foundation of the buildings are the spread foundations. Figure 4.3-8 shows the 11-story building, which has a basement floor. The settled ground consists of backfill soil and the settlement may be caused by lack of surface compaction.

The ground deformation around the foundation of the complex (refer to Section 5.2.3.12) is shown in Figure 4.3-8. This complex has four buildings which are 8-13-story reinforced concrete buildings. The types of the foundations of the buildings are the piled raft foundations which is the same type as shown in Figure 4.2-5 and Figure 4.2-6. Figure 4.3-8 shows near the column bases of the first floor in the south side building. The basement wall is arranged under the column which is shown in the foreground of the picture. The deformed ground consists of backfill soil around the basement wall. The settlement and cracks are also observed in the pavement. The damage is probably caused by oscillation during the earthquake and are often observed in other complexes.

4.4 まとめ/ Summaries

本章では，ネパールにおける建物の基礎構造に関する関係基準および構造形式を整理した．特に，近年建設数が増加している中高層集合住宅の基礎形式について，直接基礎および杭基礎の代表事例をまとめた．また，今回の調査で見られた中高層集合住宅における基礎・地盤の状況を示した．特に，基礎周りの埋土の沈下がしばしば見られたこと，人工地盤が設けられている例が多

く見られたが，人工地盤の梁に長期荷重によると思われるひび割れが見られたこと，地下外壁のひび割れによる地下水の漏水が見られたことを示した．

The details of the foundations of the Nepalese buildings and codes about the foundations enforced to the Nepalese buildings are described in this section. Especially, the representative examples of the spread foundations and piled raft foundations of the high-rise buildings are shown. Furthermore, the results of the reconnaissance survey on the foundations of the high-rise residential buildings after the seismic events are outlined. The major findings obtained from this study are summarized as follows; the settlement of backfill soil around the foundations is often observed, the most high-rise buildings in Nepal have the artificial ground and the crack was observed near the middle of the beam caused by the vertical load, the shear cracks and groundwater leakage in the basement wall were observed.

4.5 参考文献/ References

4-1) JICA: The Study on Earthquake Disaster Mitigation, Vol.1-5, 2002.
4-2) Website: http://www.geocities.jp/fromhimalaya/kentiku.html

5 建物の被害/ Building Damage

5.1 ネパールの建築基準/ Nepalese Building Standard

5.1.1 はじめに/ Introduction

　ここでは，ネパールの建物に適用される建築に関する基規準，特に耐震規定について概説する．ネパールには，Nepal National Building Code（NBC）が整備されている．基本的にはこの規準に従って設計・確認が行われるが，インドの建築基準（Indian Standard, IS）に従ってもよいこととされている．

　The building codes and standards enforced to the Nepalese buildings, especially seismic codes, are outlined in this section. Basically, Nepalese buildings are designed and their constructions are confirmed in accordance with the Nepal National Building Code (referred to as NBC, hereafter). Indian Standard (IS) is also allowed to be applied for.

5.1.2 ネパールの建築基準の概要/ Outline of National Building Code in Nepal

　1988年のネパール東部地震（M 6.7）で721名の人命が失われ，3万棟の住宅や多くの病院や学校が大きな被害を受け，建築物が中規模の地震でも非常に危険な状態にあることが明らかになった．耐震に関する知識の普及が必要との認識の下，ネパール計画・公共事業省（MPPW 旧住宅・計画省，現 MoUD 都市開発省）の都市開発住宅建築局（DUDBC 旧建築局）において，1993年にネパール国家建築基準(NBC)の原案が作成され，1994年に NBC として公表された．NBC はネパールにとって最初の耐震規定である．DUDBC はその策定時に，国連開発計画(UNDP)および国連人間居住センター（UN-HABITAT）の支援を受けている．

　この NBC は，1998年の「建築法」によって設立された MPPW の建築建設システム改善委員会により，2003年にその施行が決定され，2006年の MPPW の告示により「すべての市およびいくつかの村(VDC)で NBC の施行は義務化する」と官報に掲載された．

　2002年には，NBC の公式の施行に先立って，ラリトプール市（LSMC）がネパールで最初に NBC の施行を開始した．2004年には首都のカトマンズ市（KMC），2006年ダーラン（Dharan）市，2008年イラム（Illam）市，2010年にヘタウダ（Hetauda）市，2011年にビルグンジ（Birgunj）市とビアス（Byas）市，2012年にはブトゥワル（Butwal）市，バラトプール（Bharatpur）市，ドリケル（Dhulikhel）市，バネパ（Banepa）市とパナウティ（Panauti）市が NBC の施行を開始している（2012年までに全191市のうち12市）・その後，2013年にさらに5都市，2014年に9都市が開始して，2014年末現在で計26都市がネパールで NBC を施行している（Table 5.1.2-1, Figure 5.1.2-1 参照）．
また，Table 5.1.2-2 では NBC の成立からその後の展開に至る経緯と施行機関をまとめている．

Table 5.1.2-1 NBC Implementing Municipalities in Nepal

No.	市の名称	Name of Municipality	開始年度 Start in	Nepal year
1.	ラリトプール市	Lalitpur	2002	2059
2.	カトマンズ市	Kathmandu	2004	2061
3.	ダーラン市	Dharan	2006	2063
4.	イラム市	Ilam	2008	2065
5.	ヘタウダ市	Hetauda	2010	2067
6.	ビルグンジ市	Birgunj	2011	2068
7.	ビアス市	Byas		
8.	ブトゥワル市	Butawal	2012	2069
9.	バラトプール市	Bharatpur		
10.	ドゥリケル市	Dhulikhel		
11.	バネパ市	Banepa		
12.	パナウティ市	Panauti		
13.	ポカラ市	Pokhara	2013	2070
14.	ダンガディ市	Dhangadhi		
15.	ゴラヒ市	Ghorahi		
16.	ビラトゥナガル市	Biratnagar		
17.	ダマク市	Damak		
18.	キリトプール市	Kirtipur	2014	2071
19.	マドゥヤプール市	Madyapur		
20.	ビムダッタ市	Bhimdatta		
21.	トゥラシプール市	Tulasipur		
22.	グラリヤナ市	Gulariaya		
23.	プタリバザール市	Putali Bazar		
24.	シダルタナガール市	Siddharthanagar		
25.	トゥリユガ市	Triyuga		
26.	バドゥラプール市	Bhadrapur		

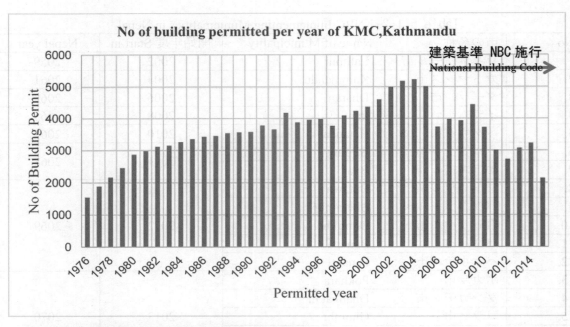

カトマンズ市の建築着工数の推移データ
(GRIPS 修士学生 Nagendra Ray Yadav がネパール語から翻訳しグラフを作成)

Figure 5.1.2-1 Number of Buildings Permitted per year by KMC

Table 5.1.2-2 Legal arrangement and responsible organizations

Legal Mechanism	Responsible organizations	Envisaged role
Building Act 1998 (Rev. 2007)	Building Construction System Improvement Committee	Devise Building Code, facilitate enforcement, disseminate code, monitor implementation, revise NBC code
	MPPW	Approve the Building Code
		Publish notice of mandatory implementation of Building Code
	DUDBC	Implement Building Code in areas outside of Municipal jurisdiction
		Supervise compliance with Building Code
	Municipalities	Ensure compliance with Building Code
Local Self Government Act 1999 (Decentralization Act)	Municipalities	Building permit (does not include provision of Building Code)
	House owners in municipal area	Comply with municipal rules and secure formal building permit before construction
National Building Code 2003	All concerned	Approved NBC
Notice of MPPW in Nepal Gazette (Feb. 13, 2006)	All municipalities, VDCs Districts Head quarter,	Implementation of Building Act

Source: - Building Act-1998, Local Self-governance Act 1999 and NBC-1994

ネパールの建築基準（NBC）は，23に分かれている．最初のNBC 000は，国際的基準の適用を含む一般原則を示している．建築基準の番号とその表題を以下のTable 5.1.2-3に示す．

Table 5.1.2-3 Code number and Code titles of NBC

Code Number	Code Title (GL: Guideline, MRT: Mandatory Rules of Thumb)
NBC 000: 1994	Requirements for State-of the- Art Design
NBC 101: 1994	Materials Specifications
NBC 102: 1994	Unit Weight of Materials
NBC 103: 1994	Occupancy Load
NBC 104: 1994	Wind Load
NBC 105: 1994	Seismic Design of Buildings in Nepal
NBC 106: 1994	Snow Load
NBC 107: 1994	Provisional Recommendation on Fire Safety
NBC 108: 1994	Site Consideration for Seismic Hazards
NBC 109: 1994	Masonry: Unreinforced
NBC 110: 1994	Plain and Reinforced Concrete
NBC 111: 1994	Steel
NBC 112: 1994	Timber
NBC 113: 1994	Aluminum
NBC 114: 1994	Construction Safety
NBC 201: 1994	MRT: Reinforced Concrete Buildings with Masonry infill
NBC 202: 1994	Mandatory Rules of Thumb (MRT): Load Bearing Masonry
NBC 203: 1994	GL for Earthquake Resistant Building Construction: Low Strength Masonry
NBC 204: 1994	GL for Earthquake Resistant Building Construction: Earthen Building (EB)
NBC 205: 1994	MRT: Reinforce Concrete Buildings Without Masonry Infill
NBC 206: 2003	Architectural Design Requirements
NBC 207: 2003	Electrical Design Requirements for (Public Buildings)
NBC 208: 2003	Sanitary and Plumbing Design Requirements.

ネパール建築基準は，さらに対応するネパールの建設産業のタイプによって以下のTable 5.1.2-4のように4つに区分することができる．

Table 5.1.2-4 Classification of NBC as per application

S.N	Type of Building Code			Purpose
1.	International State-of-Art Applicable codes: NBC 000			Applicable to large building structures. The structures must comply with existing international state-of the art building codes
2.	Professionally Engineered Buildings Applicable codes:			Building designed and constructed under supervision of engineers, buildings with plinth area more than 1,000 sq. ft, buildings having more than 3 stories, buildings with span more than 4.5 m and buildings with irregular shapes
	NBC 101	NBC 107	NBC 113	
	NBC 102	NBC 108	NBC 114	
	NBC 103	NBC 109	NBC 206	
	NBC 104	NBC 110	NBC 207	
	NBC 105	NBC 111	NBC 208	
	NBC 106	NBC 112		
3.	Mandatory Rules of Thumb Applicable codes: NBC 201, NBC 202, NBC 205			Buildings of plinth area less than 1,000 sq. ft, less than 3 stories, buildings having span less than 4.5 m and regular buildings designed and constructed by technicians in the areas where professional engineer's service is not available
4.	Guidelines of Remote Rural Building (Low Strength Masonry/Earthen Building)			Building constructed by local masons in remote areas and not more than 2 stories

Source: NNBC 000 - 1994

After 1988 earthquake magnitude of 6.7 Rector Scale in eastern Nepal resulting heavily life loss and numerous buildings including hospitals, schools were severely damaged, it was realized that most of the houses are highly vulnerable to earthquake of moderate intensities due to lack of knowledge of the earthquake safety measures. Nepal government Ministry of Physical Planning and Works (former Ministry of Housing and Physical Planning), and the Department of Urban Development and Building Construction (former Department of Buildings) drew attention for the urgent need of Nepal National Building Code. The draft of National Building Code was prepared in 1993. It was the first official document prepared which deals primarily with matters of earthquake safety of buildings.

The Department of Urban Development and Building Construction (DUDBC) of the Ministry of Physical Planning and Works (MPPW) developed the National Building Code (NBC) in 1993 with the assistance of the United Nations Development Program (UNDP) and United Nations Centre for Human Settlement (UN-HABITAT).

Nepal NBC went into force when the Building Construction System Improvement Committee (established by the Building Act 1998) authorized MPPW to implement the code. The Ministry published a notice in the Gazette in 2006 and the implementation of NBC became mandatory in all Municipalities and later some Village Development Committees (VDCs) in Nepal.

In 2002, prior to the formal entry into force of the code, Lalitpur Sub-Metropolitan City (LSMC) initiated the implementation of NBC, becoming the first Municipality in Nepal to implement the NBC. Kathmandu Metropolitan City (KMC) followed in 2004, Dharan Municipality in 2006, Illam in 2008, Hetauda in 2010, Birgunj in 2011, Byas municipality in 2011, Butwal municipality in 2012, Bharatpur in 2012, Dhulikhel in 2012, Banepa in 2012 and Panauti in 2012. Other municipalities are also applying NBC with the passage of time. In total 12 municipalities started to implement NBC by 2012 within 191 total municipalities in Nepal. Five municipalities in 2013 and nine municipalities in 2014 newly started NBC and in total 26 municipalities are implementing NBC in Nepal at the end of 2014 (Table 5.1.2-1, Figure 5.1.2.-1). Legal arrangement and responsible organizations to implement NBC are given in Table 5.1.2-2.

Nepal National Building Code has 23 parts. The first NBC is '000', which means "Requirements for State of the Art Design" and lays out general provisions of the individual building codes. For clarity, Code number and Code titles of NBC are given in Table 5.1.2-3.

Nepal Building Code is, further, classified as per application in the construction industry of Nepal, which is given in Table 5.1.2-4.

5.1.3 ネパールの耐震規定/ Nepalese Seismic Codes
主要な NBC としては，下記がある．
- ▶ **NBC 105 Seismic design of buildings in Nepal**
- ▶ NBC 114 Construction safety
- ▶ NBC 201 Mandatory rules of thumb, reinforced concrete buildings with masonry infill
- ▶ NBC 202 Mandatory rules of thumb, load bearing masonry
- ▶ NBC 203 Guidelines for earthquake resistant building construction: Low strength masonry
- ▶ NBC 204 Guidelines for earthquake resistant building construction: Earthen Building
- ▶ NBC 205 Mandatory rules of thumb, reinforced concrete buildings without masonry infill

ここでは，主として NBC 105 について概説する．

Major Nepalese seismic codes are listed below;
- ▶ **NBC 105 Seismic design of buildings in Nepal**
- ▶ NBC 114 Construction safety
- ▶ NBC 201 Mandatory rules of thumb, reinforced concrete buildings with masonry infill
- ▶ NBC 202 Mandatory rules of thumb, load bearing masonry
- ▶ NBC 203 Guidelines for earthquake resistant building construction: Low strength masonry
- ▶ NBC 204 Guidelines for earthquake resistant building construction: Earthen Building
- ▶ NBC 205 Mandatory rules of thumb, reinforced concrete buildings without masonry infill

Mainly NBC105 is introduced in this section.

5.1.3.1 適用範囲/ Scope of application
この基準の適用範囲は，床面積が 20m^2 を超える建物，高さ 5m を超える建物，一般の人が用いる用途に供するもの，その他である．逆に，この基準の適用範囲外となる建物は，原子力発電施設などの特殊な建物，橋やダムなどの土木構造物，高さ 90m を超える建物である．

The scope of application of the codes are as follows;
- The buildings that have floor areas greater than 20m^2
- The buildings of which total height is greater than 5m
- The buildings to which the public access

The structures that are out of scope are as follows;
- Special structures such as nuclear power plants
- Civil infrastructure such as bridges and dams
- The buildings of which total heights are greater than 90m

5.1.3.2 応力解析手法/ Analysis Methods
構造物の応力解析は，荷重係数法とモード解析法の 2 つがある．荷重係数法は，地震力を静的荷重として弾性解析を行い，その応力解析結果に係数を乗じて建物の応力を算出する方法である．

また，モード解析法とは，設計用スペクトルから建物の各モードの応答を推定し，その各モードの推定値を重ね合わせることにより求める．40mを超える建物，平面的・立面的不整形建物，水平強度が大きく変化する層がある建物，形状が特異な建物，特殊な重要度係数を用いる建物にはモード解析法を用いる．

The applicable structural analysis methods are 1) the seismic coefficient method and 2) the modal response spectral method. The seismic coefficient method derives design stress of a building as a stress calculated from static linear analysis multiplied by a coefficient. On the other hand, the modal response spectral method derives response of the building as the superposition of the modal responses, which is calculated with the design spectrum. The modal response spectral method should be used for the buildings with the total height of greater than 40m, irregular configurations, abrupt changes in lateral resistance and/or lateral stiffness along with height, and unusual shape, size or importance.

5.1.3.3 構造計算方法/ Design Methods and Load Combinations

構造計算は，許容応力度計算か，終局強度設計のいずれかを用いる．鉄筋コンクリート構造の場合は，終局強度設計を用いることを原則とする．

荷重の組合せは，許容応力度計算では，次のいずれかの組合せで算出される応力の最も大きいものを用いる．

- ▶ DL+LL+E
- ▶ 0.7DL+E
- ▶ DL+SL+E　　DL: Dead Load, LL: Live Load, SL: Snow Load, E: Earthquake Force

一方，終局強度設計では，次のいずれかの組合せで算出される応力の最も大きいものを用いる．

- ▶ DL+1.3LL+1.25E
- ▶ 0.9DL+1.25E
- ▶ DL+1.3SL+1.25E

The working stress method or the limit state method should be applied as the design method. In principle, the limit state method should be applied for reinforced concrete buildings.

As the load combination, the maximum load of the following combinations should be applied for the working stress method.

- ▶ DL+LL+E
- ▶ 0.7DL+E
- ▶ DL+SL+E　　DL: Dead Load, LL: Live Load, SL: Snow Load, E: Earthquake Force

On the other hand, the maximum load of the following combinations should be applied for the limit state method.

- ▶ DL+1.3LL+1.25E
- ▶ 0.9DL+1.25E
- ▶ DL+1.3SL+1.25E

5.1.3.4 設計用地震荷重/ Seismic Design Action

設計用地震荷重は，Equation 5.1.3-1に示す設計用層せん断力係数により求める．

$$C_d = C \cdot Z \cdot I \cdot K \tag{5.1.3-1}$$

ここで，C は基本地震力係数で，周期，または対象としているモードの周期に対して Figure 5.1.3-1 により求める．地盤は3つの種類（Type I～Type III）に分けられており，それぞれ，地盤の硬さ等から決まっている．

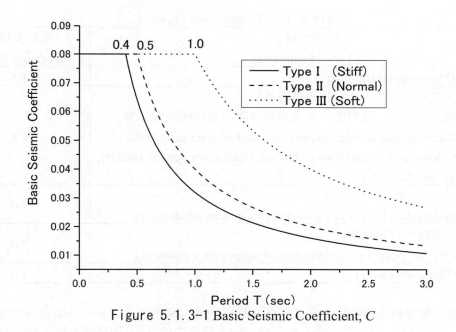

Figure 5.1.3-1 Basic Seismic Coefficient, C

また，Zは地域係数で，Figure 5.1.3-2のように0.8～1.1の値をとる．Katmandu市は1.0である．

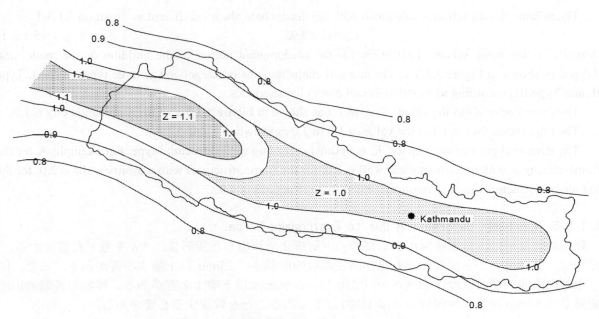

Figure 5.1.3-2 Seismic Zoning Factor, Z

Iは重要度係数でTable 5.1.3-1に示すように，1.0～2.0の値をとる．

Table 5.1.3-1 Importance Factor, I

	建物の種類 (Type of Building)	重要度係数 (Importance factor, I)
(a)	歴史建物 (Monumental Building)	1.5
(b)	地震後も継続使用性が求められる重要建物 　　例：病院，消防署，警察署，緊急車両倉庫，食料保管庫，等 (Essential Facilities that should remain functional after an earthquake 　　Example: Hospital, Fire and Police stations, Emergency vehicle shelters, Food storage structures, etc.)	1.5
(c)	ガスやガソリンの配送システム (Distribution facilities for gas or petroleum products in urban areas)	2.0
(d)	危険物質の支持・貯蔵施設 (Structures for the support or containment of dangerous substances)	2.0
(e)	他の建物 (Other structures)	1.0

K は構造性能係数で構造種別に応じて定義されている．例えば，フレーム構造（耐震壁を有するものも含む）では 1.0，組積造壁を有するフレーム構造では 2.0，組積造や壁式構造など，靭性の低い建物で 4.0 となる．

The seismic design action is calculated with the design base shear coefficient as Equation 5.1.3-1.

$$C_d = C \cdot Z \cdot I \cdot K \quad\quad\quad (5.1.3\text{-}1)$$

Where C is the basic seismic coefficient for the predominant period of the building or the mode, and defined as shown in Figure 5.1.3-1. The site soil characteristics is categorized as three types (Type I, Type II, and Type III) according to its stiffness and other characteristics.

The Zone Factor Z has the value of 0.8 to 1.1 as shown in Figure 5.1.3-2. Z for Kathmandu city is 1.0.

The importance factor, I, has the value of 1.0 to 2.0 as shown in Table 5.1.3-1.

The structural performance factor, K, is defined according to the structural type. For example, K for the frame structures with or without shear wall is 1.0, for the frame structures with masonry walls is 2.0, for the low-ductile structures such as masonry or wall-type structures is 4.0.

5.1.3.5 変形制限/ Deformation Due to Earthquake Force

構造物の変形は，荷重係数法およびモード解析法で算出した変形量に 5/K を乗じた値とする．建物は，敷地境界から少なくとも建物高さの 1/500 倍か，25mm 以上離す必要がある．また，同一敷地内の他の建物とは建物高さの 1/250 倍か，50mm 以上離す必要がある．建物の各階の層間変形量は 60mm 以下，層間変形角は 1/100 以下であることを確認する必要がある．

The deformation of the buildings is calculated as the deformation from the seismic coefficient method or the modal spectral method multiplied by 5/K. The deformation to the boundary should be less than 1/500 of the total height and 25mm. The deformation to the buildings within the site should be less than 1/250 of the total height or 50mm. The maximum inter-story drift angle should be less than 1/100 of the story height and 60mm.

5.1.4 インドの耐震規定/ Indian Seismic Codes

インドの建築基準（Indian Standard, IS）のうち，構造計算に関係する主要な基準を以下に示す．

- ➢ IS456　　Plain and reinforced concrete - Code of practice
- ➢ IS875　　Code of practice for deign loads (other than earthquake) for buildings and structures

- IS1893　Criteria for earthquake resistant design of structures
- IS13920　Ductile detailing of reinforced concrete structures subject to seismic force

IS1893に示されている設計用地震力は，設計用水平地震力係数A_hにより定義されている．

$$A_h = \frac{Z \cdot I \cdot S_a}{2R \cdot g} \tag{5.1.4-1}$$

ここで，
- Z　：地域係数は，0.1，0.16，0.24，0.36の値をとる．
- I　：重要度係数で，1.0 または 1.5 の値をとる．
- R　：応答低減係数で以下の値をとる．
  - 一般的な鉄筋コンクリートフレーム構造　　　　3.0
  - 特殊な鉄筋コンクリートフレーム構造　　　　　5.0
  - 無補強組積造　　　　　　　　　　　　　　　　1.5
  - 一般的な耐震壁構造　　　　　　　　　　　　　3.0
  - 一般的な耐震壁付き鉄筋コンクリートフレーム構造　3.0
- S_a/g：標準応答加速度係数で，Figure 5.1.4-1 による．

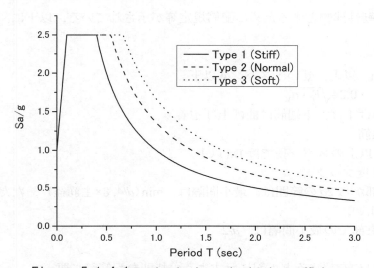

Figure 5.1.4-1 Design horizontal seismic coefficient

$Z=1.0$, $I=1.0$, $R=3.0$で計算したA_hを Figure 5.1.4-2 に示す．短周期領域で，A_hが1.0となり，NBCに比べて大きくなる．

設計方法は終局強度設計で，荷重の組合せは，鉄筋コンクリート造で，次の組合せを検討することとなる．ここで，DL: Dead Load, IL: 積載荷重, EL: 地震荷重である．

- ▶ 1.5(DL+IL)
- ▶ 1.2(DL+IL±EL)
- ▶ 1.5(DL±EL)
- ▶ 0.9DL+1.5EL

また，変形制限は，DL+ELの荷重作用時で層間変形角が1/250以下であることを確認する．

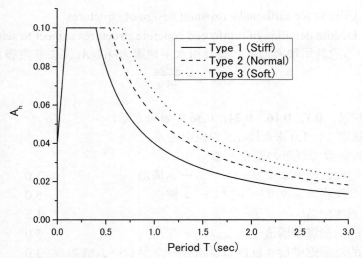

Figure 5.1.4-2 Designing horizontal seismic coefficient (Z=0.24, I=1.0, R=3.0)

IS 13920 には，靭性建物とするための配筋規定等が示されている．以下に，梁と柱の規定を抜粋する．

【梁】
- 幅：200mm 以上，せい：スパン/4 以下
- 最小主筋比 $0.24\sqrt{F_c \cdot \sigma_y}$
- 上端筋は曲げ下げ，下端筋は曲げ上げ定着
- せん断補強筋
    - 5m 以上のスパン長では D8 以上
    - 135 度フック
    - 端部から 2d の範囲は，最小間隔は，min(d/4, 8×主筋径)．ただし，100mm 以上でよい．
    - 中央部での最小間隔は，d/2

【柱】
- 軸力比で $0.1F_c$ を超えると下記に示すような特別な配筋が必要
- 最小径は 200mm 以上，ただし内法高さ 4m 以上，内法高さ 5m 以上では，300mm 以上
- 幅のせいに対する比は 0.4 以上
- せん断補強筋
    - 断面で 300mm ごとに中子筋
    - ヒンジ領域は，端部から，max(D, 内法高さ/6, 450mm)
    - 間隔は D/2 以下

The major seismic codes among the Indian Standard (IS) are listed below;
- IS456   Plain and reinforced concrete – Code of practice
- IS875   Code of practice for deign loads (other than earthquake) for buildings and structures
- IS1893   Criteria for earthquake resistant design of structures
- IS13920   Ductile detailing of reinforced concrete structures subject to seismic force

The design earthquake force defined in IS 1893 is calculated with the design horizontal acceleration coefficient, A_h as follows;

$$A_h = \frac{Z \cdot I \cdot S_a}{2R \cdot g} \quad (5.1.4\text{-}1)$$

where
    Z : Zone factor, 0.1, 0.16, 0.24 or 0.36 according to the location

I : Importance factor, 1.0 or 1.5
R : Response reduction factor as below;
- Ordinary RC moment-resisting frame (OMRF)   3.0
- Special RC moment-resisting frame   5.0
- Unreinforced masonry wall buildings   1.5
- Ordinary RC shear walls   3.0
- Ordinary shear wall with OMRF   3.0

S_a/g Average response acceleration coefficient as shown in Figure 5.1.4-1

Design horizontal acceleration coefficient with $Z=1.0$, $I=1.0$, $R=3.0$, A_h is shown in Figure 5.1.4-2. A_h becomes 1.0 for the short period range, which is greater than the demand according to NBC.

The load combination for RC buildings should be the maximum load of the following combinations, where DL: Dead Load, IL: Live Load, and EL: Earthquake Load.

- 1.5(DL+IL)
- 1.2(DL+IL±EL)
- 1.5(DL±EL)
- 0.9DL+1.5EL

As for the deformation limit, the inter-story drift angle under the load combination of DL+EL should be less than 1/250.

The specifications and details for ductile buildings are defined in IS 13920. The outline of the specifications for beams and columns are listed below;

Beams;
- Width should not be less than 200mm. Depth should not be greater than 1/4 of the span length.
- The tension steel ratio should not be less than $0.24\sqrt{F_c \cdot \sigma_y}$
- In the beam-column joint region, the top bar should be bent down and the bottom bar should be bent up for anchorage.
- As for the shear reinforcement;
    - Diameter should not be less than 8mm if the span length is greater than 5m
    - Stirrup should have 135-degree hook.
    - Spacing should not be less than 1/4 of beam depth, d and 8 times diameter, but no need to be less than 100mm in the region between $2d$ from the end of the beam. For other region, spacing should not be less than $d/2$.

Column;
- The following requirements should be applied if the design axial force ratio exceeds 0.1.
- The minimum dimension should not be less than 200mm with the clear height of 4m or greater, and 300mm with the clear height of 5m or greater.
- The ratio of the width to the depth should not be less than 0.4.
- As for the shear reinforcement;
    - The parallel legs of rectangular hoops should be spaced not more than 300mm.
    - Hinge region is the region between maximum of D, clear height / 6, and 450mm from the end.
    - Spacing should not be greater than half of the column depth.

5.2 被害の概要/ Outline of Damage
5.2.1 カトマンズ市内の被害/ Damage of Buildings in Kathmandu Valley
5.2.1.1 調査対象と地域/ Investigated Buildings and Area

　本調査では，カトマンズ市内にある低・中層鉄筋コンクリート造建物および組積造建物の被害の把握を目的として調査を行った．ただし，カトマンズ市内一体の建物を網羅することは難しいため，一部の地域の建物を調査し，被害の実態を把握することとした．調査は事前に被害が多いとの情報を得ていたカトマンズ市北西部にある Gongabu 地区およびその南西にある Sitapaila 地区を対象として実施した．

　Figure 5.2.1.1-1 に Gongabu 地区と Sitapaila 地区およびその周辺の地図を示す．Gongabu 地区は Figure 5.2.1.1-2 に示すように，リングロードと呼ばれる幹線道路の南北に広がる地域であり，リングロード周辺には多くの建物が建っている．特にリングロード北側には住宅や商業建物が密集している (Photo 5.2.1.1-1, Photo 5.2.1.1-2)．リングロード南側にはバスターミナルのほか，住宅，商業建物が存在している（Photo 5.2.1.1-3）．また，地域を縦断するように Bishhnumati 川が流れている．Sitapaila 地区は Gongabu 地区の南側にあり，リングロード沿いの建物に被害が見られた（Photo 5.2.1.1-4）．

　対象とする建物は対象地区に建つ鉄筋コンクリート造および組積造建物であり，主に大破した鉄筋コンクリート造建物の構造詳細を調査した（Figure 5.2.1.1-1 中の赤四角印）．さらに，Gongabu 地区の調査においては，特定の範囲の建物全数の調査を行い，建物の種類の分布や被害率について検討を行った．また，ネパールの建物の耐震性能評価を行うため，鉄筋コンクリート造建物1棟について設計図面を入手し，詳細な調査から，被災度の判定と耐力の推定を行った．

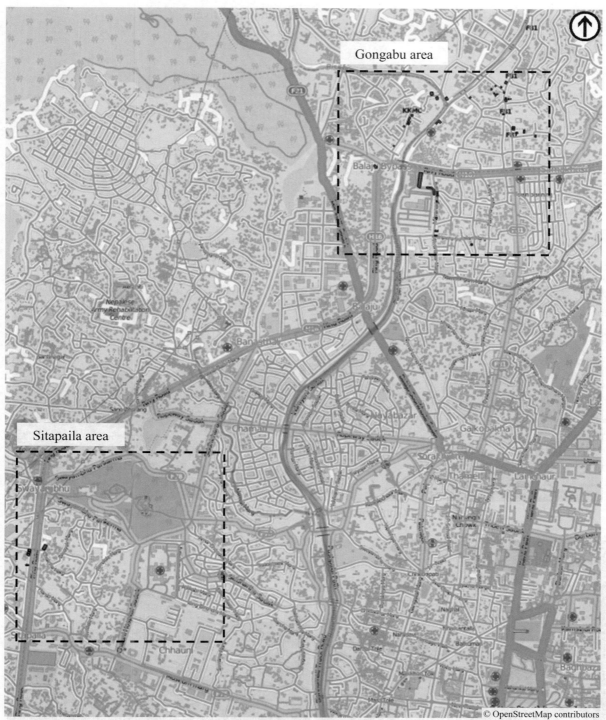

Figure 5.2.1.1-1 Investigated area

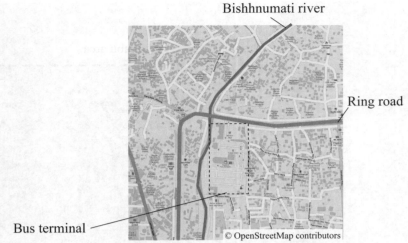

Figure 5.2.1.1-2 Gongabu area

Photo 5.2.1.1-1 Buildings in Gongabu (East)

Photo 5.2.1.1-2 Buildings in Gongabu (West)

Photo 5.2.1.1-3 Bus terminal in Gongabu

Photo 5.2.1.1-4 Buildings in Sitapaila area

In this chapter, the field investigation which was conducted in Kathmandu to assess damage to low- and mid-rise reinforced concrete buildings and masonry buildings is discussed. A part of area in Kathmandu was selected for investigation. Buildings in Gongabu area which is north-west in Kathmandu and Sitapaila area was investigated. Sitapaila area is located in the south of Gongabu area and buildings along Ring road were damaged as shown in Photo 5.2.1.1-4.

Figure 5.2.1.1-1 shows a map of Gongabu and Sitapaila area and around. The Ring road runs through the east and west in Gongabu area and many buildings can be observed along Ring road as shown in Figure 5.2.1.1-2. Especially, in the north of Ring road houses and commercial buildings are so densely packed (See Photo 5.2.1.1-1, Photo 5.2.1.1-2), on the other hand, in the south of Ring road bus terminal was found. Bishhnumati river flows north and south in Gongabu area. Sitapaila area is the south of Gongabu area and damaged buildings were observed along the Ring road.

The investigated buildings were reinforced concrete and masonry buildings in both areas and structural properties of severely damaged reinforced concrete buildings were investigated. Moreover, damage classification of all the buildings in certain area in Gongabu were conducted and types of buildings, numbers of floors, distribution and ratio of damage were assessed. Seismic capacity and damage assessment was carried out with drawings for one of those buildings to assume typical seismic capacity of buildings in Nepal.

5.2.1.2 Gongabu 地区の建物と被害/ Buildings and Damage in Gongabu Area

本節では，Gongabu 地区内の大破した建物の被害状況および構造詳細の調査を行った．各建物の位置を Figure 5.2.1.2-1 に示す．以降に各建物の詳細を示す．図中の赤印が建物の位置と形状を表している．なお，調査対象の建物は無作為に抽出を行っており，調査範囲のすべての大破した建物を調査したわけではない．

Severely damaged buildings in Gongabu area were investigated. The location was shown in Figure 5.2.1.2-1 with buildings' symbol (G1 to G24). Note that all damaged buildings were not observed but investigated buildings were selected at random in this investigation.

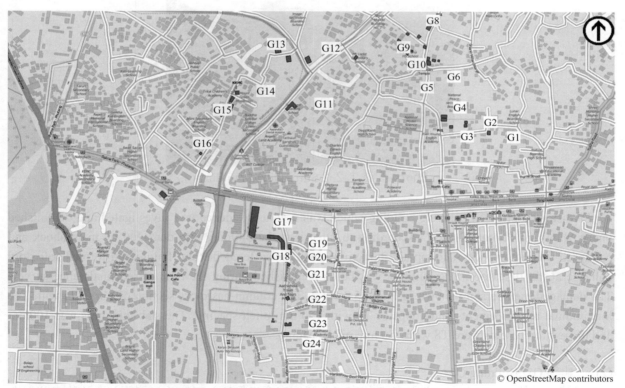

Figure 5.2.1.2-1 Investigated damaged buildings in Gongabu

(1) 建物 G1/ Building G1

5 階建ての鉄筋コンクリート造建物である．撤去作業中の写真を Photo 5.2.1.2-1 に示す．聞き込み調査によると本震時に大きな被害を受け，余震で倒壊に至ったとされている．1 階柱の柱頭・柱脚が曲げ降伏し，層崩壊している．現地到着時においては，撤去作業中であった．構造詳細を調査したところ，柱径は 9in×12in，主筋は T16，せん断補強筋は T8@150，スラブ厚 100mm，スラブ筋は T8@150 であった．被災した建物の周辺にある同規模の建物で被害を受けていないものも見られた（Photo 5.2.1.2-2）．

Photo 5.2.1.2-1 Soft first story collapse

Photo 5.2.1.2-2 Surrounding buildings

Five-story reinforced concrete building which was used as residence was investigated and demolished one is shown in Photo 5.2.1.2-1. According to interview, the building was damaged by main shock and collapsed with aftershock. The top and bottom of columns suffered flexural failure and formed soft story collapse at the first floor. The building was being demolished during the time of reconnaissance survey. The damaged members are shown in Photo 5.2.1.2-2. The column has cross section of 9in×12in with T16 longitudinal reinforcements and hoops of T8 with 150 mm pitch spacing. The slab thickness was 100mm and the reinforcements were T8 with 150 mm pitch spacing.

(2) 建物 G2/ Building G2

6 階建て鉄筋コンクリート造建物の住宅であり，完全に倒壊している．倒壊した建物の状況を Photo 5.2.1.2-3 に示す．聞き取り調査によると，本震で倒壊に至ったとされている．隣接する建物も大きな被害を受けていた（Photo 5.2.1.2-4）．

Photo 5.2.1.2-3 Collapsed building

Photo 5.2.1.2-4 Building next to collapsed one

Six-story reinforced concrete building which was also used as residence collapsed. Photo 5.2.1.2-3 shows wreckage of the building. According to interview, the building collapsed with main shock. A building next to collapsed building was damaged severely as shown in Photo 5.2.1.2-4.

(3) 建物 G3/ Building G3

6階建て鉄筋コンクリート造建物が崩壊している．鉄筋の破断面は鋭利な形状をしており，鉄筋の伸びが比較的小さかった可能性がある（Photo 5.2.1.2-5）．

Photo 5.2.1.2-5 Fractured steel reinforcing bars

Six-story reinforced building collapsed. The damaged column is shown in Photo 5.2.1.2-5. The steel had low ductility because the fracture cross section was sharp as shown in Photo 5.2.1.2-5.

(4) 建物 G4/ Building G4

5階建て鉄筋コンクリート造建物が層崩壊している．建物の外観を Photo 5.2.1.2-6 に示す．柱径は 9in×12in，柱主筋は 6-T16 であった（Figure 5.2.1.2-2）．主筋は定着されているが，鉄筋量の少ない方に倒壊しているように見られる．一方，隣接している組積造は衝突の影響で被害を受けていたが（Photo 5.2.1.2-7），地震動による大きな被害は見られなかった（Photo 5.2.1.2-8）．建物の周辺の建物は健全であった．

(a) Soft first story collapse

(b) Flexural yieldings of columns
Photo 5.2.1.2-6 Collapsed building

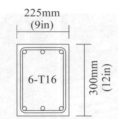

Figure 5.2.1.2-2 Cross section

Photo 5.2.1.2-7 Masonry building next to collapsed reinforced concrete building

Photo 5.2.1.2-8 Surroundings buildings

Five-story building collapsed with soft story mechanism. The appearances of the building are shown in Photo 5.2.1.2-6 and Photo 5.2.1.2-7. The diameter of column was assumed as 9in×12in and the reinforcement was 6-T16 (see Figure 5.2.1.2-2). The longitudinal reinforcements were anchored well but the building fell down in the direction of less of the reinforcements. On the other hand, masonry building next to collapsed building was crashed; however, remarkable damage was not observed (see Photo 5.2.1.2-8).

(5) 建物 G5/ Building G5

4階建て鉄筋コンクリート造建物であり，本震で倒壊している．建物の外観を Photo 5.2.1.2-9 に示す．隣接するレンガ造の建物にも被害が見られた．柱は定着部で鉄筋が抜け出した様子が見られ，柱径は 9in×12in，せん断補強筋は他の建物と同じく T8@150 であった（Photo 5.2.1.2-10）．

Photo 5.2.1.2-9 Collapsed building

Photo 5.2.1.2-10 Damage of columns

Four-story building collapsed with main shock as shown in Photo 5.2.1.2-9. The diameter of column was 9in × 12in and the hoops was T8 with 150 mm pitch spacing as well as that of aforementioned buildings.

(6) 建物 G6/ Building G6

5階建て＋地下1階の鉄筋コンクリート造建物であり，1階は店舗，2階より上が住居となっている．1階柱の柱頭部分で鉄筋が降伏し，1,2階部分が層崩壊している．建物正面の外観を Photo 5.2.1.2-11 に，層崩壊した柱を Photo 5.2.1.2-12 に，建物裏側を Photo 5.2.1.2-13 に示す．また，建物はL字型の平面形状をしており（Photo 5.2.1.2-14），Figure 5.2.1.2-3 のような平面図であると推察される．実測により調査したところ，柱径は 9in×12in であり，主筋は 8-T16，せん断補強筋は T8@150 であった．計測した長辺方向のスパンは約 3.2m，スラブ天端間高さは 2.85m，梁せいは 350mm であった．3階以上の内部の柱にもひび割れなどの被害が見られた（Photo 5.2.1.2-15）．また，短スパン梁の端部での曲げ破壊やせん断破壊が見られた（Photo 5.2.1.2-16）．

Photo 5.2.1.2-11 Front of soft first story collapsed building

Photo 5.2.1.2-12 Damage of columns at first floor

Photo 5.2.1.2-13 Back of collapsed building

Photo 5.2.1.2-14 L-shaped floor plan

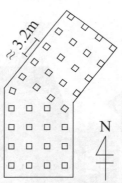

Figure 5.2.1.2-3 Assumed floor plan

Photo 5.2.1.2-15 Damage of columns above second floor

Photo 5.2.1.2-16 Damage of short span beams

Reinforced concrete building has five-story and a basement floor collapsed with soft first story mechanism. The first floor was used for store and above second floor was used for residence, which seems very common in Nepalese buildings. The appearances of the building are shown in Photo 5.2.1.2-11. Damage of column at the first floor is shown in Photo 5.2.1.2-12 and back of the building is shown in Photo 5.2.1.2-13. The building had L-shaped floor plan as shown in Photo 5.2.1.2-14. The layout of columns was assumed as Figure 5.2.1.2-4. The cross section of column was 9in×12in and the reinforcements was 8-T16 with hoops of T8@150. At the third floor columns were also damaged as shown in Photo 5.2.1.2-15. Flexural failure and shear failure were caused in short span beams (see Photo 5.2.1.2-16).

(7) 建物 G7/ Building G7

5階建て鉄筋コンクリート造＋鉄骨造ペントハウス付き建物であり，聞き取りによると本震で被害を受けた後，余震で大破した．建物の外観を Photo 5.2.1.2-17に示す．聞き取り調査によると約10年前に建築された建物であり，建物内では縫製が行われていた．2階には200台のミシンが置かれており，3，4階には大量の布や什器などがあった（Photo 5.2.1.2-18）．かなりの重量が載っていたと思われる．1階のすべての柱でせん断破壊か曲げ破壊が生じており，1層が層崩壊に近い状態であった．1階室内の状況を Photo 5.2.1.2-19に，せん断破壊した柱を Photo 5.2.1.2-20に示す．いずれのせん断破壊もレンガ壁による短柱化が原因であると思われる．1階のレンガ壁は

すべてせん断破壊しており，建物の長辺方向の壁においては水平のひび割れが，短辺方向の壁においては斜め方向のひび割れが確認された（Photo 5.2.1.2-21）．一方，2階以上においては，レンガ壁のせん断ひび割れ以外の目立った被害は見られなかった．なお，本建物の耐力評価および被災度区分判定，詳細解析については5.2.1.5項に示す．

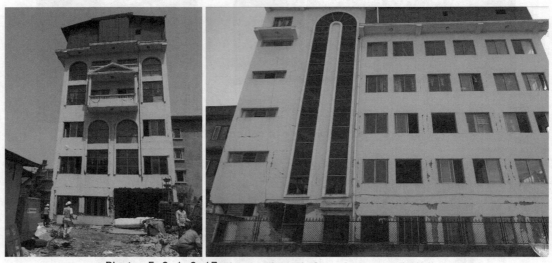

Photo 5.2.1.2-17 Five stories reinforced concrete building

Photo 5.2.1.2-18 Inside at third and fourth floor

Photo 5.2.1.2-19 Damage at first floor

Photo 5.2.1.2-20 Shear failure of columns at first floor

(a) Horizontal cracks   (b) Diagonal cracks
Photo 5.2.1.2-21 Cracks on non-structural brick walls

Five-story reinforced concrete building with steel framed pent house was damaged by main shock and seriously damaged by aftershock (Photo 5.2.1.2-17). According to interview, this building was built 10 years ago and was used for sewing products manufacturing. There were 200 sewing machines on the second floor and a large amount of cut of clothes on the third and fourth floor (Photo 5.2.1.2-18) which was assumed as heavy weight for building. Shear failure and flexural failure occurred at all the column on the first floor and soft first story mechanism was developed as shown in Photo 5.2.1.2-19. The shear failure of column was shown in Photo 5.2.1.2-20 which was assumed to be due to shortening of height by non-structural brick walls. The non-structural brick walls failed in shear and horizontal cracks and diagonal cracks were appeared on the walls in the longitudinal and transverse directions, respectively (Photo 5.2.1.2-21). On the contrary, remarkable damage was not observed on columns on the other floors. Note that assumed seismic capacity and damage assessment result conducted for this buildings are shown in Section 5.2.1.5.

(8) 建物 G8/ Building G8

　1階は店舗，2階より上が住居の7階建て鉄筋コンクリート造建物である．建物の外観を Photo 5.2.1.2-22 に示す．1，2階が層崩壊しており，かつ上部階の柱頭と柱脚においても曲げ降伏が生じていた．また，接合部の定着部分の抜け出しも見られた（Photo 5.2.1.2-23）．聞き取り調査によると，建設当初は2階建てだった建物を増築し3〜7階建てにしている．また，本震で被害を受け，余震で倒壊に至った．柱径は9in×12in，柱主筋は6-T16が配筋されており，せん断補強筋はD8@180mmであった（Figure 5.2.1.2-4）．周辺の建物においても層崩壊は免れたが1階の柱頭に被害が生じている建物が見られた．鉄骨補強により落下を防いでいた（Photo 5.2.1.2-24）．

Photo 5.2.1.2-22 Collapsed building

Photo 5.2.1.2-23 Soft story mechanism

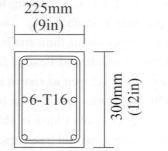

Figure 5.2.1.2-4 Cross section

Figure 5.2.1.2-24 Damage of top of column on surrounding building

Seven-story reinforced concrete building which have store on the first floor and residence above the second floors (Photo 5.2.1.2-22). The first and second floor collapsed and flexural failure occurred at the top and bottom of column. Slipping out of reinforcement of beam column joint was observed (Photo 5.2.1.2-23). According to interview, three floors added on the original two-story building and this building was damaged by main shock and collapsed with aftershock. The cross section of column was 9in×12in and the reinforcements was 6-T16 enclosed by T8 hoop with 180mm pitch spacing (Figure 5.2.1.2-5). Damage of top of column on surrounding building which was reinforced by steel frames (Photo 5.2.1.2-24).

(9) 建物 G9/ Building G9

3階建て鉄筋コンクリート造建物であり，1階は店舗であったと思われる．建物の外観を Photo 5.2.1.2-25 に示す．2階の柱頭，柱脚が損傷し中間層崩壊している．周辺道路には崩れたものと思われるレンガが散乱していた．周辺には高層の建物が建設中であったが，目立った被害は確認できなかった（Photo 5.2.1.2-26）．

Photo 5.2.1.2-25 Soft story collapse

Photo 5.2.1.2-26 No damage on building under construction

　　Three-story reinforced concrete building which have store on the first floor collapsed. (Photo 5.2.1.2-25). Top and bottom of the column on the second floor suffered flexural failure and soft story collapse mechanism was formed. Bricks were observed on the street which were assumed to be used in the wall in this building. No damage was observed on surrounding building under construction (Photo 5.2.1.2-26).

(10)　建物 G10/ Building G10

　5階建て鉄筋コンクリート造建物の中学校である．建物の外観を Photo 5.2.1.2-27 に示す．被害のため，危険（赤色）の応急危険度判定結果（Photo 5.2.1.2-28)が表示されており，使用停止中であった．調査時においては，レンガ壁のひび割れをモルタルで修復している最中であった（Photo 5.2.1.2-29）．

Photo 5.2.1.2-27 Junior high school

Photo 5.2.1.2-28 Post-earthquake temporary risk evaluation

Photo 5.2.1.2-29 Repairing of non-structural brick walls

Five-story reinforced concrete building used for junior high school was damaged (Photo 5.2.1.2-27). Post-earthquake temporary risk evaluation result of "Dangerous" with red label was displayed (Photo 5.2.1.2-28) and prohibited from entering. The damaged non-structural brick walls were being repaired (Photo 5.2.1.2-29).

(11)　建物 G11/ Building G11

　6階建て鉄筋コンクリート造建物の学校である．建物の外観を Photo 5.2.1.1-30 に示す．聞き取り調査によると本震時に 20 秒以内に倒壊している．他の建物と同じく，柱頭の曲げ破壊により層崩壊したと推察される．水道管の破損により周辺には水が広がっていたが，液状化などは確認されなかった（Photo 5.2.1.1-31）．

Photo 5.2.1.2-30 Soft story collapse

Photo 5.2.1.2-31 Wet ground in front of building

Six-story reinforced concrete building of school showed soft story collapse (Photo 5.2.1.1-30). According to interview, this building felt down within 20 seconds. It was assumed that soft story mechanism was developed by flexural failure at the end of column. Water was spread on the ground due to broken water pipe, however, liquefaction was not observed (Photo 5.2.1.2-31).

(12) 建物 G12/ Building G12
　5階建て鉄筋コンクリート造建物でありホテルとして使用されていたが，休業している．建物の外観を Photo 5.2.1.2-32 に示す．柱脚部およびレンガ壁にわずかに被害が見られた．隣接建物との境界面において施工状態が悪く，ジャンカや接合部の破壊などが見られた（Photo 5.2.1.2-33）．

Photo 5.2.1.2-32 Five-story building

Photo 5.2.1.2-33 Rock pockets and damage of beam-to-column joint

Five-story reinforced concrete building used for hotel was damaged (Photo 5.2.1.2-32). The bottom of column and non-structural brick walls were damaged. Rock pockets and damage of beam column joint were observed on the boundary surface due to poor construction (Photo 5.2.1.2-33).

(13) 建物 G13/ Building G13

7 階建て鉄筋コンクリート造建物であり，1 階が店舗に使用されている．建物の外観を Photo 5.2.1.2-34 に示す．1 階の損傷が激しく，柱脚やレンガ壁に被害が見られた．また，短辺方向に連層のレンガ壁（Photo 5.2.1.2-35）を有しており，3 階柱梁接合部から 1 階柱脚部分までレンガ壁に対角上にせん断ひび割れが生じていた．3 階の柱梁接合部および 1 階の柱脚の被害を Photo 5.2.1.2-36 に示す．1 階の柱脚は基礎との接合面がずれ，鉄筋が露出していた．接合部面は滑らかであり，コンクリートの付着は確認できなかった．鉄筋のみでせん断力を負担したことが，柱脚の破壊に繋がったと考えられる．

Photo 5.2.1.2-34 Damage of first floor column on seven stories building

Photo 5.2.1.2-35 Multi-story non-structural brick wall

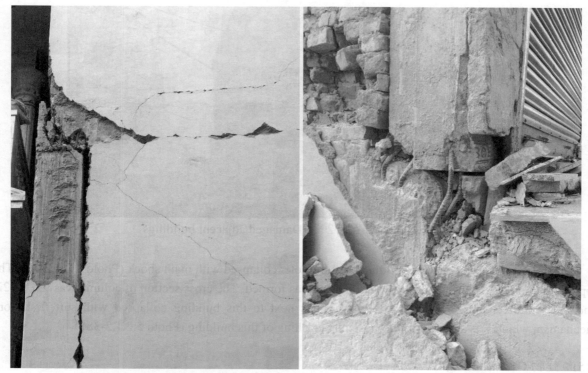

Photo 5.2.1.2-36 Damage of beam-to-column joint and bottom of column

Seven-story reinforced concrete building of which first floor was used for store was damaged. Appearance of building and non-structural brick wall in short-side direction are shown in Photo 5.2.1.2-34. Photo 5.2.1.2-35 shows diagonal shear cracks from beam-column joint on the third floor to the bottom of column on the first floor. Damage of beam-column joint and the bottom of column are shown in Photo 5.2.1.2-36. Drift between the bottom of column on the first floor and basement was observed and the reinforcement was exposed. The bottom of the column showed smooth surface and this might cause damage of bottom of column with its low bearing capacity.

(14) 建物 G14/ Building G14

6階建て鉄筋コンクリート造建物のホテルである．建物の外観を Photo 5.2.1.2-37 に示す．聞き取り調査によると，本震で倒壊している．1階の柱頭が破壊し，層崩壊している．柱径は 9in×12in，主筋は 6-T16 であった．隣接する建物 5 棟が層崩壊しており，衝突により倒壊したものもあったと思われる（Photo 5.2.1.2-38）．

Photo 5.2.1.2-37 Soft first story collapsed building

Photo 5. 2. 1. 2-38 Damaged adjacent buildings

Six-story reinforced concrete building used for hotel collapsed with main shock (Photo 5.2.1.2-37). The top of column was damaged and story mechanism was formed. The cross section of column was 9in × 12in and the reinforcements was 6-T16. Five buildings next to this building collapsed with soft first story mechanism which was assumed to be caused by crashing of this building (Photo 5.2.1.2-38).

(15)　建物 G15/ Building G15

3階建て鉄筋コンクリート造建物の住宅である．建物の外観を Photo 5.2.1.2-39 に示す．1階の柱頭・柱脚が曲げ降伏し，層崩壊している．鉄筋の定着はとれているようであった（Photo 5.2.1.2-40）．

Photo 5. 2. 1. 2-39 Soft first story collapse

Photo 5. 2. 1. 2-40 Damage of top of column

Three-story reinforced concrete building of house collapsed (Photo 5.2.1.2-39). Top and bottom of the column on the first floor suffered flexural failure and soft first story mechanism was formed. The anchorage of steels was assured (Photo 5.2.1.2-40).

(16)　建物 G16/ Building G16

5階建て鉄筋コンクリート造建物であり，他の建物と同様に1階の柱頭・柱脚が曲げ破壊し，層崩壊している．建物の外観を Photo 5.2.1.2-41 に示す．

Photo 5.2.1.2-41 Soft first story collapse

Five-story reinforced concrete building formed soft story collapse due to flexural failure at top and bottom of column on the first floor as shown in Photo 5.2.1.2-41.

(17)　建物 G17/ Building G17
　4 階建て鉄筋コンクリート造建物である．建物の外観を Photo 5.2.1.2-42 に示す．構造体には目立った被害は見られなかったが，レンガ壁は損傷が見られた．

Photo 5.2.1.2-42 Damage to non-structural brick walls

Four-story reinforced concrete building was slightly damaged (Photo 5.2.1.2-42). Remarkable damage except non-structural brick walls was not observed.

(18)　建物 G18/ Building G18
　4 階建て鉄筋コンクリート造建物であり，1 階は警察署，2 階以上は建設中であった．建物の外観を Photo 5.2.1.2-43 に示す．レンガ壁や柱および接合部などに大きな被害が見られた．エキスパンションジョイントにより，対称形の 2 棟の建物が接続されている（Photo 5.2.1.2-44）．2 階以上が建設中であるため 2 階以上にはほとんど壁はなく，相対的に 1 階の壁量が多くなっていたことから，2 階の柱の柱頭がほとんど曲げ降伏していた（Photo 5.2.1.2-45）．本震で被害が生じた．接合部内の補強筋はなく，定着も短いため，多くが破壊していた（Photo 5.2.1.2-46）．室内においては，階段の下面の鉄筋が露出し，錆びており，非常に危険な状態であった（Photo 5.2.1.2-47）．

Photo 5. 2. 1. 2-43 Three-story reinforced concrete building

Photo 5. 2. 1. 2-44 Expansion joint

Photo 5. 2. 1. 2-45 Damage at the top of column

Photo 5. 2. 1. 2-46 Damage of beam-to-column joints

Photo 5. 2. 1. 2-47 Damage of stairs

Four-story reinforced concrete building which has police office at the first floor and was under construction above second floor was damaged by main shock as shown in Photo 5.2.1.2-43. The building consisted of two buildings with expansion joint (Photo 5.2.1.2-44). Because the amount of non-structural walls was larger than the other floors, almost all the top of the column on the second floor suffered flexural failure (Photo 5.2.1.2-45). No hoops were found in beam-to-column joints and the anchorage of steels are short, consequently, many of those was severely damaged as shown in Photo 5.2.1.2-46. Inside of this building, it was danger that steels of under stairs were exposed and lusted as shown in Photo 5.2.1.2-47.

(19) 建物 G19/ Building G19

6階建て鉄筋コンクリート造建物であり，全壊している．建物の状況を Photo 5.2.1.2-48 に示す．本震で1階の柱が被害を受け，余震で全壊している．建物の4階と5階が建設中であった．他の建物と同様に柱頭の鉄筋が抜け出していた．また，周辺地盤に沈下が見られた（Photo 5.2.1.2-49）．

Photo 5.2.1.2-48 Totally collapsed building

Photo 5.2.1.2-49 Settlement of ground

　Six-story reinforced concrete building collapsed as shown in Photo 5.2.1.2-48. The column on the first floor was damaged by main shock and the building collapsed during aftershock. The fourth and fifth floors were under construction. Settlement of ground was observed around this building (Photo 5.2.1.2-49).

(20) 建物 G20/ Building G20

5階建て鉄筋コンクリート造建物の1，2階が層崩壊している（Photo 5.2.1.2-50）．柱径は 9in×12in，柱主筋は 6-T16，せん断補強筋：T8@150 であり，2階建てから5階建てに増築した建物である．

Photo 5.2.1.2-50 Soft story collapse at the first and second floors

Five-story reinforced concrete building formed soft story collapse at the first and second floors as shown in Photo 5.2.1.2-50. The cross section of the column was 9in × 12in and steels were 6-T16 enclosed by T8 hoops with 150mm pitch spacing. Three floors were added on original two-story building.

(21) 建物 G21/ Building G21
 5階建て鉄筋コンクリート造であり，1階が層崩壊している（Photo 5.2.1.2-51）．

Photo 5.2.1.2-51 Soft first story collapse

Five-story reinforced concrete building formed soft first story collapse as shown in Photo 5.2.1.2-51.

(22) 建物 G22/ Building G22
 6階建て鉄筋コンクリート造建物であり，1階が層崩壊している（Photo 5.2.1.2-52）．柱頭のコンクリートが曲げ降伏後に圧壊しており，建物内部および外部において，鉄骨柱により補強していた（Photo 5.2.1.2-53）．

Photo 5.2.1.2-52 Soft first story collapse

Photo 5.2.1.2-53 Reinforcement for collapsed column

Six-story reinforced concrete building formed soft first story collapse (Photo 5.2.1.2-52). Compression failure was observed top of the column on the first floor. The columns were reinforced with steel columns as shown in Photo 5.2.1.2-53.

(23) 建物 G23/ Building G23
7階建て鉄筋コンクリート造建物であり，1階が本震で損傷を受けた後，余震で倒壊している（Photo 5.2.1.2-54）．

Photo 5.2.1.2-54 Collapsed seven-story reinforced concrete building

Seven-story reinforced concrete building collapsed during aftershock after severe damage in main shock (Photo 5.2.1.2-54).

(24) 建物 G24/ Building G24

5階建て鉄筋コンクリート造建物が完全に倒壊していた．鉄筋の抜け出しも見られた（Photo 5.2.1.2-55）．

Photo 5.2.1.2-55 Totally collapsed five-story reinforced concrete building

Five-story reinforced concrete building collapsed totally and slipping out of reinforcement was observed (Photo 5.2.1.2-55).

5.2.1.3 Sitapaila 地区/ Buildings and Damage in Sitapaila Area

Sitapaila 地区内の大破した建物の被害状況および構造詳細の調査を行った．調査した建物の位置を Figure 5.2.1.3-1 に示す．以降に各建物の詳細を示す．

Figure 5.2.1.3-1 Location of investigated buildings

Severely damaged buildings in Sitapaila area were investigated. The location was shown in Figure 5.2.1.3-1.

(1) 建物 S1/ Building S1

4 階建て鉄筋コンクリート造建物である（Photo 5.2.1.3-1）．柱径は 12in × 12in 程度であり，主筋は 4-T16 と 4-T12 の 8 本が配筋され，せん断補強筋は T6@150 であった（Photo 5.2.1.3-2）．柱頭・柱脚の曲げ破壊および，接合部の破壊により層崩壊していた（Photo 5.2.1.3-3）．接合部の梁筋が柱コアの外側を通っており，梁のせん断補強筋は折り曲げ部で破断していた．接合部に補強筋はなかった．

Photo 5. 2. 1. 3-1 Collapsed building   Photo 5. 2. 1. 3-2 Steels in column

Photo 5. 2. 1. 3-3 Damage of bottom of column and beam column joints

Four-story reinforced concrete building collapsed as shown in Photo 5.2.1.3-1. The diameter of column was about 12in x 12in and four reinforcements of T16 and T12 were placed enclosed by shear reinforcement of T6 with 150mm pitch spacing as shown in Photo 5.2.1.3-2. Top and bottom of column suffered flexural failure and beam-column joints was damaged (Photo 5.2.1.3-3). Reinforcements of beam were anchored outside of reinforcements of column in beam column joints and shear reinforcement of beam was fractured at the corner. Shear reinforcement was not found in beam-to-column joint.

(2) 建物 S2/ Building S2

　5 階建て鉄筋コンクリート造建物が 1 階で層崩壊していた（Photo 5.2.1.3-4）．建物は層崩壊後に転倒し，隣の建物との間に隙間ができていた（Photo 5.2.1.3-5）．1 階の柱頭部分の鉄筋が抜けており（Photo 5.2.1.3-6），鉄筋の破断面から伸びが小さかった可能性がある（Photo 5.2.1.3-7）．近くには倒壊していない建物もあった（Photo 5.2.1.3-8）．

Photo 5.2.1.3-4 Soft first story collapse

Photo 5.2.1.3-5 Gap between next buildings　　Photo 5.2.1.3-6 Damage of top of column on the first floor

Photo 5.2.1.3-7 Fractured steel　　Photo 5.2.1.3-8 Non damaged building

Five-story reinforced concrete building suffered soft first story collapse as shown in Photo 5.2.1.3-4. This building felt down after soft story collapse drifted which made gap between next buildings (Photo 5.2.1.3-5). Steels at top of column pulled out from joint (Photo 5.2.1.3-6) and fractured which surface indicates short elongation of steel. (Photo 5.2.1.3-7). No damage was found near this building (Photo 5.2.1.3-8).

5.2.1.4 Gongabu 地区の建物の全数調査/ Building Survey in Gongabbu Area
(1)　調査対象地域/ Survey Area

　本調査では，5.2.1 節に示すように，建物被害が散見された Gongabu 地域を対象とした全数調査を実施した．調査を行った建物の全配置図を Figure 5.2.1.4-1 に示す．対象とする建物種別は，鉄筋コンクリート（R/C）造，組積（M）造および鉄筋コンクリート造と組積造の混合構造（M+R/C 造）とした．

Figure 5.2.1.4-1 Location of investigated buildings

　As shown in 5.2.1, whole building survey was conducted in Gongabu area where severely damaged buildings were occurred. A map of all the surveyed building is shown in Figure 5.2.1.4-1. The construction types of structures are reinforced concrete (R/C), masonry (M), and the mixed structure of reinforced concrete and masonry (M+R/C).

(2)　調査方法/ Investigation Method

　本調査では，European Seismological Commission の European Macroseismic Scale 1998（EMS-98）[5.2.1-1)]を用いて建物の被災度を調査した．調査項目は，建物種別，階数，使用用途，壁の素材，床の素材，構造形式および被災度（5 段階）である．ただし，使用用途や壁の素材，床の素材については，不明な建物が多かったとことから，本報告書において，分析の対象とはしなかった．EMS-98 では，組積造および鉄筋コンクリート構造建物の被災度は，外観上の構造部材の被害状況から Table 5.2.1.4-1 および Table 5.2.1.4-2 のように定義されている．

Table 5.2.1.4-1 Classification of damage to masonry buildings (EMS-98) [5.2.1-1]

	Grade 1: Negligible to slight damage (no structural damage, slight non-structural damage) Hair-line cracks in very few walls. Fall of small pieces of plaster only. Fall of loose stones from upper parts of buildings in very few cases.
	Grade 2: Moderate damage (slight structural damage, moderate non-structural damage) Cracks in many walls. Fall of fairly large pieces of plaster. Partial collapse of chimneys.
	Grade 3: Substantial to heavy damage (moderate structural damage, heavy non-structural damage) Large and extensive cracks in most walls. Roof tiles detach. Chimneys fracture at the roof line; failure of individual non-structural elements (partitions, gable walls).
	Grade 4: Very heavy damage (heavy structural damage, very heavy non-structural damage) Serious failure of walls; partial structural failure of roofs and floors.
	Grade 5: Destruction (very heavy structural damage) Total or near total collapse.

Table 5.2.1.4-2 Classification of damage to buildings of reinforced concrete (EMS-98)[5.2.1-1)]

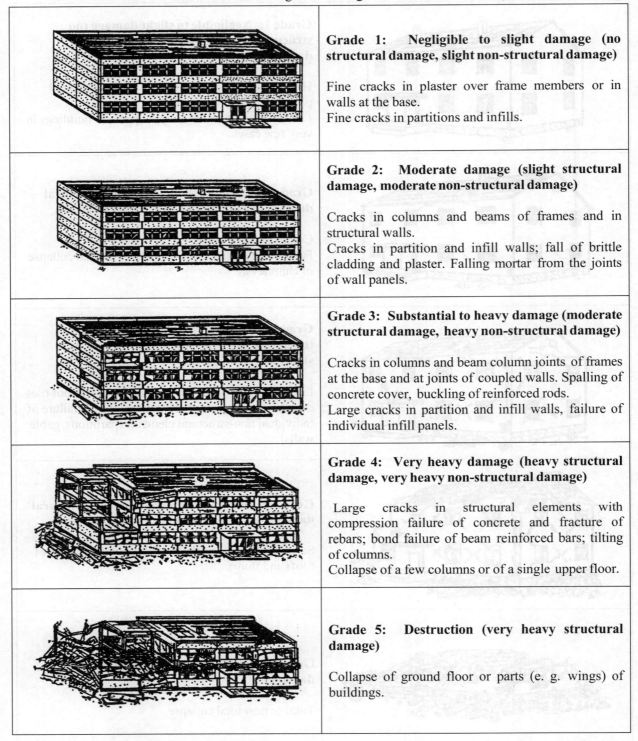

	Grade 1: Negligible to slight damage (no structural damage, slight non-structural damage) Fine cracks in plaster over frame members or in walls at the base. Fine cracks in partitions and infills.
	Grade 2: Moderate damage (slight structural damage, moderate non-structural damage) Cracks in columns and beams of frames and in structural walls. Cracks in partition and infill walls; fall of brittle cladding and plaster. Falling mortar from the joints of wall panels.
	Grade 3: Substantial to heavy damage (moderate structural damage, heavy non-structural damage) Cracks in columns and beam column joints of frames at the base and at joints of coupled walls. Spalling of concrete cover, buckling of reinforced rods. Large cracks in partition and infill walls, failure of individual infill panels.
	Grade 4: Very heavy damage (heavy structural damage, very heavy non-structural damage) Large cracks in structural elements with compression failure of concrete and fracture of rebars; bond failure of beam reinforced bars; tilting of columns. Collapse of a few columns or of a single upper floor.
	Grade 5: Destruction (very heavy structural damage) Collapse of ground floor or parts (e. g. wings) of buildings.

The damage levels of buildings were decided by European Macroseismic Scale 1998 (EMS-98), European Seismological Commission[5.2.1-1)]. Other check items are classification of structure, number of stories, building use, material of wall/floor, type of structure, and damage level (5 levels). In EMS-98, the classification of damage is defined by the external appearance of structural members as shown in Table 5.2.1.4-1 and Table 5.2.1.4-2.

(3) 調査結果/ Investigation Results
(a) 調査建物数と被災度分布/ Summary

　全調査建物の棟数および構造種別，層数ごとの内訳を Table 5.2.1.4-3 および Figure 5.2.1.4-2 に示す．また，調査建物を構造種別ごとに色分けしたマップを Figure 5.2.1.4-3 に，層数ごとに色分けしたマップを Figure 5.2.1.4-4 および Figure 5.2.1.4-5 に示す．

　調査建物総数は 1290 棟である．そのうち，75%程度の建物が鉄筋コンクリート造であり，25%程度が組積造であった．また，一部の建物で，鉄筋コンクリート造と組積造の混構造が用いられていた．層数を見ると，鉄筋コンクリート造では 3～5 階建ての建物が多かった．組積造では，1～3 階建ての建物が最も多く，おおむね 5 階建て以下となっていた．鉄筋コンクリート造建物は，リングロード（Ring road）北側のエリアに多く，その大半は 3 階以上の中層建物であった．一方で，鉄筋コンクリート造の低層建物は，リングロード西側にエリアに集中していた．また，リングロード西側のエリアは，組積造の建物が多いことも確認できる．

Table 5.2.1.4-3 Numbers of observed buildings

Number of observed buildings		1290 (one of which is steel structure)			
R/C		Masonry		Mixed structures (M+R/C)	
961 bldgs. (74.5%)		323 bldgs. (25.1%)		5 bldgs. (0.4%)	
8 stories	2	8 stories	-	8 stories	-
7 stories	24	7 stories	-	7 stories	-
6 stories	95	6 stories	1	6 stories	1
5 stories	235	5 stories	9	5 stories	1
4 stories	279	4 stories	33	4 stories	0
3 stories	214	3 stories	100	3 stories	0
2 stories	88	2 stories	61	2 stories	2
1 stories	22	1 stories	119	1 stories	1

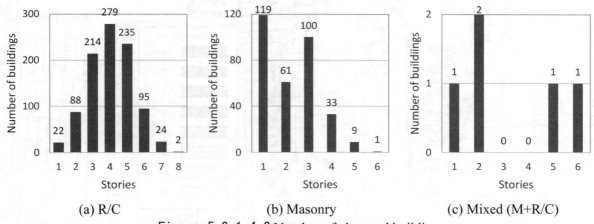

(a) R/C　　(b) Masonry　　(c) Mixed (M+R/C)

Figure 5.2.1.4-2 Number of observed buildings

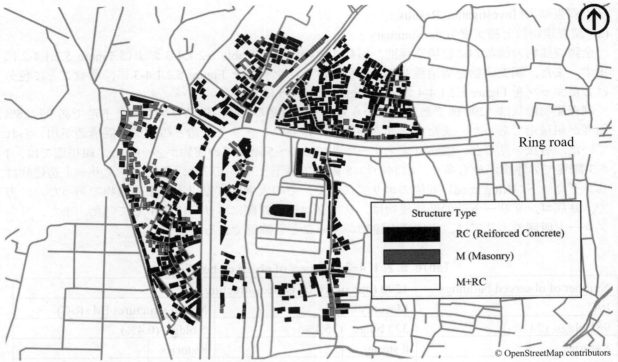

Figure 5.2.1.4-3 Structurer types of investigated buildings

Figure 5.2.1.4-4 Number of floors of reinforced concrete buildings

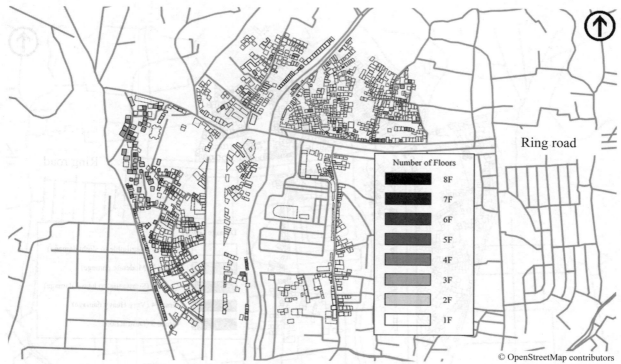

Figure 5.2.1.4-5 Number of floors of masonry buildings

EMS-98に従って被災度を判定した結果を，Table 5.2.1.4-4 および Figure 5.2.1.4-6 に示す．また，被災度ごとに色分けしたマップを，構造種別ごとに Figure 5.2.1.4-7 および Figure 5.2.1.4-8 に示す．鉄筋コンクリート造建物は，全体の 5%程度の建物が被災度 4～5 と深刻な被害となる一方で，全体の 85%程度の建物は無被害であった．一方，組積造建物は，鉄筋コンクリート造に比べて被害が大きい傾向にあり，全体の 10%程度の建物は被災度 4～5 と深刻な被害を受けていた．

Table 5.2.1.4-4 Numbers of classified buildings

R/C (961 bldgs.)		Masonry (323 bldgs.)		Mixed (5 bldgs.)	
Grade 5	29	Grade 5	16	Grade 5	1
Grade 4	20	Grade 4	16	Grade 4	0
Grade 3	22	Grade 3	11	Grade 3	0
Grade 2	76	Grade 2	39	Grade 2	2
Grade 1	817	Grade 1	241	Grade 1	2

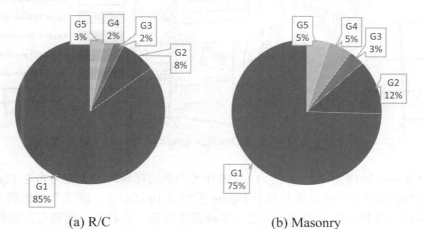

(a) R/C   (b) Masonry

Figure 5.2.1.4-6 Percentages of classified buildings

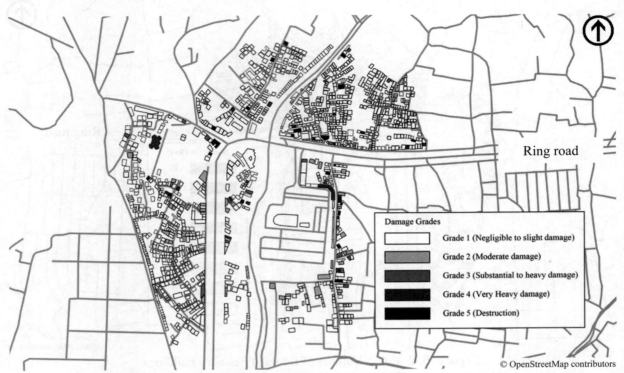

Figure 5.2.1.4-7 Damage grade of reinforced concrete buildings

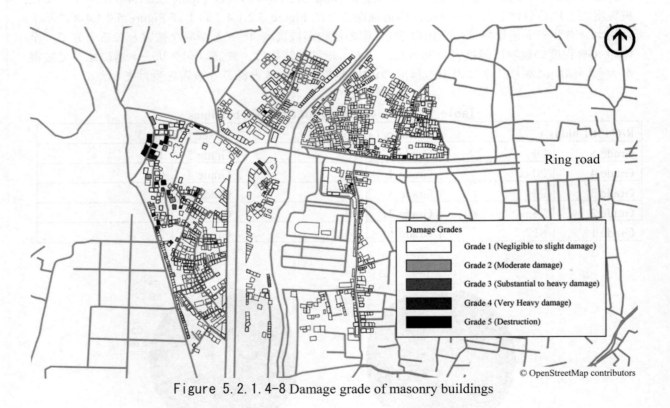

Figure 5.2.1.4-8 Damage grade of masonry buildings

　鉄筋コンクリート造建物において，1〜3階建ての低層建物の被災度分布をFigure 5.2.1.4-9に，4階建て以上の中層建物の被災度分布をFigure 5.2.1.4-10に示す．図より，低層の建物よりも4階建て以上の中層の建物の被害が大きいことが確認できる．これは，前述した建物被害の分析において示したように，ネパールの鉄筋コンクリート造建物の多くが，低層で新築した後に柱の断面

を変えずに増築を行うケースが多くあることに起因していると思われる．すなわち，増築の影響により設計時よりも上層の重量が増えることにより，増築した中層の建物ほど1層の負担せん断力が大きくなり，被害が大きくなったものと推察される．

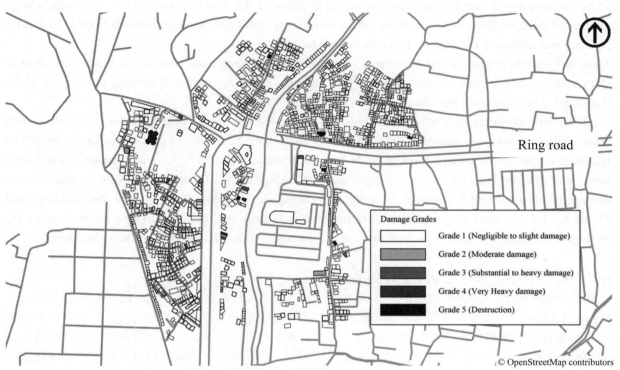

Figure 5.2.1.4-9 Damage grade of the reinforced concrete buildings (1 - 3 floors)

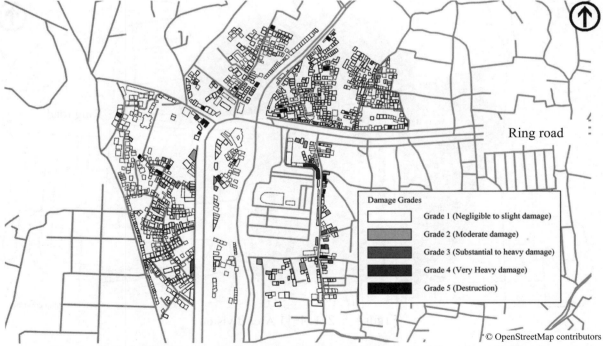

Figure 5.2.1.4-10 Damage Grade of the reinforced concrete buildings (over 4 floors)

The number of all the surveyed buildings and the number of each structural material are shown in Table 5.2.1.4-3 and Figure 5.2.1.4-2. The color-coded maps of surveyed buildings are shown in Figure 5.2.1.4-3, Figure 5.2.1.4-4 and Figure 5.2.1.4-5.

The number of all the surveyed buildings is 1290. About 75 % of them are R/C structures and about 25 % are masonry. A few buildings are the mixed structure of R/C and masonry. In R/C buildings, a large number of them are from 3- to 5-story building. In masonry buildings, most of them are from 1- to 3-story building and almost all of them are less than 6-story building.
Many R/C buildings are located in the area in the north of the Ring road. Most of them are more than 2-story building. On the other hand, low story R/C buildings are concentrated in the area in the west of the Ring road, where there are also many masonry buildings.

The result of survey by EMS-98 are shown in Figure 5.2.1.4-6 and Table 5.2.1.4-4. The color-coded maps of damage level are shown in Figure 5.2.1.4-7 and Figure 5.2.1.4-8. As to R/C buildings, about 5 % buildings are in severe damage level of grade 4 and 5, whereas about 85 % have no damage. On the other hand, masonry buildings have more damages than R/C. About 10 % of them are severely damaged whose damage levels are 4 and 5. Figure 5.2.1.4-9 shows damage level of low (1 to 3) story R/C buildings and Figure 5.2.1.4-10 shows that of medium-rise (more than 3) story R/C buildings. Those maps illustrate the damage level of medium buildings with more than 3 stories is higher than that of low story buildings.

(b) エリア別の被災度分布/ Result According to Area

建物構造や階数，被害の程度が，リングロードに区切られたブロックごとに異なることから，Figure 5.2.1.4-11のように3つのエリアに分類して被害を分析する．エリアは，リングロード北側の中層集合住宅が密集するエリア（以下，エリアAという），リングロード西側の低層戸建住宅やM造住宅の多いエリア（以下，エリアBという），リングロード南側のバスターミナル周囲の大通り沿いに中層建物の並ぶエリア（以下，エリアCという）とする．

Figure 5.2.1.4-11 Area division

エリア別の各構造種別の割合を Figure 5.2.1.4-12 に示す．エリア A，C では鉄筋コンクリート造（R/C）が約8割，組積造（M）が約2割であったのに対し，エリア B は組積造が約4割と，他のエリアに比べて多い．また，組積造と鉄筋コンクリート造の混構造もわずかに見られた．

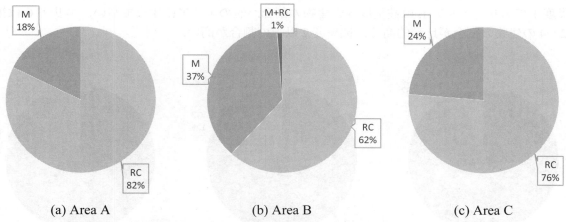

Figure 5.2.1.4-12 Percentage of structural types of buildings in each area

エリア，構造種別の層数の分布を Figure 5.2.1.4-13 および Figure 5.2.1.4-14 に示す．鉄筋コンクリート造は，エリア A では 4, 5 階建ての割合が高く，エリア B では 3, 4 階建てが，エリア C では 3～5 階建ての割合が高い．組積造は，エリア A，C では 1 階建ての割合が高く，エリア B では 3 階建ての割合が最も高く，次いで 2 階建ての割合が高い．

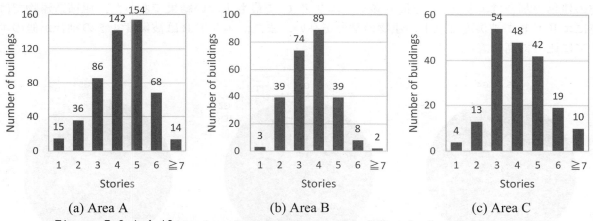

Figure 5.2.1.4-13 Number of reinforced concrete buildings by the number of stories

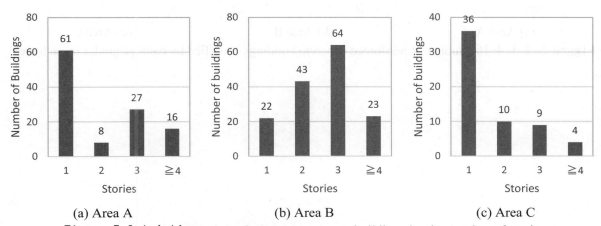

Figure 5.2.1.4-14 Number of masonry concrete buildings by the number of stories

各エリアでの建物全体の被災度の割合を Figure 5.2.1.4-15 に示す．エリア A は約 9 割の建物が被災度 1 であり，エリア B は被災度 5 の建物の割合が他のエリアに比べて高い．エリア C は被災度 2〜4 の建物の割合が比較的高く，被災度 2 以上の割合が高い．

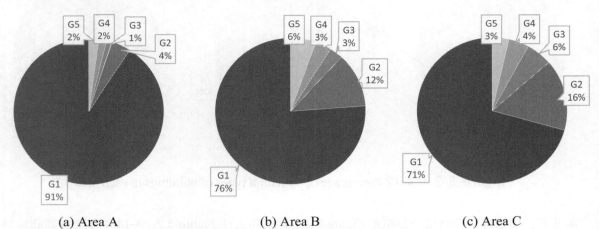

Figure 5.2.1.4-15 Number of buildings classified by damage grades in each area

各エリアでの構造種別ごとの被災度の割合を Figure 5.2.1.4-16 および Figure 5.2.1.4-17 に示す．鉄筋コンクリート造建物では，被災度 5 の割合はどのエリアも約 3〜4% であった．しかし，無被害の建物の割合はエリア A で最も多く，エリア C で最も少ない結果であった．組積造建物では，特にエリア B で被災度 2 以上の建物の割合が高い．また，エリア B は被災度 4, 5 の割合が他のエリアに比べて高い．

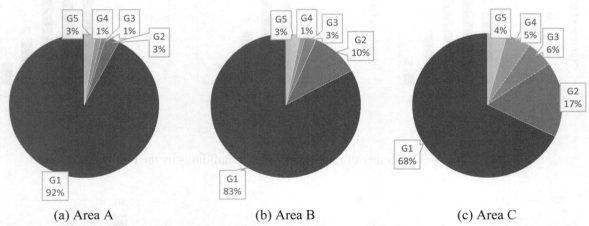

Figure 5.2.1.4-16 Number of reinforced concrete buildings classified by damage grades in each area

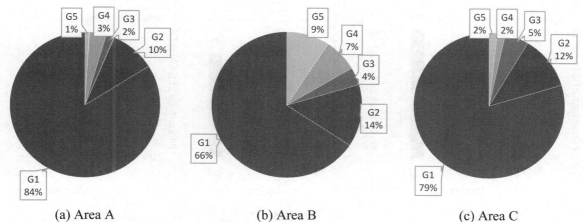

Figure 5.2.1.4-17 Number of masonry concrete buildings classified by damage grades in each area

各エリアにおける，鉄筋コンクリート造建物の被災度4以上の割合を階数別に算定した結果をFigure 5.2.1.4-18に示す．7階建て以上は被害率が高く出ているが，総数が少ないため考察からは除外する．いずれのエリアも5階建ての被害率が高い．特にエリアAでは3，4階建ての棟数が5階建ての2倍以上あるにも関わらず，被害率で見ると5階建ては約2割に被災度4以上の被害が出ており，3,4階建てには4以上の被災度の建物が少ない．

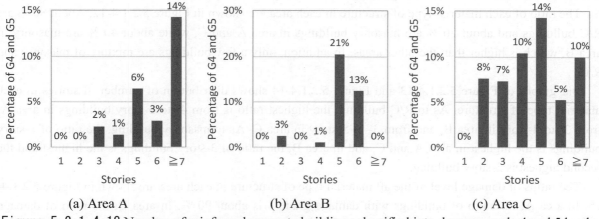

Figure 5.2.1.4-18 Number of reinforced concrete buildings classified into damage grade 4 and 5 by the number of stories

各エリアにおける，組積造建物の被災度2以上の割合を階数別に算定した結果をFigure 5.2.1.4-19に示す．4階建て以上は被害率が高く出ているが，総数が少ないため考察からは除外する．エリアA，Bは被害率の分布が酷似しており，1階建ての被害率が2階建て以上に比べて低い特徴がある．エリアA，Cとも1階建てが多いエリアであり，エリアAでは61棟，エリアCでは36棟の被害調査を行った．しかしエリアAの1階建ての被害率が7%であるのに対し，エリアCの1階建ての被害率は22%と大きい．一方でエリアCは3階建て以上の被害率が他のエリアに比べて低い特徴がある．

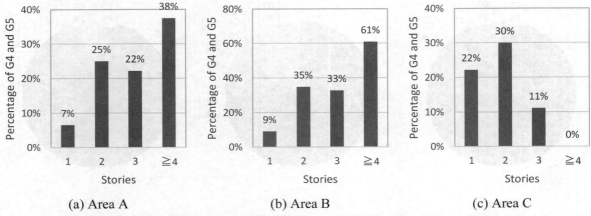

(a) Area A (b) Area B (c) Area C
Figure 5.2.1.4-19 Ratio of damaged masonry buildings by the number of floors

Since features of areas divided by the Ring road differ in building material, distribution of number of stories, and damage level of buildings, all the surveyed buildings are divided into 3 areas as shown in Figure 5.2.1.4-11. The areas are divided as follows: an area located in the north of the Ring road (area A), where medium-rise apartments are densely built; an area located in the west of the Ring road (area B), where there are low story housings and masonry buildings; an area located in the south of the Ring road (area C), where medium-rise buildings stand in rows along the street around the bus terminal.

The ratio of each material type of structure in each area are shown in Figure 5.2.1.4-12. About 80 % are R/C buildings and about 20 % are masonry buildings in area A and C, while about 40 % are masonry in area B, which is higher than the other areas. In addition, only a few buildings are mixture of masonry and R/C.

Bar graphs of Figure 5.2.1.4-13 and Figure 5.2.1.4-14 shows distribution of number of stories in each material type of structure. As to R/C building, the highest ratio is from 4- to 5-story buildings in area A, from 3- to 4-story in area B, and from 3- to 5-story in area C. As to masonry building, the ratio of 1-story buildings is the highest in area A and C, and in area B, the ratio of 3-story buildings is the highest and the second highest is 2-story building.

The ratios of damage level of the all material type of structure in each area are shown in Figure 5.2.1.4-15. In area A, the ratio of buildings with damage grade 1 is about 90 %. In area B, the ratio of damage grade 5 is higher than the other areas. In area C, the ratio of damage grade from 2 to 4 is relatively high, and the ratio of buildings whose damage level is more than 1 is higher.

The ratios of damage level of each material type of building in each area are shown in Figure 5.2.1.4-16 and Figure 5.2.1.4-17. As to R/C buildings, the ratio of damage grade 5 is about 3-4 % in all areas. The ratio of no-damaged buildings is, however, the highest in area A and the lowest in area C. As to masonry buildings, the ratio of the buildings whose damage level is more than 1 is especially high in area B, where the ratio of damage level 4 and 5 is higher than the other areas.

The ratios of R/C buildings whose damage level is more than 3 for each number of stories in each area are shown in Figure 5.2.1.4-18. The damage ratio of the buildings with over 6 floors is high because the number of those buildings is few. Hence it is excluded from consideration. The damage ratio of 5-story building is high in all areas. Above all, in area A, although the number of from 3- to 4-story buildings is more than twice as large as that of 5-story buildings, about 20 % of 5-story buildings have damage level of more than 3, and the buildings with from 3 to 4 stories whose damage level is more than 3 are few.

The ratios of masonry buildings whose damage level is more than 1 for each number of stories in each area are shown in Figure 5.2.1.4-19. The damage ratio of the buildings with over 3 floors is high because the number of those buildings is few. Hence it is excluded from consideration. The damage distribution patterns of area A and B are similar; the damage ratio of 1-story building is higher than that of buildings with 2 or more stories. Both in area A and C, there are many 1-story buildings; 61 buildings are investigated in area A, and 36 in area C. However, the damage ratio of 1-story buildings is 7 % in area A, while that in area C is 22 %. In area C, the damage ratio of the buildings with more than 2 stories is lower than that of the other areas.

(c) 各エリアの建物の特徴的な被害/ Remarkable Damage to Buildings in Each Area

Figure 5.2.1.4-20 にエリア A で被害が大きかった建物の位置を赤色で示す．また，図中の記号に対応する建物の被害状況を Photo 5.2.1.4-1 に示す．一部の鉄筋コンクリート造中層集合住宅で被害が見られた．比較的壁が少なく，弱点層となる 1 階に被害が集中し，倒壊に至る建物が散見される一方で，同規模の建物でも被害が見られないものも多数ある．

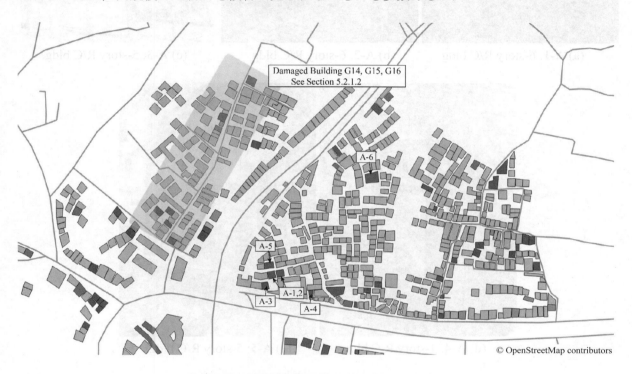

Figure 5.2.1.4-20 Area A

(a) A-1: 6-story R/C bldg.   (b) A-2: 6-story R/C bldg.   (c) A-3: 5-story R/C bldg.

(d) A-4: 4-story R/C bldg.   (e) A-5: 5-story R/C bldg.

(f) A-6: 6-story R/C bldg.

Photo 5.2.1.4-1 Severe damaged buildings on Area A

Figure 5.2.1.4-21 にエリア B で被害が大きかった建物の位置を示す．また，図中の記号に対応するエリアの被害状況を Photo 5.2.1.4-2 5.2.1.4-4 に示す．エリア B では，北側のエリアで深刻な被害が見られた．北西側のエリアでは，並立する組積造建物の大半が倒壊している．北東側のエリアでは，リングロード沿いの B-2 エリアにて，複数の中層鉄筋コンクリート造建物の倒壊が確認された．また，2 階建て鉄筋コンクリート造建物である B-3 建物でも，柱の圧縮破壊など深刻な被害が確認された．

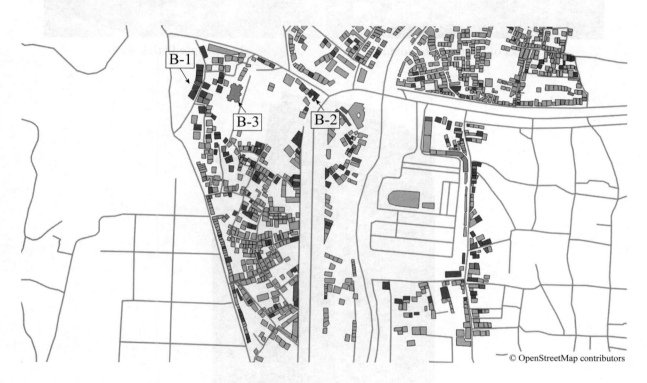

Figure 5.2.1.4-21 Area B

(a) Bricks of collapsed buildings   (b) Collapsed brick walls

(c) Severely damaged masonry building

Photo 5.2.1.4-2 Damage to masonry buildings in B-1 area of area B

Photo 5.2.1.4-3 Severely damaged reinforced concrete buildings in B-2 area of area B

(a) Front side

(b) Back side

(c) Compression failure of concrete

Photo 5.2.1.4-4 Severely damaged reinforced concrete buildings in B-3 area of area B

Figure 5.2.1.4-22 にエリア B で被害が大きかった建物の位置を示す．図中に示す被害建物については，すでに 5.2.1.2 項で示した G18～G23 の建物である．エリア C では，バスターミナル沿いの大通りに並立する中層鉄筋コンクリート造建物の一部が倒壊するなど，深刻な被害が散見された．

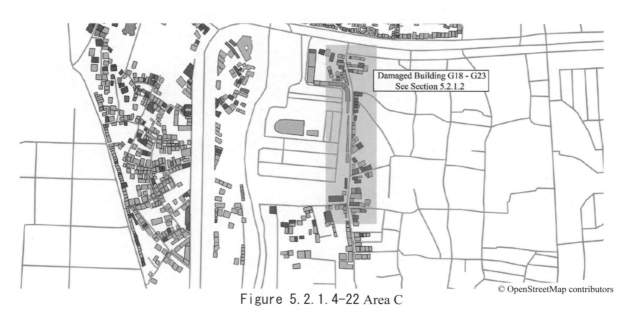

Figure 5.2.1.4-22 Area C

© OpenStreetMap contributors

In area A, there were a part of damaged medium-rise R/C apartments. Some buildings with few walls have concentrated damage at 1st story which is relatively weak, and the damage have led the buildings to collapse. On the other hand, many buildings with almost the same scale have little damage.

In area B, there were severely damaged buildings in the north area. In the northwest area, the majority of the masonry structures built side by side have collapsed. In the northeast area, in B-2 (See Photo 5.2.1.4-3) along the Ring road, several medium-rise R/C buildings have collapsed. In the R/C building B-3 with 2 floors, there were several severe damages such as shear failure in columns.

In area C, as described above, some of the medium-rise R/C buildings along the street around the bus terminal have severely damaged.

5.2.1.5 中層鉄筋コンクリート造建物の詳細調査/ Detailed Investigation of Mid-rise Reinforced Concrete Buildings

(1) 被災度区分判定/ Post-Earthquake Damage Evaluation

5.2.1.2「Gongabu 地区の建物と被害」に示した建物 G7 について被災度区分判定 [5.2.1-2)]を行った．建物平面図，立面図，断面図を Figure 5.2.1.5-1 および Figure 5.2.1.5-2 に，建物外観を Photo 5.2.1.5-1～5.2.1.5-3 に示す．建物は地上5階，ペントハウス1階の鉄筋コンクリート造の縫製工場である．建物，および被害の概要については 5.2.1.2 節(7)を参照されたい．

1階の柱に損傷が集中しており，1階の桁行方向，梁間方向それぞれにおいて被災度区分判定を行い，耐震性能残存率を算出した．なお，レンガ壁は考慮していない．それぞれの方向における各柱の損傷度を Figure 5.2.1.5-3 と Figure 5.2.1.5-4 に示す．また，損傷状況を Photo 5.2.1.5-4～5.2.1.5-17 に示す．

損傷度 V と判定された柱では，主に柱頭・柱脚において主筋が曲がり，コアコンクリートも崩れ落ちていた．また，垂れ壁・腰壁が付いている影響でせん断破壊した柱も見られた．損傷度 III と判定された柱では，比較的大きなひび割れが確認された．

最後に，各方向における耐震性能残存率を算出した（Table 5.2.1.5-1）．その結果，桁行方向の耐震性能残存率 $R=37.5\%$，梁間方向の耐震性能残存率 $R=38.9\%$ となり，両方向ともに上部構造の耐震性能残存率 R による被災度区分は大破（$R<60$）と判定された．

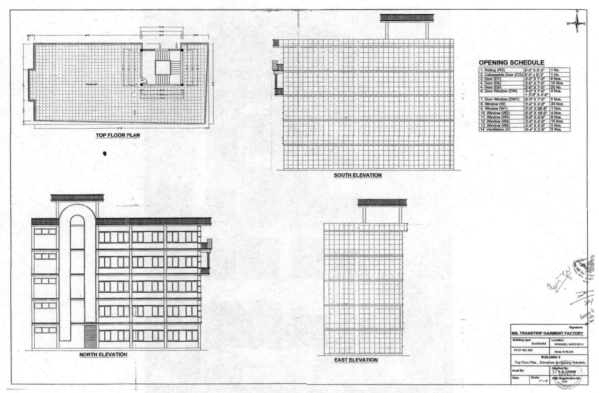

Figure 5.2.1.5-1 Top Floor Plan and elevation

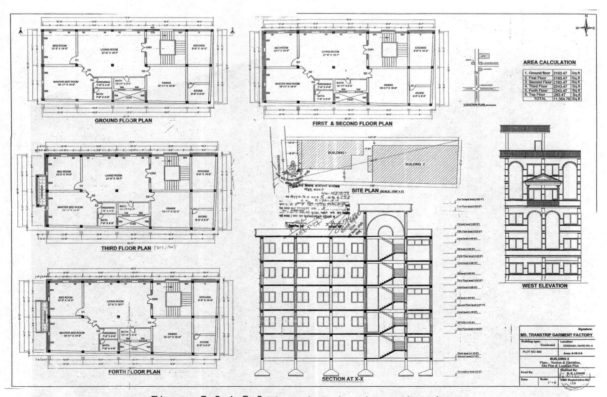

Figure 5.2.1.5-2 Floor plan, elevation, and section

Photo 5.2.1.5-1 West elevation

Photo 5.2.1.5-2 North elevation

Photo 5.2.1.5-3 South elevation

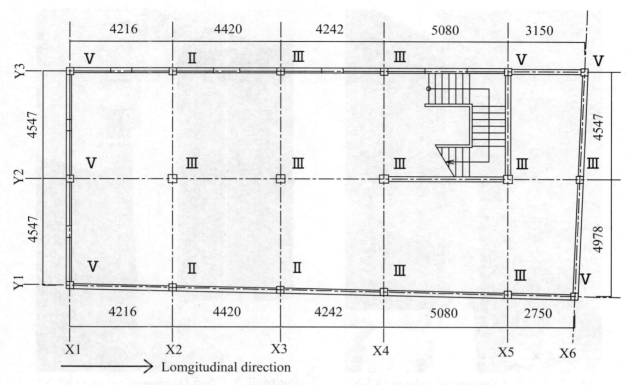

Figure 5.2.1.5-3 Damage level (1F, Longitudinal direction)

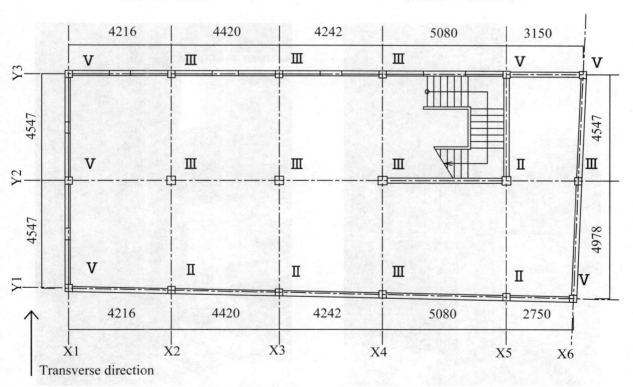

Figure 5.2.1.5-4 Damage level (1F, Transverse direction)

Photo 5.2.1.5-4 Damage of column (X1-Y1, Longitudinal direction)

Photo 5.2.1.5-5 Damage of column (X1-Y1, Transverse direction)

Photo 5.2.1.5-6 Damage of column (X1-Y2, Longitudinal direction)

Photo 5.2.1.5-7 Damage of column (X1-Y2, Transverse direction)

Photo 5.2.1.5-8 Damage of column (X1-Y3, Longitudinal direction)

Photo 5.2.1.5-9 Damage of column (X1-Y3, Transverse direction)

Photo 5.2.1.5-10 Damage of column (X5-Y3, Longitudinal direction)

Photo 5.2.1.5-11 Damage of column (X5-Y3, Transverse direction)

Photo 5.2.1.5-12 Damage of column (X6-Y1, Longitudinal and Transverse direction)

Photo 5.2.1.5-13 Damage of column (X6-Y1, Longitudinal and Transverse direction)

Photo 5.2.1.5-14 Damage of column (X3-Y3, Longitudinal direction)

Photo 5.2.1.5-15 Damage of column (X3-Y3, Transverse direction)

Photo 5.2.1.5-16 Damage of column (X3-Y2, Longitudinal direction)

Photo 5.2.1.5-17 Damage of column (X3-Y2, Transverse direction)

Table 5.2.1.5-1 Residual seismic performance ratio

Direction	Residual Seismic Performance Ratio R [%]
Longitudinal	37.5
Transverse	38.9

Post-Earthquake Damage Evaluation[5.2.1-2)] was carried out for building G7 explained in Section 5.2.1.2. The floor plan, elevation, and section are shown in Figure 5.2.1.5-1 and Figure 5.2.1.5-2. There is sewing plant building, which had 5-story masonry infilled RC frames structure. For damage on the first floor column were concentrated, Post-Earthquake Damage Evaluation in the first floor was carried out. In addition, Residual Seismic Performance Ratio was calculated. Incidentally, the masonry wall is not considered.

The damage level of column in each direction are shown in Figure 5.2.1.5-3 and Figure 5.2.1.5-4. In addition, damaged condition is shown in Photo 5.2.1.5-2 to 5.2.1.5-17.

In the column which determined damage level V, rebar was yielded in column's top and bottom and core concrete was collapsed. In addition, there was the column that shear fracture under the influence of the spandrel walls. In the column which determined damage level III, relatively large cracks occurred.

Finally, Residual Seismic Performance Ratio "R" was calculated in each direction as shown in Table 5.2.1.5-1. As a result, R=37.5% in the longitudinal direction and R=38.9% in the transvers direction. Therefore, both directions affected the Post-Earthquake Damage is determined "Severely damaged".

(2)　保有水平耐力の算定/ Lateral Seismic Capacity Prediction

5.2.1.2「Gongabu 地区の建物と被害」にて述べた，大破した 5 階建て RC 造建物 G7 を対象として，保有耐力の算定を行った．保有水平耐力の算定にあたり，材料強度はコンクリートは現地建

物で実施したリバウンドハンマーによる非破壊試験結果を，鉄筋は現地で一般的に使用されている鉄筋の引張試験結果に基づき設定した．

リバウンドハンマー試験は，Proceq 社製シュミットハンマーを用いて行った．1 階 X1-Y1 柱を対象として，柱中央部に格子状の検査点を設け，それぞれの検査点に対し 3 回リバウンドハンマーを実施した（Figure 5.2.1.5-5）．試験結果の一覧を Table 5.2.1.5-2 に示す．リバウンドハンマーの表示値の平均値は 41.5 となった．コンクリート強度推定値は，式 (5.2.1.5-1) の推定式より，41.3N/mm² となった．

$$\sigma_{estimate} = 1.3 \times R_{ave} - 18 \tag{5.2.1.5-1}$$

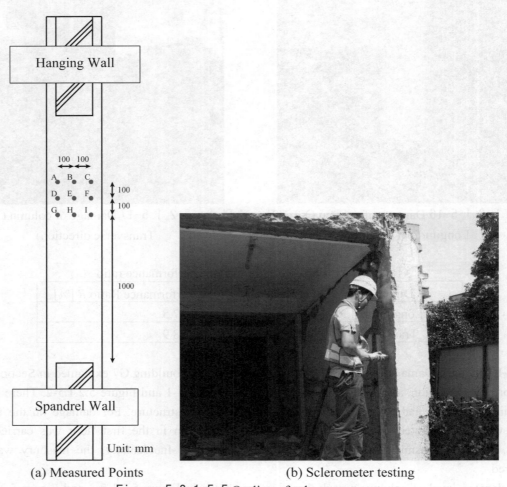

(a) Measured Points　　　　(b) Sclerometer testing

Figure 5.2.1.5-5 Outline of sclerometer test

Table 5.2.1.5-2 Results of sclerometer test (N/mm²)

A	46, 46, 48	B	45, 41, 40	C	45, 45, 46
D	43, 47, 49	E	44, 47, 48	F	48, 44, 44
G	46, 44, 43	H	44, 48, 50	I	47, 48, 45
Average : 45.6					

対象建物の被害状況および材料試験結果より，保有耐力の算定では，下記の仮定条件を設けた．
［仮定条件］
- 2 階梁，基礎梁は剛とし，柱の反曲点高さは階高中央にあるものと仮定する．
- 腰壁・垂れ壁付きの柱は，柱の可撓長さ＝内法高さとする．
- 各階荷重は，重量物が載っていた当時の状況を加味し，12kN/m² とする．

- コンクリート強度はリバウンドハンマーから得られた 40N/mm² とする.
- 主筋,せん断補強筋の降伏強度は 415N/mm² とする(Grade 415 を想定).
- 煉瓦壁の耐力は考慮しない.

柱部材の強度については,鉄筋コンクリート構造計算規準 [5.2.1-3]に従い,曲げ強度 M_u は略算式 (5.2.1.5-2) を,曲げ強度時せん断力 Q_{mu} は式 (5.2.1.5-3) を,せん断強度 Q_{su} は荒川 mean 式 (5.2.1.5-4) を用いて算定した.

$$M_u = 0.8 a_t \sigma_y D + 0.5 ND\left(1 - \frac{N}{bDF_c}\right) \quad (5.2.1.5\text{-}2)$$

$$Q_{mu} = M_u / h_0 \quad (5.2.1.5\text{-}3)$$

$$Q_{su} = \left\{ \frac{0.068 p_t^{0.23}(F_c + 18)}{M/Qd + 0.12} + 0.85\sqrt{p_w \sigma_{wy}} + 0.1\sigma_0 \right\} bj \quad (5.2.1.5\text{-}4)$$

ここに,a_t: 引張鉄筋断面積(mm²),σ_y: 引張鉄筋の降伏強度(N/mm²),b: 柱幅(mm),D: 柱せい (mm),N: 軸力(N),h_0: 柱反曲点高さ(mm),p_t: 引張鉄筋比(%),F_c: コンクリート強度(N/mm²),M/Qd: シアスパン比,p_w: 帯筋比,σ_{wy}: 帯筋の降伏強度(N/mm²),σ_0: 軸応力度(N/mm²),j: 有効せい(mm)

各柱の軸力は,Figure 5.2.1.5-6 のように各柱の負担面積を仮定し,上階荷重より算定した.算定した軸力および軸力比を Figure 5.2.1.5-7 に示す.柱の軸力比は 0.07~0.26 となり,中柱において軸力比が 0.25 程度と比較的大きな値となっていることが確認できる.

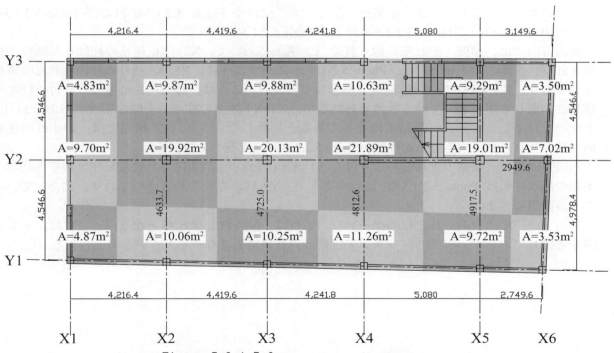

Figure 5.2.1.5-6 Support area of each column

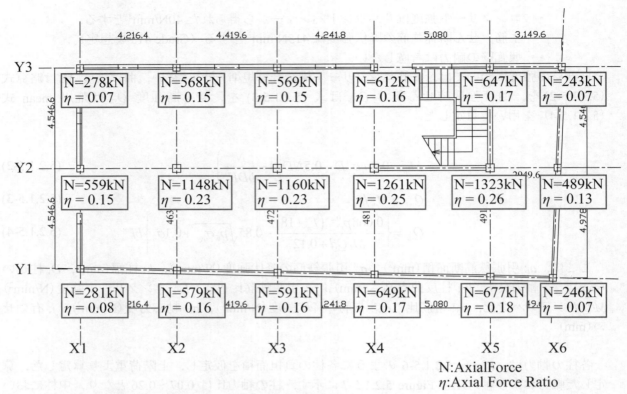

Figure 5.2.1.5-7 Estimated axial force of columns at the 1st floor

　仮定に基づいた保有耐力算定結果を，長辺方向について Figure 5.2.1.5-8 および Table 5.2.1.5-3 に，短辺方向について Figure 5.2.1.5-9 および Table 5.2.1.5-4 に示す．

　長辺方向では，腰壁・垂れ壁の取り付く Y3 構面において，X2～X6 通りの柱はせん断柱と判定される．実際の調査建物では，Photo 5.2.1.5-18 に示すように，X5, X6 通りの柱のみせん断破壊をしており，X2～X4 柱では計算結果と整合していない．これは，腰壁・垂れ壁の取り付く柱の可撓長さの取り方が影響していると考えられるが，X2～X4 通りの柱のせん断余裕度はおおむね 1.0 となっていることから，計算結果は妥当であると判断した．また，Y2 構面では，いずれの柱も曲げ柱と判定され，実際の破壊性状（Photo 5.2.1.5-19）と整合している．

　短辺方向では，腰壁・垂れ壁が取り付く X1 構面において，Y2 柱のみせん断柱と判定される．実際の破壊性状は Photo 5.2.1.5-20 に示すように，Y2 柱のみせん断破壊しており，整合していることが確認できる．

　長辺方向，短辺方向それぞれのベースシア係数は，0.29 および 0.25 となる．ここには，レンガ壁を考慮しておらず，実際のベースシア係数は，計算結果よりやや大きいと考えられる．

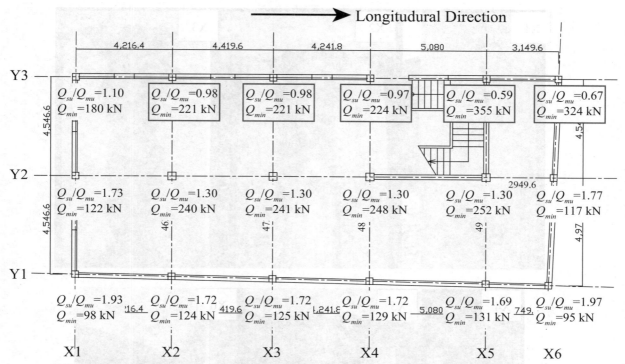

Figure 5.2.1.5-8 Calculated Results of Horizontal Strength for Longitudinal Direction

Table 5.2.1.5-3 Horizontal strength for the longitudinal direction

Position	b [mm]	D [mm]	N [kN]	h_0 [mm]	M_u [kNm]	Q_{mu} [kN]	Q_{su} [kN]	Q_{su}/Q_{mu} [-]	Q_{min} [kN]
X1-Y1	305	305	281	2750	135	98	189	1.93	98
X2-Y1	305	305	579	2750	170	124	213	1.72	124
X3-Y1	305	305	591	2750	171	125	214	1.72	125
X4-Y1	305	305	649	2750	177	129	218	1.69	129
X5-Y1	305	305	677	2750	180	131	220	1.69	131
X6-Y1	305	305	246	2750	130	95	187	1.97	95
X1-Y2	305	305	559	2750	168	122	211	1.73	122
X2-Y2	355	355	1148	2750	331	241	314	1.30	241
X3-Y2	355	355	1160	2750	332	242	315	1.30	242
X4-Y2	355	355	1261	2750	341	248	323	1.30	248
X5-Y2	355	355	1323	2750	347	252	328	1.30	252
X6-Y2	305	305	489	2750	160	117	206	1.77	117
X1-Y3	305	305	278	1500	135	180	198	1.10	180
X2-Y3	305	305	568	1500	169	225	221	0.98	221
X3-Y3	305	305	569	1500	169	225	221	0.98	221
X4-Y3	305	305	612	1500	173	231	224	0.97	224
X5-Y3	305	305	647	760	231	607	355	0.59	355
X6-Y3	305	305	243	760	184	484	324	0.67	324

Where, b: width, D: depth, N: Axial Force, h_0: height of point of contraflexure, M_u: bending strength, Q_{mu}: shear force at bending failure, Q_{su}: shear strength

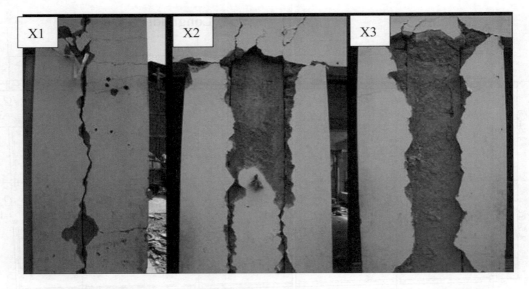

Photo 5.2.1.5-18 Damage of columns on Y3 axis

Photo 5.2.1.5-19 Damage of Columns on Y2 axis

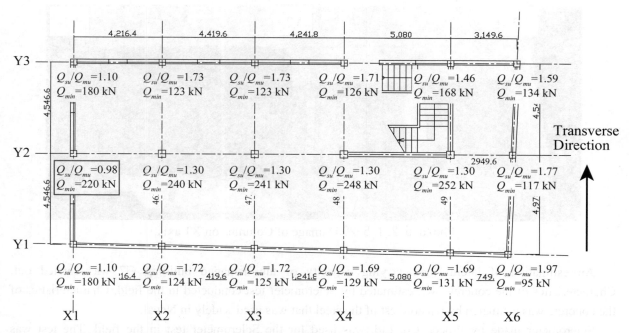

Figure 5.2.1.5-9 Calculated Results of Horizontal Strength for transverse Direction

Table 5.2.1.5-4 Horizontal strength for the transverse direction

Position	b [mm]	D [mm]	N [kN]	h₀ [mm]	M_u [kNm]	Q_{mu} [kN]	Q_{su} [kN]	Q_{su}/Q_{mu} [-]	Q_{min} [kN]
X1-Y1	305	305	281	1500	135	180	198	1.10	180
X2-Y1	305	305	579	2750	170	124	213	1.72	124
X3-Y1	305	305	591	2750	171	125	214	1.72	125
X4-Y1	305	305	649	2750	177	129	218	1.69	129
X5-Y1	305	305	677	2750	180	131	220	1.69	131
X6-Y1	305	305	246	2750	130	95	187	1.97	95
X1-Y2	305	305	559	1500	168	224	220	0.98	220
X2-Y2	355	355	1148	2750	331	241	314	1.30	241
X3-Y2	355	355	1160	2750	332	242	315	1.30	242
X4-Y2	355	355	1261	2750	341	248	323	1.30	248
X5-Y2	355	355	1323	2750	347	252	328	1.30	252
X6-Y2	305	305	489	2750	160	117	206	1.77	117
X1-Y3	305	305	278	1500	135	180	198	1.10	180
X2-Y3	305	305	568	2750	169	123	212	1.73	123
X3-Y3	305	305	569	2750	169	123	212	1.73	123
X4-Y3	305	305	612	2750	173	126	215	1.71	126
X5-Y3	305	305	647	2750	231	168	245	1.46	168
X6-Y3	305	305	243	2750	184	134	213	1.59	134

Where, b: width, D: depth, N: Axial Force, h_0: height of point of contraflexure, M_u: bending strength, Q_{mu}: shear force at bending failure, Q_{su}: shear strength

Photo 5.2.1.5-20 Damage of Columns on X1 axis

An estimation of lateral load-carrying capacity of the damaged building G7 was carried out. Characteristics of the concrete was estimated by Sclerometer test conducted in the field. Characteristics of the concrete was estimated by tension test of the steel that was used widely in Nepal.

Sclerometer made by Proceq Co. Ltd. was used for the Sclerometer test in the field. The test was conducted on 1F X1-Y1 column. We set nine inspection points on the middle height of the column, see Figure 5.2.1.5-5 (a). The test results are shown in Table 5.2.1.5-2. The average value of the test was 45.6. Due to the equation (5.2.1.5-1), an estimated compressive strength of the concrete was about 41.3 N/mm².

$$\sigma_{estimate} = 1.3 \times R_{ave} - 18 \quad (5.2.1.5\text{-}1)$$

Due to the results of the material test and damage of the building, the following assumptions is set to estimate the horizontal strength of the building.

[Assumptions]
- Beams of base floor and 2nd floor is rigid. The point of contrary flexure is on the middle height of the floor.
- The restrained area by hanging wall and spandrel wall is rigid, so that, the deformable length of the column with hanging wall and spandrel wall is equal to the clear height.
- The mass ratio of each floor is 12 kN/m² considering the situation on the earthquake.
- A compressive strength of concrete is 40N/mm².
- A yield strength of rebars is 415 N/mm².
- A strength of the brick wall is neglected.

An ultimate strength of reinforced concrete column was calculated due to AIJ standards[5.2.1-3]. The ultimate bending moment is calculated due to eq. (5.2.1.5-2), the shear force on the ultimate bending moment is calculated due to eq. (5.2.1.5-3) and the ultimate shear strength is calculated due to eq. (5.2.1.5-4).

$$M_u = 0.8 a_t \sigma_y D + 0.5 ND\left(1 - \frac{N}{bDF_c}\right) \quad (5.2.1.5\text{-}2)$$

$$Q_{mu} = M_u / h_0 \quad (5.2.1.5\text{-}3)$$

$$Q_{su} = \left\{ \frac{0.068 p_t^{0.23}(F_c + 18)}{M/Qd + 0.12} + 0.85\sqrt{p_w \sigma_{wy}} + 0.1\sigma_0 \right\} bj \quad (5.2.1.5\text{-}4)$$

A supporting area of each column is assumed as Figure 5.2.1.5-6. The estimated axial force and axial force ratio of each column is shown in Figure 5.2.1.5-7. The axial force ratio is from 0.07 to 0.26. The axial force ratio of center column is comparatively high value.

On the longitudinal direction, failure mode of X2 – X6 column on Y3 diagonal, these are with hanging wall and spandrel wall, is estimated as shear failure. In the field, X5 – X6 column on Y3 direction was damaged as shear failure, shown in Photo 5.2.1.5-18. But, X2 – X4 column on Y3 direction was damaged as bending failure. The assumption of the deformable length of the column with hanging and spandrel wall might effect to the deference of failure mode between the estimation and inspection. An estimated failure mode of the columns on Y2 diagonal are bending failure, that is agreed with the inspection results, shown in Photo 5.2.1.5-19.

On the span direction, failure mode of X1-Y2 column is only judged shear failure, which is with hanging and spandrel wall. In the field, that column was damaged as shear failure, so that, the calculation results is agreed with the inspection. (See Photo 5.2.1.5-20)

A base shear coefficient is estimated as 0.29 in longitudinal direction and 025 in transverse direction. The base shear coefficient would be larger than the calculated value, because the shear strength of brick wall was neglected in this calculation.

The calculation results of longitudinal direction are shown in Figure 5.2.1.5-8 and Table 5.2.1.5-3. The calculation results of transverse direction are shown in Figure 5.2.1.5-9 and Table 5.2.1.5-4.

5.2.1.6 市内建物調査のまとめ/ Summaries

カトマンズ市内建物の調査を行い，大破した鉄筋コンクリート造建物の構造的特徴について考察を行った．また，Gongabu 地区にある建物の全数調査を行い，建物の種類や構造形式，被害率の定量的に把握することでカトマンズ市内の建物の被害の全容の解明を試みた．その結果，鉄筋コンクリート構造の被害が組積造建物と近い割合で被害を受けていたこと，高層の建物ほど被害が大きかったことが明らかとなった．

また，現地調査から得た構造詳細を基に，ネパールで標準的な設計・施工方法によって建てられた 5 階建て鉄筋コンクリート造建物の耐震性能評価を行い，耐震性能の推定を行った．その結果，構造上は日本の建物と同程度の耐力を有していることがわかった．限られた情報により本調査ではこれ以上の推定は不可能であるが，今後より精確な評価を行うためには，入力地震動の推定や地盤の特徴を考慮した計算が必要であると考えられる．なお，8 章では詳細解析によって本調査建物の耐震性能の推定を行っている．

Structural characteristics of damaged buildings in Kathmandu valley were investigated. The numbers of buildings damaged in Gongabu area were investigated in accordance with the damage level, structural system and etc. From the result of investigation, the numbers of damaged reinforced concrete buildings were similar to that of damaged masonry buildings, and the damage is more severe when the number of stories is larger.

Additionally, seismic performance evaluation was conducted for five-story reinforced concrete building which was severely damaged. The assumed seismic performance was calculated based on assumptions given by field investigation results and the seismic capacity of the buildings is almost the same as the buildings in Japan. For further accurate investigation, seismic intensity of the ground and ground characteristic of the building is needed. Note that Chapter 8 shows the investigation of seismic capacity using analytical study of this building.

5.2.1.7 参考文献/ References

5.2.1-1) Grunthal G. (1998), European Macroseismic Scale 1998, Conseil de l'Europe Cahiers du Centre Europeen de Geodynamique et de Seismologie, Luxembourg. Available on: http://www.franceseisme.fr/EMS98_Original_english.pdf

5.2.1-2) 日本建築防災協会：震災建築物の被災度区分判定基準および復旧技術指針，2002

5.2.1-3) 日本建築学会：鉄筋コンクリート構造計算規準・同解説，2010
5.2.1-1) Grunthal G. (1998), European Macroseismic Scale 1998, Conseil de l'Europe Cahiers du Centre Europeen de Geodynamique et de Seismologie, Luxembourg. Available on:
5.2.1-2) http://www.franceseisme.fr/EMS98_Original_english.pdf
5.2.1-3) JBDPA: Post-earthquake Damage Evaluation and Rehabilitation, Japan Building Disaster Prevension Association, 2002. (in Japanese)
5.2.1-4) Architectural Institute of Japan: AIJ Standard for Structural Calculation of Reinforced Concrete Structures, 2010. (in Japanese)

5.2.2 カトマンズ市外の被害/ Earthquake Damage outside Kathmandu
5.2.2.1 調査地域と方針/ Investigation Area and Strategy

カトマンズ市外の調査は，Kathmandu 周辺に位置する Bhaktapur, Dhading, Lalitpur, Nuwakot, Sindhupalchok の各行政区にわたって実施した（Figure 5.2.2.1-1）．現地調査行程を Figure 5.2.2.1-2 の地図上に示す．同図より，調査地域は本震の震央から南東方向へ直線距離約 50km，最大余震の震央から西方向へ直線距離約 30km 以遠の範囲である．

調査の目的として，以下の項目を設定した．

【調査目的】
1) 首都郊外の建築物の特性と被害を把握する．
2) Kathmandu よりも震源に近い地域の建築物の特性と被害を把握する．
3) 各地域の類似建築物の被害状況より地震動強さを比較する．

特に上記の目的 3)を遂行するため，類似した構造特性を有する建築物として学校校舎に焦点を当て，以下の方針の下に被害調査を行った．

【調査方針】
1) 各行政区の教育委員会を通じて学校校舎の図面（標準設計図や耐震補強設計図など）を収集する．
2) 現地調査では学校校舎の構造特性や損傷を実測し，例えば，壁率と被災度の関係などを定量的に評価し得る資料を収集する．ここで，損傷した建築物の被災度は European Macroseismic Scale 1998 (EMS-98)[5.2.2-1)]に基づいて評価する．
3) 調査対象とする学校周辺では，地域の被害率を把握するため，一般建築物の特性と被害程度も区域を制限しての悉皆調査により実測する．

上記の方針に基づく調査結果の報告にあたり，現地調査で見られた学校校舎の構造形式を Table 5.2.2.1-1 にまとめ，以下では同表の略称を用いて構造形式を示すこととする．また，本調査の一部では組積構造校舎の耐震性能の一指標として壁率を評価した．壁率の定義は式 (5.2.2.1-1)のとおりである．

$$P_w = \frac{A_w}{A} \times 100 \tag{5.2.2.1-1}$$

ここで，A_w：建物の各主軸方向に有効な壁の断面積，mm^2
　　　　A：建物の壁率を評価する対象階が支持する総床面積，mm^2

(a) Map of Nepal

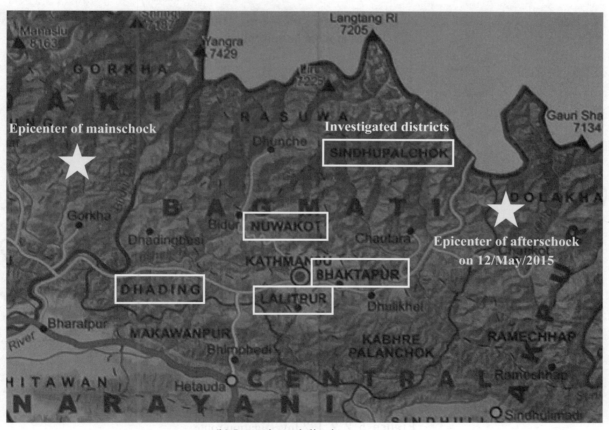

(b) Investigated districts on map

Figure 5.2.2.1-1 Investigated districts

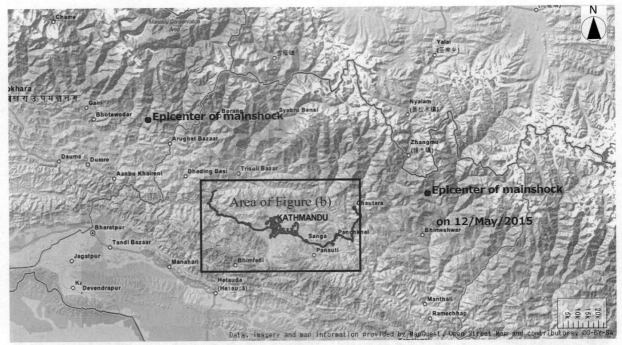

(a) Map with the epicenters

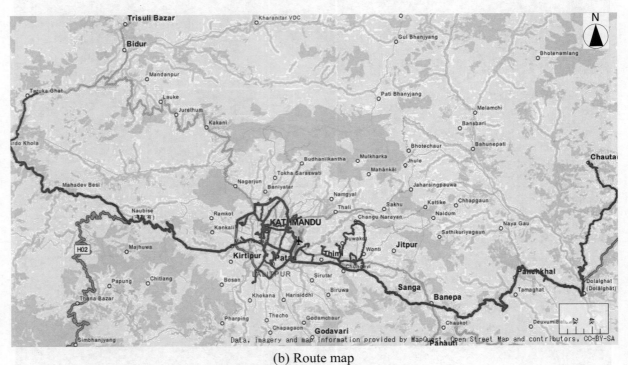

(b) Route map

Figure 5.2.2.1-2 Investigation route

Table 5.2.2.1-1 Structural systems observed in the investigated area

(a) Structural systems for masonry wall

Wall structural system		Abbreviation	Summary	Photograph
Masonry	Joint			
Stone	Mud	Stone-Mud	Wall laied stone with mud joint	5.2.2.1-1(a)
Adobe	Mud	Adobe-Mud	Wall laied adobe with mud joint	5.2.2.1-1(b)
Brick	Mud	Brick-Mud	Wall laied brick with mud joint	5.2.2.1-1(c)
Brick	Mortar	Brick-Mortar	Wall laied brick with mortar joint	5.2.2.1-1(d)
Concrete Block	Mortar	Block-Mortar	Wall laied concrete block with mortar joint	5.2.2.1-1(e)

(b) Structural systems for roof

Roof structural system		Abbreviation	Summary	Photograph
Structure	Roofing			
Timber	Galvanized iron sheet	Timber-GI	Roofing with galvanized iron sheet on timber roof truss	5.2.2.1-2(a)
Timber	Tile	Timber-Tile	Roofing with tile on timber roof truss	5.2.2.1-2(b)
Timber	Grass	Timber-Grass	Roofing with grass on timber roof truss	5.2.2.1-2(c)
Steel	Galvanized iron sheet	Steel-GI	Roofing with galvanized iron sheet on steel roof truss	5.2.2.1-2(d)
RC	RC slab	RC	Roofing with RC slab	5.2.2.1-2(e)

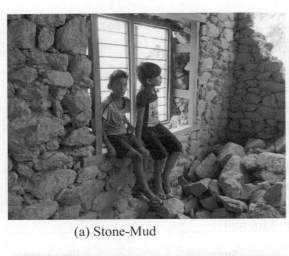
(a) Stone-Mud

(b) Adobe-Mud

(c) Brick-Mud

(d) Brick-Mortar

(e) Block-Mortar

Photo 5.2.2.1-1 Structural systems for masonry wall

(a) Timber-GI (b) Timber-Tile
(c) Timber-Grass (d) Steel-GI
(e) RC

Photo 5.2.2.1-2 Structural systems for roof

Five districts close to Kathmandu were covered by the investigation: Bhaktapur, Dhading, Lalitpur, Nuwakot, and Sindhupalchok (Figure 5.2.2.1-1). Figure 5.2.2.1-2 tracks the investigation route, which indicates that the investigation was performed beyond 50 km south-east and 30 km west from the epicenters of the main shock and the aftershock, respectively.

The objectives of the investigation were as follows:
[Objectives]
1) To obtain structural characteristics and damage of buildings outside Kathmandu.

2) To obtain structural characteristics and damage of buildings which locate closer to the epicenters than those in Kathmandu.

3) To compare seismic intensities of the investigated area based on damage to similar types of buildings.

In particular, the investigation focused on school buildings to accomplish the third objective, then was conducted according to the following strategies:

[Strategies]

1) Obtaining structural drawings, such as standard design drawing and seismic strengthening design plan, from local boards of education in the investigated districts.

2) Quantitatively measuring structural characteristics and damage of school buildings, e.g. to evaluate a relationship between wall-to-total floor area ratio and damage grade based on European Macroseismic Scale 1998 (EMS-98)[5.2.2-1].

3) Performing inventory surveys at limited areas around targeted schools to obtain damage ratios of ordinary buildings in the area.

Structural systems of school buildings observed during the investigation are summarized in Table 5.2.2.1-1 to report the investigation results in the following, where abbreviations in the table were used to identify the structural systems. A wall-to-total floor area ratio was defined by Equation (5.2.2.1-1) to evaluate the seismic performance of several masonry school buildings.

$$P_w = \frac{A_w}{A} \times 100 \qquad (5.2.2.1\text{-}1)$$

where, A_w: gross wall area of building parallel to each principal direction, mm^2; A: total floor area supported by story concerned, mm^2

5.2.2.2 学校校舎の標準設計事例/ Standard Design for Schools

Sindhupalchowk 行政区の Chautara 地区にある教育庁において，組積造による学校建物の標準設計図を入手した [5.2.2-2]．標準設計は，ネパールの教育・スポーツ省の教育局（Department of education, Ministry of education & sports, Government of Nepal）によって，山間部に建設する学校の設計図として示されたものであり，教育への支援金によって建設される小学校 (Primary school) を対象としている．公示日は 2003 年 10 月 19 日である．

標準設計の平面図を Figure 5.2.2.2-1 に示す．Figure 5.2.2.2-1(b)より，1 教室の寸法は 7200 mm×4625 mm である．壁厚は 400 mm とされている．ここで，壁の構造形式は図面上では指定されていない．Figure 5.2.2.2-1(b)より，壁にバットレスを設けて倒壊防止を図っていることがわかる．立面図を Figure 5.2.2.2-2 に示す．標準図面では平屋建ての校舎が示されている．断面図を Figure 5.2.2.2-3 に示す．屋根の構造は，亜鉛めっき鋼管で組んだトラス架構上に亜鉛めっき鋼板を葺くものであり，トラス架構の脚部は壁内部に埋め込まれている．このような屋根構造も耐震性に寄与していると考えられる．

標準設計建物の壁率を Figure 5.2.2.2-1(b)を基に算定したところ，桁行方向が 8.7%，梁間方向が 10.2%であり，梁間方向のほうが若干大きかった．ここで，壁率計算ではそれぞれの方向で耐震上有効と考えられる断面積を考慮しており，開口部の断面積は算入していない．

実際に被害を受けた校舎で，この標準設計に近い平面を持つ建物も存在した．それらを次の 1) から 3) に示す（詳しくは各項を参照）．

1) 5.2.2.4(5) 項：E 高校の平屋建て校舎は，標準設計に近い構造であった．被害は軽微であり，標準設計により耐震性が確保されていたと考えられる．

2) 5.2.2.4(6) 項：F 高校の 3 階建ての A 棟では，1 教室の寸法（7200 mm×4625 mm）はまったく同じで，3 教室が連続する形であった．A 棟は全層が倒壊するという甚大な被害を受けたが，この建物は壁厚が標準設計よりも薄く，壁のバットレスや鋼材による屋根がなかったため，標準設計よりも耐震性に劣っていた可能性が考えられる．

3) 5.2.2.4(9)項：I 高校の A 棟は，標準設計に近い構造であった．妻壁が転倒する被害を受けており，標準設計によっても耐震性が確保されない場合があることに注意が必要である．

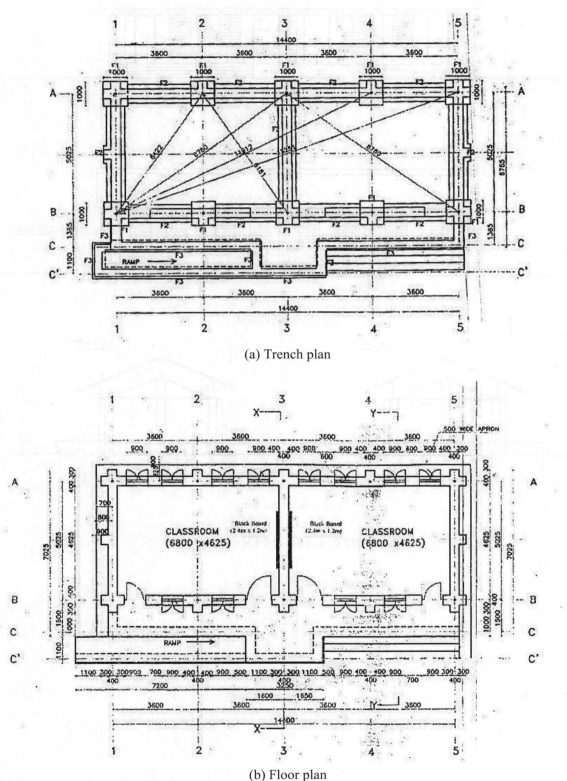

(a) Trench plan

(b) Floor plan

Figure 5.2.2.2-1 Trench plan and floor plan

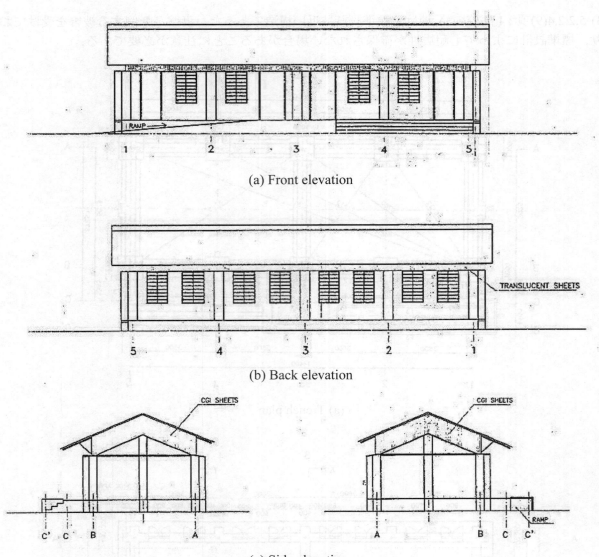

(a) Front elevation

(b) Back elevation

(c) Side elevations

Figure 5.2.2.2-2 Elevations

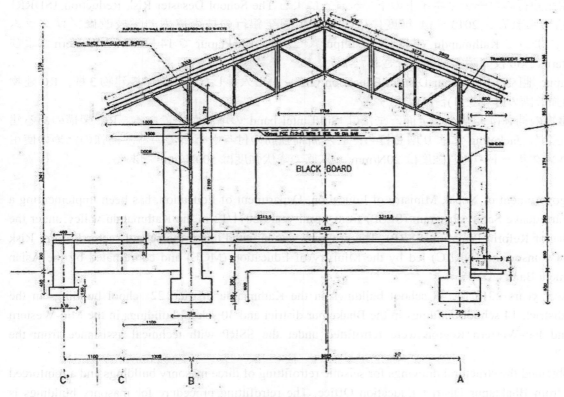

Figure 5.2.2.2-3 Section (X-X)

We obtained Nepalese standard design plans for masonry school buildings[5.2.2-2)] in the mountain region from an educational office in Chaurata, Sindhupalchowk district. The standard design was issued by the Department of Education, Ministry of Education & Sports (Government of Nepal) for the construction of primary schools in support of education. The date of issue was Oct. 19, 2003.

Figure 5.2.2.2-1 shows the plans of the standard design. According to Figure 5.2.2.2-1(b), the dimensions of a classroom are 7200 mm by 4625 mm. Wall thickness is 400 mm. The structural system of the masonry wall is not specified. According to Figure 5.2.2.2-1(b), buttresses are arranged at the walls to prevent the out-of-plane failure of the masonry walls. Figure 5.2.2.2-2 shows the elevations of the standard design. The building of the standard design is one-story high. Figure 5.2.2.2-3 shows the section of the standard design. The structural system of the roof is a trussed frame that consists of galvanizing steel pipes. Galvanized steel sheets are then used to cover the trussed frame. The bottoms of the trussed frame are embedded deeply into the wall. The described roof structure contributes constructively to the overall structural integrity and seismic performance of the building.

The wall ratios of the standard design plan are 8.7% for the longitudinal direction and 10.2% for the transverse direction.

During the Nepal earthquake, some of the school buildings that were designed using the standard design plan were damaged. The specifications of the buildings and the damage levels are described in paragraphs 5.2.2.4(5), 5.2.2.4(6), and 5.2.2.4(9). In summary, the masonry school buildings that were designed using the standard plan had a relatively high seismic performance.

5.2.2.3 学校校舎の補強設計事例/ Seismic Retrofitting Plan of School Building

ネパール教育省では，2011/12 年度から Kathmandu Valley under School Sector Reform Program (SSRP) において School Earthquake Safety Program (SESP) を実施してきた．このプログラムは，

アジア開発銀行のコーディネイトの下で教育省による The School Desaster Risk Reduction (SDRR) により始められた．2013～14 年度には，アジア開発銀行の技術協力で学校改修プログラム (SSRP) によって Kathmandu で 48 校，Lalitpur で 22 校，Bhaktapur で 14 校，Mid-Western および Far-Western で 30 校の耐震補強がなされた [5.2.2-3]．

Bhaktapur 地区の Bhaktapur District Education Office から入手した組積造学校建物 3 棟，RC 建物 1 棟の補強計画の詳細を(1)～(4)に示す．

組積造建物の補強は，壁への全面，または Sill/Lintel band の増設が主である．RC 架構のある建物は，柱梁も Jacketing により増し打ち，せん断補強筋の付与も行っている．補強のための使用材料のコンクリートの 4 週強度は $20N/mm^2$，鉄筋の降伏強度は $500N/mm^2$ である．

The government of Nepal, Ministry of Education, Department of Education, has been implementing a School Earthquake Safety Program (SESP) from fiscal years 2011/12 in the Kathmandu valley under the School Sector Reform Program (SSRP). The program was initiated under the school sector Reform Risk Reduction Consortium (NRRC) led by the Ministry of Education (MOE) and coordinated by the Asian Development Bank (ADB).

In fiscal years 2013/14, 48 school buildings in the Kathmandu district, 22 school buildings in the Lalitpur district, 14 school buildings in the Bhaktapur district and 30 school buildings in the Mid-Western region and Far-Western Region were retrofitted under the SSRP with technical assistance from the ADB[5.2.2-3].

We obtained the structural drawings for seismic retrofitting of three masonry buildings and a reinforced building from Bhaktapur District Education Office. The retrofitting procedure for masonry buildings is mainly reinforced jacketing on the face of the walls. The retrofitting procedure for the RC building is putting steel stirrups in beams and columns in addition to jacketing on the walls.

(1)　A 高校/ Higher Secondary School A

本校舎は，コの字形 3 階建て建物で，構造形式は Brick-Mortar，壁厚は 1 階 600mm，2 階 500mm，3 階 350mm である．1 階平面図を Figure 5.2.2.3-1 に示す．また，補強計画は Figure 5.2.2.3-2 に示すように一部の窓の閉塞と壁の Jacketing（縦筋は 4.75mmφ@175，一部 8mmφ@200，横筋 4.75mmφ@300），および既存木製梁と壁接合部の固定である [5.2.2-4]．なお，本建物は補強が実施される前に被災し，大きな被害を受けた．損傷状況については，5.2.2.4 (1)において後述する．

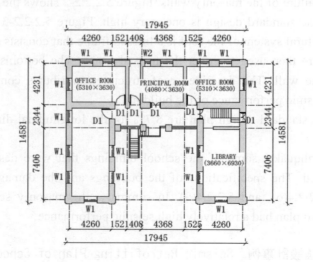

GROUND FLOOR PLAN

Figure 5.2.2.3-1　Ground Floor Plan

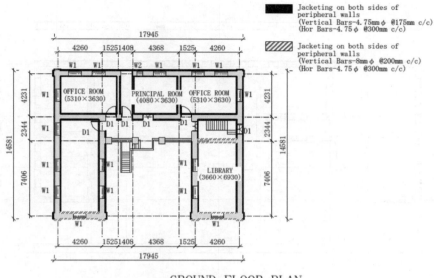

GROUND FLOOR PLAN

Figure 5.2.2.3-2　Retrofitting of Ground Floor Plan

This school building is a U-shaped plan three-story brick-mortar masonry building. Wall thickness is as follows: first floor-600mm, second floor-500mm, third floor-350mm. Figure 5.2.2.3-1 shows the first floor plan. The retrofitting plan is mainly jacketing, window obstruction and anchorage to existing wooden beams and existing walls as shown in Figure 5.2.2.3-2[5.2.2-4].

This building was damaged by the earthquake before retrofitting. The details of the damage are shown in section 5.2.2.4 (1).

(2)　B 高校/ Higher Secondary School B

本校舎は，E 字形 2 階建て建物で，構造形式は Brick-Surkli （Surkli とは Brick パウダーと Mud と籾殻の混合物である），壁厚は，620mm である．1 階平面図を Figure 5.2.2.3-3 に示す．補強計画は，それぞれ Figure 5.2.2.3-4，Figure 5.2.2.3-5 に示すように，内壁には幅 300mm の bandage （縦筋 2-7mmφ，横筋 7mmφ@150）を，外壁には全面に Jacketing （縦横筋とも 7mmφ@150）を施し，壁内外の補強部間を 2mmφの GI wire で接合している [5.2.2-3]．

なお，本建物は補強が実施される前に被災し，大きな被害を受けた．損傷状況については，5.2.2.4 (2)において後述する．

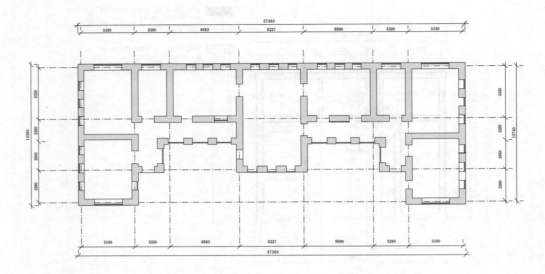

Figure 5.2.2.3-3 Ground Floor Plan

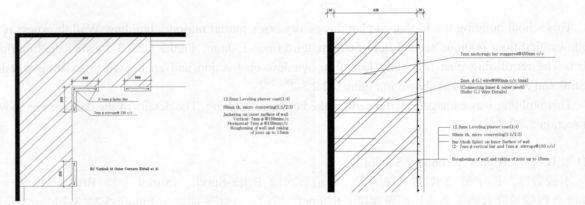

Figure 5.2.2.3-4 Vertical Splint   Figure 5.2.2.3-5 Details of Jacketing

School building B is an E-shaped two-story brick-surkhi building (surkhi is a composite material made from brick powder, lime and chaff, traditional cementitious material of Nepal). The wall thickness is 620mm. The first floor plan is shown in Figure 5.2.2.3-3. Details of the full face jacketing on the outer side, the 300mm wide bandages on the inner side of the walls and the RC vertical splints at the outer corners are shown in Figure 5.2.2.3-4 and Figure 5.2.2.3-5[5.2.2-3].

This building was damaged by the earthquake before retrofitting. The details of the damage are shown in section 5.2.2.4 (2).

(3)　C 中学校/ Secondary School C

本建物は，片廊下形式の 2 階建てである．平面図を Figure 5.2.2.3-6 に示す．構造形式は Brick-Mud と示されているが，平面図では 2 階に柱型があるので 2 階は RC の可能性が高い．補強方法は，Figure 5.2.2.3-7 に示すように，外壁は全面，内壁は敷居・まぐさ部分（Sill/Lintel Bandages）の 300mm 幅に Jacketing 増設による補強である．内壁の敷居・まぐさ部分の補強詳細を Figure 5.2.2.3-8 に示す[5.2.2-5]．

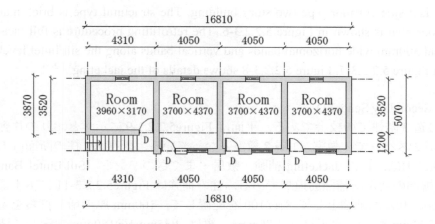

Figure 5.2.2.3-6　Ground Floor Plan

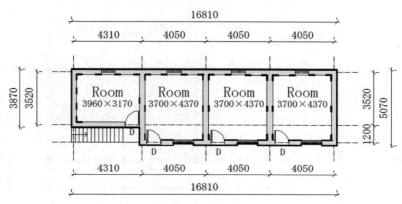

Figure 5.2.2.3-7　Retrofitting of Ground Floor Plan

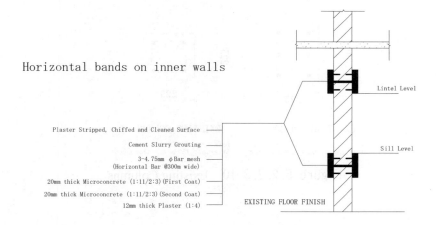

Figure 5.2.2.3-8　Details of Horizontal Bandages

This building is a side corridor type two story building. The structural type is brick-mud on the first floor. The first floor plan is shown in Figure 5.2.2.3-6. The retrofitting procedure is full face jacketing on the outer walls and 300mm wide horizontal bands and vertical bands along the sill/lintel level on the inner walls as shown in Figure 5.2.2.3-7. Figure 5.2.2.3-8 shows details of the jacketing[5.2.2-5].

(4)　D 中学校/ Secondary School D

本建物は，RC造3階建ての校舎である．平面はFigure5.2.2.3-9に示すとおりの片廊下型建物で2階以上は教室が2スパンで1教室，1層2教室となっている．既存RC柱の断面はFigure5.2.2.3-10に示す．補強計画は，柱のJacketing補強，敷居・まぐさのバンド（Sill/Lintel Bandages）付加による補強，梁端部のせん断補強筋追加である．柱の補強はFigure5.2.2.3-11に示すように，四隅にそれぞれ3-16φ，せん断補強として8φ@100を配置して，100mm厚の増し打ちをする．壁へのバンド補強は，300mm幅で，水平材3-4.75mmφ，縦は4.75mmφ@150mmを配して漆喰仕上げで，2mmφのGI wireで内外壁を接合している．梁は，端部600mmにせん断補強のための鋼材幅板を配置している（Figure5.2.2.3-12）[5.2.2-6]．

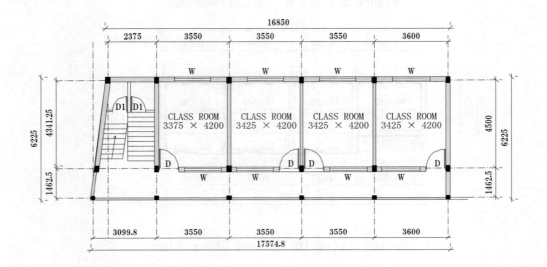

Figure 5.2.2.3-9 Ground Floor Plan

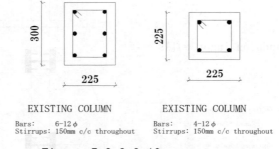

Figure 5.2.2.3-10　Existing Columns

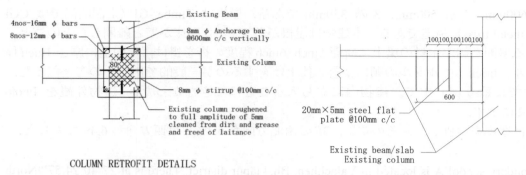

Figure 5.2.2.3-11　Column retrofit details　　Figure 5.2.2.3-12 Addition of steel straps on beams

This building is a side corridor type three story RC structure building. The first floor plan is shown in Figure 5.2.2.3-9. Figure 5.2.2.3-10 shows the bar arrangement of existing RC columns.

The retrofitting procedure is mainly jacketing on the walls and columns, attaching sill/lintel bandages and adding steel straps to beams as shown in Figure5.2.2.3-11 and 5.2.2.3-12[5.2.2-6].

5.2.2.4 学校校舎の被害事例/ Damage of Masonry School Buildings

以下では，詳細調査を実施した学校校舎の個別被害事例について報告，分析する．現地調査で見られた学校校舎の構造形式は，Table 5.2.2.1-1 において定義した略称を用いて記述する．また，壁率の定義は，式 (5.2.2.1-1)のとおりである．

Bhaktapur 行政区では，教育庁からの情報によると全 348 校，その約 1/4 が応急危険度判定で赤（危険）判定がなされた．ただし，黄色（要注意）はつけておらず，補修（補強）すれば使用できるものも含まれている．total collapse は 3〜4 棟であり，それらの学校名を得たので調査した．その結果が(1)〜(4)である．

Sindhupalchowk 行政区では，Chautara 地区の教育庁で被害情報を得た 2 校を調査した．その結果が(5), (6)である．

Dhading 行政区と Nuwakot 行政区では 3 校を調査した．その結果が(7)〜(9)である．この地域では現地での聞き取りにより被害を受けた学校を探索した．

Section 5.2.2.4 shows the damage investigation of nine schools. In this section, it uses abbreviation of structural types as shown in Table 5.2.2.1-1. Wall-to-total floor area ratios were defined equation (5.2.2.1-1).

According to the information from The Department of Educationin, Bhaktapur district, total number of schools is 348 and about one fourth school buildings were judged Red (danger) by the Post-Earthquake Safety Evaluation of Building. These buildings which were judged red (danger) are including the buildings which are possible to use after repair or seismic strengthening, however all buildings judged Red (danger) or Green (safe). The four school buildings led to total collapse. In Bhaktapur district, the investigation of these collapsed four school buildings were conducted as shown in (1) to (4).

In Chautara, Sindhupalchowk district, the investigation of two schools were conducted as shown in (5) to (6).

In Dhading district and Nuwakot district, the investigation of three schools were conducted as shown in (7) to (9).

(1)　A 高校/ Higher Secondary School A

A 高校は，Bhaktapur 行政区 Yalachhen にある．位置詳細は，27°40'24.57" N，85°25'45.09" E である．校舎は 1952 年に建設されたコの字型 3 階建て建物 1 棟である．構造形式は Brick-Mortar,

壁厚は 1 階 600mm，2 階 500mm，3 階 350mm である．屋根は Timber-GI（上記図面では CGI Sheet Roof on metal truss）構造である．本建物は屋根が落下し，3 階床が壁と離間したとのこと．床は，対面する壁間を結ぶ木材の梁上に断面 5inch×6inch 程度の桁を掛け，その上に厚さ 1inch 程度の木製パネル，brick，モルタルの順に積層し仕上げをするのが一般的であるとのことだった．調査時にはすでに取り壊し中で，建物内に立ち入ることはできなかった．建物外観を Photo 5.2.2.4-(1)-1，2 に示す．

この建物では壁率を評価した．その結果，3F の南北方向が 6.3%，東西方向が 6.4%であった．

Higher secondary school A is located in Yalachhen, Bhaktapur district. There is at 27°40'24.57" North Latitude and 85°25'45.09" East longitude. The building was constructed in 1952 and three-story brick-mortar masonry building with Timber-GI roof. The wall thickness is 350mm. The roof was collapsed by the earthquake. The demolition work of this building had already been started. Photo 5.2.2.4-(1)-1 and 2 show the overall view from south and north.

The wall-to-total floor area ratios are 6.3 % of North-South direction and 6.45% of East-West direction in third floor.

Photo 5.2.2.4-(1)-1 Sharada overall view from south   Photo 5.2.2.4-(1)-2 Sharada overall view from north

(2)　B 高校/ Higher Secondary School B

B 高校は，Bhaktapur 行政区バクタプール王宮広場に面して立地している（Photo 5.2.2.4-(2)-1）．西暦 1946 年に設立された Bhaktapur で最も古く，Nepal 国内で 4 番目に古い学校で幼稚園から大学院まである学校である．主な建物配置と写真撮影位置を Figure 5.2.2.4-(2)-1 に示す．

高校校舎は，E 字形平面の 2 階建てで，構造形式は Brick-Shurkhi（Shurkhi とは Brick パウダーと石灰と籾殻の混合物である），壁厚は 620mm である．2014 年に補強計画がなされており，その時点で壁にひび割れが見られていた．現地にいた方の証言では，地震による被害は，本震で前面壁が崩落（Photo 5.2.2.4-(2)-2），5 月 12 日の余震で背面が壊れたとのことだった（Photo 5.2.2.4-(2)-3）．基礎は Stone による組積造，屋根は Timber-GI 構造である（Photo 5.2.2.4-(2)-4）．

この建物では壁率を評価した．その結果，2F の桁行方向が 10.1%，梁間方向が 10.5%であった．

同一敷地内には補強済みの建物があり，建物接合部分のひび割れなど軽微な損傷にとどまった（Photo 5.2.2.4-(2)-5, 6）．この他の学校建物にも大きな被害はなかった（Photo 5.2.2.4-(2)-7, 8）．

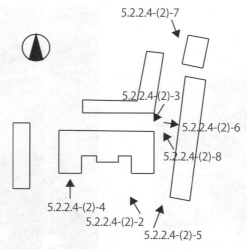

Figure 5.2.2.4-(2)-1 Site plan of school B

Photo 5.2.2.4-(2)-1 Gate of school B

Photo 5.2.2.4-(2)-2 Front side view

Photo 5.2.2.4-(2)-3 Back side view

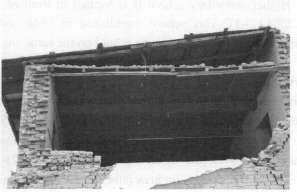

Photo 5.2.2.4-(2)-4 Out-of-plane failure of wall

Photo 5.2.2.4-(2)-5 Survived retrofitted building

Photo 5.2.2.4-(2)-6 Survived retrofitted building

Photo 5.2.2.4-(2)-7 Survived masonry building

Photo 5.2.2.4-(2)-8 Suivived masonry building

Higher secondary school B is located in front of Bhaktapur Durbar Square, Bhaktapur district (Photo 5.2.2.4-(2)-1). This school established in 1946 and the oldest school in Bhaktapur district. There is kindergarten through graduate school on the same site. Figure 5.2.2.4-(2)-1 shows the site plan of school B.

This school building is a E-shaped plan two-story brick- surki (Surki is composite material made from brick powder, lime and shaff) building with Timber-GI roof and stone masonry foundation. The wall thickness is 620mm. Front side wall was damaged by main shock (Photo 5.2.2.4-(2)-2) and back side wall damaged by aftershock (Photo 5.2.2.4-(2)-3). Photo 5.2.2.4-(2)-4 shows the second floor wall failure.

There are survived retrofitted buildings on the same site (Photo 5.2.2.4-(2)-5, 6). The other buildings on this site were not heavily damaged (Photo 5.2.2.4-(2)-7, 8)

The wall-to-total floor area ratios are10.1 % of longitudinal direction and 10.5% of span direction in the second floor.

(3) C高校/ Higher Secondary School C

C 高校は，Bhaktapur 行政区に位置している．学校はほぼ整形な校舎が校庭を囲むように建てられている（Photo 5.2.2.4-(3)-1）．RC 造 3 階建て 2 棟，RC 造 4 階建て 1 棟は無被害（Photo 5.2.2.4-(3)-2, 3）で，Brick による組積造（目地材の種別は不明）3 階建ての 1 棟が被害を受けた（Photo 5.2.2.4-(3)-4, 5）．主な被害は，Timber-Tile 構造の屋根全体の落下である．

Higher secondary school C is located in Bhaktapur district. The site plan of school C shows in Photo 5.2.2.4-(3)-1. Two three-story RC buildings and a four-story RC building were survived (Photo 5.2.2.4-(3)-2 and 3). Timber-Tile roof of three-story masonry building was collapsed (Photo 5.2.2.4-(3)-4 and 5).

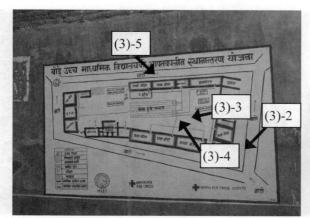
Photo 5.2.2.4-(3)-1 Site plan of school C

Photo 5.2.2.4-(3)-2 RC building

Photo 5.2.2.4-(3)-3 RC buildings (left and center)

Photo 5.2.2.4-(3)-4 Collapsed Timber-tile roof

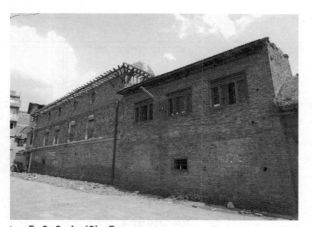
Photo 5.2.2.4-(3)-5 Back side view of Masonry building

(4) D 高校/ Higher Secondary School D

D 高校は，Bhaktapur 郊外の高台の上，27°41'35.53"N，85°24'24.08"E に立地している．校舎は Brick-Mud 構造平屋 L 字形の建物である（Photo 5.2.2.4-(4)-1）．壁厚は 350mm，内部の一部の壁厚は 210mm であった．平面図を Figure5.2.2.4-(4)-1 に示す．多くの壁が面外に倒壊し，一部の屋根

架構も落下していた（Photo 5.2.2.4-(4)-2, 3）．屋根は Timber-GI 構造である．応急危険度判定がなされており，危険（赤）が掲示されていた（Photo 5.2.2.4-(4)-4）．

この建物では壁率を評価した．その結果，桁行方向が 12.5%，梁間方向が 7.8% であった．

Photo 5.2.2.4-(4)-1 Over view of school D

Photo 5.2.2.4-(4)-2 Out-of-plane failure of wall

Photo 5.2.2.4-(4)-3 Out-of-Plane Failure

Photo 5.2.2.4-(4)-4 Red (danger) sign

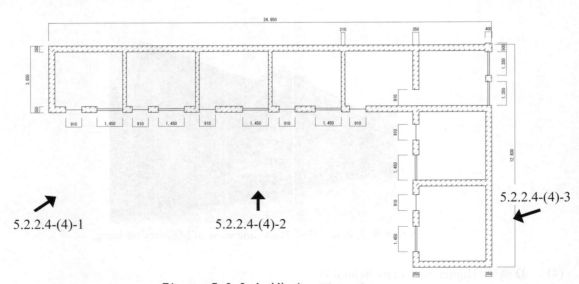
Figure 5.2.2.4-(4)-1　　Floor plan

Higher secondary school D is located on a hill in the Bhaktapur district at 27°41'35.53" North Latitude and 85°24'24.08" East longitude. The building is L-shaped single-story brick-mudmasonry with Timber-GI roof as shown in Photo 5.2.2.4-(4)-1.

Figure5.2.2.4-(4)-1 shows floor plan and the wall thickenesses are mainly 350mm and 210mm of a part of inner wall. The roof failure and out-of-plane failure of masonry wall were observed, as shown in Photo 5.2.2.4-(4)-2 and 3. The Post-Earthquake Safety Evaluation of Building of this building has done and danger (red) sign was putted. (Photo 5.2.2.4-(4)-4)

The wall-to-total floor area ratios are 12.5 % of longitudinal direction and 7.8% of span direction.

(5)　E高校/ Higher Secondary School E

Sindhupalchowk 行政区での調査を行うにあたって，まず，Chautara 地区の教育庁に立ち寄って情報を入手した．そこで入手した標準設計図については，5.2.2.2 項で述べた．ここでは，それと併せて入手した Sindhupalchowk 行政区の地図と学校数が示された図を Figure 5.2.2.4-(5)-1 に示す．同図に記入された数値は各地域の学校数を示している．同図には被害調査を行った Chautara 地区の位置を併せて示す．本調査では，Chautara 地区で 2 つの学校の被害調査を行った．それらの調査結果を本項(5)と次項(6)に示す．

教育庁での聞き取り調査結果を以下に列挙する．
・　この行政区にある 546 校のうち，確認できたものはほとんど壊れている．また，現地に行くことができず被害が確認できていない学校も多数ある．
・　建物の多くは 2 回目の地震（5 月 12 日）で被害を受けた．
・　Sindhupalchowk 行政区では学校校舎を耐震補強する計画はなかった．

Figure 5.2.2.4-(5)-1 Number of schools (Sindhupalchowk district)

本項で述べるE校は，Sindhupalchowk行政区のChautara地区に位置している．Chautara地区における位置を，後の(6)で示す学校（F校）とともにFigure 5.2.2.4-(5)-2に示す．

E校の配置図をFigure 5.2.2.4-(5)-3に示し，敷地の全景をPhoto 5.2.2.4-(5)-1に示す．敷地の北側，東側および南側の一部が崖となっている．RC造3階建ての校舎，組積造平屋建ての宿直棟，組積造平屋建ての校舎が隣接して建っていた．

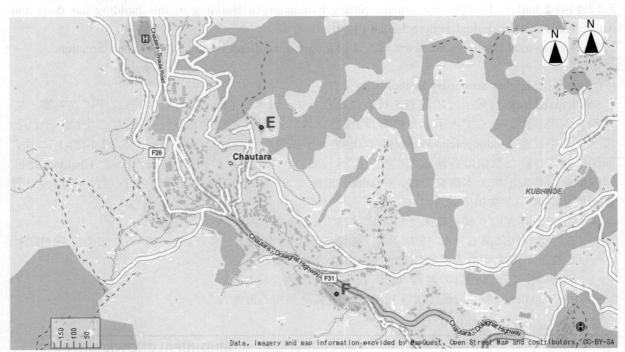

Figure 5.2.2.4-(5)-2 Locations of school E and school F

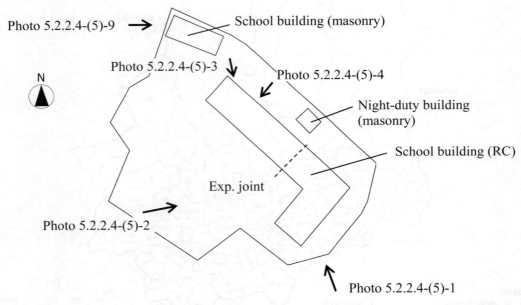

Figure 5.2.2.4-(5)-3 Site plan of school E

Photo 5.2.2.4-(5)-1 Overall view of site

RC 造 3 階建ての校舎の全景を Photo 5.2.2.4-(5)-2 に示す．この校舎には塔屋が 2 つある．エキスパンションジョイントにより 2 棟に分かれており，竣工年は西側が 2012 年，東側が 2010 年である（Figure 5.2.2.4-(5)-3 参照）．

Photo 5.2.2.4-(5)-2 Overall view of building

被害概要を以下に示す．2 階床レベルの柱梁接合部の 1 か所で，Photo 5.2.2.4-(5)-3 に示すような大きな損傷が見られた．1 階柱は壁により短柱化しているものがあり，1 か所でせん断ひび割れが見られた（Photo 5.2.2.4-(5)-4）．また，1 階の柱頭に若干の曲げひび割れが生じている箇所も見られた．しかし，構造体全体としての被害は軽微であった．壁は煉瓦造（Brick-Mortar）であり，非構造部材であった．教室境の壁（Photo 5.2.2.4-(5)-5）や外壁（Photo 5.2.2.4-(5)-6）などの多くの箇所で大きな亀裂が見られた．これらはせん断ひび割れや水平方向のひび割れであり，組積造の壁が地震力に抵抗する要素となっていた可能性もある．ただし，煉瓦造の壁が耐震性能に寄与する程度を正確に評価することは難しいといえる．

Photo 5.2.2.4-(5)-3 Damage of beam-column joint

Photo 5.2.2.4-(5)-4 Shear crack of column

Photo 5.2.2.4-(5)-5 Cracks in inner wall

Photo 5.2.2.4-(5)-6 Cracks in outer wall

　宿直棟の平面図を Figure 5.2.2.4-(5)-4 に示す．この建物は組積造の平屋建てで，壁は Stone-mud 構造である．壁厚は 600mm である．屋根は Timber-GI 構造であったと思われる．本建物の被害状況を Photo 5.2.2.4-(5)-7 と Photo 5.2.2.4-(5)-8 に示す．すべての壁が崩れ，完全に倒壊していた．本建物の壁率は桁行方向で 26.6%，梁間方向で 18.1%であり，桁行方向の方が大きかった．

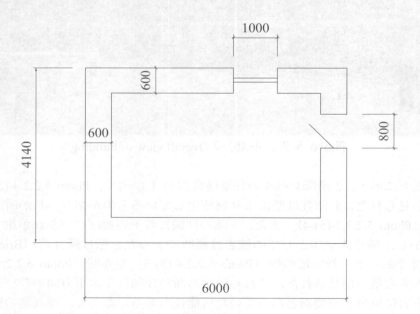
Figure 5.2.2.4-(5)-4 Plan of night-duty building

Photo 5.2.2.4-(5)-7 Night-duty building and school   Photo 5.2.2.4-(5)-8 Damage of night-duty building

　Photo 5.2.2.4-(5)-9 は敷地北西に位置する Stone-Mud 構造の壁，Steel-GI 構造の屋根を有する平屋建ての校舎である．2003 年建設の本校舎は日本の国際協力機構 (JICA) による経済支援を受けたとのことであった．桁行方向の壁はバットレス補強されており，壁とバットレスの交点において屋根を鉛直支持する鋼管が壁内部に埋め込まれていた (Photo 5.2.2.4-(5)-10)．こうした構造詳細は相対的に高い耐震性能を与えていると判断され，観察された損傷は妻壁のひび割れ程度であった．

Photo 5.2.2.4-(5)-9 Building funded by JICA

Photo 5.2.2.4-(5)-10 Steel roof support embedded in wall

Prior to the damage investigation in the Sindhupalchowk district, we visited the educational office in Chautara to obtain information about the damages to the school buildings. Figure 5.2.2.4-(5)-1 shows the map of the Sindhupalchowk district that we obtained from the educational office. The numbers on the map indicate the number of schools. We investigated two schools (school E and F) in Chautara.

The results of the inquiring survey at the educational office were as follows.

1) There were 546 schools in the Sindhupalchowk district and most schools were damaged. The educational officers could not gather the required school damage information, since it was not possible for them to access many of the school sites right after the disaster.

2) Many buildings were damaged during the second earthquake (12 May).

3) There had not been any plans to strengthen the school buildings in the Sindhupalchowk district before the earthquake.

School E was located at Chautara, Sindhupalchowk district. Figure 5.2.2.4-(5)-2 shows the locations of the schools E and F. School F is discussed in the next paragraph.

Figure 5.2.2.4-(5)-3 shows the site plan of school E. Photo 5.2.2.4-(5)-1 shows the overall view of the site. There were slopes at the north, east, and south of the site. There were three-story RC school building, one-story masonry school building, and one-story masonry night-duty building.

Photograph 5.2.2.4-(5)-2 shows the overall view of the RC school building. The building had two penthouses and an expansion joint. The west and east parts of the building were constructed in 2012 and 2010, respectively.

Photograph 5.2.2.4-(5)-3 shows a damage of the beam-column joint at the second floor level. Photo 5.2.2.4-(5)-4 shows a shear crack of a column. The shear crack occurred as the column became a short column due to the masonry spandrel wall. Slight flexural cracks occurred at the top of the first-floor columns. Overall, the damage level of the RC building was slight. The structural system of the wall was the Brick-Mortar. Photographs 5.2.2.4-(5)-5 and 5.2.2.4-(5)-6 show the cracks of inner and outer walls, respectively. The cracks in the walls were predominantly shear cracks, which suggests that during the earthquake the walls behaved as earthquake resistance elements.

Figure 5.2.2.4-(5)-4 shows the plan of the night-duty building. This was a one-story masonry building and the structural system of the wall was Stone-Mud. Wall thickness was 600 mm. Photographs 5.2.2.4-(5)-7 and 5.2.2.4-(5)-8 show the damage states of the building. The building has completely collapsed since then. The wall ratios were 26.6% for the longitudinal direction and 18.1% for the transverse direction.

Photo 5.2.2.4-(5)-9 shows a single story Stone-Mud masonry building with Steel-GI roof locating at the north-west corner in Figure 5.2.2.4-(5)-3. The building was constructed in 2003 under financial supports by Japan International Cooperation Agency (JICA). The walls along the longitudinal direction were strengthened by buttress walls. Steel roof supports were embedded at the intersections of the longitudinal and transverse walls, as shown in Photo 5.2.2.4-(5)-10. Such structural details seemed to provide relatively higher seismic performance, which resulted in slight cracks observed only to the gable wall seen in Photo 5.2.2.4-(5)-9.

(6) F高校/ Higher Secondary School F

F校はSindhupalchowk行政区のChautara地区に位置している（Figure 5.2.2.4-(5)-1参照）．現地での聞き取りによると，学校は1947年に創立され，2015年の生徒数は1307人であった．

F校の配置図をFigure 5.2.2.4-(6)-1に示す．敷地の南側と西側が崖となっている．地震前に撮影された写真をPhoto5.2.2.4-(6)-1に示す．地震後の調査時には，A棟は組積造3建て，B棟はRC造3階建てであったが，この写真では，A棟とB棟は共に組積造2階建てである．この写真は，2階部分が増築された後に撮影された写真であり（増築年は後述），その後A棟は3階が増築され，B棟は撤去後にRC造で新築するという変更が加えられたと考えられる．この学校では，A棟とB棟について詳しく調査を行った．A棟とB棟の被害状況をPhoto 5.2.2.4-(6)-2に示す．A棟は組積造3階建て，B棟はRC造3階建てであり，前者は全層崩壊，後者は1階の被害が大きいものの落階は免れており，構造形式によって被害程度に差が生じた（詳細は後述する）．

Higher Secondary School F was located in Chautara, Sindhupalchowk district (Figure 5.2.2.4-(5)-1). According to the survey, the school was founded in 1947 and it had 1307 students.

Figure 5.2.2.4-(6)-1 shows the site plan of school F. There were slopes at the south and west of the site. Photograph 5.2.2.4-(6)-1 shows a view of the site taken before the earthquake. There were some differences between the buildings in the photograph and the buildings that we investigated. Before the earthquake, third story of the building A (masonry) was added and the building B was rebuilt to a three-story RC building. Photograph 5.2.2.4-(6)-2 shows to the damage of the buildings A and B. The building A was a three-story masonry building and the building B was a three-story RC building. Building A was damaged considerably and all the three levels subsequently collapsed under their own weight, while the building B had a heavily damaged first story but it remained intact. There were significant differences in damage states depending on the structural system. These damages are discussed in later sections.

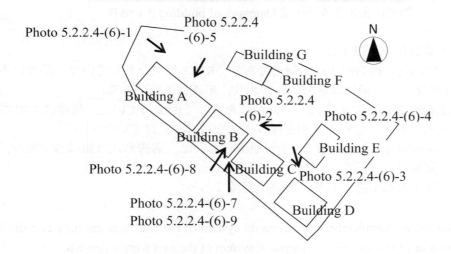

Figure 5.2.2.4-(6)-1 Site plan of school F

Photo 5.2.2.4-(6)-1 Site view (before earthquake)

Photo 5.2.2.4-(6)-2 Damages of building A and B

　A 棟と B 棟以外の被害概要を以下に示す．
　C 棟は全層崩壊していた．構造形式は組積造であり，RC スラブを有していた．階数は不明である（2 階または 3 階建て）．屋根は撤去されており，形式は不明である．
　D 棟は Photo5.2.2.4-(6)-3 に示すように，一部の壁を残して倒壊していた．階数は不明である．屋根は鉄骨トラス形式であり，部材の変形を伴う大きな被害を受けていた．
　E 棟は Photo5.2.2.4-(6)-4 に示すように，全層崩壊していた．構造形式は組積造であり，RC スラブを有していた．階数は 2 である．
　G 棟と F 棟は平屋建ての組積造であり，損傷は軽微であった．

　The building C collapsed completely. The structural system of the wall was masonry and the building had RC slabs. The number of stories and the structural system of the roof were unknown.

　The building D collapsed as shown in the Photograph 5.2.2.4-(6)-3. The structural systems of the wall and roof were masonry and Steel-GI, respectively. The roof was heavily damaged with notable deformations in steel members.

　The building E, which consisted of two stories, collapsed completely as shown in Photograph 5.2.2.4-(6)-4. The structural system of the wall was masonry and the building had RC slabs.

　Building G and F were both one-story masonry buildings and had minimal damages due to the earthquake.

Photo 5.2.2.4-(6)-3 Damage of building D

Photo 5.2.2.4-(6)-4 Damage of building E

(a) A棟/ Building A

A棟は組積造3階建てであり，2階床と3階床はRCスラブであった．建設当初は平屋建てであったが，その後2階と3階が増築された．竣工年，壁の構造形式，壁厚は各階ごとに異なっていた（Table 5.2.2.4-(6)-1）．壁厚は1階で480 mm，2階で240 mm，3階で約190 mmであった．屋根は撤去済みであり，形式は不明である．2階平面図をFigure 5.2.2.4-(6)-2に示す．ここで，2階北東面の開口形状は実測によるが，南西面は実測できなかったため，5.2.2.2項に示した標準設計のA通りと同じと仮定した．これはこの校舎の教室の大きさが標準設計と同じであったためである．なお，標準設計と比較すると教室の大きさは同じであるものの，壁厚が小さいため耐震性は劣ると考えられる．

被害状況をPhoto 5.2.2.4-(6)-5に示す．被害は1階と3階が完全に崩壊，2階は一部を残して崩壊，という甚大なものであった．本建物に付属するRC造の階段室（Figure 5.2.2.4-(6)-2参照）も，Photo 5.2.2.4-(6)-6に示すように倒壊していた．

本建物の桁行方向と梁間方向の壁率を，各階ごとにTable 5.2.2.4-(6)-2に示す．壁率は2.0%から3.5%であった．また，桁行方向と梁間方向の壁率を比較すると，各階でほぼ同程度であった．ここで，1階と3階は完全に崩壊していて開口部が確認できなかったため，次のように仮定して壁率を計算した．1階の開口部は北東面では2階と同じとし，南西面ではPhoto 5.2.2.4-(6)-1から開口幅をすべて90 cmとした．3階の開口部はすべて2階と同じとした．

Table 5.2.2.4-(6)-1 Construction year, structural system for masonry wall and wall thickness

Floor	Construction year	Structural system of wall	Wall thickness (mm)
3	2011	Block-Mortar	about 190
2	1995	Brick-Mortar	240
1	1973	Stone-Mud	480

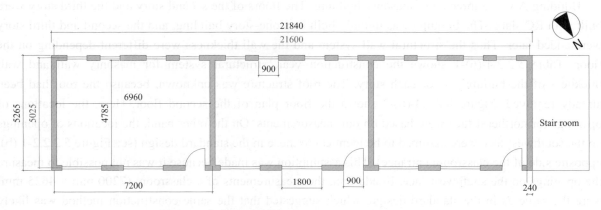
Figure 5.2.2.4-(6)-2 Floor plan (second floor)

Photo 5.2.2.4-(6)-5 Damage of building A

Photo 5.2.2.4-(6)-6 Damage of stair room

Table 5.2.2.4-(6)-2 Wall ratio

Floor	Wall ratio (%)	
	Longitudinal direction	Transverse direction
3	3.2	3.5
2	2.0	2.2
1	3.4	2.9

Building A was a three-story masonry building. The floors of the second story and the third story were built with RC slabs. The building was initially built as a one-story building, and the second and third story were added later. Thus the structural wall system and the wall thickness were different depending on the floor. Table 5.2.2.4-(6)-1 shows the construction year, structural system for masonry wall and wall thickness of the building A for each story. The roof structure was unknown, because the roof had been already removed. Figure 5.2.2.4-(6)-2 shows the floor plan of the second floor. Here, the locations of openings for northeast face were based on our measurements. On the other hand, the locations of openings on the southwest face were assumed to be identical to those in the standard design (see Figure 5.2.2.2-1 (b), opposite side of the classroom entrance). This assumption was made because it was not possible to measure the openings on the southwest face. In addition, the measurements of a classroom (7200 mm × 4625 mm) were the same as in the standard design, which suggested that the same construction method was likely used.

Photograph 5.2.2.4-(6)-5 shows the damage state of building A. The first and the third story have completely collapsed and most part of the second story had collapsed too. In addition, the RC stair room next to the building A had collapsed, as depicted in the Photograph 5.2.2.4-(6)-6.

Table 5.2.2.4-(6)-2 lists the wall ratios for the longitudinal and transverse directions of each story. The wall ratios were in the range of 2.0% to 3.5%. Here, the location of openings of the first story and the third story were unknown because they had completely collapsed. Thus the locations of openings of the first story were assumed to be same as those of the second story for the northeast face and same as Photograph 5.2.2.4-(6)-1 for southwest face (90 cm wide for each opening). The locations of openings on the third story were assumed same as those on the second story.

(b) B棟/ Building B

B棟は，鉄筋コンクリート造3階建てである．屋根の形式はTimber-GIであった（屋根スラブなし）．1階梁伏図をFigure 5.2.2.4-(6)-3に示す．ここで，現地ですべての寸法を測定できなかったため，例えばFigure 5.2.2.4-(6)-3における片持ち部材の長さは推定値であることに留意されたい．1階の柱断面図をFigure 5.2.2.4-(6)-4に示す．1階柱の断面寸法は245 mm×300 mm，主筋は4-D16+2-D12，帯筋は2-D8@150であった．なお，帯筋のフック形状は90度フックであった．柱の内法高さは2400 mmであった．大梁の断面寸法は，幅×せいが230 mm×320 mmであった．小梁は設けられていなかった．スラブ厚は120 mmであった．壁はbrick-mortarであり，壁厚は240 mmであった．

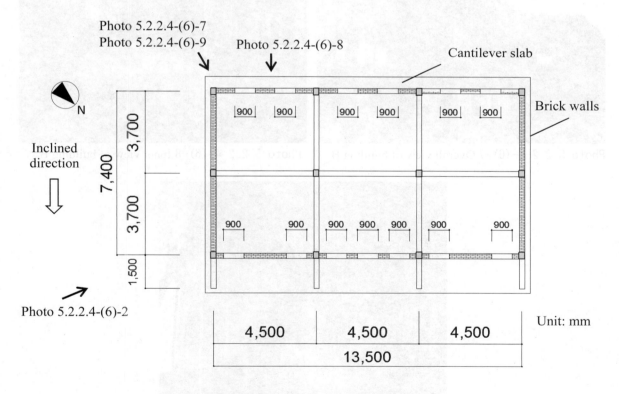

Figure 5.2.2.4-(6)-3 Beam plan (first floor)

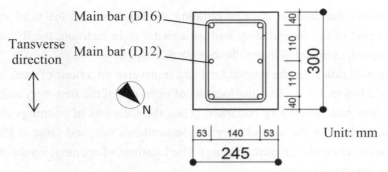

Figure 5.2.2.4-(6)-4 Column section (first floor)

　建物全景を Photo 5.2.2.4-(6)-7 に示し，1 階内部の被害状況を Photo 5.2.2.4-(6)-8 に示す．1 層のすべての柱で材端部の曲げ破壊が見られた．1 階柱頭の被害状況を Photo 5.2.2.4-(6)-9 に示すが，端部のコンクリートが圧壊して鉄筋が露出しており，主筋の座屈も見られた．建物は 1 層の柱頭・柱脚の曲げ破壊による層崩壊が生じて梁間方向（北東方向）に傾いていたが，落階には至っていなかった．2 階と 3 階の柱には大きな損傷は生じていなかった．非構造部材である煉瓦壁には各階で多くの亀裂が生じ，面外方向に倒壊した壁も見られた．

Photo 5.2.2.4-(6)-7 Overall view of building B

Photo 5.2.2.4-(6)-8 Inner view of building B

Photo 5.2.2.4-(6)-9 Damage of column

The building B was a three-story RC building. The structural system of the roof was Timber-GI. Figures 5.2.2.4-(6)-3 and 5.2.2.4-(6)-4 show the beam plan and column section of the first floor, respectively. Column section was 245 mm × 300 mm. Longitudinal reinforcements were 4-D16 and 2-D12 and hoops were 2-D8@150. Column clear height was 2400 mm. Girder section was 230 mm × 320 mm. Slab thickness was 120 mm. Structural system of the wall was Brick-Mortar and the wall thickness was 240 mm.

Photographs 5.2.2.4-(6)-7 and 5.2.2.4-(6)-8 are the overall and inner view of building B, respectively. All columns on the first floor failed in flexure at both top and bottom of the columns. Photograph 5.2.2.4-(6)-9 shows the damage state of the column top. The reinforcements exposed with buckling of longitudinal reinforcements accompanied severe concrete crushing. As a result, first-story collapse occurred and the building slanted in the transverse direction (northeast direction). However, the building did not collapse completely in vertical direction. Columns of second story and third story were not notably damaged. Masonry walls on each floor had many cracks, and some of these walls collapsed in the out-of-plane direction.

(c) B棟の保有水平耐力/ Lateral Load-carrying Capacity of Building B

RC構造のB棟について，保有水平耐力を算定した．B棟は前述のように1階の柱頭と柱脚の曲げ破壊による崩壊メカニズムが形成されていたため，1階の保有水平耐力を求めた．算定にあたって設けた仮定は，以下のとおりである．
・床の単位面積重量：11.8 kN/m^2
・屋根の単位面積重量：0.5 kN/m^2
・コンクリート圧縮強度：24 N/mm^2
・鉄筋降伏強度：415 N/mm^2
・煉瓦壁は耐力計算上無視する．

計算の結果，1階柱の長期の軸力比は0.09から0.23となり，高軸力柱は存在しなかった．柱の曲げ終局モーメントを「鉄筋コンクリート構造計算規準」の略算式により求め，反曲点位置を部材の中央と仮定して各柱の曲げ終局時せん断力 Q_{mu} を求めたところ，桁行方向で48.7 kNから66.2 kN，梁間方向で50.2 kNから71.7 kNであった．ここで，柱のせん断終局強度 Q_{su} を荒川 min 式により求めてせん断余裕（Q_{su}/Q_{mu}）を算定したところ，1.6から1.9となり，すべての柱が曲げ破壊型と判定されることを確認している．各柱の曲げ終局時せん断力を基に保有水平耐力を算定した結果，1階桁行方向で693 KN，1階梁間方向で736 kNとなった．ベースシア係数に換算すると，桁行方向で0.21，梁間方向で0.22となった．保有水平耐力は梁間方向のほうが桁行方向よりもやや大きいものの，ほぼ同程度であるといえる．被害程度は前述のように梁間方向の方が大きかったので，地震動はこの方向（北東－南西）の方が大きかったものと推察される．

The lateral load-carrying capacity for the first floor of the building B was calculated. As stated before, the first story of building B collapsed with column's flexural failure at both ends. The lateral load-carrying capacity was calculated assuming the following values: floor weight per unit area was 11.8 kN/m^2, roof weight per unit area was 0.5 kN/m^2, compressive strength of concrete was 24 N/mm^2, and yield strength of reinforcement was 415 N/mm^2. Masonry walls were neglected in the calculation.

The calculated long-term axial stress ratios of columns were in the range of 0.09 to 0.23. The ultimate flexural strengths were computed for columns employing the conventional equations in Japan, assuming double curvature deformation. The flexural strengths of columns for longitudinal direction were ranging from 48.7 kN to 66.2 kN. The flexural strengths for transverse direction were ranging from 50.2 kN to 71.7 kN. Note that the ratios of computed shear strength to computed flexural strength of each column were in the range of 1.6 to 1.9, indicating that the columns failed in flexure without shear failure. The shear strengths were computed for columns using the conventional equations in Japan. The lateral load-carrying capacity was computed as the total of the flexural strengths of the first-story columns for each direction. The lateral load-carrying capacities for longitudinal and transverse direction were 693 kN and 736 kN, respectively. Base shear coefficients for longitudinal direction and transverse direction were 0.21 and 0.22, respectively. Though the lateral load-carrying capacities for both directions were almost the same, the damage state of transverse direction was more severe than that of longitudinal direction. This indicates that the ground motion level of the transverse direction might have been greater than that of the longitudinal direction.

(d) A棟の壁のせん断応力度/ Shear Stress of Masonry Wall of Building A

次に，地震時に組積造の A 棟に作用したせん断応力度を推定した．まず，RC 造の B 棟は 1 階梁間方向で崩壊メカニズムが形成されたことから，地震時に作用した水平力の最大値は 1 階梁間方向の保有水平耐力 736 kN であると考えられる．ここで，大まかな仮定ではあるが，A 棟も B 棟と同じ 3 階建てであることから，A 棟 1 階梁間方向に作用しうる水平力の最大値は 736 kN であったと考える．この水平荷重を A 棟 1 階の梁間方向の壁断面積で除してせん断応力を求めると，0.08 N/mm^2 となる．つまり，A 棟 1 階はこれ以下のせん断応力度で崩壊したと推定することができる．ただし，これは極めて低い値であり，実際には壁の面外方向への転倒などの他の要因が層崩壊を誘発した可能性も考えられる．

For building A, the maximum shearing stress of masonry wall during the earthquake was assumed based on the lateral load-carrying capacity of the building B. Both buildings, A and B, had three stories each and were approximately of the same size. Therefore, the same lateral load, as the lateral load-carrying capacity of the building B for transverse direction (736 kN) could have acted on the first-story of the building A during the earthquake. The shearing stress of the masonry wall of building A was calculated as the lateral load divided by the cross-sectional area of the first-story walls of building A for transverse direction. As a result, the shearing stress was 0.08 N/mm^2. Therefore, we infer from this proposition that the first story of building A collapsed due to the shearing stress of 0.08 N/mm^2 or less. We also note that the shearing stress of 0.08 N/mm^2 was very low. Consequently, it is very likely that other factors, such as the out-of-plane failure of walls, might have contributed to the collapse.

(7) G 小学校/ Primary School G

G 小学校は Dhading 行政区にあり，具体的な位置は Figure 5.2.2.4-(7)-1 に示す．同小学校は Photo 5.2.2.4-(7)-1 に示すように，小学校 3 年生までの教室 1 棟の建物のみである．平面図および立面図は，Figure 5.2.2.4-(7)-2 に示す．

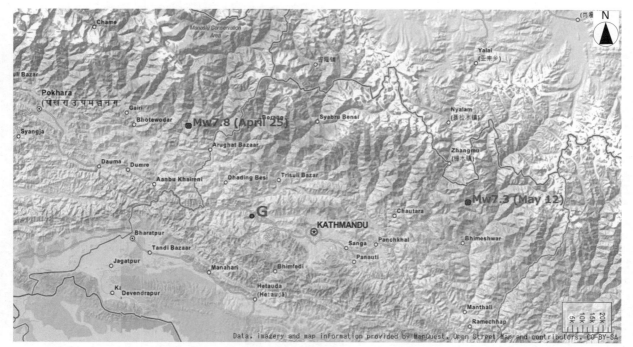

Location of G primary school: 27°46'36.56"N, 85°01'09.99"E, about 52 kilometers southeast from the epicenter of April 25th and 32 kilometers northwest from Kathmandu.

Figure 5.2.2.4-(7)-1 Location of primary school G

(a) Aerial photo

(b) Collapsed gable wall

Photo 5.2.2.4-(7)-1 Primary school G

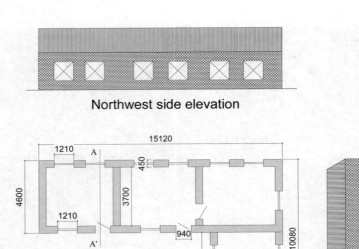

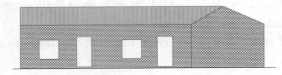

Figure 5.2.2.4-(7)-2 Floor plan and elevations of primary school G

この建物は 2007 年に建設された 1 階建ての比較的新しい建物である．壁は Stone-Mud 構造であり，壁厚は 450mm である．屋根は Timber-GI 構造である（Photo 5.2.2.4-(7)-2）．本建物の主な損傷を Photo 5.2.2.4-(7)-2 に示す．同写真(b)では，南西側の妻壁が屋内側に面外倒壊している．写真(c)は部分倒壊した東南側の教室を示す．写真(d)に隅角部の壁の崩落を，(e)に梁間方向壁のせん断ひび割れをそれぞれ示す．

本建物の桁行，梁間方向の壁率はほぼ等しく，それぞれ 11.1%，11.5% であった．

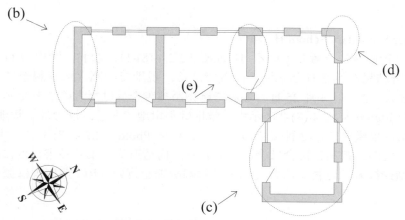

(a) Damaged parts and shooting directions of photography

(b) Out-of-plane failure of gable wall

(c) Partial collapse

(d) Collapse of wall corner

(e) Shear cracks on wall in the span direction

Photo 5. 2. 2. 4-(7)-2 Major damage to the building

This one-story building was recently built in 2007. The structural system of the wall was Stone-Mud, with a thickness of 450 mm, and the roof was Timber-GI structure (Photo 5.2.2.4-(7)-2). The major damage is shown in Photo 5.2.2.4-(7)-2: the southwest gable wall collapsed to the inside of the building as shown in (b) of the photo; (c) shows the partially collapsed classroom at the southeast side; (d) shows failure of the wall corner; and (e) shows shear cracks in the interior wall in the span direction.

The wall ratio of the building in the longitudinal and span directions were: 11.1% and 11.5%, respectively.

(8) H高校/ Higher Secondary School H

H校は Nuwakot 行政区に位置している（Figure 5.2.2.4-(8)-1）．なお，図中の G と I はそれぞれ (7)項と(9)項で調査結果が示された学校の位置である．現地での聞き取り調査によると，この学校の生徒数は 325 人であり，4 月 25 日の本震で建物が被害を受けたとのことである．

H校の配置図を Figure 5.2.2.4-(8)-2 に示す．敷地は平坦地である．校舎は，敷地東側の RC 造 2 建てと西側の組積造平屋建ての 2 棟であった．これらを Photo 5.2.2.4-(8)-1 に示す．RC 造校舎の被害は軽微であったが，組積造校舎は全壊しており，構造形式により被害程度に顕著な差が見られた．なお，組積造校舎は建物寸法の実測等の詳細調査を行い，RC 造校舎は概要調査のみを行った．

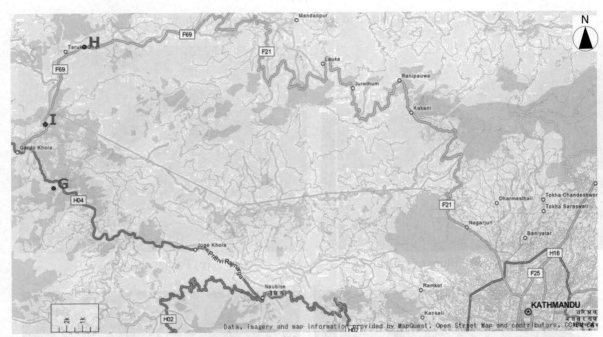

Figure 5.2.2.4-(8)-1 Location of school H

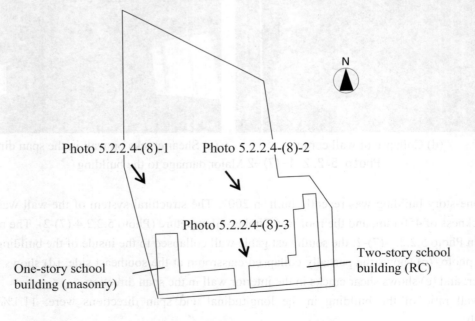

Figure 5.2.2.4-(8)-2 Site plan of school H

— 156 —

Photo 5.2.2.4-(8)-1 Site view (left: reinforced concrete, right: masonry)

　鉄筋コンクリート造校舎の全景を Photo 5.2.2.4-(8)-2 に示す．この建物では，1階隅柱の1か所で柱脚の曲げ破壊が見られた（Photo 5.2.2.4-(8)-3）．この柱の断面寸法は 230 mm×230 mm，主筋は 6-D12，帯筋は 2-D8@150 であった．なお，ここで露出した鉄筋には顕著なさびが見られ，地震発生前からある程度損傷していた可能性も考えられる．

Photo 5.2.2.4-(8)-2 Overall view of RC building

Photo 5.2.2.4-(8)-3 Damage of column

　組積造校舎は一部の壁を残して完全に倒壊していた（Photo 5.2.2.4-(8)-1 参照）．平面図を Figure 5.2.2.4-(8)-3 に示す．ここで，平面図は残存していた部分を実測することにより作成しており，開口形状などに一部推測が含まれることに注意が必要である．この建物は 1975 年ごろに建設された1階建ての校舎である．壁は Stone-Mud 構造であり，壁厚は 520mm である．屋根は Timber-GI 構造であった．本建物の損傷状況を Photo 5.2.2.4-(8)-4 と Photo 5.2.2.4-(8)-5 に示す．Photo 5.2.2.4-(8)-4 は，倒壊せずに残った壁である．

　本建物の桁行，梁間方向の壁率はほぼ等しく，それぞれ 12.2%，12.7%であった．

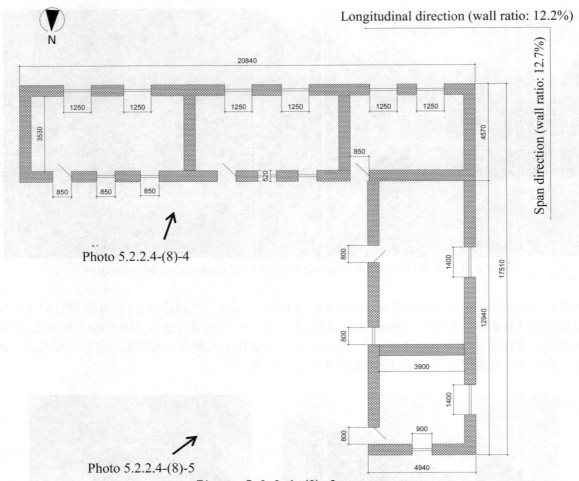

Photo 5.2.2.4-(8)-4

Photo 5.2.2.4-(8)-5

Figure 5.2.2.4-(8)-3 Floor plan

Photo 5.2.2.4-(8)-4 Damage of wall

Photo 5.2.2.4-(8)-5 Damage of class room

Higher secondary school H was located in the Nuwakot district (Figure 5.2.2.4-(8)-1). Schools G and I are discussed in other sections. According to our survey, high school H had 325 students and was damaged by the main earthquake on the 25th of April.

Figure 5.2.2.4-(8)-2 shows the site plan of school H. The ground was even. There were a two-story RC building and a one-story masonry building (Photograph 5.2.2.4-(8)-1). The damage level of the RC building was slight and that of the masonry building was severe. The masonry building has completely collapsed. There was a significant difference with respect to the structural system.

Photo 5.2.2.4-(8)-2 shows the overall view of the RC school building. Photograph 5.2.2.4-(8)-3 shows a flexure failure of the column base on the first floor. Column section was 230 mm × 230 mm, longitudinal reinforcements were 6-D12, and hoops were 2-D8@150. The reinforcements were heavily rusted.

The one-story masonry school building had completely collapsed. Figure 5.2.2.4-(8)-3 shows the floor plan of the building. Here, the wall thickness and locations of openings were based on our measurements. The building was constructed in 1975. The wall structure was Stone-Mud and the wall thickness was 520 mm. The roof structure was Timber-GI. Photographs 5.2.2.4-(8)-4 and 5.2.2.4-(8)-5 show the damage states of the building.

The wall ratios were 12.2% for the longitudinal direction and 12.7% for the transverse direction.

(9)　I 高校/ Higher Secondary School H

I 高校は Figure 5.2.2.4-(8)-1 に示した場所に所在し，Dhading 行政区に所属する．Figure 5.2.2.4-(9)-1 に示すように，本校は，2 棟の Photo 5.2.2.4-(5)-9 に示した E 学校校舎と類似の Stone-Mud 構造の壁，Steel-GI 構造の屋根を有する平屋建て校舎（Photo 5.2.2.4-(9)-1）と，1 棟の 2 階建て RC 校舎（建設中，Photo 5.2.2.4-(9)-2）の計 3 棟の校舎を有する．前者は E 学校の敷地北西の校舎同様に JICA の経済支援により建設された．E 学校では軽微な被害であったが，I 学校では妻壁の転倒が見られた（Photo 5.2.2.4-(9)-1）．一方，後者の RC 校舎の被害は軽微（EMS-98 の Grade 1）であった．

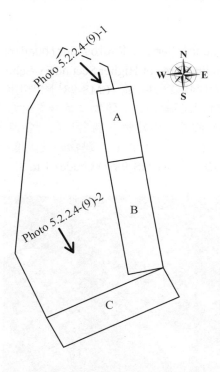

Figure 5.2.2.4-(9)-1 Site plan

Photo 5.2.2.4-(9)-1 Single story masonry building

Photo 5.2.2.4-(9)-2 2-story RC building

Higher secondary school I located in Dhading district, as shown in Figure 5.2.2.4-(8)-1. Figure 5.2.2.4-(9)-1 presents the site plan with two Stone-Mud masonry buildings with Steel-GI roof (Photo 5.2.2.4-(9)-1), which are similar to that in E school shown in Photo 5.2.2.4-(5)-9, and a two-story RC building under construction (Photo 5.2.2.4-(9)-2). The former buildings were constructed under financial supports by JICA as that in E school. Gable wall failure was observed, as shown in Photo 5.2.2.4-(9)-1, while that in E school suffered slight damage only to the gable wall. On the contrary, damage to the latter RC building was Grade 1 according to EMS-98.

5.2.2.5 特定地区の被害率/ Local Damage Ratios Surrounding the Investigated Schools
(1)　D高校周辺地区/ Surrounding Area of Higher Secondary School D

前述した D 学校周辺地区の建物について，EMS-98[5.2.2-1]判定法より被災度区分判定を行った．Figure 5.2.2.5-(1)-1 に D 学校および調査した建物に番号を付した空撮写真を示す．同図に示すように，合計 22 棟（学校建物を除く）の建物を判定した．各建物の判定結果を Figure 5.2.2.5-(1)-2(a)，被害率を同図(b)にそれぞれ示す．ただし，建物の被災度を全壊（EMS-98 の Grade 5），半壊（EMS-98 の Grade 4），半壊未満（EMS-98 の Grades 1 to 3）三段階で表示した．

Figure 5.2.2.5-(1)-1 Aerial photo of the investigated area nearby D high school

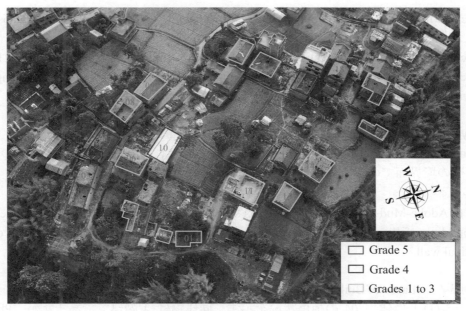

(a) Investigation results

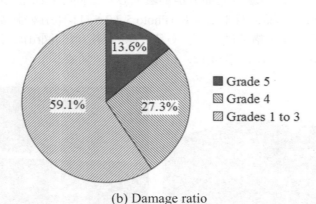

(b) Damage ratio

Figure 5.2.2.5-(1)-2 Investigation results and damage ratio

調査した 22 棟の建物の構造形式を Table 5.2.2.5-(1)-1 にまとめる．各構造形式について，典型的な破壊形式を以下で解説する．なお，各建物の名称は，Figure 5.2.2.5-(1)-1 に示す建物番号より定義する．

Table 5.2.2.5-(1)-1 Structural systems of the investigated buildings

Structural system[※1]	Masonry (Adobe-Mud)	Masonry (Brick-Mud)	RC	Total
Number[※2]	7.5	12.5	2	22
Percentage	34.1%	56.8%	9.1%	100%

※1 Refer to Table 5.2.2.1-1 for the structural systems.

※2 Building 13 had different structural systems at the south side and north side: Brick-Mud at the south side and Adobe-Mud at north side. It was counted at 0.5 for each system.

Using the methods of EMS-98[5.2.2-1)], damage assessment was conducted to the buildings at the surrounding area of higher secondary school D. Figure 5.2.2.5-(1)-1 is an aerial photo including higher secondary school D and the investigated buildings with Arabic numerals. As shown in the figure, twenty-two buildings (excluding higher secondary school D) were investigated. The investigation result of every building and damage ratio is shown in Figure 5.2.2.5-(1)-2(a) and (b), respectively. However, the damage level is indicated for three ranks: completely collapsed (Grade 5 in EMS-98), partially collapsed (Grade 4 in EMS-98), and slight to moderate damage (Grade 3 or below).

The structural systems of the investigated 22 buildings are summarized in Table 5.2.2.5-(1)-1. Typical damage patterns of every type of structural system is introduced in the following. The buildings named by Arabic numerals can be referred to Figure 5.2.2.5-(1)-1.

(a) Masonry (Adobe-Mud)構造/ Masonry (Adobe-Mud) Structure

Adobe-Mud 構造の建物の被害が大きかった．被害形態として，建物の倒壊，屋根の崩落，妻壁と桁行方向壁の境界面での鉛直方向のひび割れの貫通などが挙げられる．

Damage to Adobe-Mud structure buildings was severe. The following damage patterns were observed: collapse of buildings, falling down of roofs, and penetration of vertical cracks at the boundary of gable wall and longitudinal wall.

・ 建物の倒壊/ Collapse of Building

Photo 5.2.2.5-(1)-1 に建物 04 の損傷状況を示す．同建物は 4 階建てであったが，Photo 5.2.2.5-(1)-1(a)に示すように，建物が全壊（大部分が倒壊）した．同写真(b)に示す壁の詳細より，壁厚は煉瓦 2 個分で，480mm である．日干し煉瓦 (Photo 5.2.2.5-(1)-1(c)) の強度は測定しなかったが，非常に低いと推定できる．屋根構造は不明であり，床の構造は同図(d)に示すような木造であった．

Photo 5.2.2.5-(1)-2 に示すように，建物 12, 17 も部分的に倒壊した．

(a) View of whole building

(b) Detail of the wall

(c) Adobe

(d) Timber-made floor

Photo 5.2.2.5-(1)-1 Example of completely collapsed Masonry (Adobe-Mud) structure: Building 04

    (a) Building 12   (b) Building 17
Photo 5.2.2.5-(1)-2 Partially collapsed Masonry (Adobe-Mud) structure

 Photo 5.2.2.5-(1)-1 shows the damage to Building 04. It had been a 4-story building, which approximately completely collapsed, as shown in Photo 5.2.2.5-(1)-1. According to the wall details in Photo 5.2.2.5-(1)-1(b), the thickness corresponded to 2-bricks, which was about 480 mm. Although the strength of the adobe used in the wall (Photo 5.2.2.5-(1)-1(c)) was not tested, it was estimated to be very weak. The structural system of the roof was unknown, and the floor was made of timber as shown in Photo 5.2.2.5-(1)-1(d).

 As shown in Photo 5.2.2.5-(1)-2, Buildings 12 and 17 also collapsed partially.

・ 屋根の崩落/ Falling Down of Roofs

 Photo 5.2.2.5-(1)-3 に示すように，建物 18 の大きな損傷は屋根の崩落であった．また，写真の白枠に示すように，窓開口の両端に 2 本の縦方向のひび割れが発生した．また，建物 19 の屋根が完全に崩落した．

 Masonry (Adobe-Mud) 構造の建物を 7 棟（Table 5.2.2.5-(1)-1 で説明した混在構造の建物 13 を除く）調査した結果，Figure 5.2.2.5-(1)-3 に示すように，全・半壊率は 86%であり，この種の建物の脆弱性が示された．

Photo 5.2.2.5-(1)-3 Building 18 (roof collapse and vertical crack from the window corners)

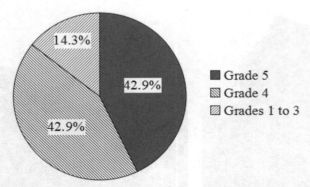

Figure 5.2.2.5-(1)-3 Damage ratio of Masonry (Adobe-Mud) structure buildings

Photo 5.2.2.5-(1)-3 shows that major damage to Building 18 was falling down of the roof. Besides, as shown in the white frame in the photo, two vertical cracks appeared at both sides of the windows. The roof of Building 19 fell down completely.

Seven Masonry (Adobe-Mud) structure buildings (except for Building 13, which was a hybrid structure building as indicated in Table 5.2.2.5-(1)-1) were investigated. Consequently, as shown in Figure 5.2.2.5-(1)-3, 86% of them completely or partially collapsed, indicating the vulnerability of this kind of structure.

・妻壁と桁行方向壁の境界面でのひび割れ/ Vertical Cracks at the Boundary of Gable Wall and Longitudinal Wall

Photo 5.2.2.5-(1)-4 に建物 13, 15 の損傷状況を示す．標記の被害形態が見られた．また，建物 02, 19 にも同様なひび割れが発生した．

(a) Building 13　　　　　　　　　　　　　　(b) Building 15

Photo 5.2.2.5-(1)-4 Crack at boundary of gable wall and longitudinal direction wall in Masonry (Adobe-Mud) structure buildings

In Buildings 13 and 15, wide cracks appeared at the boundary of gable wall and longitudinal wall, as shown in Photo 5.2.2.5-(1)-4. This type of damage was also observed in Buildings 02 and 19.

(b) Masonry (Brick-Mud) 構造/ Masonry (Brick-Mud) structure

Brick-Mud 構造の建物では，前述の Adobe-Mud 構造の建物と類似した破壊形式が見られた．Photo 5.2.2.5-(1)-5～11 に Brick-Mud 構造の建物の被害状況を示す．Masonry (Brick-Mud)構造の建物を 12 棟（Table 5.2.2.5-(1)-1 で説明した混在構造の建物 13 を除く）調査した結果，Figure

5.2.2.5-(1)-4 に示すように，半壊率は 25%であり，Masonry (Adobe-Mud) 構造より被害が小さい傾向が得られた．

Photo 5.2.2.5-(1)-5 Building 09 (crack at wall boundary)　　Photo 5.2.2.5-(1)-6 Building 10 (the third, fourth floor collapsed, but cleaned up)

(a) Longitudinal direction (slight damage)　(b) Vertical cracks on gable wall　(c) Roof (tiles falling)

Photo 5.2.2.5-(1)-7 Damage to Building 06

(a) Northwest side (slight damage)　　(b) Southside (collapse of roof, crack at walls boundary)

Photo 5.2.2.5-(1)-8 Damage to Building 07

Photo 5.2.2.5-(1)-9 Building 16 (shear crack, tiles falling)   Photo 5.2.2.5-(1)-10 Building13 (shear cracks)

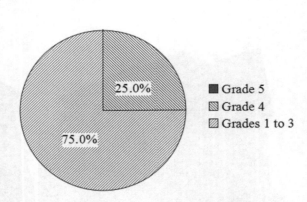

Photo 5.2.2.5-(1)-11 Building 21 (slight damage)   Figure 5.2.2.5-(1)-4 Damage ratio

In Brick-Mud structure buildings, similar damage patterns as Adobe-Mud structure were observed. Photos 5.2.2.5-(1)-5 to 5.2.2.5-(1)-11 show typical damage to this kind of buildings.

Twelve Masonry (Brick-Mud) structure buildings (except for Building 13, which was a hybrid structure building as indicated in Table 5.2.2.5-(1)-1) were investigated. Twenty-five percent of them completely and partially collapsed, as shown in Figure 5.2.2.5-(1)-4. Damage to Masonry (Brick-Mud) structure buildings was slighter than that to Adobe-Mud structure buildings.

(c) RC 構造/ RC Structures

RC 構造の建物は健全であった．Photo 5.2.2.5-(1)-12 に示す建物 11 は建設中であり，Photo 5.2.2.5-(1)-13 は完成した建物であるが，屋上に突出する RC 柱は将来の増築を想定したためのものである．

Photo 5.2.2.5-(1)-12 Building 11 (none damage)   Photo 5.2.2.5-(1)-13 Building 14 (none damage)

None damage was observed in RC structure buildings. Building 11 shown in Photo 5.2.2.5-(1)-12 was under construction. Building 14 in Photo 5.2.2.5-(1)-13 was completed, where the extruding RC columns at the second story were reserved for annex in the future.

(d) まとめ/ Summaries
1. Masonry (Adobe-Mud) 構造の建物の被害が深刻であった．
2. 瓦屋根の崩落による被害が顕著であった．
3. Masonry (Adobe-Mud)，Masonry (Brick-Mud) 構造の建物の妻壁と桁行方向壁の境界面（隅角部）で鉛直方向のひび割れが多く見られた．これは，泥による目地材の強度が非常に弱いことに起因すると推定される．地震動がより強かったり，強い余震に見舞われたりすると，建物が倒壊するおそれがある．
4. RC 構造の建物には損傷が見られなかった．

1. Masonry (Adobe-Mud) structure buildings were damaged heavily.
2. Damage due to falling down of tile roofs was remarkable.
3. Vertical cracks at the boundary of gable wall and longitudinal wall were observed in many masonry buildings, which seemed to be due to the weakness of mud joint. If the ground motion had been stronger or a strong aftershock comes, there is a vulnerability of collapse.
4. None damage was observed in RC structure buildings.

(2) F 高校周辺地区/ Surrounding Area of Higher Secondary School F

Figure 5.2.2.5-(2)-1 に調査した区域を示す．当該地域は余震の震源より南西 36km，カトマンズ北東 39km の Chautara にある．余震の震源に近いため，現地での聞き取り調査により，この地域の建物は余震による被害が大きく，本震で損傷した建物が余震により倒壊した事例が多いとのことであった．Figure 5.2.2.5-(2)-1 に示す F 学校近くの Chautara 市街地の幹線道路沿いにおいて，Figure 5.2.2.5-(2)-2 に示す 48 棟の建物を EMS-98[5.2.2-1]判定法より被災度区分判定を行った．なお，Figure 5.2.2.5-(2)-2 に番号を付した建物および全壊（EMS-98 の Grade 5），半壊（EMS-98 の Grade 4），半壊未満（EMS-98 の Grades 1 to 3）三段階で評価した結果も示している．Figure 5.2.2.5-(2)-3 の被害率より，全・半壊率は 54%であり，当該地域では建物が深刻な被害を受けた．Photo 5.2.2.5-(2)-1 は，Figure 5.2.2.5-(2)-2 に示す道路で撮影したものである．

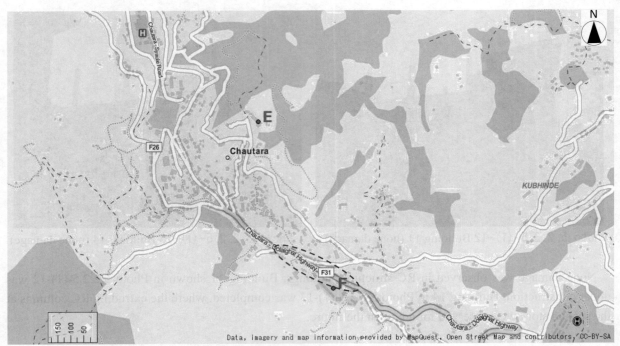

Figure 5.2.2.5-(2)-1 Investigated area

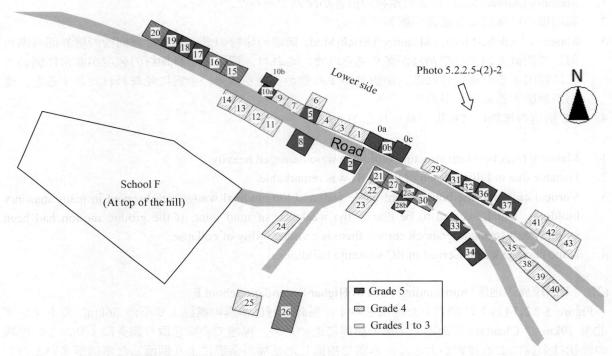

Figure 5.2.2.5-(2)-2 Investigated buildings and the damage classification (classified by three levels: completely collapsed, partially collapsed and slight to moderate damage)

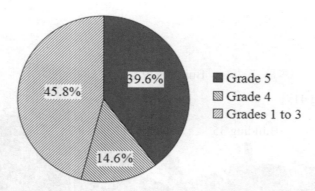

Figure 5.2.2.5-(2)-3 Damage ratio of the investigated buildings nearby F high school

Photo 5.2.2.5-(2)-1 Damage condition at the street in the central area of Chautara

　当該地域は山地であり，F 学校は山頂に位置する．Photo 5.2.2.5-(2)-2 は，Figure 5.2.2.5-(2)-2 の道路の下から撮影したものである．Photo 5.2.2.5-(2)-3 に示すように，道路北側の建物は斜面に沿って建てられ，裏側は表側より低いことがわかる．

Photo 5.2.2.5-(2)-2 Photo shot from lower position than the street (shooting direction shown in Figure 5.2.2.5-(2)-2)

Photo 5.2.2.5-(2)-3 Photo shot from the street to the west side of Building 29

　調査した建物の構造形式を Table 5.2.2.5-(2)-1 にまとめる．以下に各構造形式について被害率および典型的な破壊形式を示す．

Table 5.2.2.5-(2)-1 Structural systems of the investigated buildings

Structural system[※1]	Masonry (Stone-Mud)	Masonry (Brick-Mud)	Masonry (Brick-Mortar)	RC	Total
Number[※2]	13.5	3	1.5	30	48
Percentage	28.1%	6.3%	3.1%	62.5%	100%

※1. Refer to Table 5.2.2.1-1 for the structural systems.
※2. Buildings consisting of two types of structural systems are counted for 0.5 for each type.

Figure 5.2.2.5-(2)-1 shows the investigated area, which was in Chautara district, 36 kilometers southwest of the epicenter of the large aftershock in May 12th and 39 kilometers northeast of Kathmandu. As this area was close to the epicenter of the aftershock, damage caused by the aftershock was greater; namely, many buildings collapsed during the large aftershock after suffering damage due to the main shock, according to the field hearing survey. Damage assessment was conducted for 48 buildings shown in figure 5.2.2.5-(2)-2, which were nearby F high school and along a main street in the central area of Chautara. Figure 5.2.2.5-(2)-2 also shows the investigation results by three ranks of completely collapsed, partially collapsed, and slight to moderate damage. The damage ratio is shown in figure 5.2.2.5-(2)-3: completely or partially damaged buildings account for 54% of the evaluated buildings, indicating the severity of damage. Photo 5.2.2.5-(2)-1 shows a snapshot along the main street in Figure 5.2.2.5-(2)-2.

This area locates at a mountainous region, and F high school is at the hilltop. Photo 5.2.2.5-(2)-2 was shot from the lower position than the main street shown in Figure 5.2.2.5-(2)-2. From Photo 5.2.2.5-(2)-3, the buildings along the north side of the street were built at the slope, hence, the back side of the buildings were based lower than the front side.

The structural systems of the investigated 48 buildings are summarized in Table 5.2.2.5-(2)-1. Typical damage patterns and damage ratio of every structural system are introduced in the following.

(a) Masonry (Stone-Mud) 構造/ Masonry (Stone-Mud) Structures
調査した建物のうち，Stone-Mud 構造は 13 棟（混在構造の 1 棟を除く）であり，9 棟が全壊した．この種の建物の被害率は Figure 5.2.2.5-(2)-4 に示すように，全半壊率は 100%であり，深刻な被害を受けた．Photo 5.2.2.5-(2)-4 に Stone-Mud 構造の損傷状況を示す．

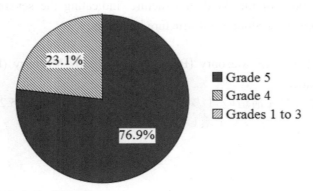

Figure 5.2.2.5-(2)-4 Damage ratio of Masonry (Stone-Mud) structures

(a) Building 30 (partial collapse)　　　　　(b) Building 02 (complete collapse)

(c) Building 28 (complete collapse)　　　　　(d) Building 33 (complete collapse)

Photo 5.2.2.5-(2)-4 Damage to Masonry (Stone-Mud) structures

Thirteen Stone-Mud structure buildings (Excluding a hybrid structure building) were investigated, and nine of them completely collapsed. As shown in Figure 5.2.2.5-(2)-4, completely or partially collapsed buildings accounted for 100% of this kind of structure, indicating the severe damage to them. Photo 5.2.2.5-(2)-4 shows the damage to Stone-Mud structure buildings.

(b) Masonry (Brick-Mud) および Masonry (Brick-Mortar) 構造/ Masonry (Brick-Mud) and Masonry (Brick-Mortar) Structures

本構造の建物を 5 棟（混在構造の 1 棟を含む）調査した．Photo 5.2.2.5-(2)-5 に示す Brick-Mortar 構造の建物 25 以外は，すべて全壊した．

(a) View of whole building　　　　　(b) Shear crack in internal wall
Photo 5.2.2.5-(2)-5 Damage to Building 25

For Masonry (Brick-Mud) or Masonry (Brick-Mortar) structure, the number of investigated buildings was 5 (Including a hybrid structure building). Excepting Building 25, which is shown in Photo 5.2.2.5-(2)-5, all completely collapsed.

(c) RC 構造/ RC Structures
48 棟の建物のうち，RC 構造はその大半を占める 30 棟である．この種の建物の被害率を Figure 5.2.2.5-(2)-5 に示す．被害形態として，建物の傾斜や倒壊，柱の曲げ破壊，壁の面外への傾斜や転倒，壁のせん断ひび割れなどが挙げられる．

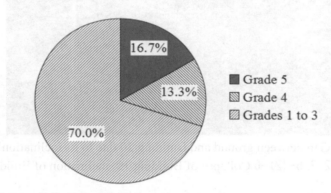

Figure 5.2.2.5-(2)-5 Damage ratio of RC structures buildings

Among the investigated forty-eight buildings in this area, thirty ones were RC structure, accounting for the great majority. Figure 5.2.2.5-(2)-5 shows the damage ratio of this kind of structure. The following typical damage patterns were observed: inclining or collapse of buildings, flexural failure of columns, inclining or out-of-plane falling of walls and shear cracks in walls.

・　建物の傾き・倒壊/ Inclining or Collapse of Buildings
Photo 5.2.2.5-(2)-6 に建物 19，20 の被害状況を示す．(a)に全体の様子，(b)に倒壊した建物 19 が建物 20 に衝突した様子，(c)に建物 20 と道路側地面の間に生じた隙間をそれぞれ示す．写真より建物 20 は 2 階建てと見えるが，実際には道路面の下に地下 1 階（Photo 5.2.2.5-(2)-6(c)）が存在し 3 階建てである．建物 19 は地下 2 階建てを含む 4 階建てであった．
Photo 5.2.2.5-(2)-7 に倒壊した建物 34，37 の被害状況を示す．建物 34 の 1 階と 2 階が層崩壊した．建物 37 は斜面下側に転倒した．

(a) Damage to Building 19 and 20

(b) Collision of collapsed Building 19 to Building 20

(c) Gap between ground and Building 20 due to its inclination
Photo 5.2.2.5-(2)-6 Collapse of Building 19, inclination of Building 20

(a) Collapse of the first and second stories of Building 34

(b) Collapse of Building 37 (6-story) – shot from the street

(c) Collapse of Building 37- shot from the lower side of the slope

Photo 5.2.2.5-(2)-7 Collapses of Building 34 and 37

Photo 5.2.2.5-(2)-6 shows damage conditions of Buildings 19 and 20: (a) is the overall view, (b) is the collapsed Building 19 crashing Building 20, (c) shows the gap between Building 20 and ground. According to Photo 5.2.2.5-(2)-6(c), it seems that Building 20 had two stories, however, it was a three-story building because actually one more story existed below the street. Building 19 had four stories.

Photo 5.2.2.5-(2)-7 shows the damage to Building 34 and 37. The first and second stories of Building 34 collapsed. Building 37 overturned to the lower side of the slope.

・ 柱の曲げ破壊/ Flexural Failure of Columns

Photo 5.2.2.5-(2)-8 に RC の柱頭曲げ破壊の例を示す．同写真(a)は建物 15 の梁間方向の中柱梁接合部および壁の被害状況を示す．1 階柱頭の主筋が座屈してコアコンクリートまで損傷し，建物の鉛直支持性能が著しく低下した状態である．同写真(b)は建物 42 の外柱頭部のカバーコンクリートの剥落，柱主筋の露出を示している．また，レンガ壁のひび割れが柱まで延伸し，柱の全せいを貫通したことがわかる．レンガ壁は非構造部材として見なされているが，柱と壁の間で力の伝達が生じたことを示している．

(a) Building 15　　　　　　　　　　　　(b) Building 42
Photo 5.2.2.5-(2)-8 Flexural failure at the top of RC columns

Photo 5.2.2.5-(2)-8 shows two flexural failure examples of RC columns. Photo 5.2.2.5-(2)-8(a) shows the damage to an interior beam-column joint and walls in the span direction of Building 15. The longitudinal rebars at the column top in the first story buckled and the core concrete was damaged, indicating that the vertical resistance deteriorated significantly. Photo 5.2.2.5-(2)-8(b) shows that the cover concrete spalled and the longitudinal rebars exposed at the top of the exterior column. Moreover, the crack in brick wall extended to RC column and penetrated the column completely: showing that transmission of force occurred between the column and the wall, although brick walls are regarded as non-structural elements when designing.

・ 壁の面外への傾きや転倒/ Out-of-plane Inclining or Falling of Walls

Photo 5.2.2.5-(2)-9 に建物 26 および 15 の損傷状況を示す．写真に示すように，壁と RC フレームの間に接合要素がないため，(a)ではブロック+レンガ壁の面外への傾き，(b)では石造壁の部分倒壊が見られた．こうした壁の面外方向への脆弱な破壊は，居住者や付近の通行者に危害を加えるおそれがあり，また，建物の構造要素の損傷が比較的小さい場合でも地震後の建物の機能を著しく低下させるため，容易な転倒を防止する取組みがとくに必要である．

(a) Inclining of exterior wall in Building 26　　　　(b) Collapse of stone wall in Building 15
Photo 5.2.2.5-(2)-9 Examples of inclination and collapse of masonry walls in RC structures

Photo 5.2.2.5-(2)-9 shows damage to Building 26 and Building 15. Since no joint element exists between walls and RC frame, the block and brick wall inclined in the out-of-plane direction, and the stone wall collapsed partially, as shown in Photo 5.2.2.5-(2)-9(a) and (b), respectively. This kind of vulnerable out-of-plane failure of walls can injure the residents or the passengers nearby, and furthermore, it will significantly decrease the function of the buildings even though the damage to structural components is relatively slight. Efforts that develop an effective method to prevent out-of-plane falling of walls is necessary.

・ 壁のせん断ひび割れ/ Shear Cracks in Walls

Photo 5.2.2.5-(2)-10 に建物 29 と 42 の損傷状況を示す．写真に示すように，RC フレームにより囲まれたレンガ壁にせん断ひび割れが見られた．こうした損傷は壁が面内方向の地震力に抵抗したことを意味しており，面外方向の損傷を抑制できれば，建物の剛性や強度を合理的に増大できる可能性がある．

(a) Wall in the span direction of Building 29　　(b) Interior wall in the span direction of Building 42
Photo 5.2.2.5-(2)-10 Shear cracks in masonry walls in RC structures

Photo 5.2.2.5-(2)-10 shows the damage to Building 29 and Building 42: shear cracks in confined walls by RC frames were observed. These damage demonstrates that the walls have resisted the in-plane seismic load, and that if out-of-plane damage could be prevented, it's possible to improve the stiffness and strength of the buildings by the existence of masonry walls.

(d) まとめ/ Summaries
1. 建物全体の全，半壊率は 54%であり，深刻な被害を受けた．
2. RC 構造の建物の被害は他の構造より比較的に軽いが，全・半壊率は 30%に達した．
3. Masonry（Stone-Mud）構造の建物では，全・半壊率は 100%であった．
4. 調査した Masonry（Brick-Mud）および Masonry（Brick-Mortar）構造の建物が少ないが，1 棟以外すべて全壊した．

1. 54% of the investigated buildings were completely or partially damaged. Buildings in this area suffered heavy damage.
2. Although damage to RC structure buildings was slighter than other types of buildings, the ratio of completely or partially damaged buildings accounted to 30%.
3. 100% of the Masonry (Stone-Mud) structure buildings completely or partially collapsed.
4. Although the number of Masonry (Brick-Mud) or Masonry (Brick-Mortar) structure buildings were limited in this area, all of them completely collapsed except for one.

(3) G 小学校周辺地区/ Surrounding Area of Primary School G

5.2.2.4 項の(7)で示した G 小学校周辺地区の建物を EMS-98[5.2.2-1)]判定法より被災度区分判定を行った．Figure 5.2.2.5-(3)-1 に G 学校および調査した建物に番号を付した空撮写真を示す．同図に示すように，当該地域は山地であり，調査した建物は点在した民家である．合計 6 棟の建物を調査した．建物の構造形式はすべて 2 階建ての Masonry (Stone-Mud) 構造であり，判定結果を Figure 5.2.2.5-(3)-2(a)，被害率を同図(b)にそれぞれ示す．前述した地区と同じく，建物の被災度を全壊，半壊，半壊未満の三段階で表示した．

Figure 5.2.2.5-(3)-1 Aerial photo of the investigated area

(a) Investigation results

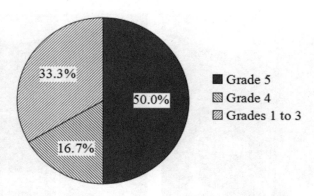
(b) Damage ratio of the investigated buildings
Figure 5.2.2.5-(3)-2 Investigation results and damage ratio

　調査した 6 棟の Masonry (Stone-Mud) 構造の民家では，全壊は 3 棟，半壊は 1 棟，半壊未満は 2 棟であった．Photo 5.2.2.5-(3)-1 に建物 1 の被害状況を示す．壁が面外方向に倒壊した．写真中の倒壊した建物の隣接建物は仮設住宅である．Photo 5.2.2.5-(3)-2 に示す建物の北側妻壁と西側桁行方向壁の隅角部に大きなひび割れが生じた．屋根の葺き材は，Photo 5.2.2.5-(3)-3 に示す石板である．2 階建てだった建物 6 が全壊し，地震後に当該位置に建てられた仮設住宅を Photo 5.2.2.5-(3)-4 に示す．

　G 小学校周辺地区は山地であり，点在した Masonry (Stone-Mud) 構造の建物を 6 棟調査した結果，3 棟が全壊，1 棟が半壊，2 棟が半壊未満であった．

Photo 5.2.2.5-(3)-1 Building 1

Photo 5.2.2.5-(3)-2 Building 3 (crack at walls boundary)

Photo 5.2.2.5-(3)-3 Stone tile used for roofing material

Photo 5.2.2.5-(3)-4 Temporary housing built at the location of collapsed Building 6

Damage levels of the buildings near G primary school, which is introduced in Section 5.2.2.4 (7), were assessed according to EMS-98[5.2.2-1)]. Figure 5.2.2.5-(3)-1 shows an aerial photo including G primary school and the investigated buildings with Arabic numerals. As shown in the photo, this area was mountainous, and the investigated buildings were scattered houses. Six buildings were investigated, all of which were Masonry (Stone-Mud) structures with two stories. The investigation results and damage ratio are shown in in Figure 5.2.2.5-(3)-2(a) and (b), respectively. Damage was defined into three grades as completely collapsed, partially collapsed and slight to moderate damage, in the same manner as the above sections.

In the investigated six Masonry (Stone-Mud) houses, three of them were completely collapsed, and one partially collapsed, and the other two were slightly or moderately damaged. Photo 5.2.2.5-(3)-1 shows the damage to Building 1: the walls collapsed in the out of plane direction. The nearby building was a temporary house. Photo 5.2.2.5-(3)-2 shows that a big crack appeared at the boundary of the north gable wall and west longitudinal wall in Building 3. Roof material was a kind of stone tile, as shown in Photo 5.2.2.5-(3)-3. The two-story Building 6 completely collapsed, and Photo 5.2.2.5-(3)-4 shows the temporary house which was built at the same location.

Primary school G located at a mountainous area. Six Masonry (Stone-Mud) structure buildings around the school were investigated: three were completely collapsed, one partially collapsed, and the other two were slightly or moderately damaged.

(4) H 高校周辺地区/ Surrounding Area of Higher Secondary School H

　H 学校周辺地区の建物の被害状況を示す．Figure 5.2.2.5-(4)-1 に H 学校および調査した建物に番号を付した空撮写真を示す．同図に示すように，合計 17 棟（学校建物を除く）の建物を判定した．各建物の判定結果を Figure 5.2.2.5-(4)-2(a)，被害率を同図(b)にそれぞれ示す．被災度区分判定の方法は，前述した地区と同じである．同地区で調査した建物の 8 割が全壊した．

Figure 5.2.2.5-(4)-1 Aerial photo of the investigated area

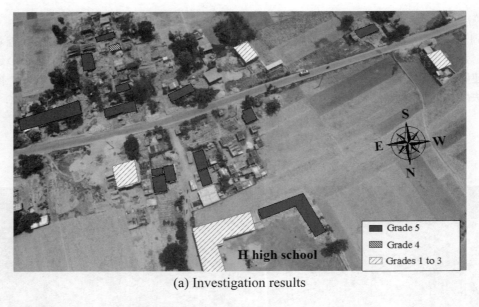

(a) Investigation results

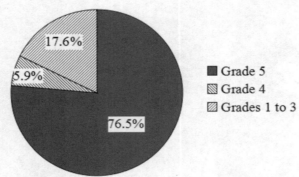

(b) Damage ratio of the investigated buildings

Figure 5.2.2.5-(4)-2 Investigation results and damage ratio

調査した地域は Figure 5.2.2.5-(4)-1 に示すように，道路沿いの平野に位置する農村である．建物の構造形式を Table 5.2.2.5-(4)-1 にまとめる．Table 5.2.2.5-(4)-1 より，石造建物がその大部分を占める 65%である．以下，各構造形式について典型的な破壊形式を示す．

Table 5.2.2.5-(4)-1 Structural systems of the investigated buildings

Structural system[※1]	Masonry (Stone-Mud)	Masonry (Block-Cement)	RC	Total
Number	11	2	4	17
Percentage	64.7%	11.8%	23.5%	100%

※1 Refer to Table 5.2.2.1-1 for the structural systems.

In this section, damage to the buildings near higher secondary school H is introduced. Figure 5.2.2.5-(4)-1 is an aerial photo including high school H and the investigated buildings. As shown in the figure, seventeen buildings (excluding school buildings) were investigated. The investigation results are shown in Figure 5.2.2.5-(4)-2(a) and the damage ratio is shown in Figure 5.2.2.5-(4)-2(b). The same assessment method as the above sections was used. In this area, about 80% of the investigated buildings completely collapsed.

The investigated area was a village along a main road. The structural systems of the investigated buildings are summarized in Table 5.2.2.5-(4)-1: Masonry (Stone-Mud) buildings accounted for 65%.

Typical damage patterns of every kind of structural system are introduced in the following.

(a) Masonry (Stone-Mud) 構造/ Masonry (Stone-Mud) Structures

Stone-Mud 構造の建物を 11 棟調査した．Figure 5.2.2.5-(4)-3 に示すように，全・半壊率は 100% であった．Photo 5.2.2.5-(4)-1 に建物の被害状況を示す．

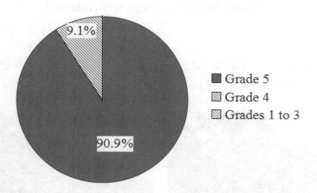

Figure 5.2.2.5-(4)-3 Damage ratio of Masonry (Stone-Mud) structure

(a) Building 9 (complete collapse)　　　(b) Building 10 (partial collapse)

(c) Building 11 (complete collapse)　　　(d) Building 14 (complete collapse)

Photo 5.2.2.5-(4)-1 Damage to Masonry (Stone-Mud) structure

Eleven Stone-Mud structure buildings were investigated, all of which completely or partially collapsed, as shown in Figure 5.2.2.5-(4)-3. Photo 5.2.2.5-(4)-1 shows the damage to this kind of structure.

(b) Masonry (Block-Mortar) 構造/ Masonry (Block-Mortar) Structures
調査した2棟のBlock-Mortar構造建物がすべて全壊であった.

Both of two investigated Block-Mortar buildings completely collapsed.

(c) RC構造/ RC Structures
RC構造の建物を4棟調査した. Photo 5.2.2.5-(4)-2に示すRCの梁がない建物6が全壊した. 残りの3棟は健全であった. Photo 5.2.2.5-(4)-3に建物4の様子を示す.

Photo 5.2.2.5-(4)-2 Building 6 (complete collapse)   Photo 5.2.2.5-(4)-3 Building 4 (none damage)

Four RC buildings were investigated. Building 6, in which RC beam did not exist completely collapsed, as shown in Photo 5.2.2.5-(4)-2. No damage was observed for the other three buildings. Photo 5.2.2.5-(4)-3 shows a view of Building 4.

(d) まとめ/ Summaries
1. 同地域では建物を17棟調査し，全半壊率は82%に達し，被害は深刻であった.
2. Masonry (Stone-Mud) 構造の割合は65%であり，全・半壊率は100%であった.
3. RC建物の損傷は軽微であった.

1. In this area, seventeen buildings were investigated, 82% of which were completely or partially damaged, showing the severe damage.
2. In the investigated buildings, masonry (Stone-Mud) buildings counted for 65%, all of which were completely damaged.
3. Damage to RC buildings were slight.

5.2.2.6 カトマンズ市外の被害の総括と日本が担える支援/ Summary of Building Damage Observed Outside Kathmandu and Prospective Japanese Supports

カトマンズ市外のBhaktapur, Dhading, Lalitpur, Nuwakot, Sindhupalchokの各行政区にわたって学校およびその周辺地域を主な対象とする現地被害調査を実施した. 首都郊外の本震の震央から南東方向へ直線距離約50km, 最大余震の震央から西方向へ直線距離約30km以遠の範囲において，建築物の特性と被害について調査した結果，以下の知見が得られた.

Onsite building damage investigation was conducted focusing on several schools and the nearby areas in five districts close to Kathmandu: Bhaktapur, Dhading, Lalitpur, Nuwakot, and Sindhupalchok. The following findings were obtained through the investigation which covered the area beyond 50 km southeast and 30 km west from the epicenters of the main shock and aftershock, respectively.

(1) 建築物の特性/ Structural Characteristics

調査対象の範囲において，建物規模は低層が中心であり，6層までの中層も見られた．建築物の構造躯体として，組積構造と鉄筋コンクリート構造（RC）が利用されていた．組積構造は組積体である石材，日干レンガ，焼成レンガ，コンクリートブロック，目地材である泥（マッド），セメントモルタルの組合せにより構成されていた．また，組積構造では増築などに伴い複数の構造が異なる組積造壁が混在して建設された事例も見られた．とくに建物高さ方向への増築も見られ，耐震性能上好ましくない増築が行われている場合も多いことがうかがえた．

一方，屋根は木材または鋼材の架構に，亜鉛メッキ鋼板，瓦，茅葺，または RC スラブであった．

Most buildings in the investigated area were low-rise: the maximum number of stories was 6 for limited medium-rise buildings.

The structural systems were masonry or RC. The former masonry buildings were constructed in combination of masonry of stone, adobe, brick, or concrete block with joint of mud or mortar. Hybrid systems with several different combinations were also applied to some buildings which resulted from expansion of the buildings. In particular, increasing number of stories might reduce the seismic performance.

On the other hand, galvanized iron sheet, tile, or grass was used for roofing on the timber or steel roof truss. Another roof system was RC slab.

(2) 被害の形態/ Earthquake Damage

(a) 組積構造/ Masonry Building

被害の形態として，建物の全体の倒壊（全壊），部分的な倒壊（半壊），組積造壁の転倒・傾斜・隅角部の鉛直ひび割れ，壁面のせん断ひび割れなどの損傷が見られた．組積造壁の損傷に着目すると，隅角部（直交する壁の境界）の鉛直ひび割れは，交差する壁のいずれか（または両方）が傾斜することによって発生していたため，壁の面外方向の地震力に起因する損傷と判断される．一方，壁面のせん断ひび割れは壁の面内方向に作用した水平力（地震力）により発生した損傷と判断される．特に前者の損傷が大きくなると，壁の転倒，屋根の崩落，建物の倒壊の原因となった事例も少なくないことを実際の被害状況が示唆していた．

This type of building suffered complete collapse, partial collapse, damage to masonry walls: overturning, tilting, vertical splitting at corner, and shear cracking. The vertical splitting initiated with orthogonal wall tilting and shear cracking seemed to be caused by lateral loads in the out-of-plane and in-plane directions, respectively. In particular, the former damage might initiate overturning of wall, falling of roof, and complete collapse of building.

(b) RC 構造/ RC Building

被害の形態として，建物の全体の倒壊（全壊），部分的な倒壊（半壊），柱・梁・接合部などの構成要素の損傷，非構造壁として用いられる組積造壁の上記同様の損傷が見られた．柱・梁は比較的細長い形状であるため，曲げによる損傷が多く，日本の既存不適格建物で見られるせん断破壊はあまり見られなかった．接合部が大きく損傷した建物では，補強鉄筋の不足や不十分な定着など，不適切な配筋が被害の原因となったことがうかがえた．

Typical damage to RC buildings included complete collapse, partial collapse, damage to structural components: column, beam, and beam-column joint, damage to nonstructural masonry walls mentioned as above. Damage to slender columns and beams were caused with flexural deformations, hence shear failure, which was commonly observed to Japanese old buildings, was not often observed in Nepalese RC buildings. Building with severe damage to beam-column joints might be attributed to inappropriate rebar arrangements such as a lack of shear reinforcement and insufficient anchorage of beam longitudinal rebar.

(3) 被害の特徴と将来の対策に向けた提言/ Typical Damage and Suggestions for Prospective Action
(a) 構造種別と被害率/ Structural System vs. Damage Ratio

学校校舎および学校周辺建物の被災度の判定結果より，組積構造が RC 構造よりも総じて被害率は高いが，RC 構造についても少なからず全壊した建物が見られた．組積構造では，強度が低いと判断される材料，すなわち組積体として石材や日干レンガ，目地材として泥を用いた構造の被害率が大きかった．建築材料の品質の管理の必要性を示唆している．被害が大きかった RC 構造では，補強鉄筋の不足や不十分な定着など，不適切な配筋に起因すると判断される被害事例も見られたため，新築建築に対しては設計，施工にわたる適切な管理，既存建築に対しては耐震診断，耐震補強により同様の被害を繰り返さない努力が必要である．

Damage ratio to masonry school buildings was higher than that to RC buildings, however, some of RC buildings completely collapse. The damage ratio of masonry buildings was higher in the case of those constructed with vulnerable materials: stone and abode for masonry and mud for joint, respectively. This indicates necessity for quality management of construction materials. Poor rebar arrangements such as a lack of shear reinforcement and insufficient anchorage of beam longitudinal rebar were observed to severely damaged RC buildings, which suggests importance of appropriate management through design to construction for new buildings and seismic evaluation/strengthening for existing buildings to prevent similar type of damage due to future earthquakes.

(b) 耐震補強の有効性/ Effectiveness of Seismic Strengthening

一部の学校校舎では，組積構造の校舎を RC 構造に耐震補強する事例があった．，同一敷地内における組積構造の校舎との被害の対比より，適切な耐震補強により組積構造の耐震性能を大幅に改善できることを示す好事例である．

One of school masonry buildings have been converted to RC moment resisting frame for the seismic strengthening. Compared to un-strengthened masonry building in the same school, earthquake damage was significantly reduced, which verifies the effectiveness of the seismic strengthening.

(c) 組積造壁の課題と可能性/ Problems and Feasible Contribution of Masonry Wall

組積構造では，建物の全半壊などの大きな被害が，組積造壁の面外方向への転倒に起因した被害事例が数多く観察された．面外方向の地震力に対する脆弱性の克服は喫緊の課題である．一方，RC 構造の建物に非構造壁として組積造壁が利用されている事例が数多く見られた．これらの事例の中には，非構造壁が面内方向の地震力の抵抗要素として構造的に寄与し，RC 躯体の変形を抑制したと想像される事例もあり，組積造壁の面外方向の容易な傾斜・転倒を抑制することで，現地で多用される組積造壁を耐震補強要素として利用できる可能性もありうる．

全半壊した学校校舎を対象に実施した壁率の評価より，組積体：焼成レンガ，目地材：泥の組積造校舎，組積体：石材，目地材：泥の組積造校舎でそれぞれ最大の壁率は，建物の総床面積に対して 12.5%，26.6%であった．本調査では調査期間の制限から壁率を評価できた校舎の数が限

られたが，データ収集の継続により壁率と被害率の関係を整理することで，将来の地震に対して脆弱（または安全）な建物の合理的な判定に寄与できる．

Sindhupalchok行政区のChautaraに位置した学校では，層降伏したと判断されたRC校舎の耐力を評価し，これに基づいて，隣接する組積構造の校舎の壁（組積体：石材，目地材：泥）のせん断強度を推定した結果，0.08N/mm² 以下と推定された．今後，材料実験結果などと比較して，評価結果の妥当性を検証する必要がある．

Severe damage to a number of masonry buildings including complete and partial collapses were initiated with out-of-plane failure of masonry walls. Upgrading of the vulnerability in the out-of-plane direction is an urgent need. On the other hand, nonstructural masonry walls applied to some RC buildings seemed to resist seismic forces in the in-plane direction, then reduce drift responses of overall buildings. Therefore, masonry walls may be structural components for seismic strengthening if the out-of-plane vulnerability can be improved.

Wall-to-total floor area ratios were evaluated for some of completely and partially collapsed masonry school buildings. The maximum values were 12.5% and 26.6% for Brick-Mud and Stone-Mud buildings, respectively. Although a small number of wall-to-total floor area ratios were evaluated due to the limited period of the investigation, further data collections are recommended to evaluate the relationship between the wall-to-total floor area ratio and the damage ratio because it can contribute to rationally screen seismically vulnerable buildings under future earthquakes.

Lateral resistance of an RC school building, which formed a story collapse mechanism, at Chautara in Sindhupalchok district was evaluated, which estimated an ultimate shear strength of 0.08N/mm² for Stone-Mud masonry walls. Further study is recommended to compare with material test results.

(d) 現地の建設環境とその改善に向けた対策/ The Local Construction Conditions and Proposed Measures for Their Improvements

地域ごとに，気象条件による要求性能の違い，材料や施工技術の入手しやすさ等により用いられる構造形式は異なってくる．今回の被災地の中でも特に運搬が制限される山間部では，現地で入手できる石や日干しレンガが用いられており，熟練した施工技術を得ることの難しさも感じられた．

石や日干しレンガの組積造であっても，適切な計画と施工技術により一定の規模に適応できる．こうした計画施工のルールについては，すでにガイドラインとしてまとめられたものがいくつか存在する（一般的なガイドライン[例えば 5.2.2-7]，地域的なガイドライン[例えば 5.2.2-8]）．しかし，一般的なルールを，具体的な地域に適応するかたちに微調整を加えて示すことは，地域それぞれで条件が異なることから，まだ十分ではない．現地の入手建材，技術を理解した上で，工学的技術を簡便に理解できるかたち，例えば，強度試験を落下試験に置き換える，現地語を用いる，ワークショップを通して認識を共有する，などして提示していくことが考えられる．今回主な調査対象とした学校校舎は，各地域に存在する建築である．その建設や修復の機会を，適切な計画施工技術を地元の専門工・住人が実践的に学ぶ機会とすることができれば，地域の技術向上に持続的に関わるものになると考えられる．

Usual building systems differ in areas with different meteorological requirements, available materials and construction skills. Conditions for transportations are obviously limited in the mountain areas among the devastated areas, we surveyed, and hence the local people have to use stones and adobe easily obtainable in their areas. We found also difficulties to access to skilled laborers.

Stones or adobe masonry structures are nevertheless applicable to certain scale of buildings, if they are used with proper planning and construction technique. There are some guidelines for these already[5.2.2.6-1].

The general rules, however, need to be further adjusted to specific local conditions. For this purpose, it is required to grasp what materials and construction skills are available, and also to propose engineered approaches easily understandable to local persons, occasionally with their language. Strength test can be replaced with fall down test, and workshops on construction site are also useful to share knowledge.

Schools can be found in almost every area, and hence, constructions or renovations of school buildings can be an opportunity for local engineer and residents to learn appropriate planning, material processing, and construction methods. This in turn provides sustainable local improvements.

5.2.2.7 参考文献/References

5.2.2-1) Grunthal G. (1998), European Macroseismic Scale 1998, Conseil de l'Europe Cahiers du Centre Europeen de Geodynamique et de Seismologie, Luxembourg. Available on: http://www.franceseisme.fr/EMS98_Original_english.pdf

5.2.2-2) Department of Education, Ministry of Education & Sports, Government of Nepal, The Project for Construction of Primary Schools in Support of Education for All, School Buildings (Mountain Region), 2003

5.2.2-3) Department of Education, Sanothimi, Bhaktapur (2015), Final Report on Detail Seismic Vulnerability Assessment, Detail Design for Retrofitting & Cost Estimate of School Building on Package B, ID No.: SSRP/DOE/2013/S/PSS-1B) (Bhaktapur District)

5.2.2-4) Department of Education, Sanothimi, Bhaktapur (2013), Structural Drawings for Seismic Retrofitting of Sharada Higher Secondary School, at Yalachhen, Bhaktapur, Nepal

5.2.2-5) Department of Education, Sanothimi, Bhaktapur (2013), Final Report, Yapivairab Lower Secondary School, Bhaktapur, Consulting Services for Detail Seismic Vulnerability Assessment and Retrofitting Design and Cost Estimate of 46 School Building in Latitpur and Bhaktapur District

5.2.2-6) Department of Education, Sanothimi, Bhaktapur (2013), Structural Drawings for Seismic Retrofitting of Jorpati Lower Secondary School, at Sanga, Bhaktapur, Nepal

5.2.2-7) Anand S. ARYA, Teddy BOEN, Yuji ISHIYAMA: Earthquake resistant non-engineered construction, UNESCO, 2014, http://unesdoc.unesco.org/images/0022/002290/229059E.pdf

5.2.2-8) Boen, Teddy: Minimum Requirements for Earthquake Resistant Masonry Building, International Organization for Migration, United States Agency for International Development, 2005

5.2.3　中高層集合住宅/ Mid- to High-rise Apartment Buildings
5.2.3.1　調査建物の位置/ Locations of the Investigated Buildings

　調査した中高層鉄筋コンクリート造建物の主な用途は，集合住宅である．調査を実施したのは，13 集合住宅で，各集合住宅には複数の棟があるため，合計 38 棟の調査を実施した．Figure 5.2.3.1-1 に，調査建物の位置を示す．各集合住宅は，A)～M)として，その位置を図に示している．建物リストを以下に示す．

- A) 3棟，軽微と思われる．立入りの許可は得られず．
- B) 3棟，軽微
- C) 2棟，軽微
- D) 1棟，軽微
- E) 5棟，小破～中波
- F) 3棟，軽微
- G) 1棟，軽微
- H) 1棟，軽微：長期荷重のひび割れ被害
- I) 4棟，軽微
- J) 軽微2棟，小破2棟 被災度区分判定実施
- K) 4棟，軽微～小破
- L) 2棟，軽微
- M) 5棟，軽微

　カトマンズ市には，その中心部に比較的整備された環状道路 (Ring road) がある．対象集合住宅は，およそこの環状道路の周辺および内側に位置している．Nepal でのこういった 10 層程度以上の集合住宅の歴史は比較的浅く，2007 年ごろから建設が始まった．ほぼ全ての構造は鉄筋コンクリート造であり，連層耐震壁は多くの場合，エレベータコアにのみ存在する．その他の間仕切り壁は，焼成レンガを積み上げてモルタルで仕上げをしたものである．内部には鉄筋等は配されていない．各調査建物の被害状況は以降に詳細を示すが，ほとんどの集合住宅では，構造部材への被害はほとんどないか，限定的である．しかし，この非構造材である間仕切り壁に甚大な被害が生じており，落下などの危険性が高かった．

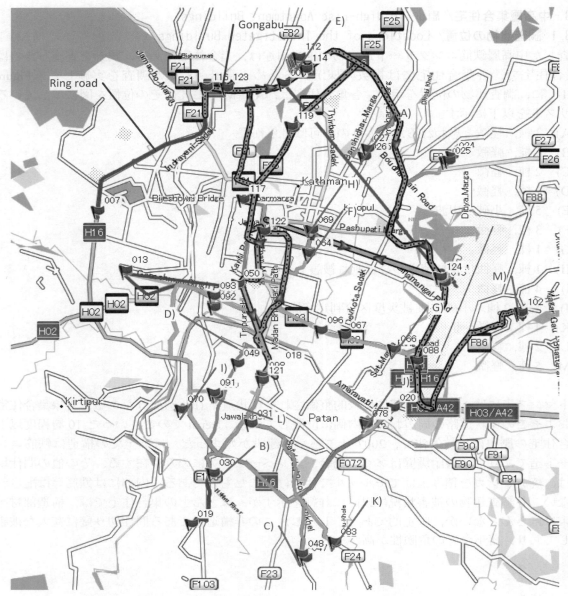

Figure 5.2.3.1-1 Locations of investigated buildings

The main usage of the investigated buildings was residence. Thirteen complexes were investigated. Since each complex has a number of buildings, 38 building were investigated in total. The locations of the complexes are shown in Figure 5.2.3.1-1. Each complex is named as A) to M), which is listed below with its damage level;

- A) Three buildings, seems slight damage but access denied
- B) Three buildings, slight damage
- C) Two buildings, slight damage
- D) Single building, slight damage
- E) Five buildings, light to moderate damage
- F) Three buildings, slight damage
- G) Single building, slight damage
- H) Single building, slight damage with cracking due to gravity load
- I) Four buildings, slight damage
- J) Four buildings, slight damage (two buildings) and light damage (two buildings). Japanese

Damage Classification method was applied.
K) Four buildings, slight to light damage
L) Two buildings, slight damage
M) Five buildings, slight damage

In the central area of Kathmandu city, there is Ring road, which is well-maintained circular road. All the investigated buildings are located close to Ring road. The history of mid- to high-rise apartment is not so long, and the construction started from 2007. Most of all buildings are reinforced concrete structure, which does not have much continuous shear walls but just around elevator core. The partition walls are made of brick with mortar finishing. No reinforcement bar is arranged in the partition walls. The details of the damage conditions of the investigated buildings are described later, but it can be summarized that the damage of structural members were not observed or very limited for the most of the investigated buildings. The damage of the non-structural members such as partition walls were, however, severe and likely to fall down.

5.2.3.2 Building A

3棟の鉄筋コンクリート造13階建て集合住宅からなる．全景をPhoto 5.3.2.2-1に示す．建物は斜面上に建っている．敷地外からは，構造部材には目立った被害は確認できなかった．一方，Photo 5.3.2.2-2に示すように，焼成レンガを積んだ非構造壁（窓枠周辺の腰壁・垂れ壁）や，R/C柱の仕上げ部に被害を確認することができた．本集合住宅では，立入りの許可を得ることができず，詳細な調査は実施できなかった．構造被害は軽微と推定される．

一方，Photo 5.4.2.2-3には，集合住宅周辺の建物状況を示す．周辺では，2層程度の組積造建物が点在しているが，軽微なひび割れが発生しているものがあるものの，倒壊や全壊建物は確認されなかった．また，ネパールでは，水道事情から全ての建物頂部に大きな高架水槽を有している．これらの高架水槽は，同写真(a)に示すように，1本柱で支えられているような構造も多い．しかし，この集合住宅周辺では，転倒などの被害は確認されなかった．

Photo 5.2.3.2-1 Full View of the building

Photo 5.2.3.2-2 Damage on non-structural elements

(a)　Elevated resevoir of a residencial house　　(b) 2-story residential masonry house
Photo 5.3.2.2-3 Structures around the complex

The complex has three buildings, which have 13 stories. The full view of the buildings is shown in Photo 5.3.2.2-1. The buildings stand on a slope. No significant structural damage was observed from outside of the complex. The non-structural walls (standing and hanging walls around window openings) and finishing of columns were, however, damaged as shown in Photo 5.3.2.2-2. Since access to the buildings was denied, detailed investigation was not able to be conducted. The damage level was evaluated as slight from the visual observation.

The buildings around the complex is shown in Photo 5.4.2.2-3. There were several 2-story masonry houses. Although some of them had cracking slightly, no collapsed house was found. Nepalese houses have water tanks on the roof as shown in the photo, because of the water supply situation. Many tanks were supported with single column as shown in the photo, but no damage was observed around the complex.

5.2.3.3 Building B

A棟，B-I棟，B-II棟の3棟からなる集合住宅で，2012年に建設された．B-I棟とB-II棟はエキスパンションジョイントを介して隣接している．敷地は川に隣接している．全景をPhoto5.2.3.3-1に示す．

There are three residential buildings, Tower A, B-I and B-II, built in 2012. Their site is next to a river as shown in Photo 5.2.3.3-1. Tower B-I and B-II stand adjacently and, they are separated with expansion joints.

(1) A 棟/ Tower A

地上 13 階，地下 2 階の RC 造建物である（Photo 5.2.3.3-2）．基準階の平面図を Figure 5.2.3.3-1 に示す．柱は約 2〜5m の不均等スパンで配置されており，断面形状は偏平である．1 階柱の断面の構造図の例を Figure 5.2.3.3-2 に示す．大半の柱は断面寸法が幅 300mm，せい 750mm となっている．主筋の位置や本数は Figure 5.2.3.3-2 に示した断面と同一のものが多いが，主筋径は柱ごとに異なっており，16φ から 32φ の範囲の主筋が用いられている．1 階では 25φ が多く用いられ，上層ほど主筋径は小さくなり，最上階では 16φ が多く用いられている．帯筋は柱頭，柱脚で 8φ@100mm，柱中央で 8φ@150mm である．RC 造壁は主にコア部に配置されており，コア部以外には 1 か所配置されているのみである．これらの RC 造壁には側柱は存在しない．壁の厚さはコア部で 230mm，コア部以外で 300mm となっている．縦筋には 12〜25φ の鉄筋が約 150〜200mm 間隔で配筋されており，横筋には 10φ の鉄筋が 200mm 間隔で配筋されている．1 階のコア部 RC 造壁の断面の構造図の一例を Figure 5.2.3.3-3 に示す．図中の a は 25φ，b は 20φ，c は 16φ の鉄筋を表しており，隅角部に近いほど太径の鉄筋が配置されている．構造図によると，梁の形状は大半が幅 300mm，せい 450mm と同一であるが，主筋量は梁ごとに異なっており，同一の梁でも例えば 16φ，20φ，25φ のように 3 種類の異なる径の主筋を使用している例も見られる（Figure 5.2.3.3-4 参照）．あばら筋は，梁端部で 8φ@100mm，梁中央部で 8φ@200mm としている箇所が大半である．コンクリートには，柱，耐力壁，地下階の梁に M-25（圧縮強度：25N/mm^2），スラブと地上階の梁に M-20 が使用されている．鉄筋には Fe500（0.2%耐力：500N/mm^2）が使用されている．

建物周囲より外観調査を行った結果，観察可能な範囲にある柱，梁，RC 造壁に目立った損傷は見られなかった．一方，レンガを組積した非構造壁には大きなせん断ひび割れが見られ，また，レンガ壁と周囲の柱，梁との境界に沿ったひび割れも多数見られた（Photo 5.2.3.3-3, 5.2.3-4）．これらのひび割れは，特に低層階に多く見られた．

Photo 5.2.3.3-1 Full view of the building

Photo 5.2.3.3-2 Full view of the building

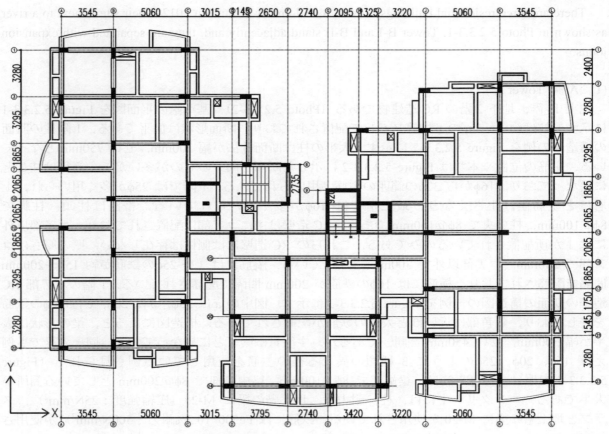

Figure 5.2.3.3-1 Typical floor plan of Tower A

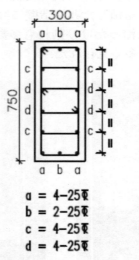

a = 4-25⊕
b = 2-25⊕
c = 4-25⊕
d = 4-25⊕

Figure 5.2.3.3-2 Column section

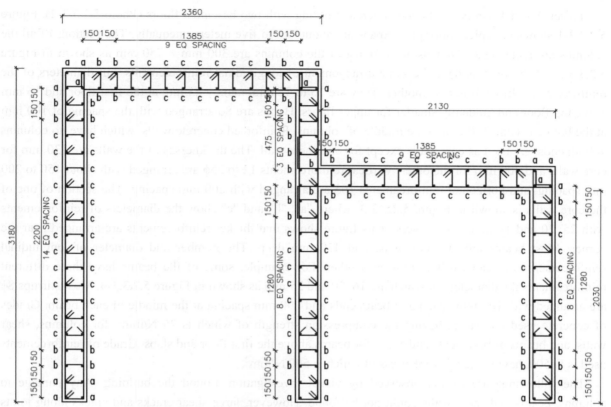

Figure 5.2.3.3-3 Shear wall section

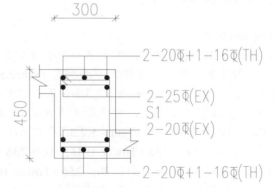

Figure 5.2.3.3-4 Beam section

Photo 5.2.3.3-3 Damage to brick walls

Photo 5.2.3.3-4 Damage to brick walls

Tower A is a 13-story reinforced concrete building with two basement floors (Photo 5.2.3.3-2). Figure 5.2.3.3-1 shows its typical floor plan. Spans are about two to five meters unequally. The sections of all the columns are rectangular. Dimensions of most of the columns are 300 mm × 750 mm as shown in Figure 5.2.3.3-2. Most columns have the same arrangement of longitudinal reinforcements, but diameters of the reinforcements differ from one another. They are 16 to 32 mm, mainly 25 mm at the first floor and 16 mm at the top floor and gradually smaller for upper floors. Hoops are 8φ arranged with the spacing of 100 mm at the both ends and 150 mm at the middle of columns. Reinforced concrete walls, which have no columns at both ends, are used as core walls except for one shear wall. The thicknesses of the walls are 230 mm for core walls and 300 mm for the other. Vertical reinforcements 12 to 25φ are arranged with about 150 to 200 mm spacing, and horizontal reinforcements 10φ are arranged with 200 mm spacing. The section of one of the core walls is shown in Figure 5.2.3.3-3, where "a", "b" and "c" show the diameters of reinforcements with 25, 20 and 16 mm, respectively. This figure shows that thicker reinforcements are arranged near the corner. Most beams are 300 mm wide and 450 mm deep. The number and diameter of longitudinal reinforcements of beams differ from each other. For example, some of the beams have three different reinforcements the diameters of which are 16, 20 and 25 mm as shown in Figure 5.2.3.3-4. Most stirrups 8φ are arranged with 100 mm spacing at beam ends and 200 mm spacing at the middle of each beam. Grades of concrete used are M-25, having the compression strength of which is 25 N/mm^2, for columns, shear walls, and beams of basements and M-20 for beams above the first floor and slabs. Grade of reinforcements used is Fe500, having 0.2 % proof stress of which is 500 N/mm^2.

The followings are results observed by visual investigation around the building. Any damage to columns, beams and shear walls could not be found. However, large shear cracks and cracks along joints between brick walls and beams/columns were observed a lot as shown in Photos 5.2.3.3-3 and 5.2.3.3-4. These cracks were heavier at lower floors especially.

(2) B-I棟，B-II棟/ Tower B-I and B-II

いずれも地上15階，地下2階のRC造建物で，エクスパンジョンジョイントを介して互いに隣接している（Photo 5.2.3.3-5）．両棟あわせた基準階の平面図をFigure 5.2.3.3-5に示す．

Tower B-I，B-IIの柱・壁配置図をそれぞれFigure 5.2.3.3-6, 7に示す．柱は約2～5mの不均等スパンで配置されており，断面形状は偏平である．地上階の大半の柱は断面寸法が幅300mm，せい750mmとなっている．主筋の位置や本数はFigure 5.2.3.3-2に示した断面と同一のものが多いが，主筋径は柱ごとに異なっており，16～32φ（Tower B-I），16～28φ（Tower B-II）の範囲の主筋が用いられている．1階では25，28φ（Tower B-I），20，25φ（Tower B-II）が多く用いられ，上層ほど主筋径は小さくなり，最上階では16φが多く用いられている．帯筋は柱頭，柱脚で8φ@100mm，柱中央で8φ@150mmである．RC造壁は，Tower B-Iではコ形が2か所と一枚壁が3か所，Tower B-IIではE形が2か配置されており，いずれの壁にも側柱は存在しない．壁の厚さはコ形，E形の壁で230mm，一枚壁で300mmとなっている．縦筋には12～25φの鉄筋が約150mm間隔で配筋されており，横筋には10φの鉄筋が200mm間隔で配筋されている．Tower AのRC壁断面（Figure 5.2.3.3-3）と同様，隅角部に近いほど太径の鉄筋が配置されている．梁の形状は大半が幅300mm，せい450mmと同一であるが，主筋量は梁ごとに異なっており，同一の梁でも例えば16φ，20φ，25φのように3種類の異なる径の主筋を使用している例も見られる．あばら筋は，梁端部で8φ@100mm，梁中央部で8φ@200mmとしている箇所が大半である．コンクリートには，柱，耐力壁，地下階の梁にM-25（低層階のRC壁に一部M-30），スラブと地上階の梁にM-20が使用されている．鉄筋にはFe500（0.2%耐力：500N/mm^2）が使用されている．

Tower B-I，B-IIについて，建物周囲，地下階の目視調査を行った．また，Tower B-Iの低層階の内部について目視調査も行った．その結果，次のような被害が見られた．Tower B-Iの1階隅柱の柱脚において表面仕上げの剥離が見られた（Photo 5.2.3.3-6）．Tower B-IIの1階外柱のうちの

1本に，柱脚位置でコンクリートが剥落し，鉄筋が露出している損傷が見られた．露出した鉄筋には，台直しによるものと思われる曲がりが見られた（Photo 5.2.3.3-7）．Tower B-I の低層階部分のごく一部の梁において，梁のせん断ひび割れ，曲げひび割れが見られた（Photo 5.2.2.3-8,5.2.2.3-9）．Tower B-I の 2 階梁のうち 1 本に，梁端で下端筋に沿ったコンクリートの剥落が見られた．梁せいの 2 倍程度の長さにわたって下端筋が露出していたが，その範囲にはあばら筋が見当たらなかった（Photo 5.2.2.3-10）．レンガを組積した外壁には，Tower A と同様に，せん断ひび割れやレンガ壁と周囲の柱，梁との境界に沿ったひび割れが多数見られ，これらのひび割れは特に低層階に多く見られた（Photo 5.2.3.3-11〜12）．建物内部の間仕切壁はレンガの組積壁からなっており，それらの壁にも外壁と同様に大きなひび割れが見られた（Photo 5.2.3.3-13）．Tower B-I，B-II 間はエキスパンションジョイントを介して隣接しているが，その接続部に位置していた天井の落下が見られた（Photo 5.2.3.3-14）．地下階では擁壁にせん断ひび割れが見られ，水が染み出した形跡が多数見られた（Photo 5.2.3.3-15）．また，地盤沈下やそれに伴うひび割れも建物周辺の敷地で見られた（Photo 5.2.3.3-16, 5.2.3.3-17）．

Photo 5.2.3.3-5 Full view of Tower B-I and B-II

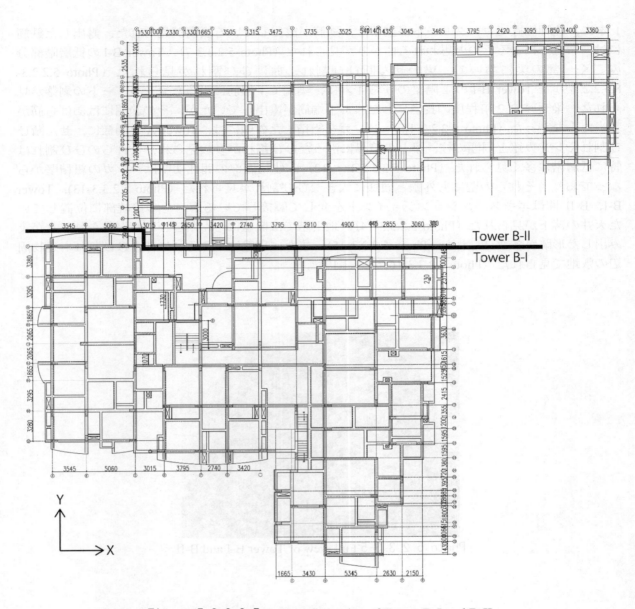

Figure 5.2.3.3-5 Typical floor plan of Tower B-I and B-II

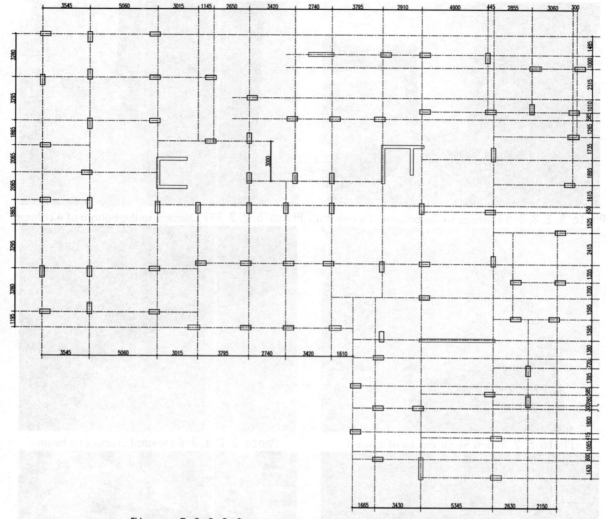

Figure 5.2.3.3-6 Layout of columns and walls of Tower B-I

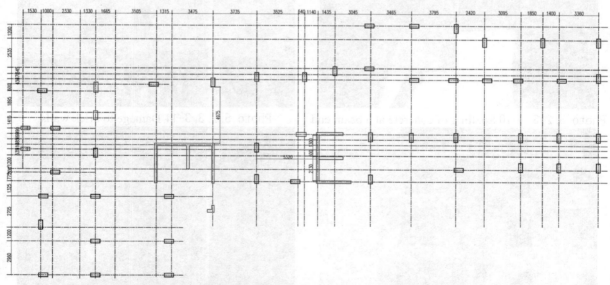

Figure 5.2.3.3-7 Layout of columns and walls of Tower B-II

Photo 5.2.3.3-6 Damage to the bottom of a column

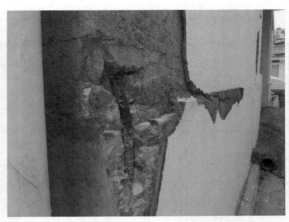
Photo 5.2.3.3-7 Damage to the bottom of a column

Photo 5.2.3.3-8 Shear cracks of a beam

Photo 5.2.3.3-9 Flexural cracks of a beam

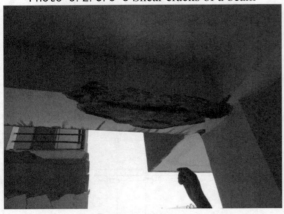
Photo 5.2.3.3-10 Spalling of concrete at a beam end

Photo 5.2.3.3-11 Damage to brick walls

Photo 5.2.3.3-12 Damage to brick walls

Photo 5.2.3.3-13 Damage to inside brick walls

Photo 5.2.3.3-14 Ceiling fall at expansion joints

Photo 5.2.3.3-15 Shear cracks to a retaining wall

Photo 5.2.3.3-16 Soil settlement

Photo 5.2.3.3-17 Cracks due to settlement

Tower B-I and B-II are 15-story reinforced concrete buildings with two basement floors (Photo 5.2.3.3-5).

These buildings stand adjacently and, they are separated with expansion joints. Figure 5.2.3.3-5 shows their typical floor plan. Spans are about two to five meters unequally. The sections of all columns are rectangular, the dimensions of most of which are 300mm x 750mm. Most columns have the same number and position of longitudinal reinforcements as shown in Figure 5.2.3.3-2. Diameters of the reinforcements differ from one another. They are 16 to 32 mm for Tower B-I and 16 to 28 mm for Tower B-II and gradually smaller at upper floors. Reinforcements frequently used at the first floor are 25ϕ and 28ϕ for Tower B-I and 20ϕ and 25ϕ for Tower B-II. At the top floor, 16ϕ is most frequently used. Hoops are 8ϕ arranged with the spacing of 100 mm at the both ends and 150 mm at the middle of columns. Reinforced concrete walls, which has no columns at both ends, are used as two U-shape core walls except for three shear walls for Tower B-I and as two E-shape core walls for Tower B-II. The thicknesses of the walls are 230 mm for the core walls and 300 mm for the others. Vertical reinforcements the diameter of which is 12 to 25 mm are arranged with about 150 mm spacing, and horizontal reinforcements 10ϕ are arranged with 200 mm spacing. Thicker vertical reinforcements are arranged near the corner the same as Tower A as shown in Figure 5.2.3.3-3. Most beams are 300 mm wide and 450 mm deep. The number and diameter of longitudinal reinforcements of beams differ from each other. For example, some of the beams have three different reinforcements the diameters of which are 16, 20 and 25 mm as shown in Figure 5.2.3.3-4. Most stirrups 8ϕ are arranged with 100 mm spacing at beam ends and 200 mm spacing at the middle of each beam. Grades of concrete used are M-25, having the compression strength of which is 25 N/mm^2, for columns, shear walls, and beams of basements and M-20 for beams above the first floor and slabs. Grade of reinforcements used is Fe500, having 0.2 % proof stress of which is 500 N/mm^2.

The followings are results observed by visual investigation around Tower B-I and B-II and inside the lower floors of Tower B-I and the basement of the two towers. Removal of finishing was observed at the bottom end of the corner column at the first floor of Tower B-I as shown in Photo 5.2.3.3-6. Spalling of cover concrete and exposure of a reinforcement were observed at the bottom end of an outer column on the first floor of Tower B-II. Photo 5.2.3.3-7 shows an exposed reinforcement bent probably for connecting reinforcements. Shear cracks and flexural cracks were observed in a few beams at lower floors of Tower B-I as shown in Photo 5.2.2.3-8 and 5.2.2.3-9. Spalling of cover concrete along the bottom bars at the end of a beam on the second floor was observed. As shown in Photo 5.2.2.3-10, any stirrups could not be found where the bars were exposed at the beam end with a length approximately double beam depth. Shear cracks on brick walls and joint cracks between brick walls and beams/columns were observed a lot as shown in Photo 5.2.3.3-11 and 5.2.3.3-12 the same as Tower A. Large cracks occurred in partition brick walls as well as exterior walls as shown in Photo 5.2.3.3-13. A ceiling fall was observed at an expansion joint between Tower B-I and B-II as shown in Photo 5.2.3.3-14. At the basement floor, shear cracks and water stain were observed in retaining walls as shown in Photo 5.2.3.3-15. Soil settlement and resultant damage were observed at the site around the buildings as shown in Photos 5.2.3.3-16 and 5.2.3.3-17.

(3) 構造計算/ Structural Desgin

固定荷重は，使用材料の重量と部材の寸法より計算している．主な材料の単位面積あたりの重量は，鉄筋コンクリート：2500 kgf/m^3，無筋コンクリート：2400 kgf/m^3，レンガ壁：1920 kgf/m^3，モルタル 2080 kgf/m^3 として計算している．

積載荷重は IS875 (Part 2) -1987$^{5.2.3-1)}$ による値を用いており，居室・台所は 0.200 tf/m^2，トイレ・浴室は 0.200 tf/m^2，倉庫は 0.300 tf/m^2，廊下・通路・ロビー・階段は 0.300 tf/m^2，屋根（歩行）は 0.150 tf/m^2，屋根（非歩行）は 0.075 tf/m^2 として計算している．

地震荷重は IS1893:2002 $^{5.2.3-2)}$ による値を用いている．地域係数 Z=0.36，重要度係数 I = 1，地盤種別 II，X，Y 方向の固有周期はそれぞれ 0.936，0.997 (Tower A)，1.010，1.041 (Tower B-I)，0.982，1.127 (Tower B-II)，応答低減係数 R = 5 を適用しており，その結果，設計用水平地震力係数 A_h は X，Y 方向でそれぞれ 0.0523，0.0491 (Tower A)，0.0485，0.0471 (Tower B-I)，0.0499，0.0435 (Tower B-II) となっている．

荷重組合せ 1.5(DL+IL)，1.2(DL+IL±EL)，1.5 (DL±EL)，0.9DL+1.5EL（DL：固定荷重，IL：積載荷重，EL：地震荷重）に対して，終局強度設計を行っている．

Dead loads were calculated from dimensions of members and unit weights of materials. Unit weights of materials mainly used were 2,500 kg/m^3 for reinforced concrete, 2,400 kg/m^3 for plain concrete, 1,920 kg/m^3 for masonry brick, and 2,080 kg /m^3 for mortar.

Live loads adopted from IS875 (Part 2) -1987 were 0.200 t/m^2 for all rooms and kitchen, 0.200 t/m^2 for toilets and bathrooms, 0.300 t/m^2 for store, 0.300 t/m^2 for corridors, passages, lobbies and staircase, 0.150 t/m^2 for accessible roof, and 0.075 t/m^2 for inaccessible roof.

Earthquake load was calculated from IS1893:2002, where zone factor Z was 0.36, importance factor I was 1, soil type was II, undamped natural periods of vibration of the structure T were 0.936 sec. and 0.997 sec. for Tower A, 1.010 sec. and 1.041 sec. for Tower B-I, 0.0499 sec. and 0.0435 sec. for Tower B-II, and response reduction factor R was 5. As the results, design horizontal seismic coefficients Ah were 0.0523 (X-direction) and 0.0491 (Y-direction) for Tower A, 0.0485 and 0.0471 for Tower B-I, 0.0499 and 0.0435 for Tower B-II.

In the limit state design, load combinations considered were 1.5(DL+IL), 1.2(DL+IL±EL), 1.5(DL±EL), and 0.9DL+1.5EL (DL: dead load, IL: live load, EL: earthquake load).

5.2.3.4 Building C

　本建物は，2015年竣工予定の鉄筋コンクリート造16階建て建物2棟から構成される．2棟共通に地下1階に駐車場を有している．2棟の間には，平屋のエントランス部を有しており，2棟との間には，5cm程度のエキスパンションジョイントを有している．全景をPhoto 5.2.3.4-1に示す．

Photo 5.2.3.4-1 Full view

　本建物は，本震により8階までの主として焼成レンガを用いた非構造壁に被害が生じ，その後，5月12日に発生した余震により，14階までの非構造壁に被害が進展したとのことである．Department of Land Housing Developmentにより応急危険度判定が実施されており，Photo 5.2.3.4-2に示すように，「Restricted Use」と判定されている．非構造壁の被害状況をPhoto 5.2.3.4-3に示す．

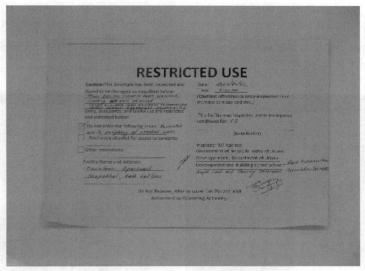

Photo 5.2.3.4-2 Yellow tag

Photo 5.2.3.4-3 Damage of non-structural walls

　1階部分は仕上げがまだ施されておらず，被害の確認が比較的容易であった．Photo 5.2.3.4-4 に 2 階床梁で確認された被害の例を示す．Photo 5.2.3.4-4 (a)は梁端部の軽微なひび割れ状況である．下端の仕上げが少しはがれ落ちていることがわかる．また，Photo 5.2.3.4-4 (b)は，比較的短い梁に軽微なせん断ひび割れが生じ，同じく仕上げがはがれ落ちている状況である．被害状況は軽微と判断できる．一方，Photo 5.2.3.4-5 は，連層耐震壁の 1 階での被害状況である．軽微なせん断ひび割れが生じ，仕上げがやはり少しはがれ落ちている．構造被害ではないが，Photo 5.2.3.4-6 に示すように，柱脚部でコンクリートを打ち継いでおり，打ち継ぎ部の処理が不十分なため，コールドジョイントが発生していることがわかる．

　本建物では，エレベータコアが偏在しているため，偏心の影響を低減するために 2 枚の連層耐震壁（Coupled shear walls）が反対側に配されている．この連層耐震壁を繋ぐ 3 階および階の梁（Coupling shear beams）にせん断の被害が生じていた（Photo 5.2.3.4-7）．この被害は，設計時から予測されていたとのことである．

(a) Slight damage at the end of beam　　　　　　(b) Slight shear cracks in the short beam
Photo 5.2.3.4-4 Damage of beams (1st floor)

Photo 5. 2. 3. 4-5 Damage of shear wall (1st floor)

Photo 5. 2. 3. 4-6 Cold joint at the bottom of a column (1st floor)

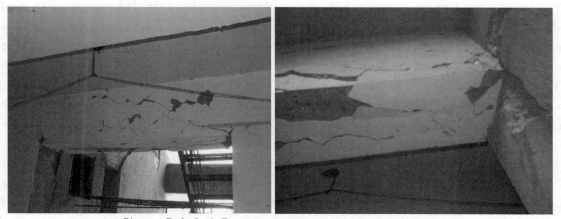

Photo 5. 2. 3. 4-7 Shear damage in the coupling beams

Photo 5.2.3.4-8 に，本集合住宅の周辺状況を示す．同(a)に示すように，周辺は農地が広がっており，隣接する建物はない．すぐ近くにある5階建てのR/C住宅（同(b)）には目立った被害は確認できず，さらに同建物の高架水槽は，1スパンの平面フレームにより支持されているが，外観からは目立った被害は確認できなかった．

(a) Buildings around the complex

(b) 5-story R/C residencial house　(c) Elevated reseivor
Photo 5. 2. 3. 4-8 Buildings around the complex

　The complex was under construction and supposed to be finished in 2015. There were two 16-story RC buildings. The underground floor of both towers are connected and used as parking space. There was a single story entrance between two towers, of which structural gaps to the towers were about 5cm. The full view of the complex is shown in Photo 5.2.3.4-1.

　The non-structural brick walls from the ground to 8th story were damaged due to the main shock, then the walls up to 14th story were damaged due to the aftershock on May 12th. The department of land housing development conducted quick inspection and evaluated as "Restricted Use" as shown in Photo 5.2.3.4-2. The damage condition of the non-structural brick wall is shown in Photo 5.2.3.4-3.

　The damage of the first story was easily investigated, since finishing was not completed yet. Photo 5.2.3.4-4 shows the observed damage of the 2nd floor beam. (a) of the photo shows slight cracks at the end of the beam. It can be observed that the finishing at the bottom of the beam fell down. The damage level was classified as slight. (b) of the photo shows a minor shear cracks in a short span beam and the finishing fell down. The damage level was also classified as slight. Photo 5.2.3.4-5 shows the damage at the bottom of the continuous shear wall. Minor cracks can be observed. Cold joint can be also observed as shown in Photo 5.2.3.4-6, since concrete was cast up to there and the surface treatment looked insufficient.

Since the location of elevator cores was close to one side, a coupled shear walls was arranged to the opposite side to avoid torsional behavior. The coupling beams of 3rd and 4th floor had shear damage as shown in Photo 5.2.3.4-7. This damage was predicted during the structural design.

Photo 5.2.3.4-8 shows the ground condition and buildings around the complex. There are field around the building and no neighboring building as shown in the Photo (a). The closest building to the complex, which was 5-story RC house, had no significant damage observed. Its water tank on the roof was supported by one-span-one-bay frame, which had no significant damage observed, either.

5.2.3.5 Building D

本建物は，2015年1月竣工の鉄筋コンクリート造11階建て建物であり，地下1階に駐車場を有している．基礎形式はパイルド・ラフト基礎と思われる．Photo 5.2.3.5-1に建物の全景を示す．他の建物でも見られるように，地下の駐車場は建物の下だけではなく建物前面部分（庭）の下にも広がっており，建物前面部分は人工地盤となっている．Department of Land Housing Developmentにより応急危険度判定が実施されており，Photo 5.2.3.5-2に示すように，「Restricted Use」と判定されている．

4.3節に示したように，本建物は全体が5cmほど沈下しているように見えた．Photo 5.2.3.5-3に地下で確認された床の損傷の様子を示す．手前が建物側，奥が人工地盤側の床となるが，建物側が下がっていることが確認できる．鉛直方向のずれは5cm程度であった．Photo 5.2.3.5-4は，1階エントランス付近で確認できた人工地盤の変形の様子である．周辺に比べて建物側が下がっていることが確認できる．4.3節でも示したように，この現象としては，建物側が下向きに変位したか，人工地盤が上向きに変位したかのいずれかと考えられる．人工地盤と人工地盤を支える柱の接合部にはひび割れが生じていた（Photo 5.2.3.5-5）．

上部構造の被害としては，非構造のブロック壁の被害が支配的であった．調査した中では，特に2階に顕著な非構造壁の被害が見られた（Photo 5.2.3.5-6）．また，鉄骨製の外階段の接合部にも被害が見られた（Photo 5.2.3.5-7, 5.2.3.5-8）．

 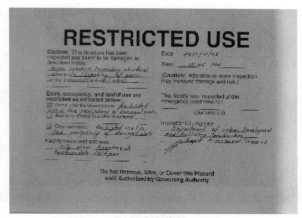

Photo 5.2.3.5-1 Full View of the building D　　　Photo 5.2.3.5-2 Yellow tag

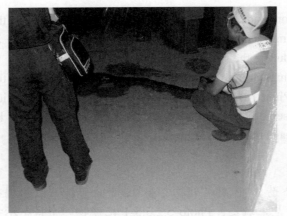
Photo 5.2.3.5-3 Cracks of a slab in the basement floor

Photo 5.2.3.5-4 Settlement of artificial ground

Photo 5.2.3.5-5 Cracks of joint between artificial ground slab and support column

Photo 5.2.3.5-6 Damage of inside brick wall

Photo 5.2.3.5-7 Damage of connection of an external steel staircase

Photo 5.2.3.5-8 Closeup of damaged connection

　The complex was under construction and supposed to be launched in 2015. There were two 11-story reinforced concrete buildings. The underground floor of both towers are connected and used as parking space. The foundation type of the building is piled raft foundation. The underground floor spreads out under not only the building but also the garden in front of the building. The ground over the underground floor is the artificial ground. The department of land housing development conducted quick inspection and evaluated as "Restricted Use" as shown in Photo 5.2.3.5-2.

It seems that the building settles about 5cm as shown in Section 4.3. The cracks in the slab of basement floor is shown in Photo 5.2.3.5-3. The slab in the front is under the building and the slab in the behind is under the artificial ground in Photo 5.2.3.5-3. It is certain that the slab in the front is lower than that in the behind. The gap between each slab is about 5cm. The deformation of the artificial ground around the entrance in 1st floor is shown in Photo 5.2.3.5-4. The building settlement is observed, (note: it is difficult to identify the location of the artificial ground.) These bump and gap is suggested that either the settlement of the buildings or the uplift of the artificial ground occurred. Cracks of joint between artificial ground slab and support column was observed (Photo 5.2.3.5-5).

The non-structural walls were damaged dominantly in the superstructure. The significant damages of the non-structural walls are observed in the second floor in this reconnaissance as shown in Photo 5.3.3.5-6. The damage of connection between the external steel staircase and the wall was observed as shown in Photo 5.2.3.5-7, 8.

5.2.3.6 Building E

2010年竣工の5棟の集合住宅からなり，配置図をFigure 5.2.3.6-1に，西面外観をPhoto 5.2.3.6-1に示す．本建物では，後述のように構造被害が見受けられ，同写真に示すようにRed Tagが貼り付けられていた．建物は，16階建てが1棟，15階建てが4棟である．建物は，写真からもわかるとおり，小高い丘の上に位置し，建設地自体も傾斜している．GPSロガーにより計測した南北軸での高度をFigure 5.2.3.6-2に示す．建物地盤面の標高差は，南北両端で15m程度あることがわかる

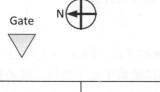

| Tower A
16F+2BF | Tower B
15F+2BF | | Tower C
15F+2BF | Tower D
15F+2BF | Tower E
15F+2BF |

Figure 5.2.3.6-1 Plan view

Photo 5.2.3.6-1 South face and Red tag

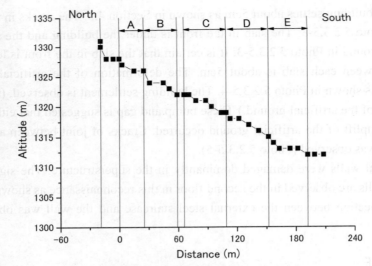

Figure 5.2.3.6-2 Elevation of the site

The complex, which was constructed in 2010, consists of 5 apartment buildings. The layout plan is shown in Figure 5.2.3.6-1, and the west face of the building is shown in Photo 5.2.3.6-1. The structural damage was observed as follows and Red Tag, which indicate that the building is unsafe, was put. Tower A has 16 stories and other towers have 15 stories. The complex located on a hill as shown in the photo, and the buildings stood on a slope. The measured slope by GPS logger is shown in Figure 5.2.3.6-2. The difference of the ground surface altitude was measured as 15m in the north-south direction.

(1) Tower A

Tower A は，地上 16 階，地下 2 階建てであり，5 棟の中で最も被害が多い．Photo 5.2.3.6-2 に西面の外観と，16 階での Tower B とのエキスパンションジョイント部に位置するト型接合部の被害を示す．接合部に大きな残留ひび割れが生じている様子がわかる．

Photo 5.2.3.6-3 には，東面の全景と梁の被害を示す．東面では特に梁に被害が多く，両端部に被害が集中していることがわかる．端部の拡大写真を見ると，せん断力による損傷が多くコンクリートが一部剥落しているが，せん断補強筋量は決して非常に少ないわけではないことがわかる．

Tower A の損傷が南北方向に多く見られたことから，安全に立ち入ることのできる地下 1 階駐車場を対象に，南北方向と東西方向の柱（壁）の長さと断面積を計測した．その結果を Table 5.2.3.6-1 に示す．長さ，断面積の合計ともに，東西方向が南北方向に対して 2 割程度多いことがわかる．

建物住戸内への立入りは許可されなかったが，例えば Photo 5.2.3.6-4 に示すように，焼成レンガを用いた非構造壁の被害は甚大であり，落下の危険性が極めて高かった．

Photo 5.2.3.6-2 South face and beam-column joint damage in the 16th floor

(a) Damage of beam ends
(b) Close-up of beam
(c) Close-up of beam end
Photo 5.2.3.6-3 Beam damage in the east frame

Table 5. 2. 3. 6-1 Column area in the basement floor of tower A (Unit: cm)

Number	EW		NS	
	Length	Area	Length	Area
1	83	2905	150	5250
2	120	4200	95	3325
3	89	3115	95	3325
4	174	6090	120	4200
5	98	3430	123	4305
6	89	3115	375	13125
7	120	4200	210	7350
8	33	1155	80	2800
9	68	2380	100	3500
10	57	1995	100	3500
11	265	9275	100	3500
12	265	9275	80	2800
13	85	2975		
14	95	3325		
15	84	2940		
16	65	2275		
17	95	3325		
18	110	3850		
Total	1995	69825	1628	56980

Photo 5. 2. 3. 6-4 Damage of non-structural wall

Tower A, which has 16 stories and 2 basement floor, suffered the severest damage. Photo 5.2.3.6-2 shows the west surface and the damage in the beam-corner column joint at 16th floor. Large residual deformation was observed at the joint.

Photo 5.2.3.6-3 shows the east face and the damage of beams. Many beams of the east frame suffered flexural damage at the ends. The close-up photo shows that although cover concrete spalled off due to shear damage, the observed stirrups shows that the amount looks not small.

Since the damage of tower A in the north-south direction was the severest, the total length and total area of the wall in the basement floor, where access was the safest, was measured. The measured amounts are shown in Table 5.2.3.6-1. It can be seen that the total length and area in the east-west direction was 20% greater than those in the north-south direction.

Although the access to the residential units were not permitted, the non-structural brick wall was observed as severely damaged and likely to fall down to the streets as shown in Photo 5.2.3.6-4.

(2) Tower B

西面外観を Photo 5.2.3.5-5 に示す．非構造壁が全壊にわたって甚大な被害を受けている．

Photo 5.2.3.6-5 West face of Tower A, Tower B, and Tower C

The west face of the tower B is shown in Photo 5.2.3.5-5. Non-structural brick walls in all stories suffered severe damage.

(3) Tower C

Photo 5.2.3.6-6 に Tower C の西面外観を示す．他の建物と同様に，非構造壁に甚大な被害が生じ，落下していることがわかる．Photo 5.2.3.6-7 には，地下階で見受けられた梁の被害を示す．同(a)は小梁の取り付く大梁の面外曲げによる被害を示す．また，同(b)に示すように，梁端部にせん断ひび割れが生じているものも見受けられた．エントランス部分では，Photo 5.2.3.6-8 に示すように，天井が落下していた．

Photo 5.2.3.6-6 West face of Tower C

(a) Damage of beam-beam joint   (b) Shear damage at the end of beam
Photo 5.2.3.6-7 Damage of beams in the basement floor

Photo 5.2.3.6-8 Damage of ceiling system

Photo 5.2.3.6-6 shows the west face of tower C. As the same as other towers, non-structural walls suffered severe damage and fell down. Photo 5.2.3.6-7 shows the damage of the beam of basement floor. Photo (a) shows the torsional damage of the girder due to the connecting beam. Photo (b) shows the shear damage at the ends of beams. The ceiling above the entrance fell down as shown in Photo 5.2.3.6-8.

(4) Tower D

Photo 5.2.3.6-9 にエントランス上部のスラブを有しない連結ばりの被害を示す．梁端で曲げによる甚大な被害を受けていることがわかる．

Photo 5.2.3.6-9 Damage of connecting beam

Photo 5.2.3.6-9 shows the damage of the connecting beam without slab above the entrance. Severe flexural damage was observed at the ends.

(5) Tower E

Photo 5.2.3.6-10 に，Tower D とのエキスパンションジョイント部の被害を示す．全階にわたって剥落，落下している部分があり，地震時の応答変形が小さくはなかったことがうかがえる．焼成レンガのサイズを計測したところ，110×240×65mm であったが（Photo 5.2.3.6-11），寸法のばらつきは大きそうであった．

Photo 5.2.3.6-10 Damage of the joint between Tower D and Tower E

Photo 5.2.3.6-11 Size of cay brick

Photo 5.2.3.6-10 shows the damage around the joint to tower D. The cover of the joint in all stories spalled and/or fell down, which shows the deformation during earthquakes was rather large. The size of the brick was measured as 110×240×65 (Photo 5.2.3.6-11), but the size looked to vary widely.

(6) 建物周辺の状況/ The Buildings Around the Complex

Photo 5.2.3.6-12 に丘の下の他の建物の状況を示す．3～5 階建て程度の RC 造（焼成レンガ壁付き）あるいは組積造が主であったが，目立った被害のある建物は確認されなかった．

Photo 5.2.3.6-12 Buildings around the complex

Photo 5.2.3.6-12 shows the buildings down the hill. Most of them were 3- to 5-story R/C with brick walls or masonry buildings. No significant structural damage was observed.

5.2.3.7 Building F

隣接する集合住宅 3 棟とやや離れて立地しているホテル棟 1 棟からなる．集合住宅は竣工後間もなく，ホテル棟は現在建設中である．全景を Photo 5.2.3.7-1,5.2.3.7-2 に示す．このうち，集合住宅 3 棟について調査した．調査時にはすでに応急危険度判定が実施されており，Restricted Use の判定を受けていた（Photo5.2.3.7-3）．

Photo 5.2.3.7-1 Full view of residential buildings　　Photo 5.2.3.7-2 Full view of a hotel tower

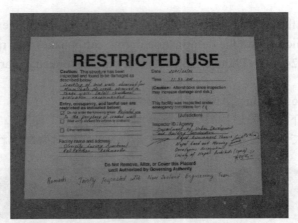

Photo 5.2.3.7-3 Result of investigation

　集合住宅はいずれも地上 18 階，地下 1 階，高さ 58m の RC 造建物で，45cm 間隔のエクスパンジョンジョイントを介して隣接している．地下階はすべての建物で共有し一つの空間となっている．各建物とも外周部に厚さ 9 インチ，内部に厚さ 12 インチの連層耐震壁を設けた耐震壁付きラーメン架構となっている．

　これらの建物の外観，地下，低層階の内部について目視調査を行った結果，次のような被害が見られた．一部の耐力壁の脚部に幅が最大 0.6mm 程度のせん断ひび割れが見られた（Photo5.2.3.7-4）．階段室の開口付き耐震壁において，開口隅角部からの斜めひび割れ（Photo5.2.3.7-5），開口脇の壁の曲げひび割れ（Photo5.2.3.7-6）が見られた．耐震壁の損傷は軽微であったが，レンガの組積壁はそれに比べ損傷が大きかった．両者の壁が隣接している箇所の損傷状況を Photo5.2.3.7-7 に示す．この壁の右半分は耐震壁，左半分はレンガ壁であり，大きな損傷の違いが見られる．

Photo 5.2.3.7-4 Shear cracks at the bottom of a shear wall

Photo 5.2.3.7-5 Diagonal cracks from the corner of an opening in a shear wall

Photo 5.2.3.7-6 Flexural cracks in a shear wall with an opning

Photo 5.2.3.7-7 Shear wall (right side) and brick wall (left side)

建物内部のレンガ内壁の損傷を Photo5.2.3.7-8 に示す．このような損傷はこの建物に限らず今回の地震により多くの建物で見られた典型的な被害である．この建物では特に 8 階以下の低層階でこのような被害が多く見られた．

建物周囲の庭の直下も一部地下階となっており，庭を支えている壁の複数に斜めひび割れが見られた（Photo5.2.3.7-9）．

Photo 5.2.3.7-8 Shear cracks of a brick wall

Photo 5.2.3.7-9 Diagonal cracks of RC walls

They have three residential buildings that stand adjacently and a hotel apart from them. The residential buildings were constructed recently, and the hotel was under construction. Appearance of these buildings were shown in Photo 5.2.3.7-1 and 5.2.3.7-2. Only the residential buildings were investigated. A quick inspection of these buildings had been conducted and the result was "Restricted Use" as shown in Photo 5.2.3.7-3.

All the residential buildings are 18-story and 58 m in height reinforced concrete structures with one basement floor, which stand adjacently with expansion joints. They have a common basement floor. Each building is a moment frame with shear walls the thickness of which are 9 inches for exterior walls and 12 inches for interior walls.

The damages observed from the visual investigation of facade, basement and interior zone at lower floors are as follows. Shear cracks were observed at the bottom of some shear walls, the maximum width of which was around 0.6 mm. At shear walls with an opening in staircase, diagonal cracks from the corner of the opening and flexural cracks beside the opening were observed as shown in Photos 5.2.3.7-5 and 5.2.3.7-6. The damage to shear walls was minor, but masonry bricks were damaged more heavily. Photo 5.2.3.7-7 shows the damage where a shear wall and a brick wall are adjacent. Right side wall is a shear wall and a left sidewall is a brick wall, which shows the difference of damage between them.

Photo 5.2.3.7-8 shows damage to an interior brick wall. Such damage was typically observed in many other buildings after this earthquake. As for this building, such damage was especially more observed at lower than ninth floor.

This building has a basement even under the garden around it, where diagonal cracks in some RC walls supporting the garden were observed as shown in Photo 5.2.3.7-9.

5.2.3.8 Building G

地上 8 階，地下 1 階（駐車場）の RC 造建物である．大通りに面した構面の窓ガラスに被害は見られないが，裏側の非構造ブロック壁は本震時（4 月 25 日）にひび割れが発生した（Photo 5.2.3.8-1）．本震後にモルタルでひび割れの補修工事をしていたところ，その後の余震（5 月 12 日）で再度同じようなブロック壁のひび割れ被害が生じた．調査時には，再度モルタルでひび割れを補修中であった．補修モルタルは，ひび割れを隠すように左官仕上げを行っているのみで，余震で簡単に同様の被害が生じる．煉瓦ブロックの非構造壁は一般的に内部空隙が多く，モルタルはひび割れ内部まで充填されているとは考えられない（Photo 5.2.3.8-2～5.2.3.8-4）．また，屋上で損傷した柱は，中心に一本だけ鉄筋が見えていた（Photo 5.2.3.8-4(b)）．

(a) View from a front street　　　　　　　　(b) Rear view. Dark color of the wall is due to mortar repair.

Photo 5.2.3.8-1 View of Building

(a) A construction worker is mixing mortar.　　(b) A reinforced concrete column and clay bricks are exposed.

Photo 5. 2. 3. 8-2 Repair of building

Photo 5. 2. 3. 8-3 Dark color is mortar repair of cracks of brick walls.

(a) A worker places mortar on cracked brick wall   (b) Column has a single longitudinal reinforcing bar.

Photo 5.2.3.8-4 Repair work

Building G is a reinforced concrete building with eight floors and one-story basement (parking space). Windows in the front facade has no damage but brick walls in the rear side had multiple cracks at the main shock on April 25th (Photo 5.2.3.8-1). Cracks were under repair when the aftershock on May 12 caused further cracks again. Construction workers were working on repairing when the AIJ team visited. Cement mortar was placed on brick surface but not filling voids of cracks (Photo 5.2.3.8-2, -3 and-4). Similar cracks are expected to happen when the building is shaken again. Damage columns on the roof had a single reinforcing bar at its center (Photo 5.2.3.8-4(b)).

5.2.3.9 Building H

直接基礎を使った地上9階，地下2階（駐車場）のRC造建物である（Photo 5.2.3.9-1）．下層5階は事務所，上層4階は集合住宅として使われている．周辺地盤が7cm程沈下していた（Photo 5.2.3.9-2）．地下2階分の駐車場を施工時，建物周辺も含めて掘削し，基礎と擁壁を施工後に埋め戻している．地盤沈下は埋戻し時の転圧不足と思われ，擁壁がひび割れていた（Photo 5.2.3.9-3）．転圧不足による地下階の被害は，他の建物でも観察された．

耐震壁とそれに連続する煉瓦ブロック非構造壁の状況をPhoto 5.2.3.9-4に示す．RC壁には被害がないが，煉瓦ブロック非構造壁には顕著なせん断ひび割れが認められる．建物隅角部で鉄筋が定着されていなかったり（Photo 5.2.3.9-5），地下駐車場の梁に長期荷重で生じたと思われる曲げひび割れ（Photo 5.2.3.9-6）が入っていたり，不適切な設計や施工の跡が確認された．周辺の建物の被害は小さかった（Photo 5.2.3.9-7）．

Photo 5.2.3.9-1 View of Building H

Photo 5.2.3.9-2 Settle around the building was about 70mm.

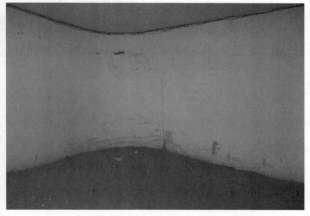

(a) A crack was 0.5mm wide.   (b) A continuous crack can be seen between a beam and a brick wall.

Photo 5.2.3.9-3 Damage of basement walls.

Photo 5.2.3.9-4 Damage of interior brick wall

Photo 5.2.3.9-5 Ninety-degree hook of longitudinal rebar is not anchored to the column core concrete.

Photo 5.2.3.9-6 Cracking of a beam of B1 floor is caused by long term loading since it is near the middle of an 8 m span. The part of the basement is under the driveway in front of the building. The beam depth was 600mm (150mm thick slab and additional 450mm depth). The other beam with 5.6 m span, whose depth is 450mm (150mm thick slab and additional 300mm depth), also had long term flexural cracking in the mid-span.

Photo 5.2.3.9-7 Nearby buildings did not show any noticeable damage.

Building H is a reinforced concrete building with nine floors and two-story basement (parking space) (Photo 5.2.3.9-1). Lower five floors are used for office and the upper four floors are used for residence. The soil settled about 70mm (Photo 5.2.3.9-2) probably because soil had not been compacted well after excavation for basement construction. Retaining walls had some cracks due to this insufficient consolidation (Photo 5.2.3.9-3).

Photo 5.2.3.9-4 shows a shear wall and a neighboring brick wall. It can be seen that the brick wall had some cracks. A hook of longitudinal bar of a beam was not anchored to the column core (Photo 5.2.3.9-5). A beam of the basement parking had some flexural cracks in the mid-span due to a long term loading (Photo 5.2.3.9-6). Neighboring buildings had minor or no damage (Photo 5.2.3.9-7).

5.2.3.10 Building I

本集合住宅は，Figure 5.2.3.10-1 に示すように，4 棟の建物からなる．建物高さは No.1 と No.2 は同一平面形状で地下のない 13 階建て，No.3 は 11 階建て（地下 1 階は駐車場），No.4 は No.1, No.2 と平面形状は類似であるが，耐震壁の量は少ない 8 階建てである．

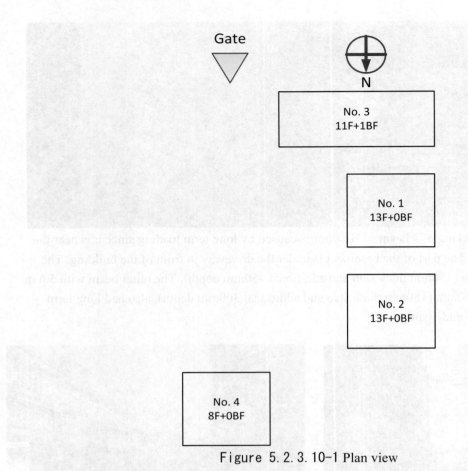

Figure 5.2.3.10-1 Plan view

　No.1 の南面，No.2 および No.3 の東面の外観を Photo 5.2.3.10-1 に示す．目立った構造被害は確認できない．Photo 5.2.3.10-2 に No.3 の周辺地盤状況を示す．建物周辺で若干沈下が確認された．これは，地下駐車場部分を掘削する際に，一回り広く掘削し，地下部構築後に建物周辺を埋め戻す際の転圧不足と考えられる．No.3 建物では，唯一地下室の立入りが可能であったが，外周地下壁に若干のひび割れを確認できた．ひび割れは南北方向の方が多かった．

(a) South face of No. 3   (b) East faces of No.1 and No.2

Photo 5.2.3.10-1 Full view of No.1, No.2, and No.3

Photo 5.2.3.10-2 Ground settlement around No.3

(a) East-West direction　　　　　　　　(b) North-South direction
Photo 5.2.3.10-3 Slight cracks in the retailing walls

　Photo 5.2.3.10-4 に No.1 の南面外観を示す．この建物では，1 階部分の柱に，Photo 5.2.3.10-5 に示すように軽微な曲げひび割れと圧縮によるかぶりの肌別れが見受けられた．また，Photo 5.2.3.10-6 に示すように，梁端では曲げモーメントによる下端仕上げの落下が見受けられたが，いずれも軽微である．No.3 と同様に，周辺地盤で Photo 5.2.3.10-7 に示すように若干の沈下が見受けられた．No.1 および No.2 では，エレベータコア部のほかに 4 枚の直交壁を有しない I 型の耐震壁が存在する．Photo 5.2.3.10-8 に示すように，これらの壁には目立った被害は見受けられず，そのため，損傷は焼成レンガを用いた非構造壁に集中していた．Photo 5.2.3.10-9 に示すように，1 階の非構造壁の被害は，モルタルにより復旧中であった．

　No.2 の南面の外観を Photo 5.2.3.10-10 に示す．平面形状，階数ともに No.1 と同じであり，被害状況もほぼ同じであった．

Photo 5.2.3.10-4 South face of No.1

Photo 5.2.3.10-5 Damage of column (1st floor)

Photo 5.2.3.10-6 Damage of beams (1st floor)

Photo 5.2.3.10-7 Ground settlement around No.1

Photo 5.2.3.10-8 Shear walls (1st floor of No.1)

Photo 5.2.3.10-9 Retrofitted non-structural wall (1st floor of No.1)

Photo 5.2.3.10-10 East face of No.2

一方，No.4 の南面外観と，1 階部分を Photo 5.2.3.10-11 に示す．本建物の平面形状は No.1 および No.2 と類似ではあるが，建物階数は 8 階であり，エレベータコア以外には耐震壁はない点が異なる．1 階柱の損傷状況を Photo 5.2.3.10-12 に示す．端部に軽微な損傷がある程度である．一方，室内の状況として，Photo 5.2.3.10-13 に 5 階の室内の被害状況を示す．焼成レンガ造の非構造壁には大きなせん断ひび割れが生じていることがわかる．その壁の影響で，短スパン化した一部の梁でせん断ひび割れが見受けられた．しかし，住民によると，同 Photo 5.2.3.10-13(b)に示すような棚からは，ものは落下しなかったと言うことであった．

Photo 5.2.3.10-11 North face and 1st floor of No.4

Photo 5.2.3.10-12 Damage of columns in the 1st floor

(a) Damage of non-structural wall (b) Nothing fell down from the cabinet

(c) Damage in the short beam
Photo 5. 2. 3. 10-13 Damages in the unit on the 5th floor

Photo 5.2.3.10-14 に周辺建物の状況を示す．4～5 階建ての組積造，あるいは R/C フレーム構造（焼成レンガ壁付き）が点在しているが，目立った構造被害は確認されなかった．

Photo 5. 2. 3. 10-14 Buildings around the complex

The complex has 4 buildings as shown in Figure 5.2.3.10-1. Towers No.1 and No.2 are identical, and have 13 stories without basement floor. Tower No.3 has 11 stories and 1 basement floor. The plan of tower No.4 is the same as those of towers No.1 and No.2, but has 8 stories and the amount of shear walls is less than those of towers No.1 and No.2.

The south face of tower No.1 and east faces of towers No.2 and No.3 are shown in Photo 5.2.3.10-1. No significant damage was observed. Photo 5.2.3.10-2 shows the ground condition around tower No.3. Little settlement was observed. The settlement is possibly because of lack of surface compaction when the basement floor was constructed, of which area is wider than that of tower No. 3. As for the basement floor, only the tower No.3 was accessible for the investigation, and minor cracks in the boundary walls were observed. The amount of cracks in the north-south direction looked more than that in the other direction.

Photo 5.2.3.10-4 shows the south face of tower No.1. Minor flexural cracks and spalling of cover concrete due to compression were observed at the bottom of the 1st story column as shown in Photo 5.2.3.10-5. It was observed that cover concrete at the bottom was spalled down as shown in Photo 5.2.3.10-6 due to flexural moment, which were minor damage. Little settlement was also observed around the building as shown in Photo 5.2.3.10-7. Towers No.1 and No.2 have 4 I shape shear walls other than the elevator core. No significant damage was observed to the I shape walls as shown in Photo 5.2.3.10-8, and the damage concentrated on the non-structural brick walls. The non-structural walls were under repair construction with mortar as shown in Photo 5.2.3.10-9.

Photo 5.2.3.10-10 shows the south face of tower No.2. As it is identical to tower No.1, the damage condition was also the same as that of tower No. 1.

The south face and close-up of 1st story are shown in Photo 5.2.3.10-11. The plan of the tower is the same as those of towers No.1 and No.2, but it has 8 stories and no shear walls except elevator core walls. The damage of the 1st story column is shown in Photo 5.2.3.10-12. Only the minor cracks were observed at the ends of the column. On the contrary, the non-structural brick walls suffered severe shear cracks. Resident said that nothing fell down from shelves shown in Photo 5.2.3.10-13(b).

Photo 5.2.3.10-14 shows the buildings around the complex. There are 4- to 5-story masonry or R/C frame buildings with brick walls, and no significant damage was observed.

5.2.3.11 Building J
(1) Tower A

　地上12階，地下2階のRC造建物である（Photo5.2.3.11-1）．基準階の平面図をFigure 5.2.3.11-2に示す．柱は約4～6mのスパンで配置されており，断面形状はほぼ正方形である．建物は応急危険度判定が実施されており，Restricted Useの判定を受けていた（Photo 5.2.3.11-2）．1階柱の断面の構造図の例をFigure 5.2.3.11-3に示す．柱の断面寸法は柱ごとにほぼ異なっており，約400×600mm～600×650mmとなっている．主筋の位置，本数，径も柱ごとに異なっており，主筋量としてはおおむね8-D25+4-D20～12-D32+4-D25程度となっている．これは主筋比2.0～2.8%程度に相当する．帯筋は4-D8@150～6-D8@75程度で，同一の柱内では，柱頭，柱脚の帯筋間隔が柱中央の帯筋間隔のおおむね半分となっている．RC造壁はコア部のみに配置されている．壁の厚さは約175mmで，側柱は存在しない．縦筋には10□の鉄筋が約200mm間隔でダブル配筋されており，横筋には8□の鉄筋が約150～200mm間隔の千鳥ダブルで配筋されている．これは，おおむね壁横筋比0.3～0.4%に相当する．1階のコア部RC造壁の断面の構造図をFigure 5.2.3.11-4に示す．梁の形状は幅が約300mmで共通となっており，せいが約500～650mmと異なっている．主筋量は梁ごとに異なっており，主筋量としては，おおむね2-D20+3-D16/2-D20～6-D25+1-D20/4-D25+1-D20程度となっている．これは，引張鉄筋比0.4～1.1%程度に相当する．あばら筋は，梁端部で8□@75mm，梁中央部で8□@175mmとなっており，これらは，あばら筋比0.2～0.4%程度に相当する．柱，梁，耐力壁のいずれも，コンクリートにはM-30（圧縮強度：30N/mm^2），鉄筋にはFe500（0.2%耐力：500N/mm^2）が使用されている．

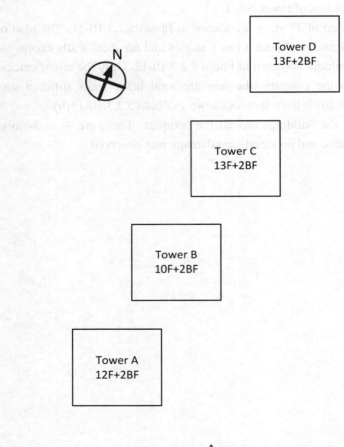

Figure 5.2.3.11-1 Plan view

Photo 5.2.3.11-1 Full view of Tower A

Photo 5.2.3.11-2 Result of investigation

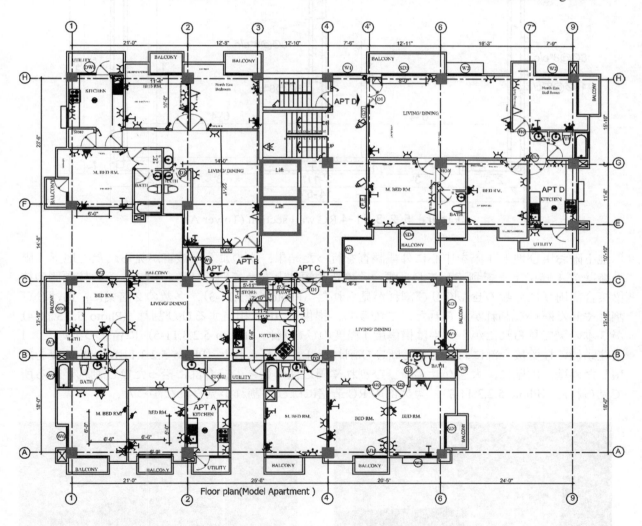
Floor plan (Model Apartment)

Figure 5.2.3.11-2 Typical floor plan (Tower 1)

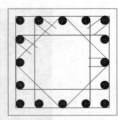

Figure 5.2.3.11-3 Column section (Tower 1)

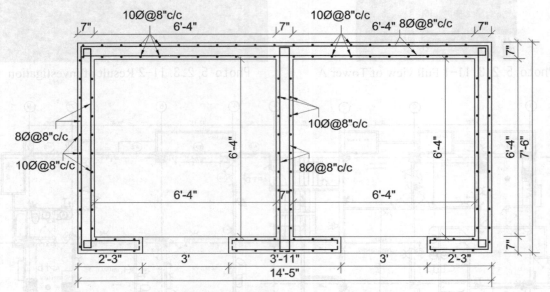

Figure 5.2.3.11-4 RC wall section (Tower A)

　地下階および地上 1 階を中心に外観調査を行った結果，次のような被害が見られた．地下 1 階の擁壁が 1 階梁下まで到達しておらず，そのため短柱となっている柱において，その柱頭側の柱梁接合部周りに無数のせん断ひび割れが見られた（Photo 5.2.3.11-3）．多数の 2 階梁に，曲げひび割れやせん断ひび割れが見られた．このうち，損傷度 II に相当するひび割れ（Photo 5.2.3.11-4）が 3 本の梁で見られたが，大半は損傷度 I 程度のひび割れ（Photo 5.2.3.11-5）に留まっていた．1 階柱頭側の柱梁接合部においてせん断ひび割れが 1 か所見られた（Photo 5.2.3.11-6）．レンガを組積した外壁，内壁に，大きなせん断ひび割れや周辺柱・梁との接合部に沿ったひび割れが至る所で見られた（Photo 5.2.3.11-7）．コア部の RC 造壁にはひび割れが見られなかった．

Photo 5.2.3.11-3 Shear craks around a joint

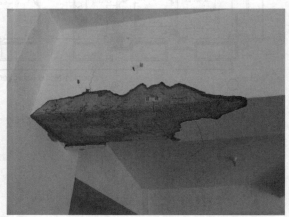

Photo 5.2.3.11-4 Flexural cracks of a beam

Photo 5.2.3.11-5 Flexural and shear cracks of a beam

Photo 5.2.3.11-6 Shear cracks of a joint

Photo 5.2.3.11-7 Damage to brick walls

　本建物の1階を対象に被災度区分判定を実施した．Figure5.2.3.11-5に，Tower Aの左右方向の被災度区分判定結果を示す．添え字のFが曲げひび割れ，Sがせん断ひび割れを示す．なお，添え字にBとあるものは，取り付く柱に比べて，梁の損傷度の方が高いため，梁の損傷度を採用したものを示している．損傷度Ⅱの柱が3本あり，このうち2本は取り付く梁の曲げひび割れが損傷度Ⅱに該当し，残りの1本は取り付く梁のせん断ひび割れが損傷度Ⅱに該当していた．残りの柱は損傷度Ⅰまたは0であった．コア部の耐震壁は損傷度0であった．耐震性能残存率 R は93%で小破と判定された．

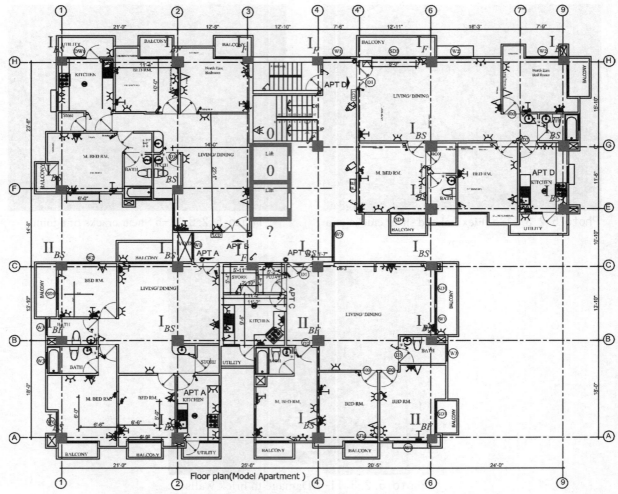

Figure 5.2.3.11-5 Damage clasification result (Tower A)

Tower A is a 12-story reinforced concrete structure with two basement floors (Photo 5.2.3.11-1). Figure 5.2.3.11-2 shows its typical floor plan. Spans are about four to six meters. A quick inspection of this building had been conducted and the result was "Restricted Use" as shown in Photo 5.2.3.11-2. The sections of all the columns are flat. Figure 5.2.3.11-3 shows an example of the section of a column on the first floor. Dimensions of most of the columns are different, which are around 400 mm×600 mm to 600 mm×650 mm. The position, number and diameter of longitudinal reinforcements are also different, which are around 8-D25+4-D20 to 12-D32+4-D25. This corresponds to 2.0 to 2.8% in ratio of longitudinal reinforcement area to gross concrete area. Hoops are around 4-D8@150 to 6-D8@75 arranged. The spacing of hoops at the both ends of a column is about half as wide as that at the center of the column. Reinforced concrete walls, which are about 175 mm thick and has no columns at both ends, are used as core walls. Vertical reinforcements 10ϕ placed in two layers are arranged with about 200 mm spacing, and horizontal reinforcements 8ϕ placed in two layers are arranged with about 150 to 200 mm spacing. This corresponds to about 0.3 to 0.4 % in ratio of horizontal reinforcement area to gross concrete area. The section of RC core wall on the first floor is illustrated in Figure 5.2.3.11-4. The beam width is about 300 mm in common, and the beam depth is about 500 to 650 mm. The number and diameter of longitudinal reinforcements of beams differ from each other. They are around 2-D20+3-D16/2-D20 to 6-D25+1-D20/4-D25+1-D20. They correspond to about 0.4 to 1.1 % in ratio of tensile reinforcement area to gross concrete area. Stirrups 8ϕ are arranged with 75 mm spacing at the beam ends and 175 mm at the middle of beams, which correspond with 0.2 to 0.4 % in ratio of shear reinforcement area to gross concrete area perpendicular to shear reinforcement within center-to-center spacing of shear reinforcement. Grades of concrete used are M-30, the compression strength of which is 30 N/mm^2, for columns, beams, and shear walls. Grade of reinforcements used is Fe500, 0.2 % proof stress of which is 500 N/mm^2.

The followings are results observed by visual investigation on the first floor and a basement floor around Tower 1. Many shear cracks were observed around a beam column joint at the top end of a short column on the first floor that is constrained by a retaining wall at the bottom end as shown in Photo 5.2.3.11-3. Bending and shear cracks were observed in many beams on the second floor. Some cracks corresponding to damage level II as shown in Photo 5.2.3.11-4 were observed in three beams, but in the other beams cracks observed were damage level I or lower. Shear cracks were observed in a beam column joint at the top end of the first floor columns as shown in Photo 5.2.3.11-6. In interior and exterior masonry brick walls, large shear cracks and cracks along joints between the walls and adjacent columns/beams were observed a lot as shown in Photo 5.2.3.11-7. There was no crack observed in reinforced concrete core walls.

Damage classification (Seismic Evaluation and Retrofit (English Version), The Japan Building Disaster Prevention Association, 2001) for the first floor of Tower A was conducted. Figure 5.2.3.11-5 shows the result of it. In this figure, suffixes F and S shows flexural and shear cracks are dominant, respectively. Then suffix B shows the damage of beams connecting the column is heavier than that of the column. This building had three damage level II columns, where two of them were classified into II because of the bending cracks of connecting beams and the other was because of the shear cracks of a connecting beam. The rest of the three columns were classified into damage level I or zero. The damage level of core wall was zero. Remaining of seismic performance R was 93 %, which means the damage of this building was minor.

(1)　Tower B

　地上 10 階，地下 2 階，屋上にエレベータ用ペントハウスを有する RC 造建物である（Figure 5.2.3.11-6）．短辺 3 スパン，長辺 4 スパンであり，2 つのエレベーターシャフトを囲むようにコア壁を配置している（Figure 5.2.3.11-7）．4 棟の中でも平面形状は最も整形に近い．一般階の階高は 3.05m（10ft）である．設計図書によると，使用したコンクリートの設計強度は 30MPa，鉄筋の規格降伏強度は 500MPa となっている．リバウンドハンマーによる 2 階梁のコンクリート強度は，40～45MPa であった．ソフトストーリーとなっている一階の状況について，被災度区分判定を行うために被害状況を確認した．主な被害は，Photo 5.2.3.11-8 に示すようにエレベータ用コア壁のせん断ひび割れ（被災度 II）と梁のせん断ひび割れ（被災度 I）であり，耐震性能残存率 R は 90%で小破の判定となった（Figure 5.2.3.11-8）．また，2 階以上の上部構造では，ブロック壁にひび割れが入っているが，構造要素に顕著な被害は確認できなかった．

　3 次元骨組モデル（SAP2000）を用いて，建物の性状を確認した．建物の基本周期は，大きなものから 1.22 秒，1.20 秒，1.04 秒であり，変形モードはねじりを伴う水平移動である．静的漸増解析をした結果を Figure 5.2.3.11-9 に示す．桁行方向と梁間方向について解析を行い，水平力の分布を逆三角形(tri)とした場合と一様(uni)とした場合の 2 つについて考察した．いずれの場合も，ベースシア係数は，0.3 を超えており，今回の地震に対しては十分な保有水平耐力を有すると判断された．同じモデルを用いて動的非線形解析を行った結果を Figure 5.2.3.11-10 に示す．地震波は，解析時点で唯一入手できた USGS の Kantipath（KATNP）における波を使用した．層間変形角が 1%，せん断力係数が耐力の 0.3 に近くなるなど，実際の被害状況を大きく見積もる結果となった．これは，主にコア壁の開口が正確にモデル化されていないためと思われる．

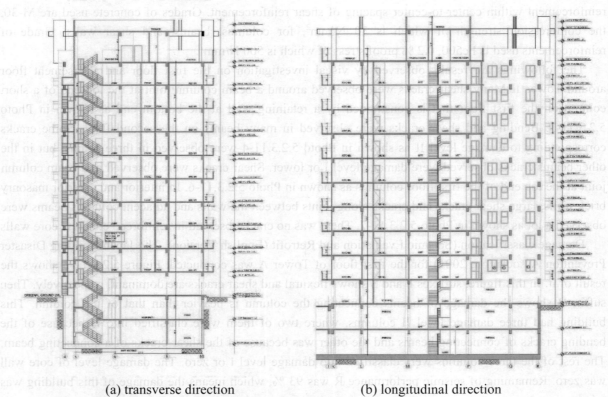

(a) transverse direction　　　　　　(b) longitudinal direction
Figure 5.2.3.11-6 Elevation of Tower B

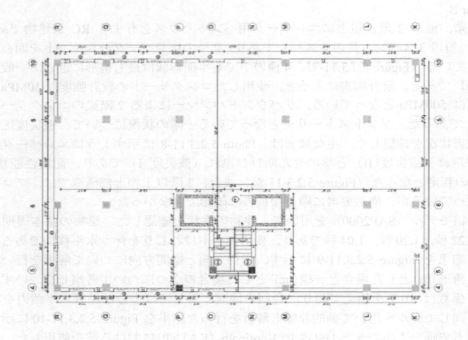

Figure 5.2.3.11-7 First floor plan of Tower B.

— 240 —

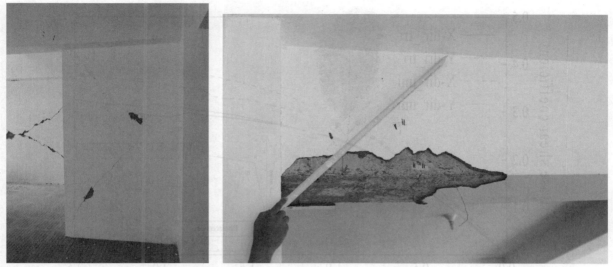

(a) The core wall (front) had minor shear cracks. Brick walls (rear) had large shear cracks.

(b) Some beams shear and flexural cracks (level I)

Photo 5.2.3.11-8 Typical damage

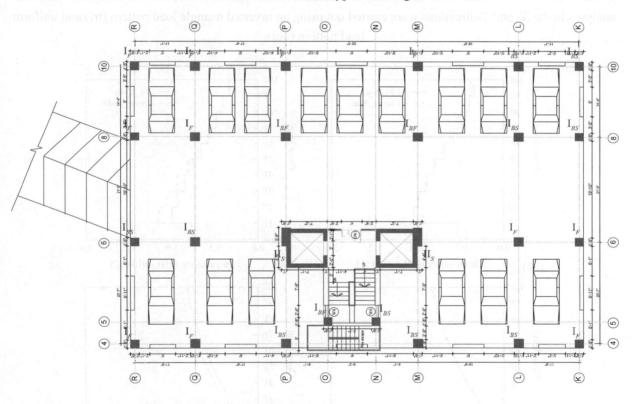

Figure 5.2.3.11-8 Damage assessment at the first floor

—241—

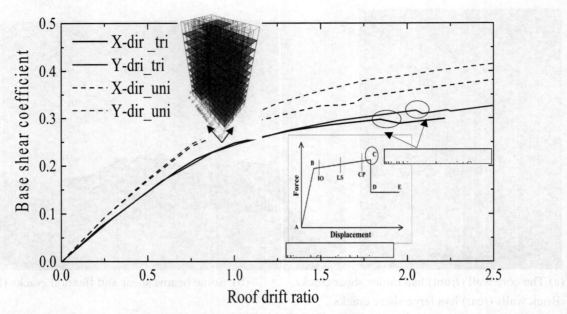

Figure 5.2.3.11-9 Base shear coefficient and roof drift ratio relation from pushover analyses. Pushover analyses in the X- and Y-directions were carried out using an inverted triangle load pattern (tri) and uniform load pattern (uni).

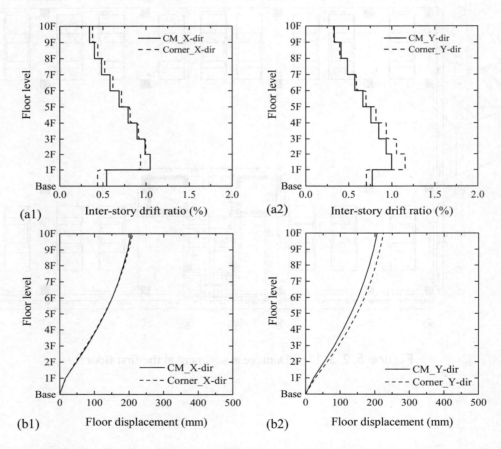

Figure 5.2.3.11-10 Peak response of superstructure under KATNP ground motion record at the center of mass CM) and a corner column (Corner)

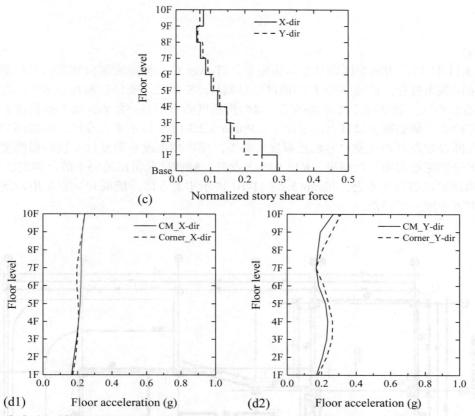

Figure 5.2.3.11-10 Peak response of superstructure under KATNP ground motion record at the center of mass CM) and a corner column (Corner) (Contd.)

Tower B is a reinforced concrete building with ten floors, one-story penthouse, and two-story basement (parking space) (Figure 5.2.3.11-6). The floor plan has four spans in the longitudinal direction and three spans with core walls around two elevator shafts (Figure 5.2.3.11-7) with minor eccentricity. An ordinary story height is 3.05 m(10ft). The design document lists concrete strength of 30MPa and steel yield strength of 500MPa. The field test with a rebound hammer showed concrete strength of the second floor beam was 40 - 45 MPa.

The damage of the first floor was evaluated using the Japanese post-earthquake damage assessment procedure (Seismic Evaluation and Retrofit (English Version), The Japan Building Disaster Prevention Association, 2001) (Figure 5.2.3.11-8). Major damage was shear cracks of core walls (Damage level II out of V) and of second floor beams (Damage level I out of V) as shown in Photo 5.2.3.11-8. Upper floor had damage to brick walls but minor or no damage to structural members.

The damage of Tower B was simulated with three-dimensional frame analysis (SAP2000). The first three fundamental periods are 1.22, 1.20, and 1.04 seconds and their mode shapes are translation with some torsion. The results of a pushover analysis are shown in Figure 5.2.3.11-9. Pushover analyses in X- and Y-directions were carried out using an inverted triangle load pattern (tri) and uniform load pattern (uni). The base shear coefficient at the ultimate stage is larger than 0.3 which is large enough to for the ground shaking of the earthquake. The same model was used for a nonlinear time history dynamic analysis using a strong motion date at Kantipath (KATNP) station (Figure 5.2.3.11-10). The maximum inter-story drift ratio was 1% and the maximum base shear was nearly 0.3 which is the capacity based on the static pushover analysis. The time-history analysis overestimated the damage of Tower 2 probably because the opening of core wall was not properly modeled.

(2) Tower C
　Figure 5.2.3.11-11 に，方向を区別せずに実施した Tower C の被災度区分判定結果を示す．図中のローマ数字が被災度を，添え字の F が曲げひび割れ，S がせん断ひび割れを示す．なお，添え字に B とあるものは，取り付く柱に比べて，梁の損傷度の方が高いため，梁の損傷度を採用したものを示している．構造被害はほとんどなく，Photo 5.2.3.11-9 に示すように，梁端部で軽微な曲げおよびせん断ひび割れが見受けられた程度である．梁の損傷度を取り付く柱の損傷度と見なして，被災度区分判定を実施した結果，R は 94% となり，軽微に非常に近い小破と判定された．
　なお，非構造壁に着目すると，Photo 5.2.3.11-10 に示すように，焼成レンガを用いた間仕切り壁は大きな被害を被っていた．

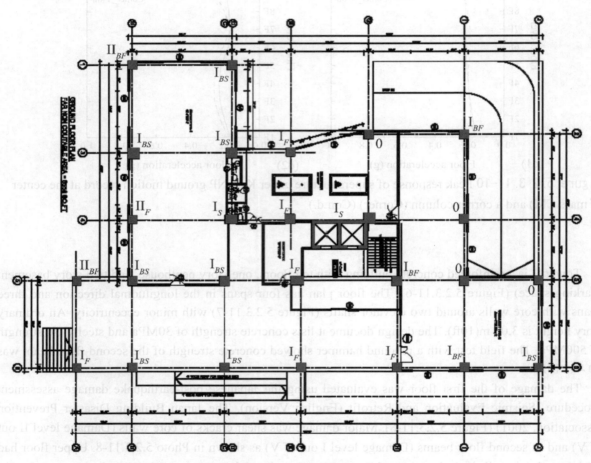

Figure 5.2.3.11-11 Damage classification result (Tower C)

Photo 5.2.3.11-9 Damage of beams

Photo 5.2.3.11-10 Damage of non-structural walls

Figure 5.2.3.11-11 shows the damage classification result of tower C. The roman number in the figure shows the damage class, "F" and "S" mean flexural and shear damage, respectively. "B" means that the damage class of beam was greater than the column connected to the beam, then the damage class of the column was replaced by that of the beam. No significant damage was observed, and only minor flexural and shear cracks were observed as shown in Photo 5.2.3.11-11. The residual seismic performance ratio, R, was calculated as 94%, which is categorized as light damage but close to slight damage.

The damage of non-structural brick walls was, however, severely damaged as shown in Photo 5.2.3.11-12.

(4) Tower D

Figure 5.2.3.11-12 に，方向を区別せずに実施した Tower D の被災度区分判定結果を示す．図中の表記は，Figure 5.2.3.11-11 と同様である．Tower C と同様に構造被害はほとんどなく，判定結果は軽微となった．

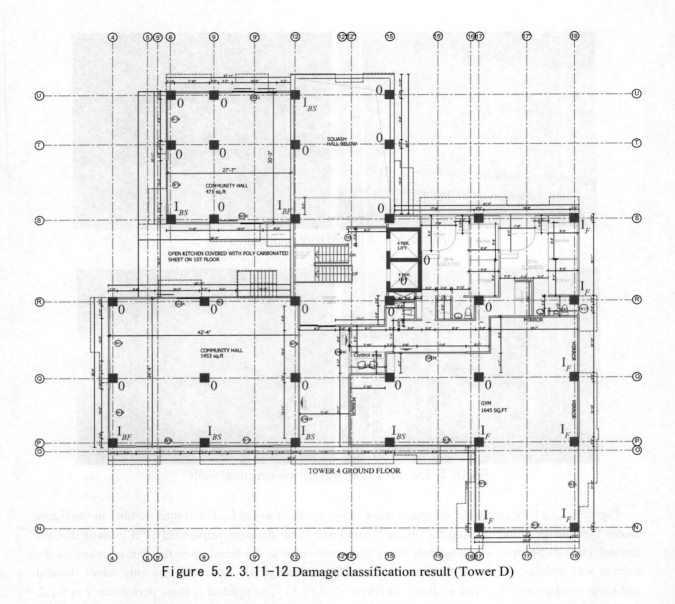

Figure 5.2.3.11-12 Damage classification result (Tower D)

Figure 5.2.3.11-12 shows the damage classification result of Tower D. The notation is the same as that in Figure 5.2.3.11-11. The structural damage is observed hardly and the result is categorized as light damage as well as Tower C.

5.2.3.12 Building K

本建物は，2007年竣工，2009年オープンの集合住宅であり，4棟の建物からなる．Photo 5.2.3.12-1 に Tower A の建物全景を，Photo 5.2.3.12-2 に Tower B～D の建物全景を示す．また，Figure 5.2.3.12-1 に建物の配置図を示す．Tower A～D の 4 棟は南北に並んでおり，それぞれの上部構造階数は Tower A：地上 16 階＋塔屋 2 階，Tower B：地上 13 階＋塔屋 2 階，Tower C：地上 11 階＋塔屋 2 階，Tower D：地上 16 階＋塔屋 2 階である．Figure 5.2.3.12-2 に示すとおり，4 棟は地下 1 階の駐車場で繋がっている．

Figure 5.2.3.12-3 に本建物の基礎伏図および基礎（フーチング・杭）の断面図を示す．設計資料によると，建物の基礎形式はパイルド・ラフト基礎となっている．不均等スパンで配置された柱のそれぞれにフーチングが配置されており，マットスラブを介して，全てのフーチングが結合されている．マットスラブの直下に杭が設置されており，杭およびマットスラブの両方を介して地盤に鉛直力を伝達している．本建物の杭の杭長は約 9m，杭径は 500mm となっており，杭主筋と

して16φの鉄筋を8本配筋し，8φの鉄筋を200mmピッチでフープ筋として配筋している．また，杭頭部はマットスラブ内に杭主筋を定着させている．

建物の被害としては，最も南に位置するTower Dの被害が最も大きく，次いでTower Aの被害が大きくなっており，4棟の中でも高層の建物で被害が大きいように見えた．以下では，Tower Dの被害を主に示す．

Figure 5.2.3.12-4にTower Dの基準階平面図を示す．ネパール国の中高層集合住宅によく見られるように，柱は不均等スパンで配置されており，柱間にはレンガを組積した非構造壁が配置されている．また，エレベータコアにはRC造の構造壁が配置されている．Photo 5.2.3.12-3にTower D東構面の被害の様子を示す．外壁がレンガを組積した非構造壁となっているのは2階以上であるが，ほぼ全ての階でせん断ひび割れが見られた．Photo 5.2.3.12-4～5.2.3.12-6にTower Dの1階ピロティ部分における被害の様子を示す．1階ピロティ部分では，柱脚および柱頭部に曲げひび割れと圧縮によるかぶりの肌別れが見られた．さらに，梁と小梁の結合部にも曲げによるひび割れが見られたが，いずれも被害程度としては軽微であった．

Figure 5.2.3.12-5に示すように，本建物にはエレベータは2基あり，それぞれのコアに配置されているRC造の耐震壁が連結梁で結合されている．連結梁のサイズは，幅が200mm，上階スラブ下端－梁下間が300mmであった．RC造の耐震壁の厚さは230mmである．Photo 5.2.3.12-7に示すように，RC造の耐震壁の被害は連結梁との接合部付近で見られ，1～3階でひび割れが確認された．一方，Photo 5.2.3.12-8, 5.2.3.12-9に示すように，連結梁には顕著なせん断ひび割れが見られ，上部建物においては最上階以外の全ての連結梁に被害が見られた．被害の大きさは，2，3階で大きいと見受けられた．一方で，地下階の連結梁およびRC造耐震壁には被害が見られなかった．Tower Cの連結梁においては，Photo 5.2.3.12-10, 5.2.3.12-11に示すように，Tower Dと同様の被害が見られたが，せん断ひび割れが生じていたのは10階までで，11階以上は梁端部の曲げひび割れとなっていた．

Photo 5.2.3.12-12に示すように，建物外側に配置されたレンガの組積による非構造壁は，最上階までせん断変形が主と思われるひび割れが見られた．Photo 5.2.3.12-13に示すように，屋上のパラペットはレンガによる組積造であったが，ひび割れが生じていた．

Photo 5.2.3.12-14に示すように，建物周辺の地盤には，地震時に沈下したと思われる形跡が認められた．沈下した地盤は地下外壁外側の埋土であり，地震時の振動によって沈下したと推測される．

本集合住宅は高層建物4棟に加えて，2～3階程度の低層建物群で形成されており，低層建物群は調査当時には建設中であった．Photo 5.2.3.12-15に示すように，低層建物群には地震による被害は見られなかった．

Photo 5.2.3.12-1 Appearance of No.1

Photo 5.2.3.12-2 Appearance of No.2 to 4

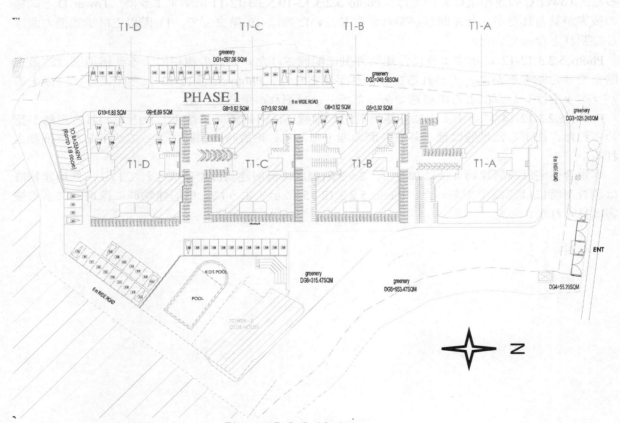

Figure 5.2.3.12-1 Site view

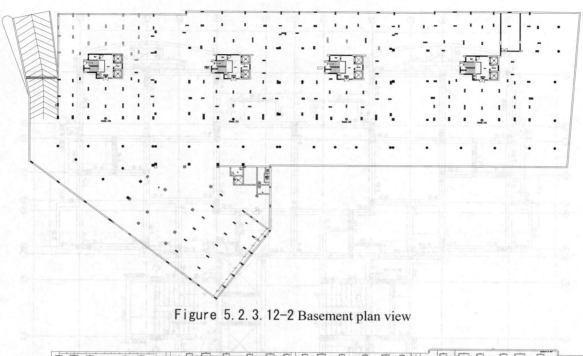

Figure 5.2.3.12-2 Basement plan view

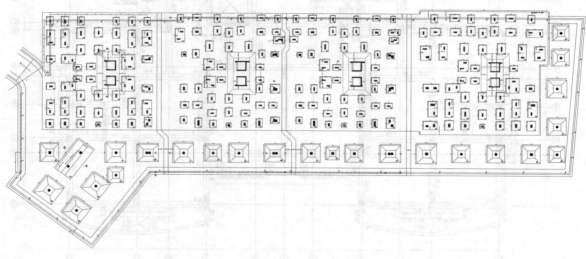

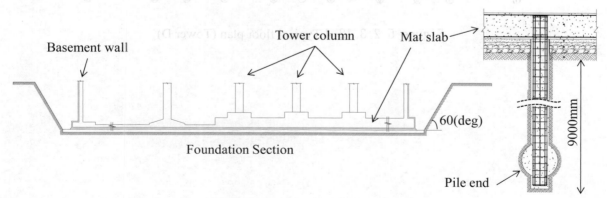

Figure 5.2.3.12-3 Foundation details (Footing plan and section, Pile section)

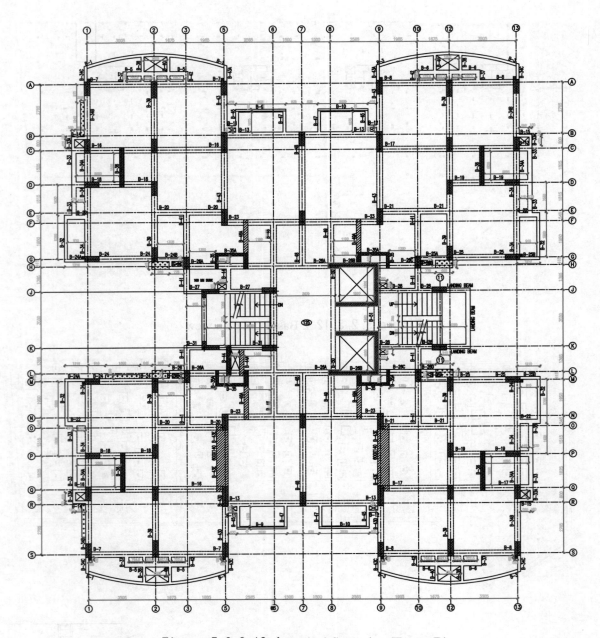

Figure 5.2.3.12-4 Typical floor plan (Tower D)

Photo 5. 2. 3. 12-3 Shear cracks of brick walls

Photo 5. 2. 3. 12-4 Damage of columns in the 1st floor of Tower D

Photo 5. 2. 3. 12-5 Damage of beams in the 1st floor (Tower D)

Photo 5. 2. 3. 12-6 Close up of the damaged beam (Tower D)

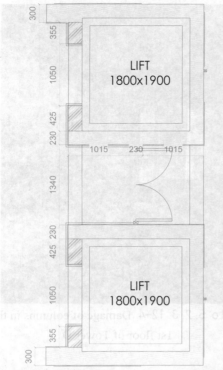

Figure 5.2.3.12-5 RC wall section (Tower D)

Photo 5.2.3.12-7 View of RC wall (Tower D)

Photo 5.2.3.12-8 Shear damage in the coupling beams (Tower D, 1st floor)

Photo 5.2.3.12-9 No damage in RC wall in the basement floor

Photo 5.2.3.12-10 Shear cracks in the coupling beams (Tower C, 1st floor)

Photo 5.2.3.12-11 Shear cracks in the coupling beams (Tower A, 1st floor)

Photo 5.2.3.12-12 Damage of non-structural walls (Tower C)

Photo 5.2.3.12-13 Damage of parapet (brick wall)

Photo 5. 2. 3. 12-14 Ground settlement around basement wall

Photo 5. 2. 3. 12-15 Buildings around the complex (No damage)

This complex is the residential buildings constructed in 2007 and opened in 2009. The complex has four buildings. The full view of Tower A is shown in Photo 5.2.3.12-1 and the full views of Towers B-D are shown in Photo 5.2.3.12-2, and the location of complex is shown in Figure 5.2.3.12-1. The buildings are arranged in the North-South direction. The number of floors of the buildings is respectively as follows; Tower A is 16-story, Tower B is 13-story, Tower C is 13-story and Tower D is 16 story (note: this number does not contain the penthouse floor). The buildings have a common basement floor.

The section and the plans of the foundations, which are footings and piles, are shown in Figure 5.2.3.12-3. The types of the foundations of the buildings are the piled raft foundations according to the specification. Footings are arranged under columns which are arranged unequally. A mat slab connects the footings. Piles are embedded under the mat slab and the piles and the mat slab support the buildings. The pile length is about 9m and diameter is about 500mm. 8 vertical reinforcements 16ϕ are arranged and hoops 8ϕ are arranged with 200mm spacing. The vertical reinforcements are fixed in the mat slab at the pile caps.

The typical plan of Tower D is shown in Figure 5.2.3.12-4. Columns are arranged irregularly in the same way of many other buildings in Nepal. The non-structural brick wall is arranged between two columns. The reinforced concrete wall is used as core wall.

Large damages according to the earthquake were observed in Tower D, which is located in South of this complex. Damages of Tower A were slightly smaller than that of Tower D. It seemed that the 16-story buildings in this complex suffered large earthquake damages. In the following, the damages of Tower D are shown.

The damages of non-structural brick walls in the east side of Tower D are shown in Photo 5.2.3.12-3. This building has non-structural outer brick wall above 2nd floor and the shear cracks of the walls were observed in all floors as shown in Photo 5.2.3.12-3. The damages of columns and beams in 1st floor of Tower D are shown in Photo 5.2.3.12-4 to 6. Spalling of cover concrete and flexural cracks were observed at the bottom and top end of outer columns, since concrete was cast up to there and the surface treatment looked insufficient. The flexure cracks at the beam joint were observed. These cracks are slight.

This building has two elevators and reinforced concrete walls used as core walls. A coupling beam connect two core walls. The coupling beam has about 200mm width and 300mm depth. The reinforced concrete wall has about 230mm width. Shear cracks in the reinforced concrete wall were observed near the connection between the beam and the wall at the 1st - 3rd floor. On the other hand, the shear cracks in the coupling shear beam were observed at the 1st-15th floor in the superstructure, and it seemed that the cracks at the 2nd and 3rd floor were large. These cracks were not observed in the basement floor.

Damages in coupling beams were observed in Tower A and C as shown in Photo 5.2.3.12-10 to 11, which were similar to the damages in Tower D. Shear cracks in the coupling beam were observed below 10 floor and only flexure cracks were observed above 11 floor in Tower C. Shear cracks of non-structural outer walls in Tower C were observed in all floors as shown in Photo 5.2.3.12-12.
Parapet of the roof is a brick wall where slight cracks were observed as shown in Photo 5.2.3.12-13.

A ground settlement around the foundation of the complex was observed as shown in Photo 5.2.3.12-14. The settled ground is backfilling soil around outer basement wall and it seems that the settlement was occurred by oscillation during the earthquake.

This complex has many low residential houses which are 2-3 story buildings under construction as shown in Photo 5.2.3.12-15. No damage was observed in these houses.

5.2.3.13 Building L

直接基礎で，地上 14 階＋塔屋 1 階，地下 1 階（駐車場）の RC 造建物 2 棟からなる（Photo 5.2.3.13-1, Figure 5.2.3.13-1, 5.2.3.13-2）．Figure 5.2.3.13-1 の A-A 断面が 2 つの建物を区切る位置である．インドの IS コードに従って設計した建物は，全体の平面形状としてはほぼ対称形だが，それぞれの棟は 45° 方向には対称，-45° 方向には非対称となっている．2010 年から工事を始めて 2015 年 5 月に竣工予定であり，地震時点で住民はいなかった．1 階のみ，部材の損傷度を判定し損傷が認められた部材にのみ損傷レベルを付して Figure 5.2.3.13-1 に示した．(C)は柱，(B)は梁，(W)は壁に関わる損傷を示し，F1 は損傷度 1 の曲げひび割れ，S1 は損傷度 1 のせん断ひび割れ，W1 は損傷度 1 の耐震壁におけるせん断ひび割れを示す．部分的に図面と記号の部材が対応していない部分があるのは，部材が施工時に変更されているためである．耐震壁が比較的多く配置されており，ブロック壁のひび割れ被害は 9 階まで観察されるが，全体の損傷程度は小さい．地下駐車場で，上部が庭となっているスパン 9m の梁中央付近に，長期荷重によるひび割れが認められた．

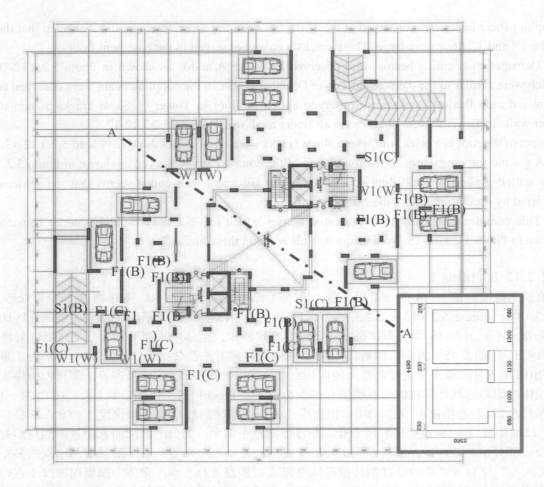

Figure 5.2.3.13-1　Floor plan of the first floor (Insert shows core wall dimensions)
(C): column, (B): beam and (W): wall

(a) East side

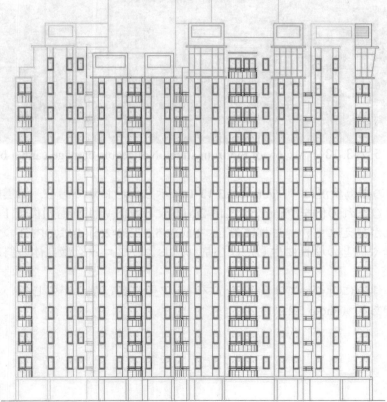

(b) South side

Figure 5.2.3.13-2 Elevation

Photo 5.2.3.13-1 A view of the front street. Noticeable damage cannot be seen.

　1階の構造部材の損傷状況は，Figure 5.2.3.13-1 に示したとおりである．耐震壁のせん断ひび割れと梁のせん断ひび割れの例を Photo 5.2.3.13-2(a)(b)に示す．いずれも損傷度 I のひび割れであり，写真ではひび割れが見えにくい．これに対し，Photo 5.2.3.13-2(c)(d)は，内部のブロック壁の損傷を示している．梁や柱との境目に生じたひび割れ，およびブロック壁自体の斜めひび割れなどが顕著である．

　周辺の建物は，建物に近づいてよく見るとブロック壁にひび割れが生じているが，構造部材はほとんど無被害である（Photo 5.2.3.13-3）．

(a) Shear wall had minor shear cracks.

(b) Beam had a shear crack at the end.

(c) Brick walls had severe cracks

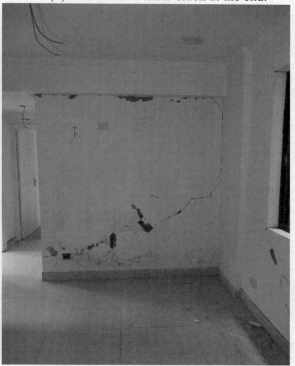
(d) Brick walls diagonal cracks

Photo 5. 2. 3. 13-2 Damage of internal members

Photo 5. 2. 3. 13-3 Neighboring buildings had minor or no damage.

Twin buildings of Building L are a reinforced concrete building with mat slab. They have fourteen floors with a single story penthouse and one story basement (parking space) as shown (Photo 5.2.3.13-1). Figure 5.2.3.13-1 shows A-A section which separates twin buildings. The buildings were designed using the Indian code and have been under construction since 2010. As it was to be completed in May, no residents were in the buildings at the time of shaking. Damage was evaluated for the first floor members and marked on Figure 5.2.3.13-1. (C) is for columns, (B) for beams and (W) for walls. Then, F1 stands for flexural damage I, S1 for shear damage I and W1 for wall shear damage I. Members without any specific explanation had no damage. Although brick walls had cracks up to ninth floor, the structural members did not suffer minor or no damage probably due to large amount of shear walls. Some beams of underground parking had a flexural cracking in their mid-span due to long term loading.

Damage in Figure 5.2.3.13-1 is shown in photos. Photo 5.2.3.13-2(a)(b) shows the shear cracks of a shear wall and a beam. Their damage levels are minor (W1 and S1) and hard to see clearly in these photos.

5.2.3.13-2(c)(d) shows damage of interior brick walls. Cracks are distinctive along the interface of structural members and in brick walls themselves as shear cracks. Neighboring buildings had minor or no damage to structural members but several cracks to brick walls (Photo 5.2.3.13-3).

5.2.3.14 Building M

パイルド・ラフト基礎上に，地上17階，地下1階のRC造建物が5棟建っている（Figure 5.2.3.14-1）．もともとの計画では敷地内に10棟を建設予定であったが，計画変さらにより5棟（Photo 5.2.3.14-1）に縮小された．工事開始は2010年である．地震時には150家族が住んでいたが，地震後の応急危険度判定（黄色判定）を受け半数の世帯が自主的に避難し，残った75世帯ほどが継続して生活している．全ての建物で，構造部材の被害は梁端の曲げひび割れ程度（Photo 5.2.3.14-2の左側にこの梁がコア壁に挟まれたつなぎ梁であることを示した）であり，建物全体としては無被害または軽微の部類である．しかし，ブロック壁の被害が各棟で顕著であり（Photo 5.2.3.14-3），住民に不安を与えている．被害を受けたブロック壁のひび割れ周辺をはつり，ワイヤーメッシュを釘で貼り付けて，エポキシ塗布後，無収縮モルタルを塗って補修していた（Photo 5.2.3.14-4）．北東－南西方向に被害が目立ち，H棟が最も被害が大きかった．ただし，H棟でも梁端の曲げひび割れと，ブロック壁の被害がほとんどである．

他の建物と同様に，地上でドライブウェイ下の地下駐車場の梁が，長期耐力不足のため鋼板補強されていた（Photo 5.2.3.14-5）．周辺建物は，ほとんど無被害であった（Photo 5.2.3.14-6）．

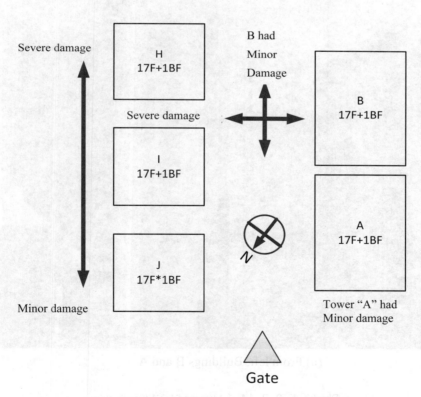

Figure 5.2.3.14-1 Plan of apartment complex

(a) From left, Buildings J, I and H

(a) From left, Buildings B and A

Photo 5. 2. 3. 14-1 View of buildings

Photo 5.2.3.14-2 A crack can be seen at the slab-beam interface (cold joint) of a coupling beam.

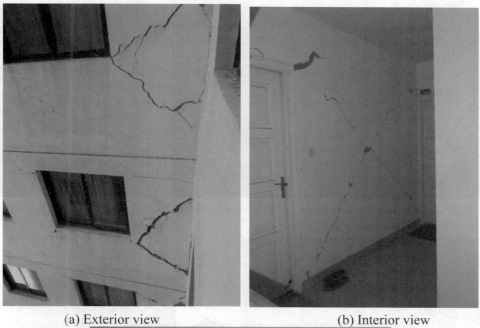

(a) Exterior view   (b) Interior view

(c) Damage above a door opening
Photo 5.2.3.14-3 Damage to brick walls

Photo 5. 2. 3. 14-4 Cracked brick wall was repaired with wire mesh, epoxy, and non-shrinkage mortar.

Photo 5. 2. 3. 14-5 Multiple beams of B1 parking were reinforced by steel plate to stop long-term cracks.

Photo 5. 2. 3. 14-6 Neighboring buildings have minor or no damage.

Buildings M is an apartment complex of five reinforced concrete buildings with seventeen floors and one story basement standing on piled raft (Figure 5.2.3.14-1). Ten buildings were originally planned to be built but five are completed as Photo 5.2.3.14-1. One hundred fifty families were living at the time of earthquake but half of them evacuated after the city declared as 'Be careful to use (yellow tag)' damage. Major structural damage was flexural cracks at beam ends or some cracks at cold joints (Photo 5.2.3.14-2) and overall damage is minor. However, damage to bricks are extensive at both exterior and interior walls as can be seen in Photo 5.2.3.14-3. Some brick wall damage was repaired by wire mesh, epoxy and non-shrinkage mortar (Photo 5.2.3.14-4). Damage due to north-east and south-west shaking was distinctive and Tower H had most severe damage although damage was almost limited to brick walls.

As other buildings, some beams of underground parking had flexural cracking in the mid-span due to long-term loading and few of them had steel plate reinforcement on their lower face (Photo 5.2.3.14-5). Neighboring building had minor or no damage (Photo 5.2.3.14-6).

5.2.3.15 まとめ/ Conclusions

- RC造中高層建物（地上10～18階程度）は，RCフレーム＋コア壁を基本に，連層耐震壁が追加で配置され（ないものもある），構造体を構成している．外壁や間仕切壁にはレンガ壁が用いられており，それらは構造要素としては考慮されていない（薄い偏平柱は，梁主筋の定着がとれないものもある）．
- 一部の建物において，梁の曲げ・せん断による損傷，圧縮柱の損傷，コア壁のせん断による損傷，柱梁接合部の損傷が見られたが，それらを除けば，構造体の損傷は軽微であった（変形制御設計の重要性）．
- レンガ壁（外壁および内壁）の被害は大きく，調査した全建物でせん断破壊・ひび割れが見られ，一部崩落も見られた．落下したレンガにより死傷者が出ている．（レンガ壁の取扱いは，今後の技術支援で最も大きな課題である．）
- 構造被害が多く見られた建物5棟（うち4棟は同一敷地内）の地上1階を対象に，被災度区分判定を実施した結果，R=96%，90%，94%，97%（以上，同一敷地内），98%であり，軽微3棟，小破2棟であった．
- R=90%の建物について，立体骨組を用いた非線形荷重増分解析を行った結果，耐力はベースシア係数で約0.3程度であった．
- 外壁を構成する非構造レンガ壁の落下防止策は，緊急の課題である．
- 高層集合住宅では，非構造レンガ壁の損傷により，住宅としての機能が失われており，ネパールで施工可能な補修・補強方法の提案が必要である．
- 壁が比較的多いと思われる建物においても，レンガ壁の損傷は防げておらず，耐震壁の増築やダンパー設置では，対策が追い付かないと思われる．

- R/C middle- to high-rise buildings, which have 10 to 18 stories, consist of R/C moment resisting frame with continuous core walls. Brick masonry walls are used for partition walls and external walls, which are not considered as structural elements.
- Generally, structure itself did not suffer severe damage, while a limited numbers of buildings suffered flexural and/or shear damages in beams, damages in the columns, shear damages in core walls, and damages in beam-column joints.
- Brick masonry walls suffered severe damages. That damage was very common and observed in most of all buildings. Some walls fell down and killed passengers.
- The Japanese damage classification method was applied for five buildings (four buildings located in the same complex). The results were R=96%, 90%. 94%,97%, and 98%, which were classified as slight damage (3 buildings) and minor damage (2 buildings).

- Base shear coefficient obtained by 3D non-linear dynamic response analysis of buildings which R of 90% was 0.3.
- It is the urgent and critical issue to prevent damage and falling down of non-structural brick walls.
- Especially for high-rise apartment buildings, the rooms were not able to be used continuously due to the damage of brick walls. A retrofitting technique for Nepalese brick walls is required.
- Even a structure has many R/C walls, it was observed that brick walls were severely damaged. It shows that additional R/C wall or installing damping device cannot solve the problem.

5.2.3.16 参考文献／ References

5.2.3-1) Indian standard: IS875(Part 2)-1987
5.2.3-2) Indian standard: IS1893:2002

5.2.3.17 謝辞／ Acknowledgements

5.2.3節で用いた図面や建物情報は，各建物管理者のご厚意により提供いただいた．

The drawings and building information shown in Section 5.2.3 were kindly provided by the building owners.

6 歴史都市の被害状況/ Damage to Historical Cities

6.1 カトマンズ盆地の世界文化遺産の概要/ Summary of World Heritages in Kathmandu Valley

　カトマンズは，国を興したPrithvi Narayan Shah国王以前の中世の間にkhaldoの谷として知られるようになった．その文化的でかつ古の美術工芸品で豊かに彩られたこの特筆すべき場所は，ネパールの文化的，政治的な中心地である．カトマンズ谷は，東をSangha Bhanjyangに，西をBad-bhanjyangに，北をPanchmaneに，そして南をPharpingに縁取られている．お椀のような形をした谷は4つの山に囲まれ，カトマンズ，ラリトプール，そしてバクタプールの3つの地区から成っている．そこには1つの大都市，1つの都市郊外，そして3つの地方市域が含まれる．

　文化遺産はカトマンズ谷の基本的アイデンティティになっており，古の寺院や宗教的な場所そして文化財を誇りとしている．さらに緑の丘とそれを取り巻くヒマラヤの景観がこの谷の魅力を高めている．この谷にはたくさんの寺院，神社，僧院，仏塔，広場，木造芸術やその他の種類の文化遺産が存在している．また，カトマンズ谷は異なる宗教的背景を持つ人々の信仰の中心でもある．パシュパティナート寺院，クリシュナ寺院，そしてチャングナラヤン寺院はヒンズー教の聖なる場所と考えられており，一方で仏教徒にとって，スワヤンブナートの仏塔とボーダナートの仏塔はきわめて重要である．イスラム教徒にとって広く知られたジャメ・モスクがあり，街中にはキリスト教のコミュニティによって建てられた数多くの教会がある．古のネパール王朝が置かれたハヌマンドーカ王宮やさまざまな王宮は，観光者によく知られた中心的で魅力的な場所になっている．独特のネパール文化を映し出す祭りや伝統そしてその他の祭事は，カトマンズをさらに魅力的で魅惑的なものにしてきた．

　首都として，カトマンズは国の教育と経済の中心になっている．首都圏外の数多くの人々にとってカトマンズは夢をかなえ，そしてより高い学びを追求するための場所として注目されている．このため，生活者と交通渋滞でますます混み合ってきている．このまちはすべての地域，民族そして民族的背景が融合する場所であり，それは明らかなる文明と文化的様式をよく反映している．カトマンズはネパールを訪れる観光者にとって好まれる目的地の1つとなっている．

（参考："Introduction of World Heritage Site: Heritage of Kathmandu Valley", Dhoju Publication House, pp.7）

　Kathmandu used to be known as Khaldo 'valley', during the medieval period before King Prithvi Narayan Shah unified the country. This landmark place, considered rich for its cultural and ancient artifacts, is the cultural and political heart of Nepal. The Kathmandu valley is bounded by Sangha Bhanjyang in the east, Bad-bhanjyang in the west, Panchmane Bhanjyang in the north and Pharping in the south. The bowl-shaped valley, surrounded by four mountains, constitutes three districts- Kathmandu, Lalitpur and Bhaktapur. It has one metropolitan city, one sub-metropolitan cities and three municipalities. Cultural heritage is the principal identity of the Kathmandu valley which boasts of ancient temples, religious sites and cultural artifacts. The landscape of the green hills and the vista of the Himalayas in its surroundings add to the attractions of this valley. The valley is home to many temples, shrines, monasteries, stupas, squares, wooden arts, and other sorts of artifacts. The Kathmandu valley is also a center of faith for people from different religious backgrounds. The Pashupatinath Temple, Krishna Temple and Changunarayan Temple are considered the important holy places for Hindu devotees while, for the Buddhists, Swoyambhunath Stupa and Boudhanath Stupa are very important. There is a famous Jame Mosque for the Muslims and the city also has many churches built by the Christian community. The Hanumandhoka palace, the ancient seat of Nepalese royalty, and various ancient palaces are the main attractions of the city popular among tourists. Festival, traditions and other rituals reflecting uniqueness of Nepali culture have made

Kathmandu more attractive and alluring. Being the capital, Kathmandu is the educational and commercial center of the country. Many people outside the capital regard Kathmandu the place of realizing one's dreams and pursuing higher studies. Consequently, it is more crowded with heavy traffic and full of life. The city is the melting point for people of all the religions, races and ethnic backgrounds, and it is well reflected in its distinct civilization and cultural patterns. Kathmandu is one of the preferred destination for tourists visiting Nepal. (Reference "Introduction of World Heritage Site: Heritage of Kathmandu Valley", Dhoju Publication House, pp.7)

6.2　世界文化遺産の被害／Damage to World Heritages

Figure 6.2-1 にカトマンズ盆地の 7 つの世界文化遺産の位置を示す．Changunarayan Hindu Temple は入場禁止のため，現場周辺での聞き取り調査を行った．これを除く 6 か所を対象に調査し，各敷地内の建物を EMS-98[5.2.2-1]判定法より被災度区分判定を行った．本節では，各世界文化遺産の被害状況を示し，被害の特徴をまとめる．

世界文化遺産の建築物は多種多様であるが，本節では大きく Newar-Tower（ネワール様式の多重塔），Newar-Building（ネワール様式の一般建築），Masonry（組積造建築），Others（その他）の 4 種類に分けてそれぞれの被害の特徴を説明する．Photo 6.2-1 に以上の各種建築物の代表的な写真を示す．

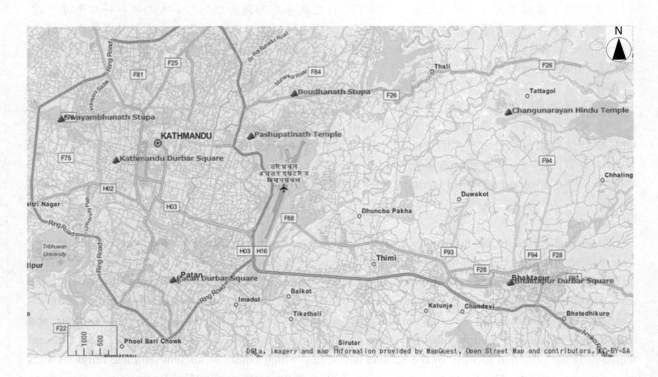

Figure 6.2-1 Location of world cultural heritages in Kathmandu valley

(a) Newar-Tower

(b) Newar-Building

(c) Masonry

(d) Others

Photo 6.2-1 Structural systems categorized in this section

Figure 6.2-1 shows seven world heritages located in Kathmandu valley. As no permission to enter Changunarayan Hindu Temple, interviews were conducted to the local people near the temple. Field investigations on buildings were conducted in the other six sites, applying the method of EMS98[5.2.2.1-1)] to the damage evaluation. This section summarizes damage to every heritage and the damage characteristics.

Buildings in the heritages were of a great variety. In this section, the buildings are categorized into four types: Newar-Tower (multi-story tower in Newar style), Newar-Building (normal building in Newar style), Masonry (brick or stone masonry), and Others (such as statues and religious symbols). Photo 6.2-1 shows typical samples for all types of buildings.

6.2.1 Kathmandu Durbar Square

Kathmandu Durbar Square はカトマンズ盆地の中心に位置し，3 つの Durbar Square（ほかに Patan Durbar Square, Bhaktapur Durbar Sqare）の中，規模が一番大きい王宮広場である．この歴史遺産では，42 棟の建物に対して，前述した方法を用いて被災度区分判定を行った．Figure 6.2.1-1 に同歴史遺産の平面図を示す．なお，各建物の被害状況の記述の便宜上，建物に番号を付した．被災度区分判定の結果も同図に示す（被災度判定がなされた建物が調査できた建物である）．被害率を Figure 6.2.1-2 に示す．ただし，同図では全壊（EMS-98 の V），半壊（EMS-98 の IV）および半壊未満（EMS-98 の III 以下）の三段階で表示した．Table 6.2.1-1 に調査した 42 棟の建物の構造形式を示す．各構造形式の損傷状況について，以下で解説する．

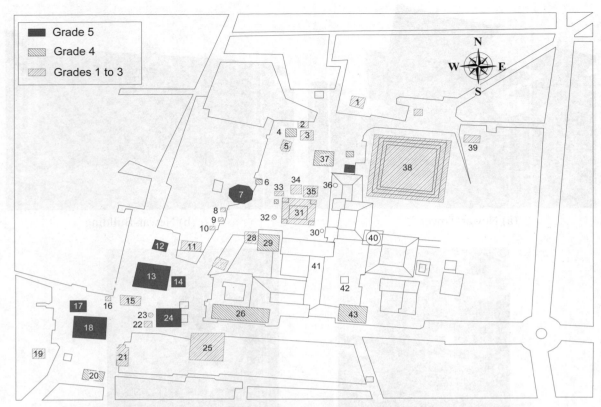

Figure 6.2.1-1 Site plan of Kathmandu Durbar Square and investigation results

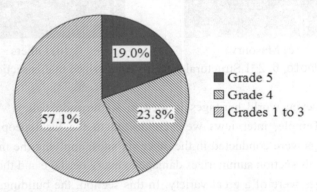

Figure 6.2.1-2 Damage ratio of the investigated structures

Table 6.2.1-1 Structural systems observed at Kathmandu Durbar Square

Structural system	Newar-Tower	Newar-Building	Masonry	Others	Total
Number	19	10	6	7	42
Percentage	45%	24%	14%	17%	100%

Kathmandu Durbar Square locates at the center of Kathmandu valley, and is the largest among three Durbar Squares (the other two are Patan Durbar Square and Bhaktapur Durbar Square). In this heritage site, forty-two buildings were investigated including the damage assessment according to the method as described above. Figures 6.2.1-1 and 6.2.1-2 show the assessment results and the damage ratio, respectively. Table 6.2.1-1 summarizes the structural systems of the investigated forty-two buildings. Damage to every type of structural system is illustrated in the following.

6.2.1.1 Newar-Tower 構造/ Newar-Tower structures

Kathmandu Durbar Square では，Newar-Tower 構造の建物が大きな被害を受けた．Figure 6.2.1-3(a)の被害率に示すように，全・半壊率は 52%に達した．Photo 6.2.1-1 に建物の被害の様子を示す．建物 13 が完全に倒壊し，基壇のみが残されていた．建物 3 が被害を受け，余震を備える対策として，木材のサポートが設置されていた．この種の余震への対策は世界文化遺産の建築のみならず，一般的な組積造住宅でもよく見られた．

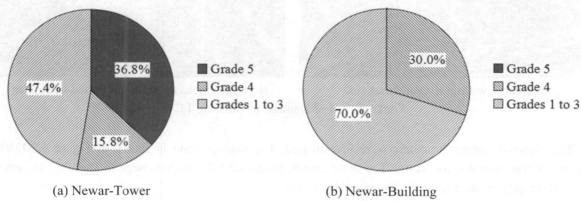

(a) Newar-Tower   (b) Newar-Building
Figure 6.2.1-3 Damage ratio of Newar type structures

(a) Building 13: complete collapse   (b) Building 3: supported by timber after earthquake
Photo 6.2.1-1 Damage to Newar-Tower structures

In Kathmandu Durbar Square, Newar-Tower structure buildings suffered heavy damage. As shown in Figure 6.2.1-3(a), 52% of this type of structure completely or partially collapsed. Photo 6.2.1-1 shows the damage conditions. Building 13 completely collapsed, only leaving the foundation. Building 3 suffered damage, thus, timber supports were applied to resist aftershocks, which was common not only for heritage buildings but also for general masonry residential houses.

6.2.1.2 Newar-Building 構造/ Newar-Building Structures

Newar-Building 構造の建物を 10 棟調査した．被害率を Figure 6.2.1-3(b)に示す．Newar-Tower 構造より被害率が低かった．Photo 6.2.1-2 に建物 11 の被害状況を示す．壁に大きなひび割れが発生し，木材のサポートが設置されていた．

(a) Overview from the southeast side　　　　　(b) Lage cracks on walls supported by timber
Photo 6.2.1-2 Damage to Building 11

Ten Newar-Building structures were investigated. The damage ratio is shown in Figure 6.2.1-3(b), which is lower than that for Newar-Tower structures. Photo 6.2.1-2 shows damage to Building 11, where the walls largely cracked and were supported by timber.

6.2.1.3 組積造/ Masonry Structure

調査した 6 棟の組積造の建物のうち，全壊・半壊各 1 棟，半壊未満は 4 棟であった．Photo 6.2.1-3 に組積造の被害状況を示す．

(a) Building 22: Supported by timber　　　　　(b) Building 5: no structural damage
Photo 6.2.1-3 Damage to masonry structures

In six investigated Masonry structure buildings, one completely collapsed, one partially collapsed, and the other four were slightly or moderately damaged. Photo 6.2.1-3 shows damage to Masonry structures.

6.2.1.4 その他/ Others

前述した 3 種類以外の構造物の被害状況を Photo 6.2.1-4 に示す．同写真(a)の西洋式の建築では外壁が部分倒壊し，半壊であった．写真(b)に示す建物の下部は Newar-Building 構造で，上部に Newar-Tower 構造の混合構造であるため，Others として分類した．写真に示すように，Newar-Tower 構造部分の上層部が倒壊した．

(a) Building 26: wall collapse   (b) Building 43: top floors of west (left) tower collapased

Photo 6.2.1-4 Damage to other structures

Damage to other buildings except for the above three types are shown in Photo 6.2.1-4. External walls of a western architectural building shown in Photo 6.2.1-4(a) collapsed partially. Building 43 shown in Photo 6.2.1-4(b) was a hybrid structure with Newar-Building structure at the bottom part and Newar-Tower structure at the top, so it was categorized as "Others". As shown in the photograph, the top story of the Newar-Tower structure collapsed.

6.2.1.5 地盤の常時微動計測結果/ Microtremor Mesurement on the Site

周辺地盤に対して，水平 2 成分，鉛直 1 成分の常時微動計測を行った．計測には速度計を用いた．

寺院の敷地内西側の地盤で常時微動計測を行った．H/V スペクトルを Figure 6.2.1-4 に示す．NS, EW 共に 1Hz 以下での卓越が見られた．

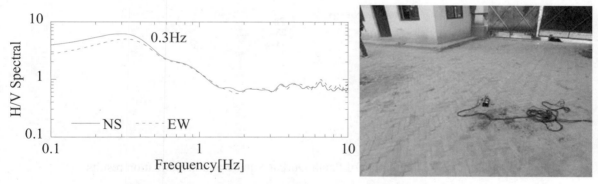

Figure 6.2.1-4 H/V spectrumat Kathmandu Durbar Square

A velocity sensor that could measure one vertical component and two horizontal components was used. Figure 6.2.1-4 shows the resultant H/V spectra for the NS and EW directions near Building 7. The natural frequencies were below 1 Hz for both directions.

6.2.1.6 まとめ/ Summaries
1. Kathmandu Durbar Square では，建物の全・半壊率は 43%であった．
2. Newar-Tower 構造の建物の全・半壊率が最も高く，52%に達した．全壊した建物が 8 棟のうち，Newar-Tower 構造の建物はその 88%を占める 7 棟であった．

1. In Kathmandu Durbar Square, 43% of the invesitgated buildings completely or partially collapsed.
2. Damage ratio of Newar-Tower structure buildings was the highest: completely or partially collapsed buildings accounted for 52%. Seven of eight completely collapsed buildings were Newar-Tower structure, accounting for 88%.

6.2.2 Patan Durbar Square

Patan Durbar Square では，24棟の建物を調査した．Figure 6.2.2-1 に同世界文化遺産の平面図を示す．Figure 6.2.1-1 と同様に，カラーで表示された建物が調査したものであり，色分けにより建物の被災度判定の結果を示す．被害率を Figure 6.2.2-2 に示す．Table 6.2.2-1 に調査した建物の構造形式を示す．各構造形式の損傷状況について，以下に説明する．

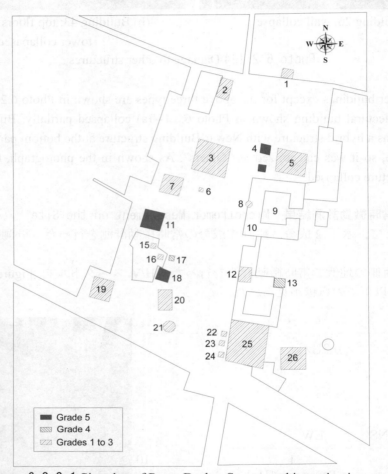

Figure 6.2.2-1 Site plan of Patan Durbar Square and investigation results

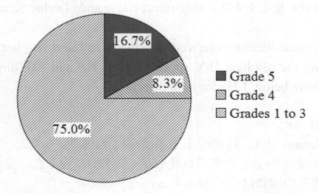

Figure 6.2.2-2 Damage ratio of structures in Patan Durbar Square

Table 6.2.2-1 Structural systems observed at Patan Durbar Square

Structural system	Newar-Tower	Newar-Building	Masonry	Others	Total
Number	7	3	4	10	24
Percentage	29%	13%	17%	42%	100%

In Patan Durbar Square site, twenty-four buildings were investigated. Figure 6.2.2-1 shows the site plan of this heritage in the same manner as Figure 6.2.1-1. The resultant damage ratio is shown in Figure 6.2.2-2. Table 6.2.2-1 summarizes the structural systems of the investigated buildings. In the following, damage to buildings is illustrated for each structural system.

6.2.2.1 Newar-Tower 構造/ Newar-Tower Structures

Newar-Tower 構造の建物は7棟調査したうち，4棟が全壊した．Photo 6.2.2-1 には全・半壊した建物の例を示す．Photo 6.2.2-2 の半壊未満の建物3 では，内部のレンガ壁が倒壊した．

(a) Building 11: complete collapse　　　　　　(b) Building 13: collapsed top of tower

Photo 6.2.2-1 Completely or partially damaged buildings

(a) Overview from the west side　　(b) Collapse of interior wall

Photo 6.2.2-2 Damage to Building 3

In the investigated seven Newar-Tower structure buildings, 4 of them completely collapsed. Photo 6.2.2-1 shows examples of completely or partially collapsed ones. Photo 6.2.2-2 shows a lightly damaged building, in which the internal brick wall collapsed.

6.2.2.2 Newar-Building 構造/ Newar-Building Structures

Newar-Building 構造を3棟調査した．3棟とも外から構造的な被害は確認できなかった．

Three Newar-Building structures were investigated, and no structural damage was observed to all of them.

6.2.2.3 組積造/ Masonry Structures

調査した4棟の組積造の建物がすべて半壊未満であった．Photo 6.2.2-3 の(a)，(b)にそれぞれレンガ造，石造の構造物を示す．

(a) Building 16: constructed with brick　　(b) Building 21: constructed with stone
Photo 6.2.2-3 Damage to masonry structures

The investigated four Masonry buildings were slightly or moderately damaged. Brick and stone masonry buildings are shown in Photo 6.2.2-3(a) and (b), respectively.

6.2.2.4 その他/ Others

Photo6.2.2-4 に石柱と鐘楼の被害状況を示す．同写真(a)の石柱の上端部が地面に落下した．同写真(b)に示す鐘楼は健全であった．

(a) Structure 17: falling of top of stone monument　　(b) Structure 20: bell tower without damage
Photo 6.2.2-4 Damage to other structures

Photo 6.2.2-4 shows damage to a stone column and a bell tower. In the photograph (a), the top part fell down to the ground. In the photograph (b), the bell tower had no damage.

6.2.2.5 地盤の常時微動計測結果/ Microtremor Mesurement on the Site

周辺地盤に対して，水平2成分，鉛直1成分の常時微動計測を行った．計測には速度計を用いた．

寺院の敷地裏手東側の地盤で常時微動計測を行った．H/Vスペクトルを Figure 6.2.2-3 に示す．NS, EW 共に約 1Hz 以下での卓越が見られた．

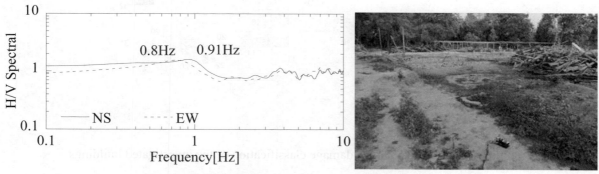

Figure 6.2.2-3 H/V spectrum at Patan Durbar Square

A velocity sensor that could measure one vertical component and two horizontal components was used. Figure 6.2.2-3 shows the resultant H/V spectra for the NS and EW directions at the eastern ground of the site. The natural frequencies were below 1 Hz for both directions.

6.2.2.6 まとめ/ Summaries
1. Patan Durbar Square では，調査した建物の全・半壊率は25%であった．
2. 全壊した4棟の建物がすべて Newar-Tower 構造であった．

1. In Patan Durbar Square, 25% of the investigated buildings completely or partially collapsed.
2. All of four completely collapsed buildings were Newar-Tower structure buildings.

6.2.3 Bhaktapur Durbar Square

Bhaktapur Durbar Square は Kathmandu から東約 13km 離れたマッラ王国時代（12世紀～18世紀）の1つの都であった Bhaktapur に位置する．同世界文化遺産では，17棟の建物を調査した．敷地の建物配置図および調査した建物の被害率をそれぞれ Figure 6.2.3-1, 6.2.3-2 に示す．調査した建物の全・半壊率は35%であった．調査した建物の構造形式を Table 6.2.3-1 に示す．

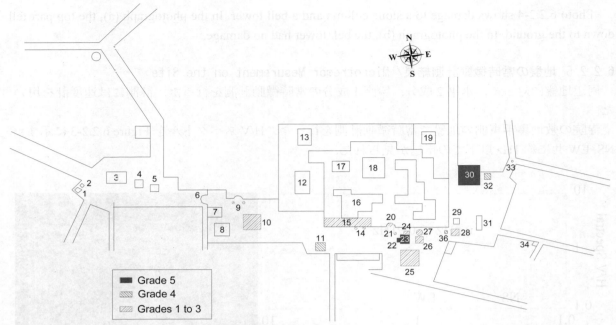

Figure 6.2.3-1 Site plan and damage classification of the investigated buildings

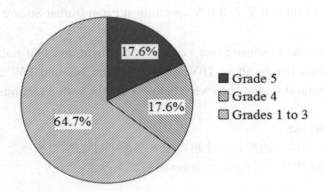

Figure 6.2.3-2 Damage ratio of investigated buildings

Table 6.2.3-1 Structural systems of the investigated buildings

Structural system	Newar-Tower	Newar-Building	Masonry	Others	Total
Number	3	1	6	7	17
Percentage	18%	6%	35%	41%	100%

Bhaktapur Durbar Square locates at Bhaktapur, which was one of the capitals in Malla period (from 12th to 18th century) and locates 13 km east of Kathmandu. In this heritage, seventeen buildings were investigated. The site map and damage ratio of investigated buildings are shown in Figure 6.2.3-1 and Figure 6.2.3-2, respectively. 35% of the investigated buildings completely or partially collapsed. The structural systems are summarized in Table 6.2.3-1.

6.2.3.1 調査結果/ Investigation Results

Newar-tower 構造の建物を 3 棟調査し，全・半壊はなかった．この種の構造の被害がほかの 2 つの Durbar square より少なかった．また，Newar-building 構造を 1 棟調査した結果，大きな損傷はなかった．

同所の被害の特徴として，組積造の被害がより深刻であり，調査した6棟のうち，全壊は2棟，半壊は3棟であった．Photo 6.2.3-1～6.2.3-3に被害を受けた組積造の例を示す．Photo 6.2.3-1に示す建物30が完全に倒壊した．Photo 6.2.3-2に示すように，建物11の上部が壊れた．Photo 6.2.3-3に示すレンガ造建物28の壁が倒壊した（黄色い枠内部分）．その隣の石造の塔の最上端が折れた．

Photo 6.2.3-1 Building 30: complete collapse

Photo 6.2.3-2 Building 11: partial collapse

Photo 6.2.3-3 Building 28 (white one): wall collapsed; Building 36 (stone tower): tip bended

Three Newar-tower structures were investigated, and no one was completely or partially collapsed. Damage to this kind of structure was slighter than those in the other two Durbar Squares. One Newar-building structure was investigated, which suffered no obvious damage.

One of the typical damage characteristics in this heritage site was severe damage to Masonry structures. Two of five investigated buildings were completely collapsed, and the other three were partially collapsed. Photos 6.2.3-1 to 6.2.3-3 show damage to Masonry buildings. Building 30 in Photo 6.2.3-1 completely collapsed. Top part of Building 11 collapsed as shown in Photo 6.2.3-2. Photo 6.2.3-3 shows that the wall of Building 28 collapsed (within the yellow circle), and the tip of the nearby stone-made masonry building fractured.

6.2.3.2 まとめ/ Summaries
1. Bhaktapur Durbar square では，Newar-tower 構造の建物が Kathmandu Durbar Square および Patan Durbar Square より被害が少なかった．
2. 組積造の建物の全・半壊率は83%であり，被害は深刻であった．

1. In Bhaktapur Durbar square, damage to Newar-tower structure buildings was slighter than those in Kathmandu Durbar Square and Patan Durbar Square.
2. Damage to Masonry buildings was heavy: 83% of the investigated ones completely/partially collapsed.

6.2.4 Swayambhunath Temple

Swayambhunath Temple は Kathmandu 市内の丘の上に位置する 2500 年以上の歴史を持つ仏教の聖地である．中央のストゥーパはネパール仏教の最も重要な仏塔である．2008 年～2010 年に大修復を行った．

ここでは建物を 37 棟調査した．同世界文化遺産の平面図および調査した建物の被害率をそれぞれ Figure 6.2.4-1, 6.2.4-2 に示す．Swayambhunath Stupa 敷地内に歴史建築物だけでなく，店舗やレストランなどの商業用建築も多数混在する．ここで調査した建物にはこれらの商業用建築も含まれている．Table 6.2.4-1 に調査した建物の構造形式を示す．組積造の建物はその 81%を占めている．以下に敷地中央のストゥーパおよび組積造の被害を解説する．

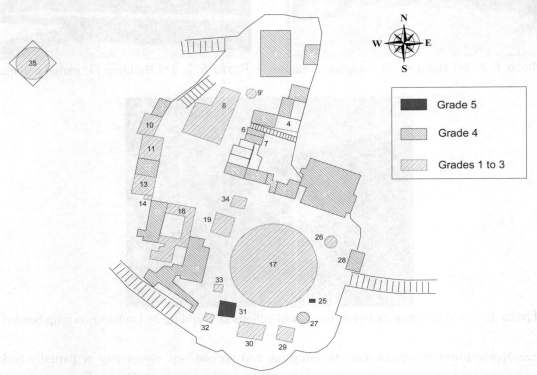

Figure 6.2.4-1 Site plan and investigation results

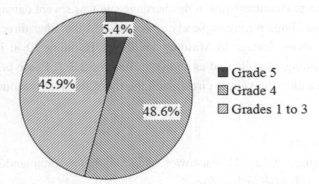

Figure 6.2.4-2 Damage ratio of investigated buildings

Table 6.2.4-1 Structural system of the investigated buildings

Structural system	Newar-Tower	Newar-Building	Masonry	Others	Total
Number	1	0	30	6	37
Percentage	3%	0%	81%	16%	100%

Swayambhunath Temple is a Buddhist sanctuary with 2500 years' histories. It locates at the top of a small hill in Kathmandu. The Stupa is the most important pagoda for Nepal Buddhism. During 2008 to 2010, extensive repair was conducted.

In this site, thirty-seven buildings were investigated. The site plan and the damage ratio of investigated buildings are shown in Figure 6.2.4-1 and Figure 6.2.4-2, respectively. In Swayambhunath Stupa site, except for historic buildings, a lot of commercial buildings such as shops or restaurants also existed. It should be noted that the investigated buildings in this site included the commercial buildings. Table 6.2.4-1 shows the structural systems of the investigated buildings. Masonry buildings accounted for 81%. Damage to the Stupa and masonry buildings is mentioned in the following.

6.2.4.1 ストゥーパ/ Stupa

ストゥーパの構造形式は外部から確認できなかった．Photo 6.2.4-1 に示すように，大きな被害は見られなかった．

Photo 6.2.4-1 Building 17 (stupa): no obvious damage

Structural system of the Stupa is unknown. As shown in Photo 6.2.4-1, no obvious damage was observed.

6.2.4.2 組積造/ Masonry Structure

組積造の被害率を Figure 6.2.4-3 に示す．全・半壊率は 63%であり，甚大な被害を受けた．Photo 6.2.4-2～6.2.4-5 に被災した組積造の建物の例を示す．Photo 6.2.4-2 の建物 1 の北面妻壁の上部が面外に倒れた．Photo 6.2.4-3 の建物 9 の 1 階と 2 階の境界面に大きなひび割れが発生し，面外方向のずれが生じた．Photo 6.2.4-4，6.2.4-5 に示す建物 24，27 が部分的に倒壊した．

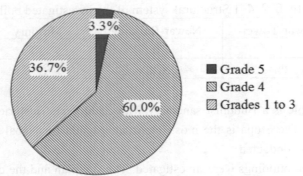

Figure 6.2.4-3 Damage ratio of masonry buildings

(a)Overview from the southwest side

(b) Partial collapse of gable wall on the north side

Photo 6.2.4-2 Damage to Building 1

Photo 6.2.4-3 Damage to Building 9

Photo 6.2.4-4 Damage to Building 24

Photo 6.2.4-5 Damage to Building 27

Damage ratio of Masonry structure buildings is shown in Figure 6.2.4-3. 63% of them were completely or partially collapsed, showing the severe damage. Photos 6.2.4-2 to 6.2.4-5 show examples of the damaged masonry structure buildings. Top part of the north gable wall in Building 1 collapsed in the out-of-plane direction, as shown in Photo 6.2.4-2. Photo 6.2.4-3 shows that a large crack appeared at the boundary of the first and second story, which resulted in a gap between the stories. Building 24 in Photo 6.2.4-4 and Building 27 in Photo 6.2.4-5 partially collapsed.

6.2.4.3 地盤の常時微動計測結果/ Microtremor Measurement Results on the Site

周辺地盤に対して，水平2成分，鉛直1成分の常時微動計測を行った．計測には速度計を用いた．

小高い丘の上にある寺院の敷地内の地盤で常時微動計測を行った．H/V スペクトルを Figure 6.2.4-4 に示す．NS, EW 共に約 3.59Hz での卓越が見られた．

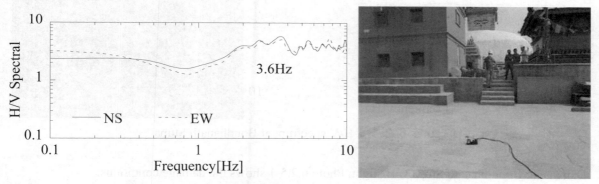

Figure 6.2.4-4 H/V spectrum at Swayambhunath Temple

A velocity sensor that could measure one vertical component and two horizontal components was used. Figure 6.2.4-4 shows the resultant H/V spectra for the NS and EW directions at the southern ground of Building 30. The natural frequencies were about 3.6 Hz for both directions.

6.2.4.4 まとめ/ Summaries

Swayambhunath Temple では，組積造が調査した建物の 81%を占めていた．その全・半壊率は 63%であり，甚大な被害を受けた．

At Swayambhunath Temple site, Masonry structure buildings accounted for 81% of all investigated buildings. This kind of structure suffered heavy damage: 63% of them completely or partially collapsed.

6.2.5 Boudhanath Stupa

Bouddhanath Stupa の損傷は軽微であった．Photo 6.2.5-1 に被害状況を示す．

周辺地盤に対して，水平 2 成分，鉛直 1 成分の常時微動計測を行った．計測には速度計を用いた．寺院西側付近の敷地の地盤で常時微動計測を行った．H/V スペクトルを Figure 6.2.5-1 に示す．NS, EW 共に 1Hz 未満での卓越が見られた．

(a) Overview　　　　　　　　　(b) Slight damage to masonry structure on dome

Photo 6.2.5-1 Damage to Bouddhanath stupa

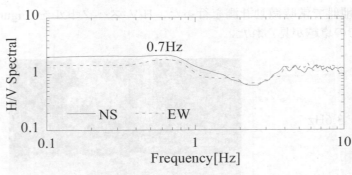 

Figure 6.2.5-1 H/V spectrum at Boudhanath Stupa

Damage to Bouddhanath Stupa was slight. Photo 6.2.5-1 shows the damage conditions.

A velocity sensor that could measure one vertical component and two horizontal components was used for a microtremor measurement. Figure 6.2.5-1 shows the resultant H/V spectra for the NS and EW directions at the northern ground of Stupa. The natural frequencies were below 1 Hz for both directions.

6.2.6 Pashupatinath Hindu Temple

Pashupatinath Temple は，ヒンズー教の寺院である．その中核部分にはヒンズー教徒のみ入場可能であり，近づけなかったが，Photo 6.2.6-1 に示す離れた高台からの観察より大きな損傷は見られなかった．同世界文化遺産で調査した 9 棟の建物および色分けして被災度区分判定の結果を Figure 6.2.6-1 に示す．Figure 6.2.6-2 に調査した建物に基づいて算出した被害率を示す．

Photo 6.2.6-1 Main building of Pashupatinath temple

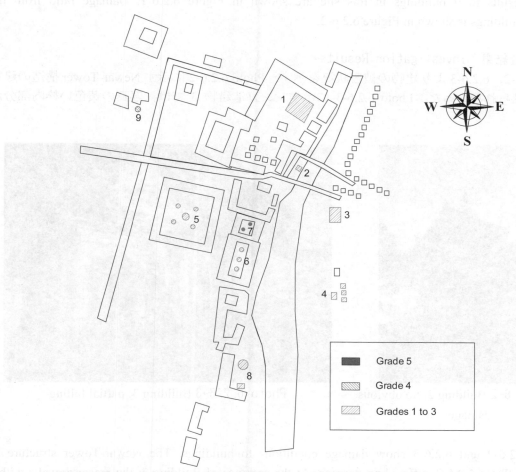

Figure 6.2.6-1 Site plan and damage classification of the investigated buildings

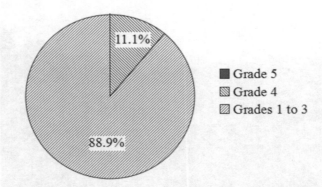

Figure 6.2.6-2 Damage ratio of investigated buildings

Pashupatinath Temple is a Hindu temple. Entry to the core area is not permitted except for Hindus. Observed from a nearby hill, as shown in Photo 6.2.6-1, no obvious damage was found. The damage assessment results to 9 buildings in this site are shown in Figure 6.2.6-1. Damage ratio from the investigated buildings is shown in Figure 6.2.6-2.

6.2.6.1 調査結果/ Investigation Results

Photo 6.2.6-2, 6.2.6-3 より建物の被害状況を示す．Photo 6.2.6-2 に示す Newar-Tower 構造の建物 2 に損傷は見られなかった．Photo 6.2.6-3 に示すレンガ造建物 3 では，写真の黄色い枠内部分が崩壊した．

Photo 6.2.6-2 Building 2: no obvious damage

Photo 6.2.6-3 Building 3: partial falling

Photos 6.2.6-2 and 6.2.6-3 show damage conditions to buildings. The Newar-Tower structure of Building 2 in Photo 6.2.6-2 suffered no damage. At the entrance of Building 3, the masonry walls within the yellow circle in Photo 6.2.6-3 collapsed.

6.2.6.2 地盤の常時微動計測結果/ Microtremor Measurement Results on the Site

周辺地盤に対して，水平 2 成分，鉛直 1 成分の常時微動計測を行った．計測には速度計を用いた．

寺院西側付近の敷地の地盤で常時微動計測を行った．H/V スペクトルを Figure 6.2.6-3 に示す．NS, EW 共に約 3.4Hz での卓越が見られた．

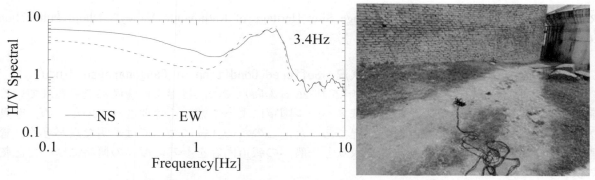

Figure 6.2.6-3 H/V spectrum at Pashupatinath Hindu Temple

A velocity sensor that could measure one vertical component and two horizontal components was used. Figure 6.2.6-3 shows the resultant H/V spectra for the NS and EW directions near Building 1. The natural frequencies were about 3.4 Hz for both directions.

6.2.6.3 まとめ/ Summaries

Pashupatinath Temple の被害は小さかった.

Damage to buildings in Pashupatinath Temple site was slight.

6.2.7 Changunarayan Hindu Temple
6.2.7.1 チャングナラヤン寺院の概要/ Outlines

　チャングナラヤン寺院は，バクタプールから約 6km，カトマンズからは約 22km 離れた，海抜にして 1540m の丘の上に建てられている．この二重屋根を持つ寺院はナラヤンの化身であるビシュヌ神に捧げられたものであり，複数の腕をもつタントラ神が浮き彫りされた精緻な屋根の支柱を持つ建物である．Licchavi 時代に建造されたネパール最古の寺院であると信じられている．
　いつ，どのようにしてこの寺院が今ある場所に現れたのかについては確たる証拠はないが，古の書物に紀元前 6 世紀以前にこの寺院が建てられたことが書かれていたとされている．すなわち，この建物は紀元前 521 年の Licchavi King Mandev の時代に「Bijay Stambha」が建立したとする説がもっとも有力である．ここを訪れるものは，両側にそれぞれ異なった古美術品を売る手工芸品店が建ち並ぶ通りをバス停を基点に 300m ほど歩くことになる．この同じ通り沿いには古の発掘品を観察することのできるチャング博物館も立地する.
　(参考："Introduction of World Heritage Site: Heritage of Kathmandu Valley", Dhoju Publication House, pp.61）

Among seven world heritage sites declared by the UNESCO in the Kathmandu Valley, Changu Narayan Temple is one of them. It lies on a hilltop approximately 6 km north of Bhaktapur and 22 km from Kathmandu. It lies at an altitude of 1540 meters from the mean sea level. This double-roofed temple is dedicated to Vishnu in his incarnation as Narayan and is exceptionally beautiful, with amazingly intricate roof struts depicting multi-armed Tantric deities. It is believed to be constructed during the Licchavi period and is regarded as the oldest temple in Nepal. There is no authentic information about when and how this temple came into existence nevertheless the popular belief says that the temple was built before 6th century BC as recorded in ancient inscription. This is best exemplified 'Bijay Stambha' built at the time of Licchavi King Mandev in 521 BS. One needs to walk a distance of 300 meter to reach the temple premises from the bus park and there are many handicraft shops selling different antique items on either side of the road. There is also a Changu Museum to observe ancient archeological items on the same path.

(Reference: "Introduction of World Heritage Site: Heritage of Kathmandu Valley", Dhoju Publication House, pp.61)

6.2.7.2 チャングナラヤン寺院の被害状況/ Suffered Condition of Cangunarayan Hindu

われわれ調査団が現地を訪れた 2015 年 5 月 26 日の時点では，世界文化遺産に登録されている寺院の敷地内部にある本堂とその周辺はネパール国軍によって厳しく管理されていたため，写真の撮影や近寄っての確認ができない状況であった．このため詳細については不明な点が多く，管理をしていた軍人に対する簡単な聞き取りと一般への報道内容を参考に被害の概略について記載する．

山頂の寺院へと繋がる参道は階段の多いほぼ 1 本道になっている．伝統的な民家が建ち並ぶ参道には多くの手工芸品店やみやげ物店，飲食店などが建ち並んでいたが，歴史ある参道の建物の多くが地震によって被害を受けおり（Photo 6.2.7-1），日干しレンガと泥モルタルで作られた一部の建物が倒壊した瓦礫は，参道を塞ぐ状況にまでなっていた（Photo 6.2.7-2）．

寺院の周囲は僧院によって取り囲まれており，これらの僧院も甚大な被害を受けていた．4 月 25 日の本震で一部崩壊が起こり，5 月 12 日の余震で傷んでいた部分が完全に崩壊したとのことである（Photo 6.2.7-3）．

現在の寺院そのものは 1700 年代に再建された建物であるが，ヒンズー教の特徴を色濃く表現した二重屋根を持つパゴダ（Pagoda）形式である．木造のフレーム構造を持ち，フレームの開口部はレンガによって充填される複合構造になっている．木造部が垂直荷重を伝え，レンガ造部も垂直荷重を伝えるとともに水平力を支える役割を果たしていると思われる．

本殿建物については，遠方より一見する範囲では大きな被害は認められなかったが（写真撮影不可），建物周囲から無数のサポートが斜めにかけられていた．これらは建物を正立させ余震に備えるための処置とのことであった．

この寺院と同様の建築形式を持つ他の例を参考にすると，地震によって建物全体の倒壊は免れたものの，木造フレームに囲まれたレンガ壁にひび割れや剥落，一部崩壊が起こってフレームと壁の間に隙間が生じてしまったために水平力に対する抵抗力が減少し（Photo 6.2.7-4），余震に対してこの水平力を補助する必要からサポートで横から支えているものと考えられる．チャングナラヤン寺院の場合，これらの支柱は建物外部からだけではなく，内側からも同様に架けられているとの説明であった．

境内となる本堂周囲の屋外空間では，軍が崩落した部材の整理と管理を行っており，民間人の避難者等の姿は見られなかった．

Photo 6.2.7-1 Damaged building along approach

Photo 6.2.7-2 Debris on approach

Photo 6.2.7-3 Partially damaged exterior wall of monastery

Photo 6.2.7-4 Damage to buildings in Patan Durbar Square

In 26th May 2015 when we arrived at the site, it was difficult to make research in detail and take photos of main temple because of guarding by army. Therefore, you should remind that the contents of this report are limited with possible information from interview research to soldiers and published news in websites.

The main approach route connecting to the mountain top temple is only one with many stairs. Before the earthquake, there were many traditional buildings used as handcraft and souvenir shops, hotels or restaurants. But because of serious damage by the earthquake (Photo 6.2.7-1), some parts of road were blocked by debris from old masonry buildings with dried bricks and mud mortal (Photo 6.2.7-2).

There are series of monasteries surrounding the main pagoda and they also got serious damage. The parts of buildings were damaged by the first shock in 25th April, and these part were totally collapsed by the aftershock in 12th May (Photo 6.2.7-3).

The main temple is two stories pagoda with Hindu style which was rebuilt in 1700s. This building has hybrid structure of wooden timber frame and brick walls which are filled up the face surrounded by wooden timber. It seems that the vertical weight was mainly supported by wooden timber and horizontal shock was mainly supported by brick wall in the same time. Main pagoda was prohibited to be researched in detail but we could see that many scaffoldings from every direction were set for keeping the building shape in the right way against aftershocks.

Referring the architectural style of similar other temples, earthquake shock made damages to brick wall surrounded by frames, and made gaps between walls and frames. Originally, combination of flames and walls can bring forth of shock proof performance, but once it has gaps because of damage in walls, the whole building loses the needed shock proof performance (Photo 6.2.7-4). The main pagoda looked not so seriously got damage from exterior view, but the soldier said that it needed support with many scaffoldings not only from outside but also from inside of buildings for preparation of aftershocks.

In the case of Changunarayan Hindu Temple, the open space around the main pagoda was guarded by the army, and it didn't used as evacuation spaces for local peoples one month after the main shock.

6.2.7.3 復興へ向けて想定される課題/ The Possible Challenges for Rehabilitation

前述のように，一見すると本殿そのものはレンガ壁に隙間が開いたりしてはいるものの倒壊を免れており，遠目には大きな被害を受けたようには見えないが，構造上のポイントとして，木造

フレームの壁面内がレンガなどで隙間なく充填されることによってはじめて水平方向の耐力が発現できる形式であるため，元通りの耐力を発現させるためには，理想的には一度すべてを解体して，レンガ壁と木造フレームを隙間なく組み直す必要がある．

さらに詳しい調査が必要だが，一部のレンガ壁を崩すだけの力が全体に加わっているために，木造フレーム部分自体にもジョイント部などに損傷がある可能性があり，その場合は緻密な彫刻が施された部材そのものを入れ替える必要も出てくる．伝統的なネワール様式の彫刻を施すことのできる職人は減り続けているとも言われており，解体と再構築に必要な高額なコストと職人の確保という大きな課題を抱えている．

The main pagoda seems to be needed the reconstruction after total disassembly of frames and brick walls, for getting back the shock proof performance, at least same to the original condition.

And if the joint of masonry members also got some damages because of strong stress which could break even in the brick walls, the wooden members with detailed carving should be replaced. The number of well-trained craftsmen who can rebuild the wooden parts with traditional "Newar" style is reducing now, so it will have serious challenges for taking much time and money, and continuing the traditional cultural values.

6.2.7.4 地盤の常時微動計測結果/ Microtremor Measurement Results on the Site

周辺地盤に対して，水平2成分，鉛直1成分の常時微動計測を行った．計測には速度計を用いた．

チャングナラヤン寺院の敷地裏手西側の地盤で常時微動計測を実施した．H/V スペクトルを Figure 6.2.7-1 に示す．NS, EW 共に約 2.4Hz での卓越が見られた．

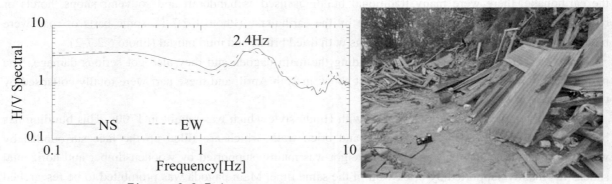

Figure 6.2.7-1 H/V spectrum at Changunarayan Hindu Temple

A velocity sensor that could measure one vertical component and two horizontal components was used. Figure 6.2.7-1 shows the resultant H/V spectra for the NS and EW directions at the western ground of the site. The natural frequencies were about 2.4 Hz for both directions.

6.3 世界文化遺産の周辺地域の被害/ Suffered Condition of Residents' Area Surrounding World Heritages

6.3.1 Patan Durbar Square の周辺住区の被害/ Suffered Condition of Residents' Area Surrounding Patan Durbar Square

6.3.1.1 パタン・ダルバール・スクエア周辺住区の被害状況/ The Suffered Condtion

今回の緊急調査においては，当該の周辺住区の中でも(1)ジャタプル（Jhatapol）地区，(2)ナグバハル（Nagbahal）地区，(3)イラナニ（Iranani）地区の一部のみを調査するに留まった．周辺住区全般については，言及できる状況にないことを補足する．

The research in this time was limited within parts of (1) Jhatapol District, (2) Nagbahal District and (3) Iranani District, so as that please remind that these outcomes written in below don't explain about regular conditions in all districts in Patan area.

(1) ジャタプル(Jhatapol)地区の被害状況/ The Condition of Jhatapol District

この地区の調査においては，立命館大学歴史都市防災研究センター（現，歴史都市防災研究所）が，京都大学，ネパール・トリブバン大学と協働し，震災の前から実施していた，立命館大学GCOE カトマンズプロジェクトの研究成果および研究データを活用した．これに含まれる詳細地図を参考に今回の悉皆調査を実施している．

上記のプロジェクトで地震の前に詳細調査を行った 91 棟の建物を対象に，EMS-98[5.2.2-1)]判定法より被災度区分判定を行った．Figure 6.3.1-1 に建物に番号を付けた調査地域の地図を示す．Figure 6.3.1-1 および Photo 6.3.1-1（撮影方向は Figure 6.3.1-1 に示す）に示すように，同地域の建物は独立ではなく，隣棟と近接または一体的に建てられたものが多い．

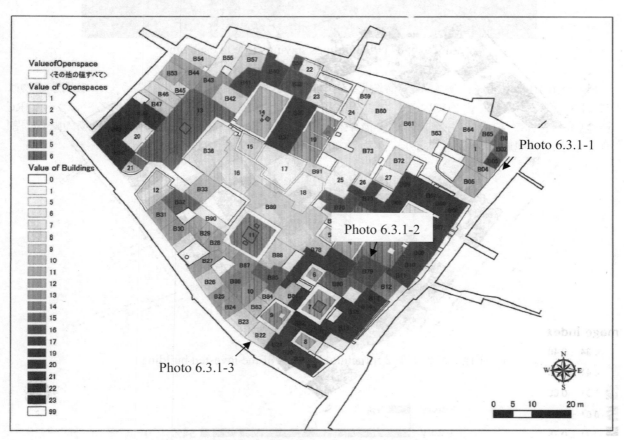

Figure 6.3.1-1 Site plan of the investigated region

Photo 6.3.1-1 Buildings staying close to each other

　Figure 6.3.1-2 に調査した建物の構造形式の割合を示す．全 91 棟の建物のうち，組積造建物は 77 棟で全体の 85%を占めている．なお，組積造建物はすべて焼成レンガ造である．ほかに，RC 造建物は 14%の 13 棟，トラス構造建物 1 棟であった．Figure 6.3.1-3 に調査した建物の階数の割合を示す．同地域は市街地であり，建物の 80%が 4 階建て以上である．

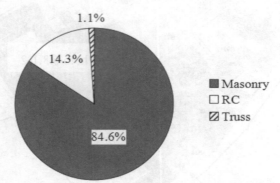

Figure 6.3.1-2 Structural systems of the invested buildings

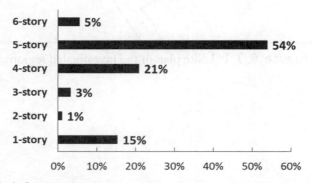

Figure 6.3.1-3 Distribution on number of stories of the investigated buildings

Figure 6.3.1-4 に調査した建物全体の被害率を示す．同図に示すように，Grade 5 の全壊した建物はなかった．Grade 4 の半壊した建物が 15%であった．以下に建物の構造形式，築年数，増築の有無の視点から建物の被害状況を分析する．

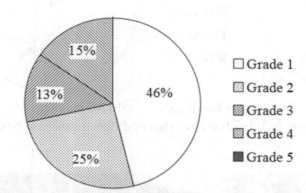

Figure 6.3.1-4 Damage ratio of all the investigated buildings

For the damage research of all buildings in this district, we used detailed maps from the outcomes in 2011 by Research Center for Disaster Mitigation of Urban Cultural heritage, Ritsumeikan University (Recent name is Institute of Disaster Mitigation for Urban Cultural Heritage) with Kyoto University and Tribhuvan University in Nepal.

In this study, post-earthquake damage evaluation by EMS-98[5.2.2-1)] was applied to 91 buildings which were investigated aforementioned project. Figure 6.3.1-1 shows map of investigated buildings. The numbers on the map represent id of buildings. The buildings in this area were built with adjacent buildings not independent as shown in Figure 6.3.1-1 and photo 6.3.1.-1.

Figure 6.3.1-2 shows the proportion in structural systems. In 91 buildings, 85% of 77 ones were masonry buildings. In addition, all the masonry buildings were made of bricks. 14% of 13 buildings were RC structure. Figure 6.3.1-3 shows the proportion in number of stories. 80% of the buildings were of four or more stories.

Fig 6.3.1-4 shows damage ratio of all the investigated buildings. There are no collapsed buildings classified into Grade 5 but 15% buildings of Grade 4 collapsed half. In the following, damage to the buildings is analyzed in terms of structural system, building age and extension history.

(a) 構造形式/ Structural System

Figure 6.3.1-5 に構造形式別の被害率を示す．同図に示すように，組積造建物の被害が RC 造建物より大きかった．Photo 6.3.1-2 に組積造建物の被害例として建物 79 を示す．東北側の壁に大きなひび割れが発生し，面外への傾きが見られた．また，建物の倒壊を防ぐために，木材を使って壁を支持していた．Photo 6.3.1-3 に RC 造建物 22 の被害状況を示す．柱のかぶりコンクリートが剥落し，主筋が露出していた．同建物にこれを除く損傷は見られなかった．

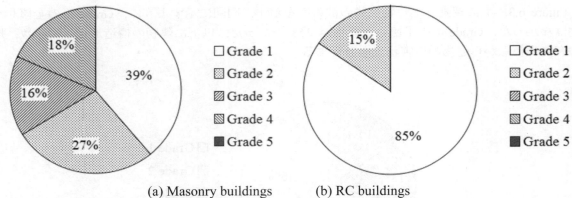

(a) Masonry buildings (b) RC buildings
Figure 6.3.1-5 Damage ratios of different structural types

Photo 6.3.1-2 Damage to masonry structures: Building 79 (Grade 4)

Photo 6.3.1-3 Damage to RC structures: Building 22 (Grade 2)

Figure 6.3.1-5 compares the damage ratios among the structural systems. As shown in the figure, damage to masonry buildings was more severe than that to RC buildings. Photo 6.3.1-2 shows an example of damage to masonry Building 79. A large crack appeared in the northeast wall due to out-of-plane tilting of the orthogonal wall was observed. To prevent collapse of the building, timber supports were installed around the building. Photo 6.3.1-3 shows limited damage to an RC building: cover concrete of a column spalled and the longitudinal rebar exposed. In this building, no other damage was observed.

(b) 築年数/ Building age

調査した建物の築年数を 80 年超，30〜80 年，30 年未満の 3 段階に分け，各段階の割合を Figure 6.3.1-6 に示す．同図より，80 年前に建設された建物が一番多い 42%を占めている．Figure 6.3.1-7 に建設年代別の各構造形式の割合を示す．築年数が浅い建物ほど RC 造建物の割合が大きくなる傾向が見られる．Figure 6.3.1-8 に年代別の建物の被害率を示す．同図より，古い建物の被害率が高いことがわかる．

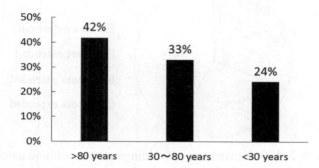

Figure 6.3.1-6 Building ages of the investigated buildings

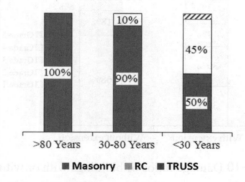

Figure 6.3.1-7 Structural systems for every building age

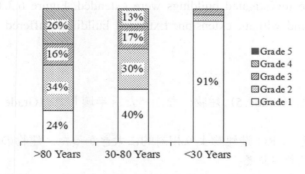

Figure 6.3.1-8 Damage ratios for every building age

The investigated buildings were classified into three periods by building ages: more than 80 years, 30 to 80 years, and less than 30 years. The proportion of number of buildings constructed in every period is shown in Figure 6.3.1-6. Buildings with building age of more than 80 years accounted for the highest ratio of 42%. Figure 6.3.1-7 shows the proportion of applied structural systems in each period, which indicates that more RC buildings have been constructed in recent years. Figure 6.3.1-8 presents the damage ratios of the buildings in every building age. The older buildings suffered more severe damage.

(c) 増築の有無/ Extension History

同地域では建物の増築事例がよく見られた．Figure 6.3.1-9 に建物の増築状況を示す．同図より，58%の建物が増築されていた．Figure 6.3.1-10 に増築有，無別の建物の被害率を示す．増築された建物は，明らかに増築なし建物より被害率が高いことがわかる．

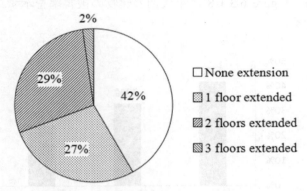

Figure 6.3.1-9 Distribution of buildings with or without extension

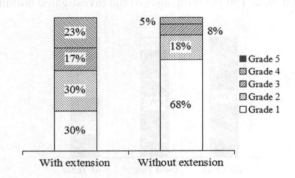

Figure 6.3.1-10 Damage ratios of buildings with or without extension

In this area, extension of buildings was commonly seen. Figure 6.3.1-9 shows the conditions related to the extension. 58% of the investigated buildings were extended. Figure 6.3.1-10 compares the damage ratios of buildings with and without extension. Extended buildings suffered heavier damage than non-extended ones.

(d) まとめ/ Summaries
1. 同地域では倒壊した（Grade 5）建物はなかった．半壊した（Grade 4）建物の割合は 15% であった．
2. 組積造建物の被害率は RC 造建物より相対的に大きかった．建物の構造形式が被害率に与える影響は大きいと判断される．
3. 古い建物ほど被害率が大きい傾向が得られた．長寿命建物の維持管理が歴史都市の地震防災上重要であることを示唆している．
4. 同地域では，増築された建物が調査した建物全体の 58% に達し，増築された建物の被害率は増築がない建物より大きかった．

なお，上述の立命館大学 GCOE カトマンズプロジェクトにおいて 2011 年に実施した各建物の調査結果に含まれる被災前の写真と，今回の現地での同一カ所の被災状況とを比較する範囲では，

地震による影響により，被災前から存在していたひび割れが広がっていたり新たにひび割れが入ったりした建物が散見された（Photo 6.3.1-4）．

しかし一方で，特に両側側面が他の建物に接しているような立地の場合には，両側の建物が相互に支え合い，地震によるひび割れの拡大が抑制されたと思われるケースも存在した（Photo 6.3.1-5）．ただし，この現象の解明についてはさらなる詳細調査が必要である．

Photo 6.3.1-4 Crack opening on masonry wall　　Photo 6.3.1-5 Possible effects of adjoining buildings on crack opening

1. In this area, no building completely collapsed (Grade 5). Fifteen percentage of the buildings partially collapsed (Grade 4).
2. Masonry buildings suffered heavier damage than RC ones. It seemed that the structural system of buildings had significant impact to their damage ratio.
3. Older buildings suffered heavier damage, indicating the importance of management for long life buildings in earthquake disaster prevention of historic urban cities.
4. In this area, extended buildings accounted for 58% of the investigated ones. Damage to the extended buildings was higher than that to non-extended ones.

And we found many cases of buildings which have new or wider cracks than the before from the comparison of photographs in between 2011 by the Kathmandu Project in Ritsumeikan GCOE program and 2015 by this research (Photo 6.3.1-4).

On the other hand, especially in some cases of buildings pinched by other buildings from both sides, these cracks in the buildings' wall didn't grow than the before (Photo 6.3.1-5). But for understanding this phenomenon, more detailed research must be needed.

(2) ナグバハル（Nagbahal）地区の被害状況/ The Condition of Nagbahal District
当該地区はパタン旧市街地内でも最大規模クラスの広場（square, courtyard）に面しており，ヒッティ（Hiti）と呼ばれる伝統的な共同水場を持つコミュニティ地区である（Photo 6.3.1-6）．

広場側から広場に面した建物群を目視で観察した範囲では倒壊した建物は見られなかったが，一部の建物では，支柱により広場側から建物ファサードを支えることで，余震に備えるべく応急的に補強の施された建物も見られた（Photo 6.3.1-7）．

Photo 6.3.1-6 Hiti in Nagbahal square

Photo 6.3.1-7 Damaged building temporarily supported

広場に面した範囲では，倒壊に至る深刻な建物被害はなかったにもかかわらず，多くの住民が屋外または建物1階で生活をしていた．伝統的な生活形態では建物は上階ほど清浄な場所と考えられているため，主に最上階にリビングが置かれて普段はそこで生活することが一般的である．しかし今回聞取りした範囲では，地震発生以降1か月を経た調査時点においても無数に体感できる余震があるため，住民は常に大きな余震を恐れて暮らしているとのことであった．このため日中は屋外の広場や何時でも逃げ出すことのできる建物1階部分で生活し（Photo 6.3.1-8），夜間は広場の中央にある小さな寺院とパティ（Pati：屋根のあるコミュニティの集会所）をとりまく緑地公園のエリアに常設したテントで寝泊まりをしているとのことである（Photo 6.3.1-9）．

Photo 6.3.1-8 Residents outside residences

Photo 6.3.1-9 Camping in communitiy park

震災直後は，この緑地公園部分のみならずレンガで舗装された通路を含む広場全体にテントを仮設して，建物には極力立ち入らないようにしてテントを中心に生活していたとのことであり，調査時点の直前まで広場はテントで一杯になっていたため，時には交通や生活の障害にもなっていたが，おおむね1か月を機に就寝時のみテントで眠る方針に変更し，テントの数を集約して広場の機能を回復させたとのことである．

水の確保については，震災以前には水道や海外からの支援を得て再整備されたヒッティ（伝統的な共同の水場）を水源として生活しており，さらにコミュニティ独自の工夫により，揚水ポン

プを介してヒッティから常に一定量をタンクに貯留できるシステムを構築していた（Photo 6.3.1-10）.

このため，震災後の一定期間のみは停電のためにポンプが機能せずに人力で水を汲み上げて利用していたが，電源復旧後はシステムを修理してタンクから簡易水道のようにヒッティの水が利用できているとのことであった．水道が機能しない状況下でも伝統的な共同の水場であるヒッティがあったお陰で水に困らずに避難生活を送ることができているとのことである．

伝統的で文化的なコミュニティ活動の核となっている歴史ある広場空間と水場空間とが，震災後にもコミュニティの安全と生活を支える重要な要素として，機能し続けていることを確認することができた．

Photo 6.3.1-10 Community water supply

The Nagbahal district is a community area facing one of the largest courtyards within the old city of Patan and having traditional water supply facility named "Hiti" in the courtyard (Photo 6.3.1-6).

There looked to be no collapsed building but surface of a few buildings were supported by scaffoldings for preparation of aftershocks (Photo 6.3.1-7).

Most of dwellers in houses facing the courtyard were living in outdoor or only in ground floor in day time, in spite of no serious damage in their houses. They believe that the rooms in upper floor are more sacred place than in lower floor. Because of that, they mainly spend time at the living room in top floor for usual life style. Although, still now as one month after the earthquake, they have been able to feel many aftershocks and that situation kept the most of people living in ground floor in day time (Photo 6.3.1-8) and sleeping in tents at the courtyard surrounding small temple and "Pati" as roofed community space in night time (Photo 6.3.1-9).

Right after the earthquake, they said that most of people were living in tents using all the space of courtyard including brick pavement space. But sometimes those spaces with full of tents made traffic problems, so they decided to change the space for tents in minimum size and revive the original function of courtyard, one month after the earthquake.

For seeking life water, they were using water resource from traditional water place (Hiti) which was revived by the support of United States before the earthquake, and it was already modified with outer additional reservoir by their community members (Photo 6.3.1-10).

Because of that, they have been able to use the water resource continuously, even after the disaster which made serious damage in the city water systems.

The fact was shown that these historic courtyard and water place as the important core elements for traditional community activities were also utilized as important resources for saving peoples' life even after the disaster.

(3) イラナニ (Iranani) 地区の被害状況/ The Condition of Iranani District

当該地区は，上記のナグバハル地区の南側に隣接する，およそ半分の面積を持つ広場に面したコミュニティを有する地区であり，広場の一角に共有の井戸（Photo 6.3.1-11）と小さなパティを持つ地区である．さらに広場の南側が「Golden Temple」と呼ばれる著名なヒンズー寺院に隣接しており（Photo 6.3.1-12），北西角部にも別の僧院を擁しており，住民の多くが宗教的なつながりを持ってコミュニティが構成されている．

Photo 6.3.1-11 Community well   Photo 6.3.1-12 Golden temple with minor damage to roof

この地区についても，基本的には上記のナグバハル地区と同様に夜間は広場の一角に集約したテントで生活しており，日中もパティの周囲にタープを張って日陰を作り，素早く避難することが困難な高齢者を中心として，広場を拠点に生活を送っていた（Photo 6.3.1-13）．

生活のための水源についても，伝統的な井戸水を利用して従前と変わらずに給水ができているとのことであった．

Photo 6.3.1-13 Pati in Iranani square

This district is occupied by community people facing a courtyard with half area of Nagbahal, and has public underground well (Photo 6.3.1-11) and small "Pati" in the courtyard. The south side of courtyard is facing the popular Hindu temple called "Golden Temple" (Photo 6.3.1-12) and north side is facing another monastery because of religious community relationship.

In the case of this district, most of dwellers and especially elder persons who were difficult to quick evacuate were living in the courtyard with tents for night time and tarp surrounding the "Pati" for day time (Photo 6.3.1-13), same to the condition of Nagbahal District. For securing life water, traditional water supply as underground well could be utilized same to the condition before the earthquake.

6.3.1.2 パタン市の歴史的建物の被害と微動測定結果/ Damage and Vibration Characteristics of Heritage Structures in Patan

(1) 地震以前の建物の振動測定調査/ Outline of Survey

2009 年 9 月 16〜18 日に，トリブバン大学（IOE），NSET（National Safety for Earthquake Technology - Nepal）の協力を得て，パタン市内の Rhada Krishna Temple 三重塔（1668 年建設，1992 改修 [6.3-1]），Kumbeswar Temple 五重塔，4 階建ての木造住宅（Lalitpur Sattle）を対象とした微動測定を実施した．塔の構造は，壁が焼成レンガにマッドモルタル目地，小屋組，床と軸組の一部は木造の木骨レンガ造である．

Microtremor measurements of heritage structures before the earthquake were performed in September 16-18, 2009, in cooperation with Tribhuvan University and NSET. The measurement was operated on three-storied pagoda of Rhada Krishna Temple (constructed in 1668, restored in 1992)[6.3-1], five-storied pagoda of Kumbeswar Temple, and four-storied timber residential building of Lalitapur Sattle. Of those historical buildings, the pagodas were constructed by bricks with mud mortar joints and timber members.

In order to survey the damage due to the Gorkha Earthquake in 2015, the authors operated on-site inspection at the sites on August 10 to 14.

(2) 地震被害調査/ Survey Result

2015 年 8 月 10 日から 14 日にかけて前述の調査対象建物の被災状況を調査した．微動測定を実施した結果を地震被害と併せて Figure 6.3.1-11 に示す．三重塔は並進運動の固有振動数は EW, NS 方向でほぼ一致している．五重塔の並進運動固有振動数は図示した EW 方向と比べて NS 方向の方が高く，1 次 2.02Hz，2 次 4.50Hz，3 次 7.32Hz であったが，振動モード形はほぼ同じであった．Photo. 6.3.1-14 に示す 4 階建の木造住宅は，両側を組積造住宅建築に挟まれた構造であり，1 次固有振動数は 3.5Hz であった．

三重塔は 2015 年 4 月 25 日の本震で倒壊し，五重塔は，5 月 12 日余震により五重の部分が倒壊した．その後，倒壊した五重部分は解体され，四重までの構造が残されている．初重のレンガ壁には顕著な損傷は目視では確認されず人々が出入している．組積造に挟まれた木造中層住宅は外見無被害であったが，組積造部分はレンガ造壁に顕著な亀裂が発生し，構造修復が必要である．

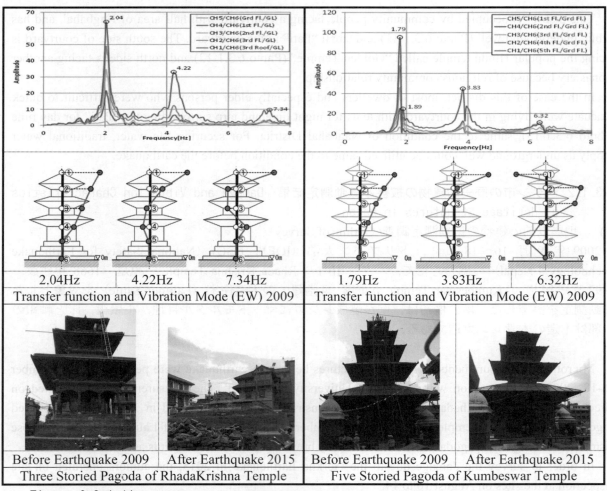

Figure 6.3.1-11 Fundamental dynamic characteristics of multi-storied pagodas before earthquake, compared with earthquake damage

(a) Before Earthquake September, 2009   (b) After Earthquake August, 2015
Photo 6.3.1-14 Multi storied wooden houses (Lalitapur Sattle) before and after earthquake

The fundamental dynamic characteristics given by the microtremor measurements of the pagodas are summarized in Figure 6.3.1-11 together with the pictures of before and after the earthquake. The 3-story pagoda of Rhada Krishna Temple, the natural frequencies of translational modes in EW direction was nearly equal to those in NS direction. On the other hand, the 5-storied pagoda of Kumbeswar Temple, the natural frequencies of translational modes in NS direction was higher than those in EW direction. The natural frequencies of translational modes in NS direction were 2.02Hz for 1st mode, 4.50Hz for 2nd mode, and 7.32Hz for 3rd mode. However, the vibration mode shapes in NS direction agreed with those in EW direction. The fundamental natural frequency of the traditional timber residential building shown in Photo. 6.3.1-14 was 3.5Hz. Shown in Photo 6.3.1-14, this timber residential building was combined with the both side masonry residential buildings.

From the result of the damage investigation, the 3-storied pagoda totally collapsed by the main shock of April 25. The 5-storied pagoda structurally survived against the main shock, but from the aftershock on 12th May the 5th (top) story collapsed and dismantled as shown in Figure 6.3.1-11, for the future reconstruction. But for the remaining structure, there were no visible cracks in the brick wall of the 1st story. Many people were seen to go inside to pray. At the timber residential building shown in Photo. 6.3.1-14, no damage was visible from the exterior. However, the side masonry residential building suffered serious damage. Structural cracks in need of repair were seen in the brick walls by the earthquake.

(3) まとめ/ Summaries

2009年にパタン市で実施した歴史的建物の微動調査の結果と，当該建物の被災状況を報告した．本調査のほか，世界文化遺産の塔等の微動調査が，BijayaJaishi ら [6.3-2]，Manjip SHAKYA ら [6.3-3]によってなされている．地震被災前の振動調査データは貴重であり，今後の被害原因の究明と再建および保存修復計画の検討に役立つことが期待される．

The report describes the results of microtremor measurements of heritage structures in Patan in 2009 and their damage by the earthquake. Similar research has been operated and reported by Bijaya Jaishi et al.[6.3-2] and Manjip SHAKYA et al.[6.3-3]. These data can be expected to be used for the restoration plan from an earthquake engineering point of view.

(4) 復興へ向けて想定される課題/ Challenges for the Recontruction of Historic Area

このように，上述の範囲においては，数々の文化遺産建物が倒壊してしまった王宮広場そのものの被害状況に比すれば，住居をはじめとする建物に関する倒壊被害はまだ少なかったものと思われる．その一方，一部の建物ではひび割れや部分的な損傷など（Photo 6.3.1-15），余震によりさらに被害が拡大する可能性を伴う深刻な状況にある．このため復興に向けて，将来の地震に対して安全が確保できるレベルにまで補修を行うためには，多くの時間と費用を要することが懸念される．

Photo 6.3.1-15 Partial collapse in the top story

Within the part of these research results, the number of collapsed buildings in residential areas seemed not so much than the case of heritage buildings in Durbar Square. Although, many residential buildings still had cracks and partly damages with serious risk of breaking down by continuous aftershocks (Photo 6.3.1-15). It is worried that it needs much money and time to rehabilitate all the buildings and to keep the safety against future earthquake.

6.3.2 Bhaktapur Durbar Square の周辺住区の被害/ Suffered Condition of Residents' Area Surrounding Bhaktapur Durbar Square

6.3.2.1 バクタプール・ダルバール・スクエア周辺住区の被害状況/ The Suffered Condition

今回の緊急調査においては，限られた時間の中で訪問できた範囲が限定されるため，周辺住区の記載内容については，普遍的なものではないことを補足する．

はじめに訪問できたのは，世界文化遺産地区の王宮広場へのメインアプローチから東側の住区である．近代に都市化されたと考えられ，RC 造の建物を多く含み，二車線の道路で区画されたエリアとなっていた．1 階部分を店舗に利用している建物の一部には，木製の支柱で応急的に外壁が支えられた例が見られた（Photo 6.3.2-1）．

次に訪問した世界文化遺産地区の西側から旧市街に入るルート上では，数多くのレンガ造の住居が被災しており，特に上階の壁面が屋根ごと崩壊している例が散見された（Photo 6.3.2-2）．道路幅員の狭い街路については，倒壊した建物のガレキによって道路全体が閉塞している場所もあり（Photo 6.3.2-3），手作業によるガレキ処理の作業が続けられていた．

総じて前述したパタン・ダルバール広場周辺よりも住区部分の被害の程度は大きいように見受けられ，震災後 1 か月を経てもなお瓦礫の撤去と清掃作業が続けられていた．

Photo 6.3.2-1 Exterior walls temporarily supported

Photo 6.3.2-2 Buildings suffering damage to the upper stories

Photo 6.3.2-3 Debris on narrow street

   The research in this time was limited within some parts of district, so as that please remind that these outcomes written in below don't explain about regular conditions in all the area of Bhaktapur.
The first investigated area was eastern part from the main approach route to the world cultural heritage site of Durbar Square. It seemed modern developed area with brocks of many RC buildings and wide roads with double road lanes. Parts of buildings which used the ground floors as shops were supported the facades by temporary wooden scaffoldings (Photo 6.3.2-1).
   On the western part along the route to the world cultural heritage site, many brick houses were damaged and some of buildings were collapsed especially at the upper floors' walls and roofs (Photo 6.3.2-2). Some narrow streets were completely blocked with debris (Photo 6.3.2-3). The damaged level looked more serious than the case of residential area around Patan Durbar Square, and the road cleaning works with peoples' hands were ongoing still one month after the earthquake.

6.3.2.2 復興へ向けて想定される課題/ Challenges for the Recontruction of Historic District

　調査できた範囲内においては，地震により継続使用が困難となった建物が1か月を経過した時点においても数多く残されており，危険建物の撤去や瓦礫の処理作業が市民の手でいまだ継続されている状況であった．一方で世界文化遺産地区を含む地域の住区については，国軍が動員されて組織的にガレキの撤去作業が行われたとのことで（Photo 6.3.2-4），応急対応の進捗にも大きな地域格差が見受けられた．

　一部で伝統的な歴史ある建物がすべてその古さのために被災したかのような報道があるが，実際には地震発生の以前からメンテナンスがゆき届いている場合は，古い建物であっても被害が少ない例も見られる（Photo 6.3.2-5）．文化財関係者によれば，それにもかかわらず風評被害によって歴史ある建物が見捨てられ，拙速にRC造の建物がもてはやされる社会的な傾向も生じているとのことであり，歴史的地域の復興のためには慎重な対応が求められるとの指摘がされていた．

　一方，現地の技術者によると，一般住宅では上層が増築された建物も多く，増築は何世代にもわたり進められることも珍しくないとのことである．その結果，建物の上層ほど新しい技術が取り入れられているが，下層が耐震性能の低い素材，技術により建設された建物も数多く見られた（Photo 6.3.2-6）．建物下層に対する配慮のない増築の危険性を住民が理解できる取組みを行うことも将来の地震に備える復興には不可欠な課題である．

Photo 6.3.2-4 Street cleared debris

Photo 6.3.2-5 Historic building suffering minor damage

Photo 6.3.2-6 Building extended vertically

Within the research area, many residential buildings which become impossible to use were still remained. On the other hand, the residential areas within the world cultural heritage site were already cleaned up by the systematic works of national army (Photo 6.3.2-4). There was qualitative difference in emergency correspondence between the areas in the world heritage site and outside.

There were less damaged old and historic buildings because of adequate maintenance (Photo 6.3.2-5), but most of journalism pointed out that all the historic buildings had vulnerabilities. Some heritage managers said that most of people believed the wrong information that old buildings were dangerous and only the new RC buildings could survive because of careless journalism. Careful responses were needed for rehabilitation of historic districts.

Local engineers pointed out the social problem that many buildings were added upper floors during many generations (Photo 6.3.2-6) and most of lower parts were built without structural consideration of additional weight. It must be indispensable for future to educate the local people for understanding the risk of additional upper building without any structural consideration.

6.3.3 Dharahara 塔の被害と再建へ向けて想定される課題/ Challenges for the Recontruction of Dharahara Tower

Kathmandu Durbar Square 周辺に立地する Dharahara 塔は 1835 年に創建された．この塔は，その後の 1934 年の地震により倒壊し，1936 年に再建されたが，今回の地震により再び倒壊した．再建後の塔は高さが約 60m の Brick-Shurkhi（Brick パウダーと石灰と籾殻の混合物）構造であった．

カトマンズの主要な観光資源の 1 つであったため，地震時にも多数の観光客が訪れており，60 人程度の犠牲者があったとのことである．過去の地震により繰り返し被害を受けている建物であり，将来の地震により同様の被害を繰り返さないため，再建にあたっては適切な耐震性能を確保し，人命の保護を優先する対策が望まれる．

Photo 6.3.3-1 Dharahara tower before the earthquakes
(Left: original and right: the second towers)

Photo 6.3.3-2 Collapased tower

Dharahara tower located close to Kathmandu Durbar Square was originally built in 1835. This tower has been reconstructed in 1936 after the collapse during the 1934 earthquake. However, it collapsed again by the latest main shock. The height and structural system of the last tower were approximately 60 m and Brick- Shurkhi (Shurkhi: mixture of brick powder, lime and rice husk) structure.

More than 60 persons died because the tower was one of the most major tourist attractions. Upgrading the seismic performance is necessary when it is rebuilt, not to repeat similar damage and loss of human lives.

6.3.4 謝辞/ Acknowledgements

The authors express sincere gratitude to Director Amod Dixit (NSET), Professor Jishnu Suberi (Tribhuvan University), Dr. Suman Rajbhandari (Nepal Engineering College), Dr. Narsingh Rajbhandari (Tribhuvan University), Mr. Radha (NSET), Dr. Hiroshi Imai, Members of Fujita Laboratory of the University of Tokyo: Dr. Shiro Watanabe, Dr. Ayako Maeshima, Mr. Hiroki Nakashima, Mr. Daichi Higashi and Mr. Takahiro Toyoda.

6.3.5 参考文献/ References

6.3-1) Timber Conservation Problems of the Nepali Pagoda Temple, R. Ranjitkar and E. Theophile, ICOMOS International Wood Committee (IIWC), 8th International Symposium ICOMOS, 1992

6.3-2) Bijaya Jaishi et al.: Dynamic and seismic performance of old multi-tiered temples in Nepal, Engineering Structures 25, ELSEVIER, pp1827-1839, 2003

6.3-3) Manjip SHAKYA et. al.: PREDICTIVE FORMULATION FOR THE ESTIMATION OF THE FUNDAMENTAL FREQUENCY OF SLENDER MASONRY STRUCTURES, Proc. of 2nd European Conference on Earthquake Engineering and Seismology, 2014

6.4 歴史都市の被害が示す教訓/ Lessons Learnt from the Damages in Historic Districts

6.4.1 7つの世界文化遺産において/ From the Cases of Seven World Curutural Heritage Sites

入場制限がなされた Changunarayan Hindu Temple を除く 6 つの世界文化遺産において，各敷地内の建物の被害状況を観察するとともに，EMS-98 判定法より被災度区分判定を行って，世界文化遺産で見られる建築の被害の傾向を分析した．Kathmandu Durbar Square, Patan Durbar Square ではネワール様式の多重塔建築（本報では Newar-Tower 構造と表記）の被害が顕著であった．一方，Bhaktapur Darbar Square, Swayambhunath Temple では組積造建築を中心に深刻な被害が見られた．調査を実施した 6 つの世界文化遺産の中で上記の 4 つの被害がとくに大きかった．Bhaktapur Durbar Square を除く上記世界文化遺産の敷地内で実施された常時微動計測結果は，Kathmandu Durbar Square, Patan Durbar Square では地盤の周期が相対的に長く，各敷地の地盤条件が建築物の被害の傾向に大きく影響した可能性を指摘できる．

必ずしも古い建物すべてに被害が集中したわけではなく，施工精度と維持管理が十分な場合には軽微な被害で済んでいる事例も見られた．担当の保存修復建築家によると，Patan の王宮建築では補修作業が完了した部分は倒壊を免れた一方で，予算が付かずに今後に補修予定だった場所のみ倒壊したとのことである．

Onsite investigations were performed in six World Cultural Heritage Sites except for Changunarayan Hindu Temple where entry was prohibited. Damage characteristics of several types of buildings in the heritage sites were investigated through the post-earthquake damage evaluation by EMS-98. Newar-Tower structures were severely damaged in Kathmandu Durbar Square and Patan Durbar Square. In contrast, Masonry structures suffered significant damage in Bhaktapur Durbar Square and Swayambhunath Temple. Heavy damage to heritage structures was observed particularly in the above four sites. Microtremor measurement results, conducted in Kathmandu Durbar Square, Patan Durbar Square, and Swayambhunath Temple, indicated that ground conditions (ground motion characteristics) might affect the different tendency in damaged structures observed in each heritage site.

There were less damaged old buildings with well accurate development and continuous maintenance. In the case of Patan Durbar Square, a conservation architect showed us the evidence that only the damaged part of palace building was not repaired before the earthquake because of limitation in budget.

6.4.2　2つの歴史地区において/ From the Cases of Two Histric Districts

現地の建築家によれば，被害の少なかった宮殿建築などについては，レンガ造の角部が開かぬようL字型木材（ナゴル：Naagol）を入れた上で木製の飾り帯で水平方向に縛る工夫や，レンガの粉末や籾殻などを配合した目地材（シルキ：Shurkhi）を使用し，奥にテーパーの付いたレンガを積むことで，十分な目地材を充填しつつ見た目の目地の細さを表現する手法など，伝統的な施工技術が採用されているとのことであるが，これらの伝統的技術の中には耐震上も有効な技術が含まれていると考えることもできる．

一般民家についてはバクタプールの被害が大きく，分棟形式で日干しレンガでできた建物に被害が集中しており，特に短辺側（多くは道路側）の壁面が面外に押し出されて倒壊した事例が多数見られた．

パタン歴史地区では，建物の細分化と高層化が進んでおり地震に対する危険性が高まっていた．一方で，個別の建物同士が隣接して連棟化していたためか，バクタプールより被害は軽微なケースが見受けられた．しかしながらそのような場合であってもひび割れが随所に見られるため，余震に対する対策は不可欠となっている．

歴史的な広場や水場も避難所など防災資源として利用されるなど，災害時にもコミュニティの活動を支える重要な役割を果たしており，これらの将来にわたる保全は防災上も大きな意味を持つと考えられる．

Local architects pointed out that less damaged palace buildings were built with traditional knowledge for shockproof performance. For example, L-shaped wooden parts called "Naggol" connecting two brick walls at the corner will be able to stabilize the weak point of brick buildings, and joint mortal called "Shurkhi" including brick powder, limestone and rice husks filled in between tapered bricks will be able to keep enough strength for fastening bricks. These traditional construction technologies are possible to be effective measures for shockproof performance.

There seemed to be serious damages in "separated or individual" residential buildings with dried mud bricks in Bhaktapur. Many buildings lost the facade walls with short width which seemed to be pushed toward outside because of earthquake shocks.

On the other side, the risks of buildings seemed to be increasing because of vertical addition and dividing housing lots, but some of "touching side by side" residential buildings seemed not to get serious damage because of mutual support by holding between neighbor buildings. Even in these cases, it must be needed to repair cracks for keeping safety in future.

Traditional and historic open spaces as "Squares" and water places as "Hitis" and public wells were supporting local evacuees' life and used as disaster mitigation resources for community activities. It must be very important to maintain and keep them for future generations not only for conservation of cultural value but also for disaster mitigation of historic districts.

7 人的被害/ Human Damage
7.1 はじめに/ Overall Human Casualty Conditions

2015年ネパール・ゴルカ地震（Mw 7.8）は，ネパール時間4月25日（土）午前11時56分に発生した．最大クラスの余震（Mw 7.3，震央はKodariから南東19km）が5月12日（火）ネパール時間の午後12時50分に発生し，さらに被害が拡大した．地震による被害はネパールだけでなく，周辺国のインド，中国（チベット），バングラディシュ等に広がっている．Table 7.1-1[7-1]に本震と最大余震（5月12日）による人的被害を示す．本稿では人的被害・住宅被害の統計資料を基に地理的分布や年齢，性別等の影響を検討し，建物被害との関係を考察する．

地震による人的被害は死者8,713人，負傷者22,493人，家屋全壊が505,577棟に達する（Table 7.1-2）（UN reliefweb サイト[7-2]より，2015年6月5日現在ネパール政府発表統計）．女性の割合が死者では55.2%と高く，負傷者では47.5%とやや低い．耐震性の低いレンガ造，日干しレンガ造が多数倒壊し，都市部で一部RC構造が倒壊し，多くの人的被害につながった．

Table 7.1-1 Numbers of human casualty in the main shock and the largest aftershock

	Nations	Apr. 25, 2015 Mainshock	May 12, 2015 Aftershock
Dead	Nepal	8471	218
	India	130 #1	62
	China	27	1
	Bangladesh	4	2
	Total	8632	283
Missing	Nepal	276 #2	
	China	3	
	Total	279	

#1: Jagran, Patna Daily #2: Nepal Police 19.05.2015

Update on 20.05.2015 (Source:[7-1])

http://earthquake-report.com/2015/04/25/massive-earthquake-nepal-on-april-25-2015/

Table 7.1-2 Total number of human loss and injury by sex (as of June 5, 2015 reported by Nepal government)

	Dead	Injured	Dead (%)	Injured (%)
Female	4808	10676	55.2	47.5
Male	3902	11544	44.8	51.3
Unknown	3	273	0.0	1.2
Total	8713	22493	100.0	100.0

The 2015 Gorkha, Nepal earthquake (Mw 7.8) occurred on Saturday, April 25, at 11:56 a.m. Nepali local time. The largest aftershock (Mw 7.3) occurred at 19km SE of Kodari on Tuesday, May 12 at 12:50 p.m. Nepali local time, causing more structural damages and human casualties. The human losses occurred not only in Nepal, but also in neighbouring countries of India, China (Tibet), and Bangladesh (Table 7.1-1).

Damage statistics for housing damages and human casualties were collected and emergency response of local municipalities for building damage inspectionsa were studied in relation to seismic building code enforcement. In this section, human casualty characteristics are investigated in regard to geographical distribution, age and sex distribution, relation with housing damage conditions based on damage statistics.

Nepal government reported total earthquake damage as 8,713 people killed, 22,493 people injured, 505,577 houses heavily damaged as of June 5, 2015 (Ref.: UN reliefweb[7-2]). Table 7.1-2 indicates sex breakdown of human loss and injury. Female share 55.2% majority of human loss, while they share 47.5% of injury, mainly due to the earthquake occurrence time during day time on Nepali holiday of Saturday, when more males tend to stay outdoors than females. Many rural houses of stone or adobe masonry with mud mortar were collapsed causing human losses. In urban area of Kathmandu valley, some RCC frame and infill brick buildings were collapsed causing human losses.

7.2 人的被害の統計および地理的分布 / Statistics of Human Casualty and Geographical Distribution

7.2.1 郡別の人的被害地理的分布 / District-wise Human Casualty Distribution

ネパール政府被害統計により，郡別の死者・負傷者数を Figure 7.2-1, 7.2-2 に示す．死者はカトマンズ盆地の東，山岳地帯にあるシンドパルチョーク (Sindhupalchok) 郡で 3,440 人に達して最大であり，死亡率も 1%を超えている．カトマンズ盆地のカトマンズ(Kathmandu)郡で 1,221 人，バクタプール (Bhaktapur) 郡で 333 人を数え，盆地の中では Bhaktapur 郡の家屋全壊率が高い．一方，負傷者数は Kathmandu 郡が 7,864 人と最大で，盆地内のラリトプール(Lalitpur)郡 3,052 人，Bhaktapur 郡 2,101 人と多く，都市部では病院施設が多く負傷者を治療したこと，郡部では病院が少ない上に被災して収容困難な状況となったことが推察される．

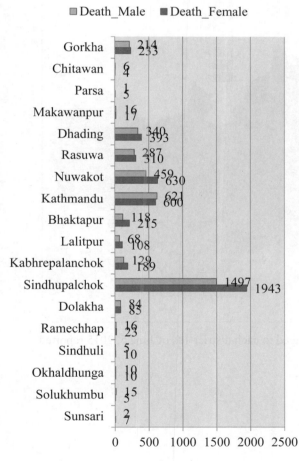

Figure 7.2-1 Number of human loss by districts and sex (as of June 5, 2015 reported by Nepal government)

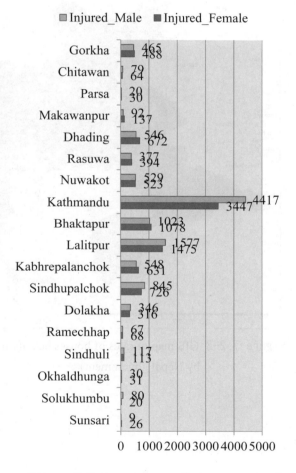

Figure 7.2-2 Number of injury by districts and sex (as of June 5, 2015 reported by Nepal government)

郡別の家屋全壊率と死亡率の地図を Figure 7.2-3, 7.2-4 に示す．家屋全壊率は山岳地帯のラスワ (Rasuwa) 郡から ヌワコット (Nuwakot) 郡，シンドルパルチョーク (Sindhupalchok)郡，ドラカ (Dolakha)郡まで東西 150km 以上にわたる地域が，50%を超えて激甚な被害となったことがわか

る．カトマンズ盆地の Kathmandu 郡，Bhaktapur 郡，Lalitpur 郡の中では Bhaktapur 郡の家屋全壊率が高い．死亡率については，北部山岳地帯の Sindhulpalchok 郡と Rasuwa 郡で死亡率 1%を越え，同じく山岳地帯のダーディング(Dhading)郡も死亡率が高い．カトマンズ盆地の Bhaktapur 郡，Kathmandu 郡，Lalitpur 郡で死亡率は 0.12%未満となっている．

　郡別の統計を基に，家屋全壊率と死亡率の XY プロットを Figure 7.2-5 に示す．Sindhupalchok 郡や Rasuwa 郡は家屋被害も 100%～80%と高く，死亡率が 1.2～1.4%に達する一方，全壊率が 100%でも死亡率がやや低い Nuwakot 郡や Dolakha 郡がある．東部で 5 月 12 日（火）正午すぎに最大クラス余震（Mw 7.3）があり，この余震震源に近い Dolakha 郡では余震で全壊した家屋が多く，テントや野外の仮設シェルターにいた住民の犠牲が少なかったことの影響かと思われる．ネパール政府の被害統計発表 [7-2)]によれば，Dolakha 郡の住家被害は，5 月 11 日付報告で全壊 5,000 戸，半壊 35,000 戸，6 月 5 日付報告で全壊 48,880 戸，半壊 3,120 戸と大幅に増加・悪化している．

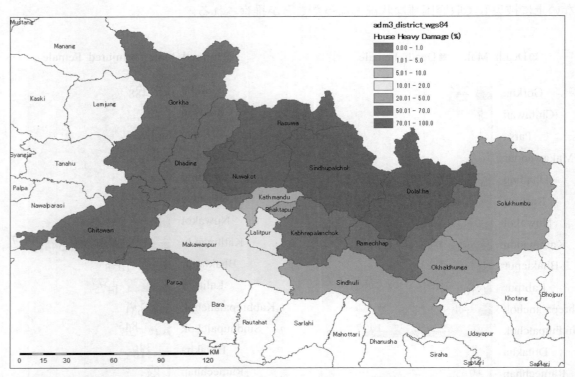

Figure 7.2-3　GIS map of rates of houses heavily damaged in each district (as of June 5, 2015 reported by Nepal government)

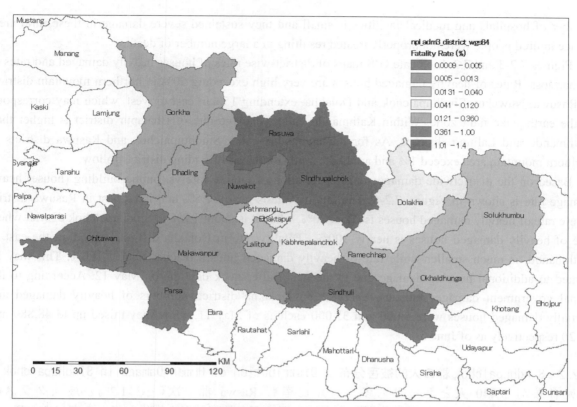

Figure 7.2-4 GIS map of human loss rates in each district (as of June 5, 2015 reported by Nepal government)

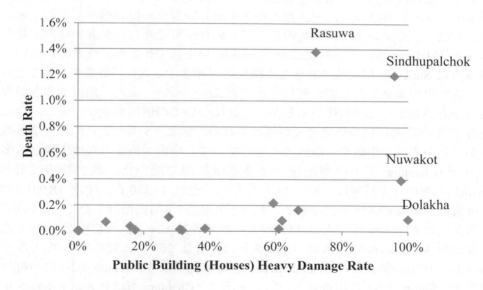

Figure 7.2-5 Relation of rate of houses heavily damaged and rate of human loss by district

Figure 7.2-1 indicates district-wise human loss and injury distribution by sex. As for the human loss, Sindhupalchok district sustained maximum number exceeding 3,400, while Kathmandu district is 1,221 human loss, Bhaktapur district is 333 human loss in metropolitan Kathmandu valley. In the valley, Bhaktapur district and the municipality sustained the heaviest housing and human loss compared to Kathmandu district, and Lalitpur district. As for the number of injury (Figure. 7.2-2), Kathmandu district counted maximum of 7,864, Lalitpur district did 3,052, and Bhaktapur district did 2,101 in the Valley. The number of hospitals and medical facilities is small and they sustained severe damage in these rural area. Hence injured people were not properly treated resulting in a large number of death.

Figures 7.2-3 and 7.2-4 indicate GIS maps of district-wise rates of houses heavily damaged and rates of human loss. Rates of heavily damaged houses are very high exceeding 50% in northern mountain districts of Rasuwa, Nuwakot, Sindhupalchok and Dolakha, extending 150km east to west, which may correspond to the earthquake fault zone. Within Kathmandu valley, damage rate of Bhatapur district is higher than Kathmandu and Lalitpur districts. As for human fatality rates, Sindhulpalchok and Rasuwa districts in northern mountain area exceed 1% and are higher and Gorkha and Dhading districts follow.

Based on the districtwide damage statistics, relation of fatality rate vs. public building (house) heavy damage rate is shown in Figure. 7.2-5. The fatality rate is nearly 1.5% and is highest in Rasuwa district where rate of heavily damaged houses is about 70%, while it is about 1.2% in Sindhupalchok district where rate of heavily damaged houses is nearly 100%. Fatality rate in Dolakha district located on the east of Kathmandu, is much smaller while rate of heavily damaged houses reaches almost 100%. This may be related to additional housing damage due to the major aftershock daytime on May 12. According to the Nepal government damage statistics report [7-2], in Dolakha district, numbers of heavily damaged and partially damaged houses were 5,000 and 35,000 each as of May 11, while they raised up to 48,880 and 3,120 respectively as of June 5.

7.2.2 Sindhupalchok 郡の人的被害分布 / Distribution of Human Damage in Sindhupalchok

死者数が 3,440 人ともっとも多く，死亡率も Raswa 郡に次いで 1.2%と最大クラスの Sindhupalchok 郡について，郡警察署から市町村別の死者数統計表を提供していただいた．Figure 7.2-6 の地図に市町村別死者率を棒グラフで，2011 年国勢調査による住宅壁材料のセメントモルタル・レンガまたは石積みの割合を茶色から緑の濃淡で示す．なお，この郡において，壁材料のセメントモルタル以外はほとんど，泥モルタルのレンガまたは石積みである．死亡率は郡の東部より西部で高く，セメントモルタルの割合が低い村や町で死亡率が高い傾向が見られる．また，メラムーチ（Melamuchi）市から北部の Sunkoshi 川上流で死亡率，死者数が高いことが目立つ．2014 年 8 月に Sunkoshi 川地域で大きな土砂災害（死者 156 人）[7-3]が発生したことの影響も考えられる．土砂災害の多発した北部の町村などで死亡率が高い．また，地震動強さが東部より震央に近い西部の方が強かった可能性があるが，これについての情報が少ないので，今後のアンケート震度調査 [7-4]や地震動評価の研究進展が期待される．また，5 月 12 日の最大余震は本震より揺れは小さかったが本震で中破や大破被害を受けていて，余震で倒壊した住宅建物も多いという話をチョータラ（Chautara）市での郡地域開発事務所訪問で聞いた．政府被害統計 [7-2]によれば，Sindhupalchok 郡の住家被害は，5 月 11 日付報告で全壊 44,310 戸，半壊 18,991 戸であったが，6 月 5 日付報告で全壊 63,885 戸，半壊 2,751 戸と全壊が 1.4 倍に増加したことがわかる．

郡庁所在地の Chautara 市（人口 15,606 人）は死者数 124 人，死亡率が 0.8%と比較的小さく，第二の都市の Melamuchi 市（人口 5,230 人）は死者数 264 人，死亡率 5.0%と高くなっている．2011 年人口・住宅国勢調査の Sindhupalchok 郡統計表 [7-5]より，Figure 7.2-7 に市町村別の家屋壁材料の割合を，Figure 7.2-8 に屋根材料の割合を示す．Chautara 市はセメントモルタルのレンガ組積造が多い一方，Melamuchi 市は泥モルタルのレンガ組積造が多く，死者数を多くした要因と考えられる．Figure 7.2-8 によれば屋根材料も，Chautara 市では瓦ぶき傾斜屋根と RCC（鉄筋コンクリート）屋根が多く，Melamuchi 市では波板トタン屋根が多く，Chautara の方が住宅の質が高いことがうかがわれる．

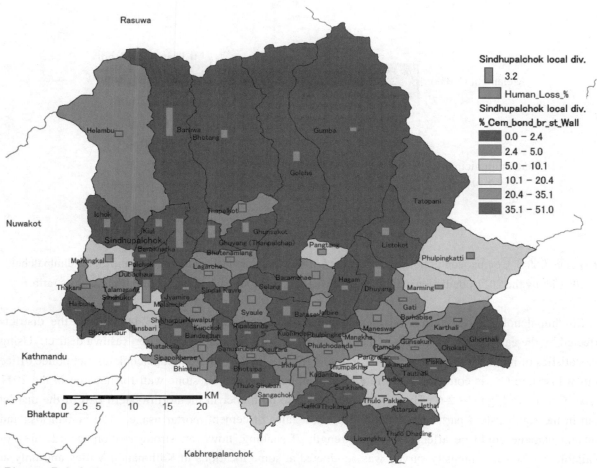

Figure 7.2-6 Human loss % in Sindhulpalchok district based on the district police statistics and % of cement mortar bonded brick or stone wall houses in Nepal census 2011.

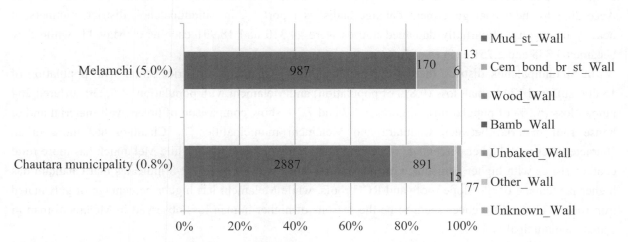

Figure 7.2-7 Comparison of house wall material in Melamchi and Chautara municipalities, Sindhulpalchok district by the 2011 population and housing sensus. (Percent for each municipality is human loss ratio.)

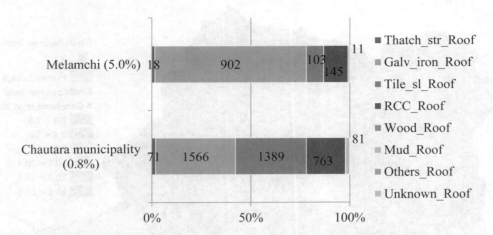

Figure 7.2-8 Comparison of house roof material in Melamchi and Chautara municipalities, Sindhulpalchok district by the 2011 population and housing sensus. (Percent for each municipality is human loss ratio.)

Sindhupalchok district suffered largest number of human loss reaching 3,440 among the districts affected by the earthquake, and average fatality rate of 1.2% is second highest after Rasuwa district. Using the statistics of human loss in cities, towns and villages provided by the Sindhupalchok district police office, human loss rate (%) is compared with rate of cement bonded brick or stone wall for housing in the 2011 Nepal Census in Figure 7.2-6. Human loss rates tend to be higher in the northwestern part of the district than in the southeastern part, corresponding to lower rates of cement mortar usage. The human loss and housing damage could be affected by the strength of shaking, however, strong motion records are not available and seismic intensity survey was conducted at some locations in Kathmandu Valley and only at Chautara in Sindhupalchok by the author[7-4], so that extensive seismic intensity survey would be important and useful. In the western part of the district, there is Sun Koshi River valley where severe landslide claimed 156 human lives in August 2014 (ref. 7-3). Land failure occured in a similar scale in the area. According to the Nepal goverment damage statistics report [7-2], in Sindhupalchok district, numbers of heavily damaged and partially damaged houses were 44,310 and 18,991 each as of May 11, while they became 63,885 and 2,751 each as of June 5.

In Sindhulpalchok district, there are 2 municipalities. Chautara, a district center with population of 15,606 suffered 124 human loss (0.8% of population) and Melamchi with population of 5,230 suffered 264 human loss (5.0% of population). Figures 7.2-7 and 7.2-8 show comparison of house wall material and of house roof material between Chautara and Melamchi municipalities[7-5]. Chautara has more urban characteristics with higher percentage of cement bond brick or stone walls while Melamuch has more rural characteristics with higher percentage of mud mortar stone wall. Figure 7.2-8 indicates that Chautara has higher percentage of tile slope roofs and RCC roofs, while Melamchi has higher percentage of galvanated iron roofs. Those differences seem to be the reasons of higher human loss observed in Melamchi than in Chautara municipality.

7.2.3 人的被害の年齢性別分布 / Distribution of Human Damage by Age Group and Distinction of Sex

ネパール警察が 5 月 20 日現在の死者名簿（住所，性別，年齢等）8,279 人分をウェブに公表している[7-6]．そのうち，年齢の判明している 7,822 人について，年齢性別分布を集計した（Figure 7.2-9）．死者は乳幼児と子どもと 75 歳以上の高齢者に目立って多いこと，多くの年代で男性より女性の犠牲者が多いことがわかる．

また，死者が 100 人以上発生した 10 の郡について，2011 年国勢調査の年齢性別の人口を集計した（Figure 7.2-10）．国勢調査による年齢分布は子どもと若い世代が多く，高齢者の人口は少ない．65 歳以上の高齢化率は 5.9%（男性 5.7%，女性 6.1%）となり，日本の 2010 年国勢調査における高齢化率 23.0%に比べ，非常に低い．

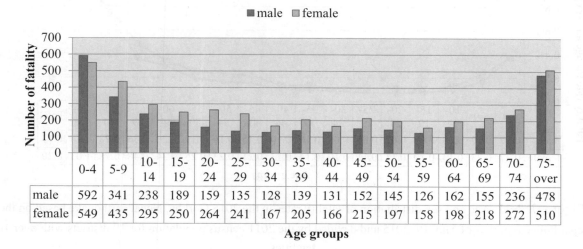

Figure 7.2-9 Age and sex histogram of fatality in the 2015 Gorkha, Nepal earthquake based on the Nepal Police report as of May 19, 2015 (N=7846, excluding age or sex unknown).

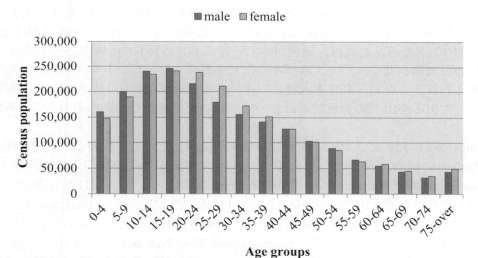

Figure 7.2-10 Age and sex distribution of population in the 10 districts most affected (Source: 2011 Nepal National Cencus)

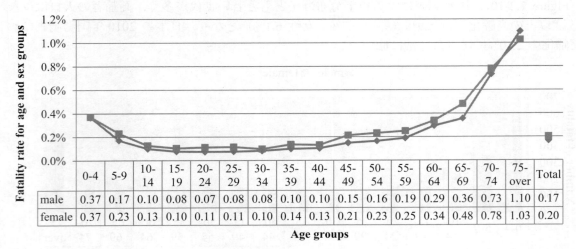

Figure 7.2-11 Age and sex distribution of fatality rates in the 2015 Gorkha, Nepal earthquake based on the Nepal Police report as of May 19, 2015 and devided by the 2011 census population for 10 districts with over 100 fatalities.

地震による年齢区分別死者数（Figure 7.2-9）を国勢調査の年齢別人口（Figure 7.2-10）で割って算出した年齢別死亡率を Figure 7.2-11 に示す．死者数は乳幼児から 9 歳までの子ども，70 歳以上の高齢者に多く，死亡率も高齢者が著しく高い．男女合わせた平均死亡率に対して 0〜4 歳は 2.1 倍，70〜74 歳は 4.2 倍，75 歳以上は 5.9 倍の死亡率になっている．死者における 65 歳以上の割合は，23.7％となる．これは，地震がネパールにおける休日の土曜正午前に起こったことで，若い世代の在宅率が低く，一方，高齢者の在宅率が高くなったことや，地震時の避難行動などの影響が考えられる．なお，東日本大震災の津波および既往地震による人間被害の年齢等依存性については，太田・小山[7-7]の分析結果において，乳幼児や高齢者の死亡率が高くなる傾向が示されている．

Figure 7.2-1 において，郡別の死者数を男女別に示したところ，多くの郡で女性の方が男性より死者数が多い傾向にあった．その中で，女性の割合が特に高い Bhaktapur 郡，死者数最大の Sindhupalchok 郡や Nuwakot 郡，首都の Kathmandu 郡について，2011 年国勢調査における郡の男女人口と死者数の男女比率を Table 7.2-1 と Figure 7.2-12 に示す．Bhaktapur 郡では人口比が男女半々であるのに比べて，女性の犠牲者が多く，死者における男女の割合は，女性が 55.2％，男性が 44.8％となっている．山間部の Sindhupalchok 郡や Nuwakot 郡では人口に占める女性の割合が 52％とやや高いが，それ以上に死者のうち女性の割合が前者で 56.5％，後者で 57.9％と高い．死亡者の女性割合が高いのは，在宅率の高さや，子どもを守る行動などで，屋外避難が遅れた影響が考えられる．男性人口のやや多い Kathmandu など都市部では，死者数の割合は男性がやや多い．カトマンズ盆地のカトマンズ市では，倒壊した建物が住宅に限らず，歴史建物など観光先や，商業建物も多かったことの影響が考えられる．非補強のレンガやアドベの組積造住宅において，妻壁の上部から破壊し，屋根や上階部分が崩壊していく被害パターンが多いこと，ネパールの住宅では上の階に台所や食事スペースをおく傾向があることが，女性の死者率の高さに影響した可能性もあると思われる．

Table 7.2-1 Comparison of gender breakdown for number of fatality and population for rural districts of Sindhupalchok and Nuwakot, and urban districts of Bhaktapur and Kathmandu in Kathmandu valley. Number of fatality from national report as of 05 June 2015.

district	Fatal_Female	Fatal_Male	Pop_Female	Pop_Male
Sindhupalchok	56.5%	43.5%	52.2%	47.8%
Nuwakot	57.9%	42.1%	52.3%	47.7%
Bhaktapur	64.6%	35.4%	49.9%	50.1%
Kathmandu	49.1%	50.8%	48.2%	51.8%

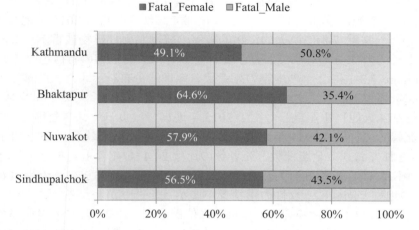

Figure 7.2-12 Sex breakdown of number of human loss as of June 5, 2015 for 2 urban districts in Kathmandu valley and 2 rural districts (Nuwakot and Sindhupalchok) in mountain region.

Nepal police department reliesed the list of people who lost lives in the earthquake as of May 20, 2015 with age, sex, district name in the official website [7-6]. The list contains 8279 cases and age and sex distribution are shown in Figure 7.2-10. Numbers of fatality are much higher for babies, infants and small children less than 10 year old and for elderly people over 75 years old. Also number of human loss is higher for female than for male. Figure 7.2-9 indicates age and sex histogram of the population by the national census 2011 for 10 districts suffering more than 100 people losing lives. Compared to Japan, population is much younger with peak groups between 10 and 24 year old. Fatality rate for each age and sex groups are shown in Figure 7.2-10. Fatality rate is much higher for females and for elderly group of 75 year and over (5.9 times more than average) and for small children under 5 year old (2.1 times more than average). Those tendency seems to be affected by location of the people at the time of the earthquake, that is, at 11:56 a.m., few minutes before noon in Nepali time, on Saturday, April 25, 2015. Elderly and small children and women seem to stay inside vulnerable houses than working age groups and men. Especially, we may note that not Sunday, but Saturday is a weekly holiday in Nepal. Ohta and Koyama [7-7] analyzed age dependance of human loss at the 2011 Great East Japan Earthquake in comparison to other earthquake disasters and indicated higher fatality rates for infants and elderly population are common.

Figure 7.2-1 indicated number of human loss is higher for females than for males in many affected districts. Out of those, Table 7.2-1 and Figure 7.2-12 compares sex breakdown of human loss in 2 urban districts of Kathmandu and Bhaktapur in Kathmandu valley, and 2 rural districts in Nuwakot and Sindhupalchok. In Kathmandu district, breakdown of human loss is almost equal for females and males, while in Bhaktapur, Nuwakot and Sindhupalchok, females show much higher death percentage than males. The difference is highest for Bhaktapur. The reason of very high human loss for female in Bhaktapur is not known and local civil engineers and municipal historical building official had no specific information of any building with many female occupants being collapsed and increase female human losses. The main cause of higher female fatality may be the fact that females tended to stay indoors when the earthquake happened around noon time of Saturday. Also, in traditional houses of Nepal, kitchens and living rooms are placed at upper floors while ground floors are used for animals and storage. In brick and adobe masonry buildings, out of plane failure of end walls occur from the top of the walls causing severer damage at upper floors and roofs and that might have affected more human loss of females.

7.3 過去の地震との比較/ Comparison with the Past Earthquakes
7.3.1 1934年ネパール・インド国境地震/ 1934 Nepal India Border Earthquake

1934年ネパール・インド国境地震（Mw 8.1）は1月15日（08:43 UTC）ネパール時間で午後2時24分に発生した．震源は首都カトマンズより東部であり，今回の2015年地震の震源域のほぼ東隣に位置していた．文献7-8)には人的，物的被害の統計および建物被害が，文献7-9)には緊急救援の状況が詳しくとりまとめられており，これを参考に人的被害の特徴を見ていく．

Table 7.3-1, Figure 7.3-1 に2つの地震の死者数と地理的分布を示す．人的被害は，インド・ビハール州を中心に死者7,188人，ネパールでは死者8,519人（そのうちカトマンズ盆地で4,296人，東部山岳地帯で3,974人他）を記録した[7-8]．2015年地震ではカトマンズ盆地で1,731人，山岳地帯で6,981人を記録している．1934年地震におけるネパールでの家屋・寺・公共施設等の全壊は207,704棟と報告されており，全壊棟数と死者数の比は24.4棟/死者1人あたりとなる．

また，ネパールにおける死者8,519人のうち，男性3,850人（45.2%），女性4,669人（54.8%）となり，2015年の地震と同様に，女性の犠牲者が多かったことがわかる．

1934年地震の断層はカトマンズ盆地より東部に位置していたので，79年を経て，都市部の住宅耐震性改善に比べ，郡部の住宅が日干し煉瓦（アドベ）造・泥モルタルレンガ組積造などが多く脆弱なことがうかがわれる．

Table 7.3-1 Comparison of number of human loss in the 1934 Nepal-Bihar border earthquake and the 2015 earthquake

	The 1934 EQ	The 2015 EQ
Kathmandu Valley	4296	1731
East Mountain Region	3974	4007
West Mountain Region	65	2866
Others	184	108
India	7188	130
Total	15707	8842

— 320 —

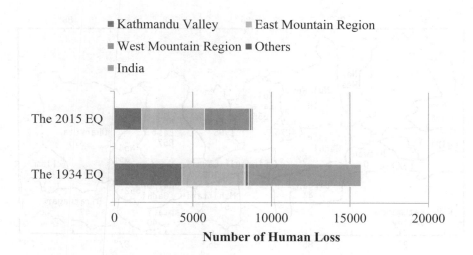

Figure 7.3-1 Comparison of regional distribution for the number of human loss in the 1934 Bihar-Nepal and in the 2015 Gorkha, Nepal earthquakes

1934年地震における死者数の地理的分布を Figure 7.3-2 に示す．死者数はカトマンズ盆地でも，パタン郊外，バクタプール市内，東部山岳地帯の East No.4 地域，同 No.3 地域で多い．なお，Figure 7.3-2 の地方区分と現在の行政区域の対応は，およそ下記のとおりである．

- No. 1 East　　Bagmati region 北部（Sindhupalchowk 郡や Kabhrepalchowk 郡）
- No. 2 East　　Janakpur region 北部（Dolakha 郡や Ramechhap 郡）
- No. 3 East　　Sagarmatha regon 北部（Solukhumbu 郡や Okhaldhunga 郡）
- No. 4 East　　Sagarmatha region 東部と Koshi region 西部
- Dhankuta　　Koshi region と Mechi region

地域別・男女別の死者数を Figure 7.3-3 に示す．特に，バクタプール市内，東部 No.3, No.4 地域で女性の犠牲者が多い傾向が見られる．その推定される原因として，1934 年の時代にも田舎の方が男女の役割，家事と農作業など，家内と屋外作業の差異が大きかったことが考えられる．

1934 年地震の物的・人的被害統計表（Figure 7.3-3 の地域区分による）を基に，死者数と全壊住宅数の関係を Figure 7.3-4 に示す．全壊住宅数と死者数の比（グラフの傾き）が 10～20 近い地域と，2～3 くらいの地域がある．

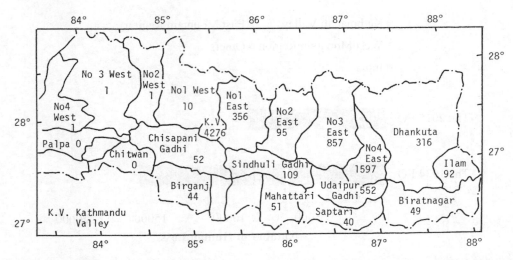

Figure 7.3-2 Geographical distribution of number of human loss in Nepal in the 1934 Nepal-Bihar earthquake. Numbers in each zones indicate number of human loss. (Source of the figure from 7-11) Fujiwara et al, 1989, and original data of the number of fatalities in Nepal from the Ref. Pandey)

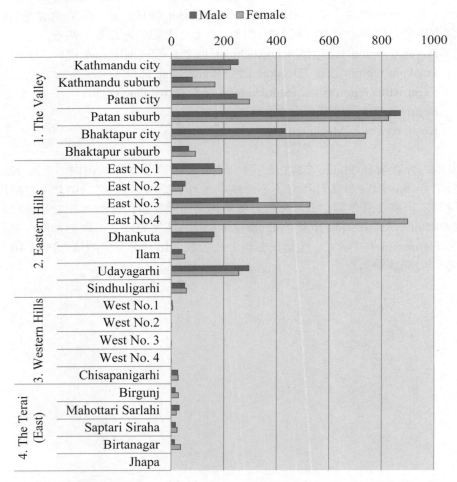

Figure 7.3-3 District distribution of human loss in the 1934 Nepal India border earthquake (Ref. 7-7).

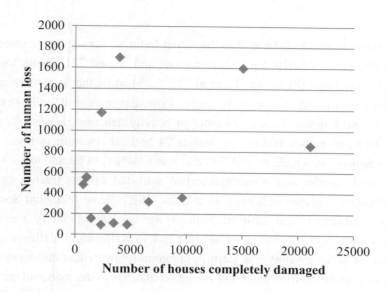

Figure 7.3-4 Relation of number of heavily damaged houses to the number of human loss in the 1934 Nepal India border earthquake (each point is area and district indicated in Figure 7.3-3).

The 1934 Nepal India border earthquake (Mw 8.1) occurred on January 15 at 8:43 UTC, which is 2:24 in Nepali time. The epicenter was located east of Kathmandu valley and the fault zone was located right next to the east from the 2015 Gorkha, Nepal earthquake. Housing damages and human casualty distributions are compared for the two earthquakes here based on references 7-8) and 7-9).

Table 7.3-1 and Figure 7.3-1 compare geographical distribution of human loss for the two large earthquakes. In the 1934 earthquake, more human loss occurred in Kathmandu valley and in East Mountain Region [7-8], while in the 2015 earthquake, more human loss occurred in Mountain Region. At the time of the 1934 earthquake, Kathmandu valley was outside of the fault zone, and was close enough to suffer tremendous collapse of houses and temples. In the 2015 earthquake, Kathmandu valley was located just above the fault plane, and human losses were smaller there than rural districts. It suggests that houses and buildings in urban Kathmandu valley have been somehow improved in seismic strength, as more houses and buildings use brick masonry with cement mortar for walls and confined reinforced masonry buildings became common rather than old and rural mud mortar brick, stone or adobe masonry houses.

7.3.2 1988年ネパール・インド国境地震/ 1988 Nepal India Border Earthquake

1988年8月21日午前4時45分（ネパール時間）に，ネパールとインドの国境，北緯26°755，東経66°616を震源とするMw 6.9の地震が発生した．ネパール国内で死者721人が発生し，インドのビハール州で死者282名があった（藤原ほか[7-10), 7-11)]）．被害の多くはネパール東部の山岳地帯で発生し，カトマンズ盆地でもバクタプールなどで古いレンガ造建物の倒壊があり，死者8名となった．家屋倒壊は53212棟，倒壊棟数と死者数の比は，全体で74棟/死者1人あたりとなる．郡別にみると，死者のもっとも多いSunsari郡で（2494/138=18棟），死亡率はSunsari郡で（138/344594人=0.04%）であった．

この地震発生を契機に，ネパールでは地震防災への関心が徐々に高まり，1993年に防災NGOのNSET-Nepalが発足するなどの動きが見られた．また，2001年インド・グジャラート大地震が発生し，ネパール政府からの要請により，JICAによるカトマンズ盆地地震防災対策調査が2001年から2002年にかけて実施された．一方で，交通が不便で生活の厳しい山岳地帯から，首都のカトマンズ盆地への人口移動が進み，レンガ組積造において泥モルタルからセメントモルタルの普及など，建築材料の改善が見られる一方，建物の密集，住宅やアパート上階への増築など防災上の課題も増えてきたと思われる．

The 21 August 1988 earthquake (Mw 6.9) in the Nepal-India border region occurred at the epicenter of 26.755 deg North Latitude and 66.616 deg East Longitude and caused 721 human loss in Nepal and 282 human loss in Bihar state, India (Fujiwara, T., et al.[7-10, 7-11]). Most of the heavy damages occurred in the eastern mountain regions of Nepal and there were some damages and collapses in Baktapur city, Kathmandu valley causing 8 human losses. Number of heavily damages houses was 53,212 and average number of heavily damaged houses per human loss is 74 houses/ one human loss. The most severely damaged district was Sunsari, in which, human loss rate was 0.04% (138 human loss / 344,594 population).

The 1988 Nepal-India border region earthquake had activated various interest in seismic safety and technologies for earthquake registant buildings, so that the NSET-Nepal (National Society for Earthquake Safety- Nepal) was established, and national policies for earthquake safety was started. Japanese international cooperation project for evaluating seismic risk in Kathmandu Valley was conducted around 2000, and importance of seismic safety and retrofit, community awareness etc. were published by JICA. However, migration of population from rural and mountain districts to the metropolitan area of Kathmandu valley increased vulnerability by higher population and building density and add-in floors above existing masonry or RCC buildings.

7.4 カトマンズ盆地の都市 （カトマンズ，ラリトプール，バクタプール） / Municipalities in Kathmandu Valley (Kathmandu, Lalitpur, Bhaktapur)

まず同じカトマンズ盆地に位置する3都市，カトマンズ市，ラリトプール市，バクタプール市の死者数を区ごとのデータを比較する（Figure 7.4-2〜7.4-4）．なお，これら3都市の位置関係は Figure 7.4-1 に記載している．

いずれの図も同じ区分で色分けしており，3つの図を比較して以下のことがわかる．

1. カトマンズ市の15区（137名死亡）を筆頭に，6区（同66名），16区（53名）および29区（91名）に被害が集中しており，同市のほか，区やラリトプール市には，20名以上の死者が出た区はない．
2. 古い建物の多く集中するこれらの都市の中心市街地では，比較的死者数が少ない．
3. 被害が集中している区が，カトマンズ市の場合は北西と北東部，バクタプール市の場合（とラリトプール市でも）南東部に多く見られる．
4. ラリトプール市の人的被害が他の2都市と比べると全体的に少ない．
   （なぜこれらの被害の特徴が見られるかは現在詳細調査中）

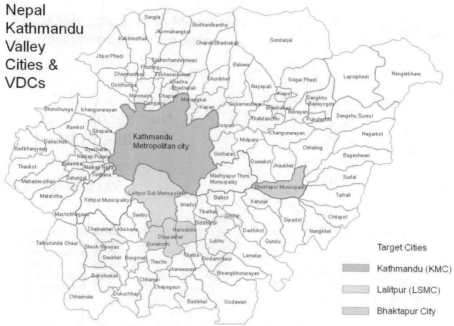

Figure 7.4-1 Three Target Cities in Kathmandu Valley
(VDC: Villedge Development Committee)

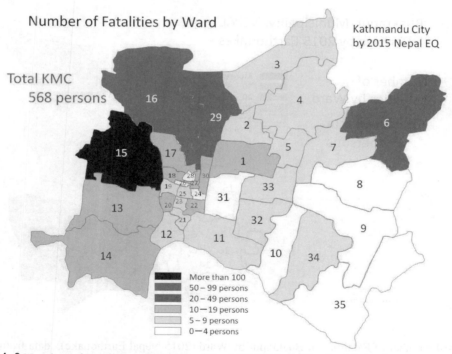

Figure 7.4-2 Number of Fatalities of KMC by Ward (2015 Nepal Earthquake), data from municipality

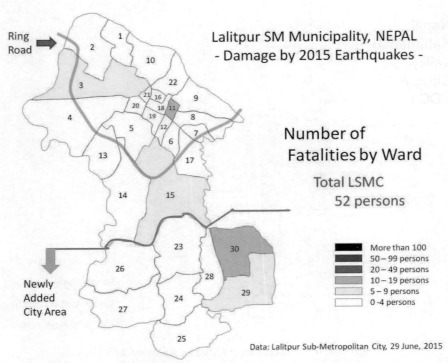

Figure 7.4-3 Number of Fatalities of LSMC by Ward (2015 Nepal Earthquake), data from municipality

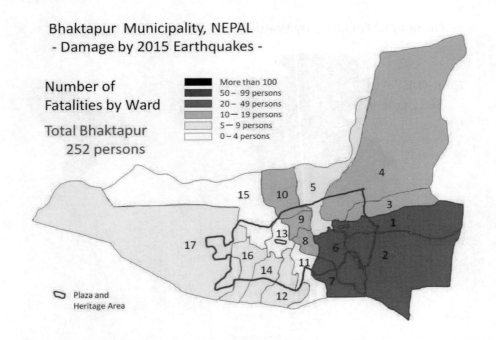

Figure 7.4-4 Number of Fatalities of Bhaktapur by Ward (2015 Nepal Earthquake), data from municipality

　次に同じ3都市の人的被害を絶対数ではなく，人口比率との関係で見ると，次のFigure 7.4-5～7.4-7のようになる．

　これらについても Figure 7.4-1 で見られた4つの特徴が，やや明確さは薄れるが見られる．この3都市では人口に対する死者の率がいずれの区でも1％以下であり，バクタプール以外の2都市の多くの区は0.1％以下であった．

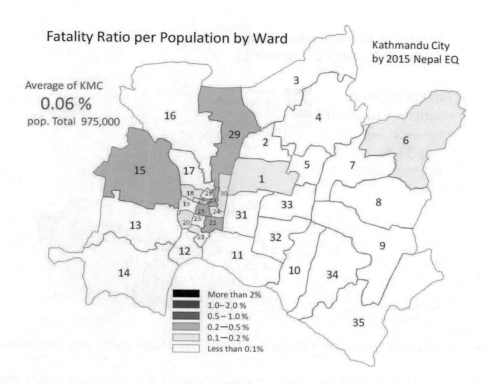

Figure 7.4-5 Ratio of Fatalities of KMC by Ward (2015 Nepal Earthquake), data from municipality

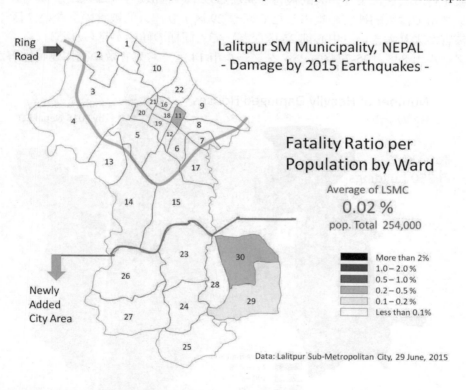

Figure 7.4-6 Ratio of Fatalities of LSMC by Ward (2015 Nepal Earthquake), data from municipality

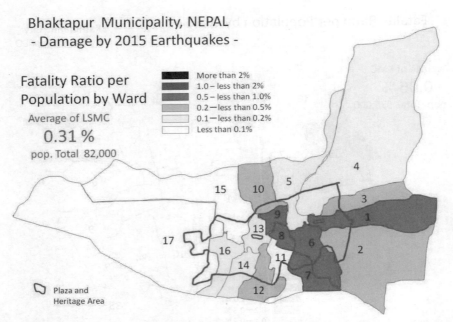

Figure 7.4-7 Ratio of Fatalities of KMC by Ward (2015 Nepal Earthquake), data from municipality

同様に建物被害を区ごとに見ると，Figure 7.4-8～7.4-10 のようになる．これら3都市の建築物重大被害比較を行うことにより，人的被害と異なる以下の特徴が見られる．
1. カトマンズ市では人的被害の集中した6区や29区より，人的被害の少ない7区や14区の方が建物被害がより大きい（中心部25区など）でも同様の傾向が見られる）．
2. ラリトプール市8区，25-27区，バクタプール市14区でも死者数の割に建物被害が大きい．

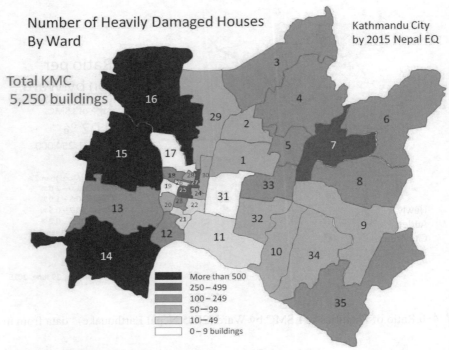

Figure 7.4-8 Number of Heavily Damaged Houses of KMC by Ward (2015 Nepal Earthquake), data from municipality

—328—

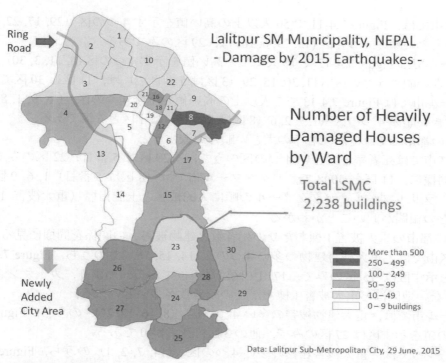

Figure 7.4-9 Number of Heavily Damaged Houses of LSMC by Ward (2015 Nepal Earthquake), data from municipality

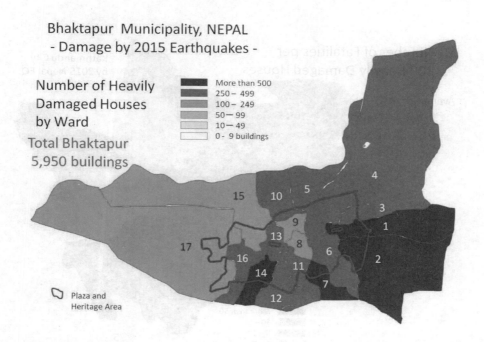

Figure 7.4-10 Number of Heavily Damaged Houses of Bhaktapur by Ward (2015 Nepal Earthquake), data from municipality

　人的被害と建物被害との関係を，重大被害100棟あたりの死者数という指標で見ると，以下のFigure 7.4-11～7.4-13のようになる．これらの図から，後にまとめるような特徴がうかがえる．
　これら3つの図と，まず死者数の絶対値とを比較すると，

1) カトマンズ市では，Figure 7.4-11 で 50 人以上の高い値を示す 4 つの区 (29, 17, 22, 19) のうち，人的被害の大きい順の 4 つの区 (15, 29, 6, 16) は，29 区のみである．
2) ラリトプールでは Figure 7.4-12 で 10 人以上の高い値を示す 4 つの区 (6, 11, 3, 30) のうち，人的被害の大きい順の 4 つの区 (11, 30, 15, 29 (3 区は 5 番目)) は，11 区と 30 区である．
3) バクタプール市では Figure 7.4-13 で 7 人以上の高い値を示す 4 つの区 (6, 9, 1, 8) のうち，人的被害の大きい順の 4 つの区 (1, 7, 2, 6 (8 区は 5 番目) は 1 区と 6 区である．
同様に 3 つの都市でそれぞれ死者率の大きい順と比較すると，
4) カトマンズ市では死者率の大きい 4 つの区のうち，(29 区は 5 番目) 22 区のみで，ラリトプール市では同様に，11 区と 30 区で，バクタプール市では (8 区は 5 番目) 1, 6, 9 区であり，カトマンズ，ラリトプール，バクタプールの順に人的被害と上記指標（重大被害 1 棟あたりの死者数）との相関が低いことがわかる．
また，3 つの都市の重大被害 1 棟あたりの死者数と建物被害との関係を同様に見ると，
5) カトマンズ市では，重大被害建物の多い 4 つの区 (14, 15, 16, 25) のうち，Figure 7.4-11 で 10 人以上の値を示す区は 15 区のみで，17, 19 区は最下位である．つまり，カトマンズ市では建物被害が少ない地区ほど重大被害 1 棟あたりの死者数が多いといえる．
6) ラリトプール市では，重大建物被害の多い 4 つの区 (8, 16, 12, 27) のうち，Figure 7.4-12 で 2 人以上の値を示す区は 27 区のみで，他の 3 区は死者が 0 である．
7) バクタプール市では，重大被害建物の多い 4 つの区 (14, 7, 2, 1) のうち，Figure 7.4-13 で 10 人以上の値を示す区はないが，7, 2, 1 の 3 つの区はいずれも 5 人以上である．これらの結果から，特徴的な区において何が生じたのかをさらに調査・分析する計画である．

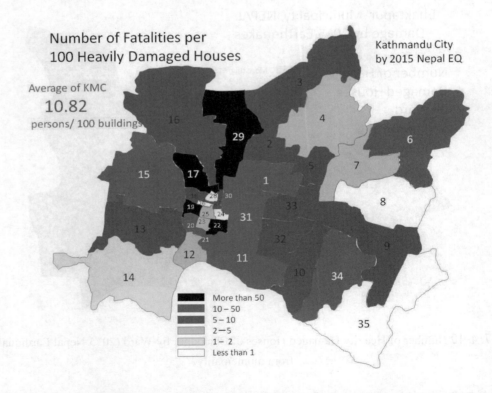

Figure 7.4-11 Number of Fatalities per 100 Heavily Damaged Houses of KMC by Ward (2015 Nepal Earthquake), data from municipality

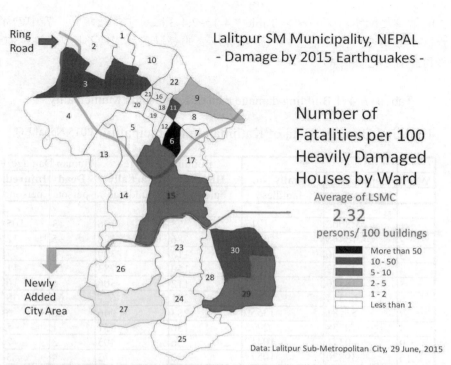

Figure 7.4-12 Number of Fatalities per 100 Heavily Damaged Houses of Lalitpur SMC by Ward (2015 Nepal Earthquake), data from municipality

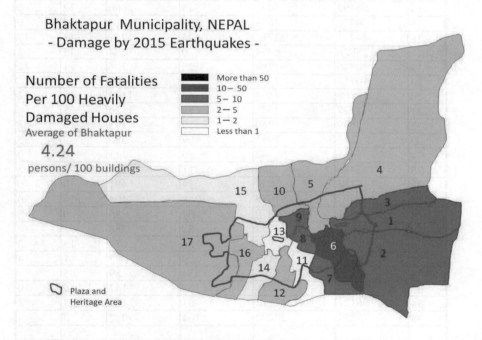

Figure 7.4-13 Number of Fatalities per 100 Heavily Damaged Houses of Bhaktapur city by Ward (2015 Nepal Earthquake), data from municipality

建物および人的被害に関するデータを Table 7.4-1～7.4-3 に示す．ただし，表中の死亡者数が死亡者の死亡した区か，あるいは死亡者の（戸籍等）公的登録されている区のどちらであるかは不明であり，今後再調査が必要である．

Table 7.4-1 Building damage data of Kathmandu Municipality

Building Damage Data of Kathmandu Municipality 2015 Nepal EQ

Ward	Population	Family No.	Building Damage		Human Damage	
			Heavily	Partially	Dead	Injured
	person	families	buidings	buildings	person	person
1	8008	1917	73	196	13	105
2	13448	3599	86	198	5	12
3	34866	9145	113	320	8	7
4	47362	12030	150	783	5	11
5	18320	4774	112	306	6	16
6	60344	15434	241	627	66	38
7	51581	13559	283	946	8	6
8	10738	2773	130	351	1	5
9	40371	10417	56	405	3	2
10	39820	10571	50	73	4	3
11	17765	4416	25	189	6	1
12	13262	3173	130	400	5	11
13	40456	10207	188	1208	15	14
14	58495	15472	743	2060	12	0
15	54476	14093	555	1010	137	0
16	84441	22715	694	1251	53	17
17	25926	6394	9	1284	13	2
18	10746	2746	128	376	11	12
19	10711	2632	8	102	6	
20	10968	2844	57	1144	15	22
21	13727	3389	39	1120	7	
22	5699	1250	19	195	16	8
23	8357	1991	169	380	5	35
24	3488	742	59	113	0	0
25	3486	788	311	200	7	15
26	4133	947	34	491	0	0
27	7592	1888	268	124	16	0
28	5611	1370	67	85	0	5
29	45052	12252	58	786	91	
30	8563	1914	58	679	15	8
31	16211	4112	9	77	1	4
32	33316	9298	54	89	5	
33	25694	6876	107	147	6	10
34	66121	17772	63	164	7	8
35	76299	20792	104	912	0	3
Total	975453	254292	5250	18791	568	380

Analyzed by GRIPS Disaster Management Policy Program (Tokyo)
Data from Disaster Management Director of Kathmandu (on 2 June, 2015)
Data on population and family numbers are based on Nepal National Census 2011

Table 7.4-2 Building damage data of Lalitpur Municipality

Building Damage Data of Lalitpur Municipality   2015 Nepal EQ

Ward	Population	Family No.	Building Damage		Human Damage	
			Heavily	Partially	Dead	Injured
	person	families	buidings	buildings	person	person
1	8434	2221	38	61	0	0
2	19061	4839	30	306	0	4
3	14082	3528	17	340	5	10
4	15367	3913	53	186	0	3
5	6404	1516	6	122	0	2
6	6780	1563	6	470	4	2
7	7849	1839	15	176	0	0
8	11400	2816	410	232	0	5
9	13908	3484	45	384	1	18
10	6554	1729	14	112	0	0
11	4458	1010	27	427	12	11
12	5891	1342	223	253	0	2
13	14867	3772	19	221	0	0
14	21232	5438	0	0	0	0
15	13858	3480	82	822	8	14
16	4362	858	242	340	0	3
17	10644	2678	90	109	0	0
18	5777	1200	68	788	0	0
19	7385	1774	3	198	0	0
20	7721	1978	7	346	0	1
21	4659	1143	23	252	0	2
22	10109	2460	20	300	0	0
23	7002	1854	28	375	0	4
24	2424	571	51	441	0	12
25	3252	753	117	317	1	0
26	5813	1377	139	336	0	0
27	4279	1020	214	94	4	0
28	2872	756	109	35	0	2
29	4159	1070	74	310	6	21
30	3705	911	68	156	11	15
	(220802).	(54581).				
Total	254308	62893	2238	8509	52	131

Data from Executive Officer of Lalitpur (on 26 June, 2015)
Data on population and family: based on National Census 2011
Numbers of ( ): before consolidation of Ward 23 to 30 to LSMC

Table 7.4-3 Building damage data of Bakhtapur Municipality

Building Damage Data of Bakhtapur Municipality   2015 Nepal EQ

Ward	Population	Family No.	Building Damage		Human Damage	
			Heavily	Partially	Dead	Injured
	person	families	buidings	buildings	person	person
1	4805	972	513	155	43	56
2	6694	1456	527	66	33	66
3	3427	697	290	78	15	21
4	11011	2632	307	343	14	18
5	5141	1124	322	66	8	14
6	3126	604	252	66	29	43
7	4437	960	564	156	34	35
8	3138	620	214	162	16	12
9	2071	405	152	42	13	6
10	4509	899	421	69	10	11
11	3287	629	304	126	3	4
12	3782	761	428	26	9	19
13	2225	417	345	111	3	5
14	4466	954	584	60	8	1
15	6044	1374	237	199	3	2
16	3684	793	260	159	6	15
17	9901	2342	230	208	5	69
Total	81748	17639	5950	2092	252	397

Data from Executive Officer of Bakhtapur (on 31 May, 2015)
Analysed by GRIPS Disaster Management Policy Program (Tokyo)
Data on population and family numbers are based on National Census 2011

Figure 7.4-2 to Figure 7.4-4 show the comparison of three cities in Kathmandu Valley, i.e. Kathmandu Metropolicatn City (KMC), Lalitpur Sub-Metropolitan City (LSMC), and Bhaktapur municipality. All figures are colored under the same standard (level) of classification and easily compared, and the findings are as follows; (In addition, Figure. 7.4-1 shows the location of 3 target cities in the Valley)

1) Number of fatalities concentrates on Ward 15 (137 fatalities), following ward 29 (91 fatalities), ward 6 (66 fatalities) and ward 16 (53 fatalities) and other wards in Kathmandu KMC, and Lalitpur LSMC have no more than 20 fatalities.
2) These cities have old area where old buildings are concentrated, however those old areas had comparatively less casulaties.
3) The human damage concentrated areas are located in north-west and north-east areas in Kathmandu city, while south-east areas are heaviliy affected in Bhaktapur (and also in Lalitpur LSMC) munisipality.
4) Lalitpur LSMC has less human damages compared with other two cities.

(The reasons why these phenomena can be observed are now investgated based on detailed data by GRIPS.)

Figure 7.4-5 to Figure 7.4-7 show the ratio of fatalities per total population (National Census 2011). The figures identify almost similar characteristics seen in Figure 7.4-2 to Figure 7.4-4. Every ward shows the ratio of fatalities less than 1%, and most of wards in Kthmandu and Lalitpur cities have less thna 0.1 % ratio of casualties.

Figure 7.4-8 to Figure 7.4-10 show number of building damages by ward in three cities. When compare the damages of houses, some characteristcs other than human damage can be seen as mentioned last part.

1) In Kathmandu (KMC) city, building damage in ward 7 and ward 14 where the less human damages observed are more severe compared with ward 6 and ward 29 where more human damages recorded. (In central area like ward 25 has similar characteristics.)
2) In Lalitpur LSMC, ward 8, wards 25-27 and in Bhaktapur ward 14 have less fatalities, however they have comparatively heavier housing and building damages.

Figure 7.4-11 to Figure 7.4-13 show the "Number of Fatalities per 100 Heavily Damaged Houses" by Ward in Kathmandu (KMC), Lalitpur (LSMC) and Bhaktapur municipality. The detailed analysis from these three figures are described in the latter parts. The original data collected from three municipalities are also shown at the last part of this section.

The following 7 points show tentative analysis results from the data collected from KMC, LSMC and Bhaktapur municipalities after the 2015 Nepal Earthquake.

Firstly, the comparison of these three figures (Figure 7.4-11 to Figure 7.4-13) shows;
1) In Kathmandu (KMC), within the highest 4 wards (No. 29, 17, 22, 19) of Figure. 7.4-11 that have more than 50 persons, only ward 29 is included in the highest 4 wards (No. 15, 29, 6, 16) of fatality.
2) In Lalitpur (LSMC), within the highest 4 wards (No. 6, 11, 3, 30) of Figure. 7.4-12 that have more than 10 persons, ward 11 and ward 30 are included in the highest 4 wards (No. 11, 30, 15, 29 (Ward 3 is 5th)).
3) In Bhaktapur municipality, within highest 4 wards (No. 6, 9, 1, 8) of Figure.7.4-13 that have more than 7 persons, ward 1 and ward 6 are included in the highest 4 wards (No. 1, 7, 2, 6 (ward 8 is 5th)) of fatality.

Similarly, the followings are analyzed from comparison of ratio of fatalities in three municipalities;
4) Among the highest 4 wards of fatality ratio in Kathmandu (KMC), only ward 22 (ward 29 is 5th) is included (in the Figure. 7.4-11 highest 4 wards). In Lalitpur (LSMC), ward 11 and ward 30 are included while in Bhaktapur municipality ward 1, ward 6 and ward 9 (ward 8 is 5th) are included (in each Figure. 7.4-12 and 7.4-13 highest 4 wards). That means the correlation between human damage and the indicator of Figure. 7.4-11 to 7.4-13 become lower in order of Kathmandu (KMC), Lalitpur (LSMC) and Bhaktapur municipality.

In addition, correlation between the above-mentioned indicator (casualties per 100 heavily damaged houses) and number of heavily damaged houses can be analyzed similarly in three municipalities as;
5) In Kathmandu (KMC), within highest 4 wards (No. 14, 15, 16, 25) of heavily damaged houses, only Ward 15 shows more than 10 persons in Figure. 7.4-11, while ward 17 and ward 19 are the lowest. This means that in Kathmandu (KMC), the wards with less housing damage had a larger number of fatalities because of one heavily damaged house (building).
6) In Lalitpur (LSMC), within highest 4 wards (No. 8, 16, 12, 27) of heavily damaged houses, only ward 27 shows more than 2 persons in Figure. 7.4-12, while other three wards have no casualty.
7) In Bhaktapur municipality, within highest 4 wards (No. 14, 7, 2, 1) of heavily damaged houses, there is no ward that shows more than 10 persons, however ward 7, ward 2 and ward 1 have more than 5 persons.

The author has a plan to investigate and to analyze what happened and occurred in the characteristic wards.

Data of building and human damages are shown in Table 7.4-1 to 7.4-3. Note that it is unknown whether the ward represent the place of death or registered ward of casualties.

7.5 まとめ/ Summaries

2015年ネパール・ゴルカ地震における人的被害・住家被害について，死亡率と全壊率の郡別の分布を示した．人的・物的被害はカトマンズ盆地より山岳地帯の北部に高く，地震断層の及ぶ東西約150kmにわたり激甚な状況であった．郡別では，最大の3400人を超える死者が発生したシンドルパルチョーク郡の人的被害分布では，東部より西北部の死亡率が高く，国勢調査による住宅壁のセメントモルタル・レンガ積みの割合が低い地域，つまり泥モルタルの割合の高い地域で死亡率が高い傾向が見られた．また，郡庁所在地のチョータラより第2の市であるメラムーチの死亡率が高く，より農村的な泥モルタルレンガ組積造の構造や材料の影響が考えられる．

年齢性別の人的被害を見ると，死者数の男女割合は45%対55%と，女性の方が多く，年齢別死亡率では全世代平均に対して乳幼児が2.1倍，75歳以上の高齢者が5.9倍と著しく高くなり，地震発生時間（4月の土曜日の正午前）の在宅率の影響がうかがわれる．

過去の大地震における人的被害を見ると，1934年ネパール・インド国境地震（Mw 8.1）は震源断層が今回より東の，カトマンズ盆地の外側に位置していたが，ネパールで8,000人超（そのうちカトマンズ盆地で4000人余り）の死者が発生し，女性の死者数が多かった．2015年地震は断層上にカトマンズ盆地が位置しているが，地震動の性質か，建物にセメントモルタルの普及，RCC建物の増加等で地震に強くなったためか，カトマンズ盆地で今回は比較的人的被害が少ない．

カトマンズ盆地におけるカトマンズ・バクタプール・ラリトプールの3市について，自治体から区別の被害統計データの提供を受け，家屋全壊数と全壊率，死者数と死亡率，家屋の重大被害100棟あたり死者数を地図に示した．3つの市ではバクタプールの全壊率，死亡率が共に高い．この3都市では人口に対する死者の割合がいずれの区でも1%以下であり，バクタプール以外の2都市の多くの区は0.1%以下であった．

Macro distribution of houses heavily damaged and human loss by district-wise statistics are examined in the maps for the 2015 Gorkha, Nepal earthquake. Housing damages and human losses are devastating and were much higher in northern mountain region of 150km EW corresponding to the earthquake fault zone than in Kathmandu valley. Maximum human loss occurred in Sindhulpalchowk district exceeding 3,400 and GIS distribution of human loss rates in Sindhulpalchowk seems to correspond weaker housing types with mud mortar brick or stone masonry by the 2011 census. Gender breakdown of human loss is 55% female and 45% male. Age and sex distribution of human loss per census population indicates higher rates for infants (2.1 times more than average) and elderly people (5.9 times more for 75 year and older than average), suggesting that polulation located inside of houses around noon time of Saturday, Nepali holiday affected such pattern. Looking back the 1934 Nepal-India border earthquake (Mw 8.1), human loss rates were higher for female than male in the same way. Human loss in Kathmandu valley in 1934 was larger compared to the 2015 event, which may be affected by different strong motion characteristics and improved seismic strength of cement mortar masonry houses and RCC buildings common now in Kathmandu valley compared to rural brick or stone masonry houses with mud mortar.

In the Kathmandu valley, ward-wise damage statistics data were collected from 3 municipalities of Kathmandu, Bhaktapur, and Lalitpur. Damage distribution maps are indicated for the rates of heavily damaged houses, rates of human loss, ratio of human loss per 100 heavily damaged houses in 3 cities. Human loss percentageas are less than 1%, and most of wards in Kthmandu and Lalitpur cities have less thna 0.1 % ratio of casualties.

7.6 謝辞/ Acknowledgements

本調査にあたり，地方開発省（前ラリトプール市長）Tara Bahadur Karki 氏，バクタプール市長 Rijal Uddhav 氏，カトマンズ市防災課長 Bir Bahadur Khadka 氏に多大な協力を頂きました．ここに感謝の意を表します．

The authors express sincere gratitude to former Executive Officer, Lalitpur Sub-Metropolitan city (LSMC), Mr. Tara Bahadur Karki (MOFALD); Executive Officer, Mr. Rijal Uddhav (Bhaktapur city); and Director of Disaster Management Section, Mr. Bir Bahadur Khadka (Kathmandu Metropolitan city).

7.7 参考文献/ References

7-1) http://earthquake-report.com/2015/04/25/massive-earthquake-nepal-on-april-25-2015/ （2015.07.31 閲覧）

7-2) Nepal earthquake- humanitarian data exchange: https://data.hdx.rwlabs.org/group/nepal-earthquake （2015.07.31 閲覧）

7-3) Circle of blue, Himalayas strike again: deadly landslide in Nepal, 06 Aug. 2014 http://www.circleofblue.org/waternews/2014/world/nepal-landslide-hydropower/ （2015.11.30 閲覧）

7-4) Murakami, H., Guragain, R., Pradhan, B., Adhikari, S., Basyal, G., Mori, S.: Seismic intensity questionnaire survey for the 2015 Gorkha, Nepal earthquake – Preliminary results and damage observations -, Int. Symp. Japan Association for Earthq. Engr., 2015.

7-5) District Profile Data Collection, Demography, 23 Census 2011 District Sindhupalchowk.xlsx http://un.org.np/data-coll/ （2015.8.30 閲覧）

7-6) Record of the people who died in the 2015 Nepal earthquake (last recorded at 2015-05-19), Nepal police.

7-7) 太田裕，小山真紀：2011 年東日本大震災に伴う人間被害の激甚性　既往地震群との対比でみる死者発生の年齢等依存性，日本地震工学会論文集，15, 2, pp.11-23, 2015

7-8) Pandey, M. R. and Molnar, P.: The distribution of intensity of the Bihar-Nepal earthquake of 15 January 1934 and bounds on the extent of the rupture zone, Journal of Nepal Geological Society, 5, 1, pp.22-44, 1988.

7-9) Brahma Shumsher J.B. Rana: The great earthquake in Nepal (1934 A.D.), Ratna Pustak Bhandar, Kathmandu, 136pp.

7-10) Fujiwara, T., Sato, T., Kubo, T., Murakami, H. O., Reconnaissance report on the 21 August 1988 earthquake in the Nepal-India border region, No. B-63-4, Research Report on Natural Disasters, Supported by the Japanese Ministry of Education, Science and Culture, 121 pp., 1989.

7-11) 藤原悌三，佐藤忠信，久保哲夫，村上ひとみ：1988 年ネパール・インド国境地震の災害調査，京都大学防災研究所年報，第 32 号 A, pp.71-95, 1989

7-1) http://earthquake-report.com/2015/04/25/massive-earthquake-nepal-on-april-25-2015/ (2015.07.31)

7-2) Nepal earthquake- humanitarian data exchange: (2015.07.31) https://data.hdx.rwlabs.org/group/nepal-earthquake

7-3) Circle of blue, Himalayas strike again: deadly landslide in Nepal, 06 Aug. 2014 http://www.circleofblue.org/waternews/2014/world/nepal-landslide-hydropower/ (2015.11.30)

7-4) Murakami, H., Guragain, R., Pradhan, B., Adhikari, S., Basyal, G., Mori, S.: Seismic intensity questionnaire survey for the 2015 Gorkha, Nepal earthquake – Preliminary results and damage observations -, Int. Symp. Japan Association for Earthq. Engr., 2015.

7-5) District Profile Data Collection, Demography, 23 Census 2011 District Sindhupalchowk.xlsx http://un.org.np/data-coll/ (2015.8.30)

7-6) Record of the people who died in the 2015 Nepal earthquake (last recorded at 2015-05-19), Nepal police.

7-7) Ohta, Y. and Koyama, M.: Severity of mortality in the 2011 East Japan Giant Earthquake age-dependancy in comparison with past major earthquakes, Journal of Japan Association of Earthquake Engineering, 15, 2, pp.11-23, 2015.

7-8) Pandey, M. R. and Molnar, P.: The distribution of intensity of teh Bihar-Nepal earthquake of 15 January 1934 and bounds on the extent of the rupture zone, Journal of Nepal Geological Society, 5, 1, pp.22-44, 1988.

7-9) Brahma Shumsher J.B. Rana: The great earthquake in Nepal (1934 A.D.), Ratna Pustak Bhandar, Kathmandu, 136pp.

7-10) Fujiwara, T., Sato, T., Kubo, T., Murakami, H. O., Reconnaissance report on the 21 August 1988 earthquake in the Nepal-India border region, No. B-63-4, Research Report on Natural Disasters, Supported by the Japanese Ministry of Education, Science and Culture, 121 pp., 1989.

7-11) Fujiwara, T., Sato, T., Kubo, T., and Murakami, H. O.: Survey report of the 21 August 1988 earthquake on Nepal-India border region, Annuals, Disas. Prev. Res. Inst., Kyoto Univ., No. 32A, pp. 71-95, 1989.

8 詳細調査建物の解析／Numerical Analysis

8.1 解析の概要／Outline of Analysis

ここでは，調査で入手した配筋等の情報を基に，2つの建物について詳細な解析を実施した．1つ目の建物は，建物を3次基にモデル化し，非線形静的増分解析および非線形地震応答解析を実施した．もう1つの建物では，被害の大きかった一方向について，仮想仕事法を用いて建物のベースシア係数を検討した．

In this chapter, detailed analysis with two buildings was conducted referring to the drawings and structural documents obtained during the investigation. For one of the buildings, 3D dynamic analysis was conducted. For the other building, the method of the virtual work was applied to calculate the base shear coefficient of the damaged direction.

8.2 Gongabu 地区の建物 G7／Building G7 in Gongabu

8.2.1 検討建築物／Target Building

検討に使用する建築物は，5.2.1.2「Gongabu 地区の建物と被害」に示した建物 G7 である．建物は地上5階，ペントハウス1階の鉄筋コンクリート造の縫製工場である．建物，および被害の概要については 5.2.1.2 節(7)および 5.2.1.5 節を参照されたい．

各階荷重は，聞き取り調査から得られた当時の状況（2階には200台のミシンが置かれており，3,4階には大量の布があった）を加味し，12kN/m^2 とした．コンクリート強度はリバウンドハンマーから得られた 40N/mm^2 とした．主筋およびせん断補強筋の降伏強度は，ネパールに流通する鉄筋の材料試験結果から 490N/mm^2 とした．部材断面を Table 8.2-1 および Table 8.2-2 に示す．また，材料特性を Table 8.2-3 に示す．柱の断面・配筋は，実測調査の結果から，実際の建物と同様のものとした．梁の断面は，実測調査の結果から決定した．梁の配筋は，本建物の付近で同規模の建物の配筋を参考にするとともに，柱の損傷被害が大きいことを鑑み，柱よりも曲げ耐力が大きくなるように決定した．各階の柱・梁部材の断面および配筋は等しいものとした．解析モデルおよび平面図を Figure 8.2-1 と Figure 8.2-2 に示す．

Table 8.2-1 Analysis Model Specifications (Column)

	C1	C2	C3
Column dimensions (mm)	305×305	305×305	355×355
Column longitudinal rebar	8-ϕ25	8-ϕ20	8-ϕ25
Column hoop	ϕ10@100 - 2 legs	ϕ10@150 - 2 legs	ϕ10@150 - 2 legs

Table 8.2-2 Analysis Model Specifications (Beam)

	All
Beam dimensions (mm)	280×400
Beam longitudinal rebar	4-ϕ25
Beam stirrup	ϕ10@100 - 2 legs

Table 8.2-3 Material Property

Compressive strength of concrete (N/mm^2)	40.0
Tensile strength of concrete (N/mm^2)	4.0
Young's modulus of concrete (N/mm^2)	28058
Yield strength of reinforcing bar (N/mm^2)	490
Young's modulus of reinforcing bar (N/mm^2)	205000

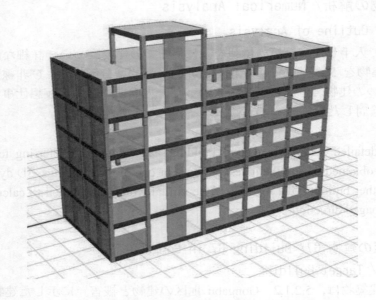

Figure 8.2-1 Structural model (3D)

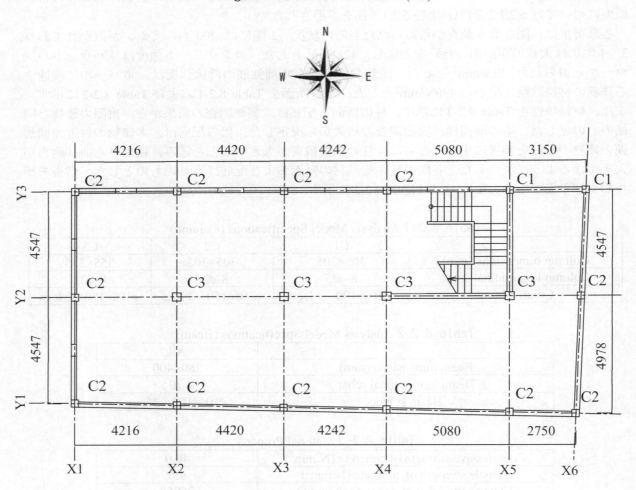

Figure 8.2-2 Floor plan

Sample building is a sewing plant consist of five-story masonry-infilled RC frames structure (G7) (Section 5.2.1.2). Each floor load was set to 12 kN/m². The concrete strength was set to 40 N/mm². Cross sectional properties of the reinforced concrete components of the structure are listed in Table 8.2.1-1 and Table 8.2-2. In addition, the material properties are shown in Table 8.2-3. The analytical model and floor plan are shown in Figure 8.2-1 and Figure 8.2-2.

8.2.2 解析モデル/ Analysis Model

解析には，汎用ソフト SNAP Ver.6[8-1]を用いた．解析モデルは，1階柱脚を固定とした立体フレームモデルとした．柱はマルチスプリングモデル，梁は材端バネ付きビームモデル，壁は3本柱モデル[8-2]によってモデル化した．X1構面の壁は開口周比が大きいため，モデル化せず，腰壁・垂れ壁の高さを柱の剛域としてのみ考慮した．柱および梁部材のスケルトンカーブは曲げひび割れ点および曲げ降伏点を折れ点としたトリリニア型とし，曲げ降伏時の剛性低下率は菅野式[8-3]を用いて算出した．履歴特性は武田モデル[8-4]とし，除下時剛性低下指数は柱が 0.4，梁が 0.5 とした．柱，梁のせん断バネの復元力特性はバイリニア型とした．壁のせん断バネにおけるせん断応力度－せん断変形角関係は，文献 8-5)を参考に，せん断変形角θ_w=0.5rad.において，最大せん断応力度τ_w=0.73N/mm²に達し，その後はその耐力を保持するものとした．復元力特性は Figure 8.2-3 に示すようなバイリニアスリップとした．壁の軸バネの復元力特性は弾性とした．減衰は瞬間剛性比例型として，減衰定数 h=0.03 とした．

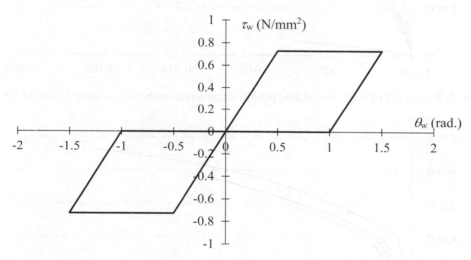

Figure 8.2-3 Restoring force characteristics of wall

The analysis was computed on SNAP Ver.6 [8-1]. The analysis model was three dimensional frame model with the first-story column base fixed. The column was modeled as multi-spring model. The beam was modeled as end-spring beam element. The masonry wall is modeled was Kabeyasawa model [8-2]. As for the skeleton curve of the column and beam member, Tri-linear model was used. The calculation of stiffness decreasing rate at the bending yield was used is the formula by Sugano[8-3]. As for the restoring force characteristics of the column and beam member, Takeda model[8-4] was used. As for the restoring force characteristics of the shear spring for the column and beam member, bilinear model was used. In addition, as for the masonry wall member, bilinear-slip model[8-5] was used (Figure 8.2-3). Restoring force characteristics of the axial spring for the wall was elastic. Tangent stiffness-proportional damping was used and the damping ratio was set to h=0.03.

8.2.3 建物性状 / Building Properties

モデルの固有周期を Table 8.2-4 に，静的増分解析結果を Figure 8.2-4 および Figure 8.2-5 に示す．NS 方向よりも EW 方向の方が，層せん断力，初期剛性ともに大きくなっている．これは EW 方向の方が壁量が多いためである．

Table 8.2-4 Natural Period

	First Mode	Second Mode
Natural Period (s)	0.76	0.27

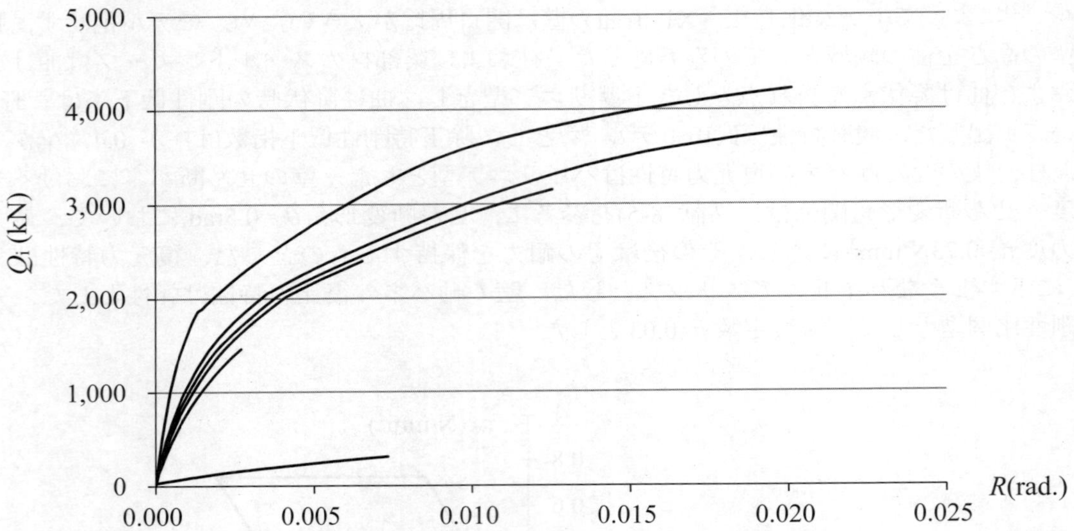

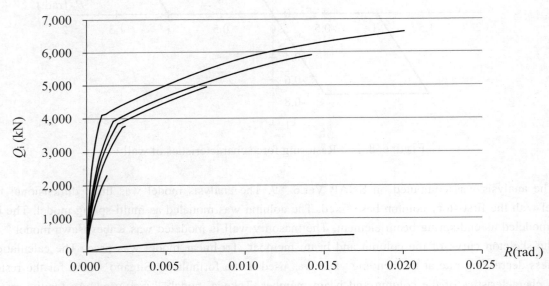

Figure 8.2-4 Result of static and elastic plastic incremental analysis (Capacity Curve of NS direction)

Figure 8.2-5 Result of static and elastic plastic incremental analysis (Capacity Curve of EW direction)

The natural period of analysis model is shown in Table 8.2-4. The result of static and elastic-plastic incremental analysis is shown in Figure 8.2-4 and Figure 8.2-5.

Story shear force and initial stiffness of EW direction is larger than NS direction. Because of there were large quantities of masonry walls in the EW direction.

8.2.4 検討用入力地震動/ Input Ground Motion

入力地震動として，2015 年 4 月 25 日に，カトマンズ市内（カトマンズ盆地）で観測された強震記録を用いた．これは，アメリカ地質調査所（USGS）が公開している加速度記録である．加速度の時刻歴波形を Figure 8.2-6 および Figure 8.2-7 に示す．観測された NS 波，EW 波をそれぞれ建物の NS 方向（Transverse direction），EW 方向（Longitudinal direction）に入力した．

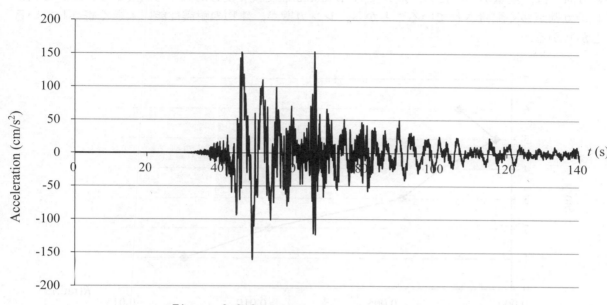

Figure 8.2-6 Input ground motion (NS direction)

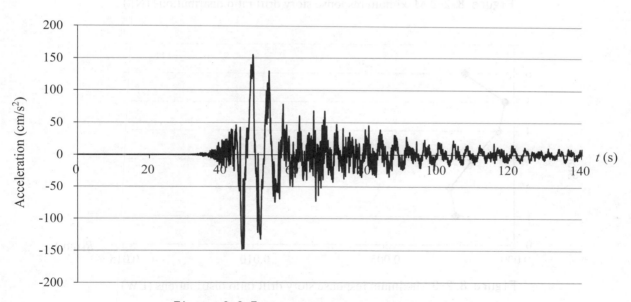

Figure 8.2-7 Input ground motion (EW direction)

Strong motion records that have been observed in the Kathmandu city (Kathmandu Valley) were used for input ground motion, which U.S. Geological Survey (USGS) publicized on the Web. The time history waveforms of acceleration are shown in Figure 8.2-6 and Figure 8.2-7.

8.2.5 解析結果/ Analysis Result
8.2.5.1 最大応答層間変形角/ Maximum Response Story Drift Ratio

非線形地震応答解析より得られた NS, EW, それぞれの方向における高さ方向の最大応答層間変形角 R を Figure 8.2-8 および Figure 8.2-9 に示す.

NS 方向では, 応答層間変形角が 1 階で最大となり, 1/33rad.程度まで変形している. 一方, EW 方向では, 壁量が多いため, 最大でも 1/400rad.程度まで変形が抑えられている. EW 方向にはレンガ壁が多く配置されていることから, レンガ壁が, 建物の耐震性能に大きく寄与していることがわかる.

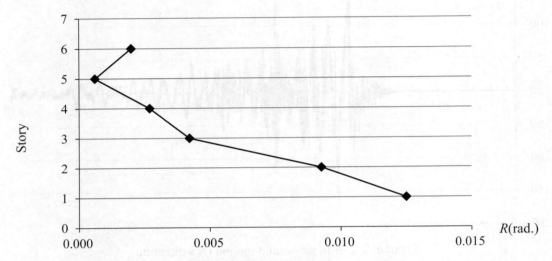

Figure 8.2-8 Maximum response story drift ratio distributions (NS)

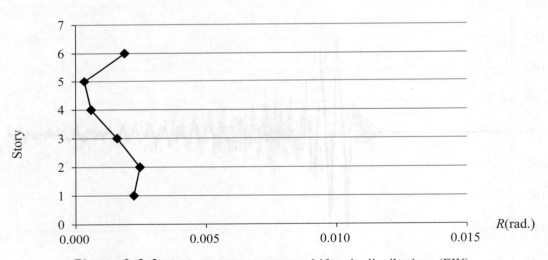

Figure 8.2-9 Maximum response story drift ratio distributions (EW)

The maximum response story drift ratio distributions in each direction obtained from the analysis are shown in Figure 8.2-8 and Figure 8.2-9.

The maximum response story drift ratio in the NS direction (Transverse direction) was 1/33 rad. On the other hand, the maximum response story drift ratio in the EW direction (Longitudinal direction) was only 1/400 rad. As there were large quantities of masonry walls in the EW direction, it indicates that masonry wall contributes to the seismic performance of buildings.

8.2.5.2 損傷状況/ Damage Condition

解析より得られた地震後の損傷状況の分布を Figure 8.2-10 および Figure 8.2-11 に示す．

NS 方向においては，1 階で曲げ破壊した柱が多く見られ，実際の損傷状況と良い対応を示している．EW 方向における Y3 構面 1 階の一部の柱では，実際の破壊状況と異なり，せん断破壊している柱が見られる．

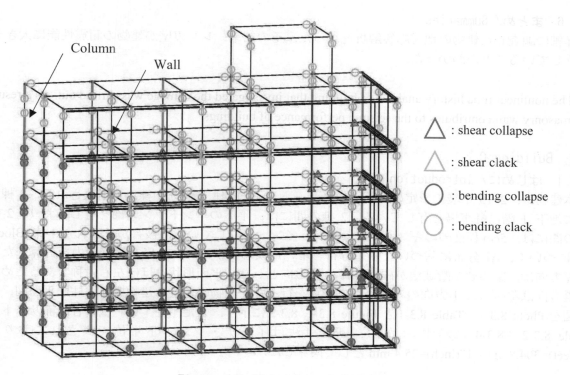

Figure 8.2-10 Damaged condition (NS)

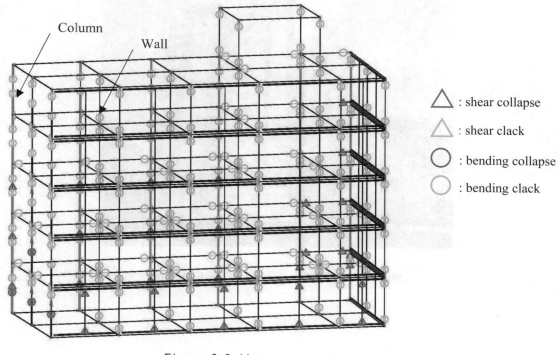

Figure 8.2-11 Damaged condition (EW)

The damaged condition in each direction obtained from the analysis is shown in Figure 8.2-10 and Figure 8.2-11. There were many flexural yielding columns in the NS direction in the damaged condition of the analysis, which showed good correspondence to the actual damage. While some of the columns on the first floor in Y3 Plane in the EW direction in the analysis results failed in shear, which were different from the actual damaged condition.

8.2.6 まとめ/ Summaries

詳細に調査した建物の地震応答解析を行った．その結果，レンガ壁が建物の耐震性能に大きく寄与していることがわかった．

The nonlinear time history analysis of building that investigated the damage was carried out. As a result, the masonry wall contributes to the seismic performance of buildings.

8.3 Building C
8.3.1 はじめに/ Introduction

本建物は，2015 年竣工予定の鉄筋コンクリート造 16 階建て建物 2 棟から構成される．2 棟共通に地下 1 階に駐車場を有している．2 棟の間には，平屋のエントランス部を有しており，2 棟との間には，5cm 程度のエキスパンションジョイントを有している．被害が見られた 1 棟 (Block-B) について，Ai 分布に基づいた外力分布を用いた仮想仕事法により保有水平耐力を計算した．計算方向は，梁のせん断破壊が確認された X 方向とした．平面形状はほぼ左右対称であるため，地震方向は左→右の 1 方向のみについて計算を行った．建物の全景，建物概要と柱壁平面図，梁伏図を Photo 8.3-1, Table 8.3-1 と Figure 8.3-1, 8.3-2 に示す．また，柱・梁・壁の各断面リストを Table 8.3-2〜8.3-4 に示す．　なお，断面寸法はインチ・フィート単位で表されており，1'(feet)=304.8 mm , 1"(inch)=25.4 mm として換算した．

Photo 8.3-1　Whole view of the buildings

Table 8.3-1 Outline of the building

Structure	Reinforced concrete	
Structural type	Frame with shear walls	
Dimensions	16-story with 1 basement floor	
	Longitudinal	35.9m
	Transversal	32.4m
	Story height	1 to 16 story : 2.8m (total 44.8m)

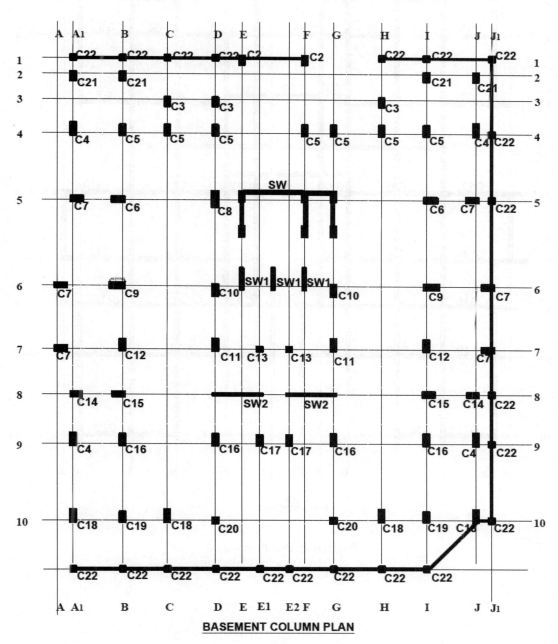

Figure 8.3-1 Plan view

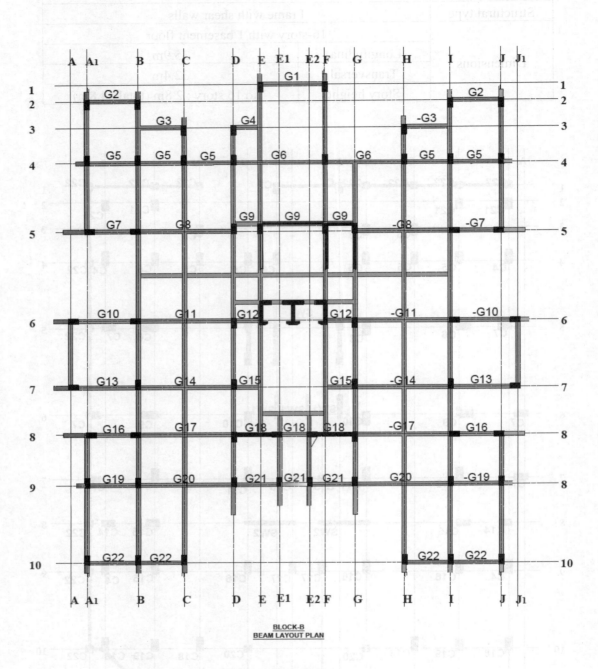

Figure 8.3-2 Plan view

Table 8.3-2 Column list

	C2	C3	C4	C5	C6	C7	C8
15F	16[406] × 28[711]	16[406] × 28[711]	16[406] × 32[813]	16[406] × 32[813]	32[813] × 16[406]	32[813] × 16[406]	16[406] × 44[1118]
Bar	20φ-12	25φ-4+20φ-8	25φ-4+20φ-8	25φ-8+20φ-4	25φ-8+20φ-4	25φ-8+20φ-4	25φ-16
14F							
Bar							→
13F							18[457] × 44[1118]
Bar							25φ-18
12F							
Bar							→
11F							18[457] × 44[1118]
Bar	↓	↓	↓	↓	↓	↓	25φ-24

*1 Round bar with diameter of 8mm was used for shear reinforcement with spacing of 100mm in the region of 750mm from the end and 150mm in the other region.
*2 Concrete strength: Fc=29 for BF-3F, Fc=24 for 4-11F, Fc=19 for 12-15F.   *3 1inch=25.4mm

Table 8.3-2 Column list (Contd.)

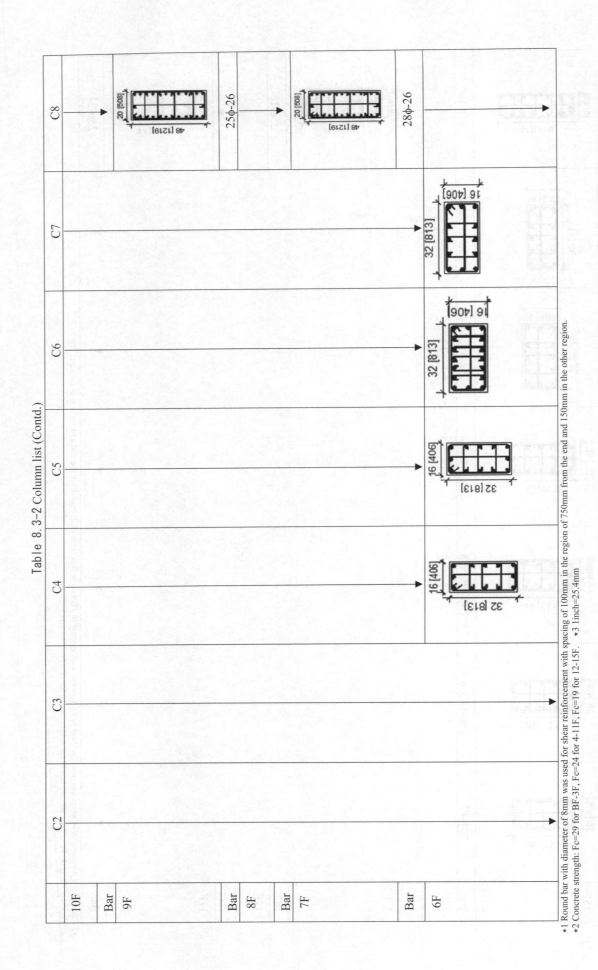

*1 Round bar with diameter of 8mm was used for shear reinforcement with spacing of 100mm in the region of 750mm from the end and 150mm in the other region.
*2 Concrete strength: Fc=29 for BF-3F, Fc=24 for 4-11F, Fc=19 for 12-15F. *3 1inch=25.4mm

Table 8.3-2 Column list (Contd.)

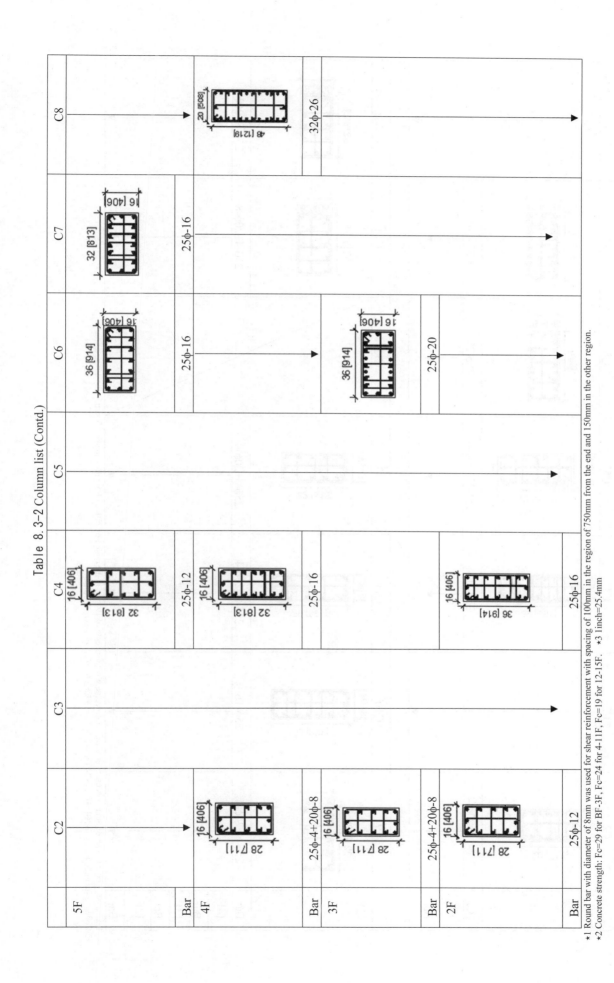

*1 Round bar with diameter of 8mm was used for shear reinforcement with spacing of 100mm in the region of 750mm from the end and 150mm in the other region.
*2 Concrete strength: Fc=29 for BF-3F, Fc=24 for 4-11F, Fc=19 for 12-15F.   *3 1 inch=25.4mm

Table 8.3-2 Column list (Contd.)

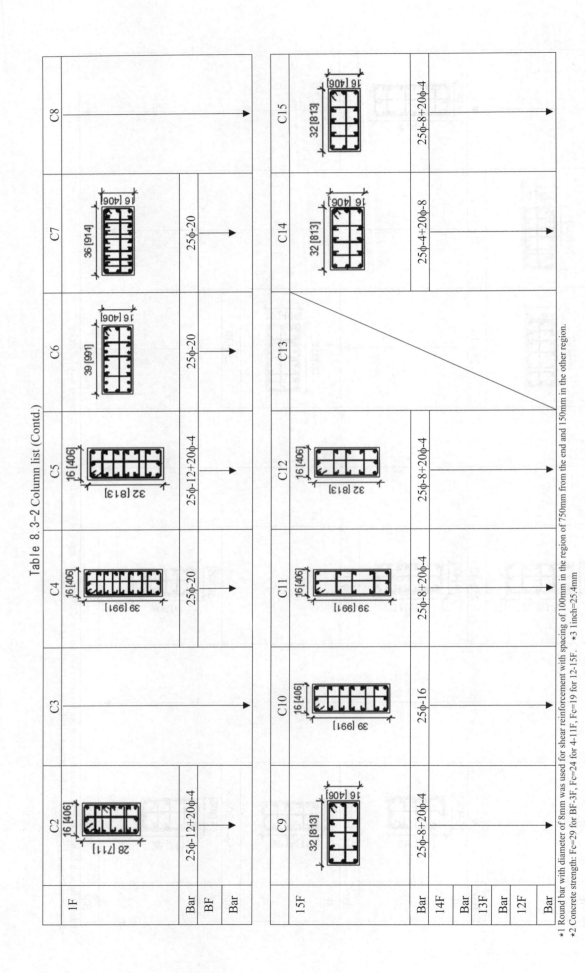

Table 8.3-2 Column list (Contd.)

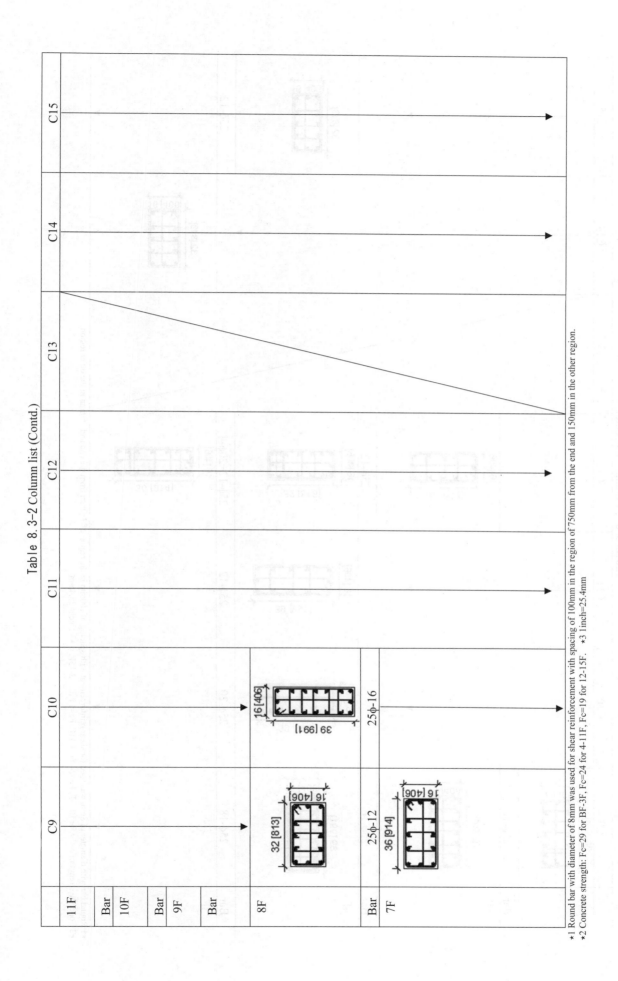

*1 Round bar with diameter of 8mm was used for shear reinforcement with spacing of 100mm in the region of 750mm from the end and 150mm in the other region.
*2 Concrete strength: Fc=29 for BF-3F, Fc=24 for 4-11F, Fc=19 for 12-15F.   *3 1inch=25.4mm

Table 8.3-2 Column list (Contd.)

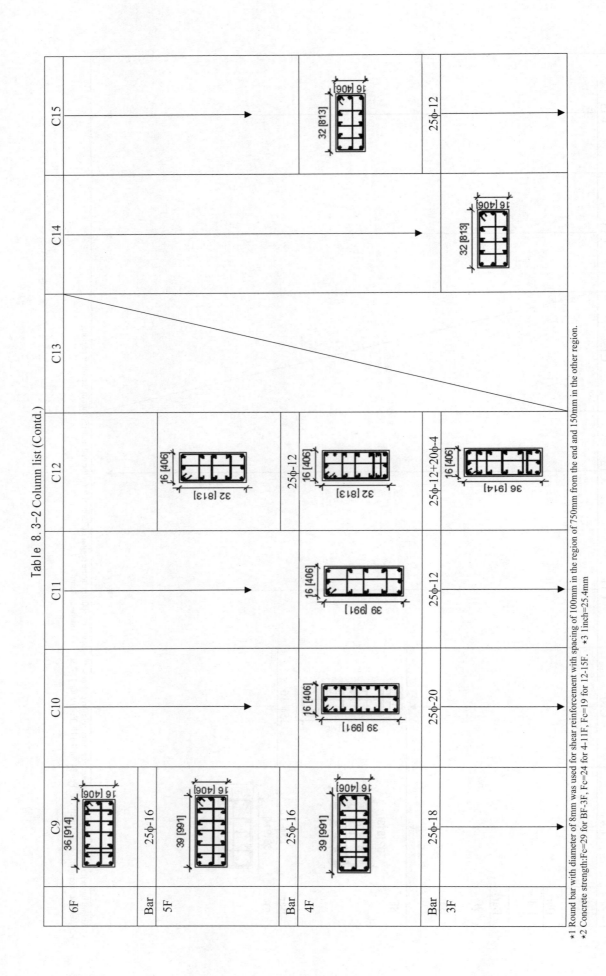

*1 Round bar with diameter of 8mm was used for shear reinforcement with spacing of 100mm in the region of 750mm from the end and 150mm in the other region.
*2 Concrete strength:Fc=29 for BF-3F, Fc=24 for BF-3F, Fc=24 for 4-11F, Fc=19 for 12-15F. *3 1inch=25.4mm

Table 8.3-2 Column list (Contd.)

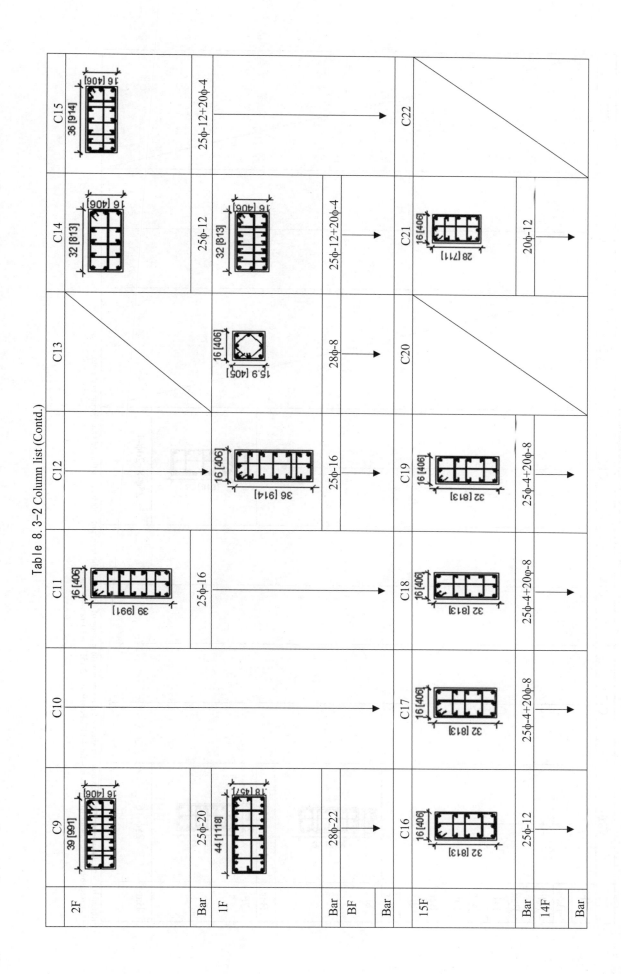

Table 8.3-2 Column list (Contd.)

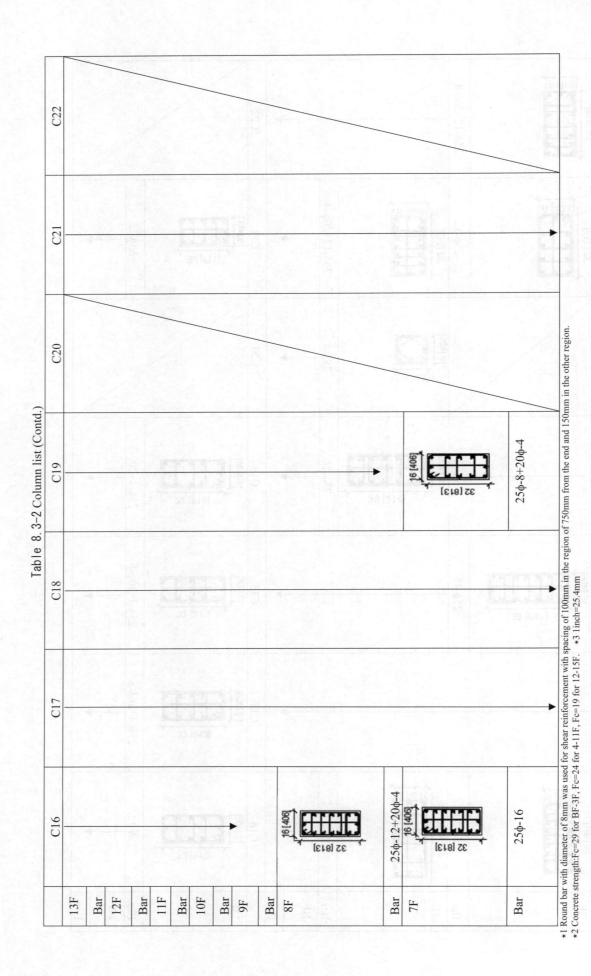

*1 Round bar with diameter of 8mm was used for shear reinforcement with spacing of 100mm in the region of 750mm from the end and 150mm in the other region.
*2 Concrete strength:Fc=29 for BF-3F, Fc=24 for 4-11F, Fc=19 for 12-15F. *3 1inch=25.4mm

Table 8.3-2 Column list (Contd.)

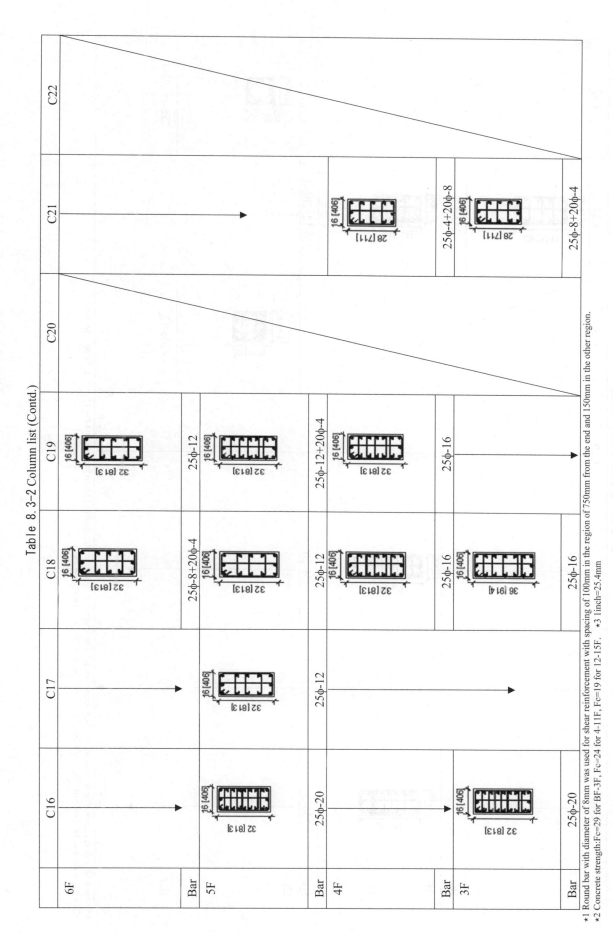

*1 Round bar with diameter of 8mm was used for shear reinforcement with spacing of 100mm in the region of 750mm from the end and 150mm in the other region.
*2 Concrete strength: Fc=29 for BF-3F, Fc=24 for 4-11F, Fc=19 for 12-15F.　*3 1inch=25.4mm

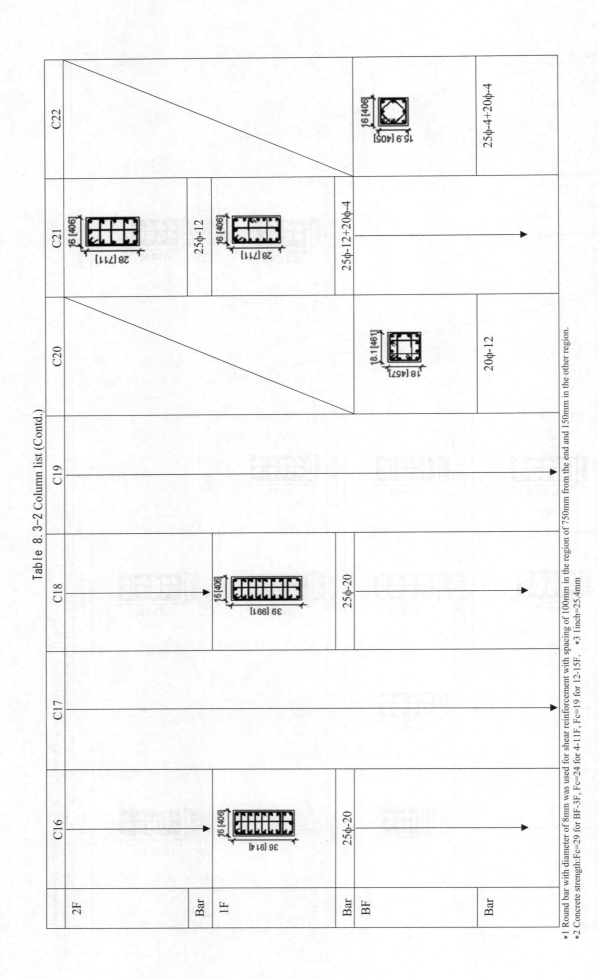

Table 8.3-2 Column list (Contd.)

Table 8.3-3 Beam list

Name	G1		G2		G3	
Location	End	Center	End	Center	End	Center
	(2-250, 4-200)	(3-250, 4-200)	(2-250, 4-200)	(3-250, 4-200)	(3-250, 3-200)	(2-250, 3-200)
B x D	301 x 508		301 x 508		301 x 508	
Name	G4		G5		G6	
Location	End	Center	End	Center	End	Center
	(2-250, 3-200)	(2-250, 3-200)	(4-250, 4-200)	(2-250, 4-200)	(5-250, 4-200)	(2-250, 3-200)
B x D	301 x 508		301 x 508		301 x 508	
Name	G7			G8		G9
Location	Outer	Center	Inner	Outer	Center	Inner	All
	(2-250, 4-250)	(4-250, 4-250)	(5-250, 4-250)	(5-250, 4-250)	(2-250, 4-250)	(7-250, 4-250)	(7-250, 4-250)
B x D	301 x 508			301 x 508			301 x 508

*1 Details are the same for all stories *2 Round bar with diameter of 8mm was used for shear reinforcement with spacing of 100mm in the region of 1116mm from the end and 150mm in the other region.

Table 8.3-3 Beam list (Contd.)

Name	G10			G11			G12	
Location	Outer	Center	Inner	Outer	Center	Inner	All	
	4-25φ / 4-25φ	2-25φ / 4-25φ	5-25φ / 4-25φ	5-25φ / 4-25φ	2-25φ / 4-25φ	8-25φ / 4-20φ	8-25φ / 4-20φ	
B x D	301 x 508			301 x 508			301 x 508	
Name	G13			G14			G15	
Location	End	Center		End	Center		All	
	4-25φ / 3-25φ	2-25φ / 3-25φ		4-25φ / 3-25φ	2-25φ / 3-25φ	5-25φ / 3-25φ	5-25φ / 3-25φ	
B x D	301 x 508			301 x 508			301 x 508	
Name	G16			G17			G18	
Location	Outer	Center	Inner	Outer	Center	Inner	All	
	8-25φ / 4-20φ	4-25φ / 4-25φ	2-25φ / 4-25φ	2-25φ / 3-25φ	4-25φ / 3-25φ	5-25φ / 3-25φ	5-25φ / 3-25φ	
B x D	301 x 508			301 x 508			301 x 508	

*1 Details are the same for all stories *2 Round bar with diameter of 8mm was used for shear reinforcement with spacing of 100mm in the region of 1116mm from the end and 150mm in the other region.

— 360 —

Table 8.3-3 Beam list (Contd.)

Name	G19			G20		G21
Location	Outer	Center	Inner	End	Center	All
B x D	301 x 508			301 x 508		301 x 508
Name	G22					
Location	End	Center				
B x D	301 x 508					

*1 Details are the same for all stories *2 Round bar with diameter of 8mm was used for shear reinforcement with spacing of 100mm in the region of 1116mm from the end and 150mm in the other region.

Table 8.3-4 Wall list

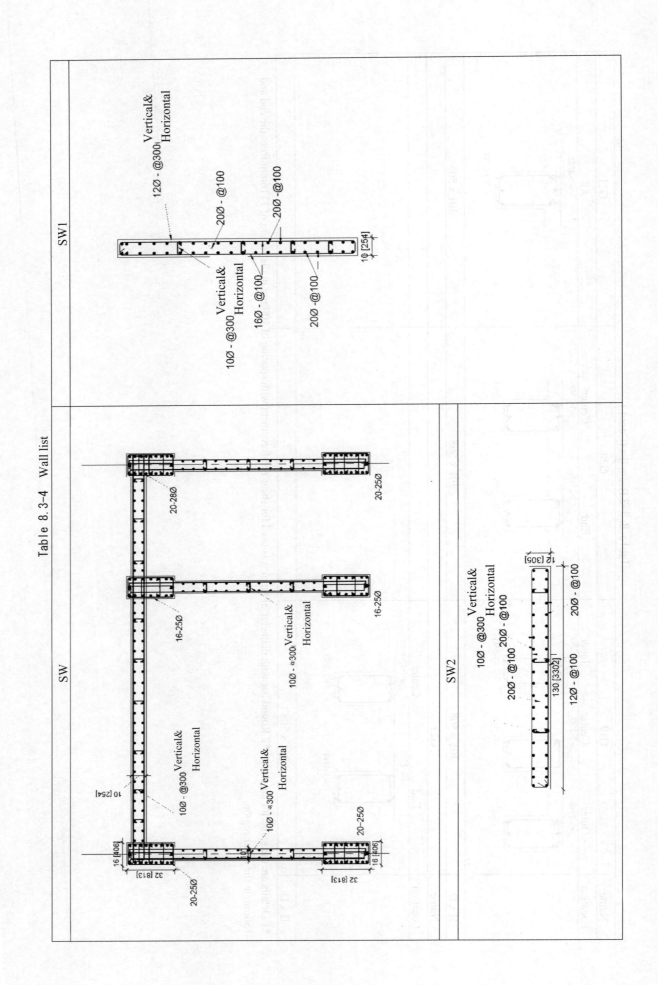

The complex has two buildings, which are 16-story reinforced concrete buildings constructed in 2015. There is a single-story entrance hall between two buildings, which is separated with structural gap of 5 cm between buildings. The virtual work method with the lateral external force distribution based on Ai Shape defined in Japanese Building Standard was applied for the building C, which was damaged due to the earthquake. The calculated direction was X-direction, of which beams were failed in shear. The lateral force was applied in the direction from left to right. The whole view of the buildings is shown in Photo 8.3-1. The outline of the building is shown in Table 8.3-1. Plan view with columns and beams are shown in Figure 8.3-1 and 8.3-2. The details of columns and beams are shown in Table 8.3-2 to 8.3-4. Since the length was shown in the unit of feet and inch on the original drawings, they were converted to mm as 1' (feet)=304.8 mm and 1" (inch)=25.4 mm.

8.3.2 材料強度/ Material Properties
8.3.2.1 鉄筋強度/ Steel Bar Strength

鉄筋は異形鉄筋で，鉄筋の径は European size である．降伏強度および引張強度は，現地で採取した鉄筋を用いて引張試験を行って求めた．なお，T28，T32 は柱の主筋に用いられているが，材料強度は引張試験を行っていないため不明とした．計算上は T25 と同じ強度と仮定している．Table 8.3-5 に鉄筋の詳細について示す．

Table 8.3-5 Steel bar strengths

Material	Type	Diameter	Yield strength (N/mm^2)	Tensile strength (N/mm^2)
Bar	T8	φ8	655	772
	T10	φ10	528	616
	T12	φ12	571	678
	T16	φ16	500	608
	T20	φ20	473	589
	T25	φ25	534	653
	T28	φ28	NA	NA
	T32	φ32	NA	NA

Deformed bars were applied for main bars, of which diameter was European size. Steel bar samples were taken from the building to obtain yield and tensile strengths. Since the samples of T28 and T32 were not able to be obtained, the strength was assumed to be the same as T25. Strength of steel bars are shown in Table 8.3-5.

8.3.2.2 コンクリート強度/ Concrete Strength

コンクリート強度については，ネパールではキューブ圧縮試験により定義されている．そこで，キューブ強度からシリンダー強度への換算は以下に示す式により行い，それぞれの強度を Table 8.3-6 のように求めた．
コンクリート材料試験換算圧縮強度
① キューブ供試体断面寸法 75×75，長さ 150mm の場合

$f_{CB} = f_B - 2.0$

② キューブ供試体断面寸法 100×100，長さ 200mm の場合

$f_{CB} = f_B - 1.0$

③ キューブ供試体断面寸法 125×125，長さ 250mm の場合

$f_{CB}=f_B-1.0$

ここで，

f_{CB}：シリンダー強度 (N/mm^2)

f_B：キューブ強度 (N/mm^2)

Table 8.3-6 Concrete strength

Material	Story	Cube strength (N/mm^2)	Cylinder strength (N/mm^2)
Concrete	GF to 2nd	30	29
	3rd to10th	25	24
	11th to 15th	20	19

Concrete strength shown on the original drawings was measured with cubic concrete samples. Therefore, the cylinder concrete strength was calculated with the following function from the cube strength. The calculated strength is shown in Table 8.3-6.

1) For cube specimen size of 75×75 mm and length of 150 mm

$f_{CB}=f_B-2.0$

2) For cube specimen size of 100×100 mm and length of 200 mm

$f_{CB}=f_B-1.0$

3) For cube specimen size of 125×125 mm and length of 250 mm

$f_{CB}=f_B-1.0$

Where;

f_{CB}: Cylinder test strength (N/mm^2)

f_B: Cube test strength (N/mm^2)

8.3.3 部材耐力の計算/ Ultimate Strength of Members
8.3.3.1 梁のせん断終局強度/ Ultimate Shear Strength of Beams

梁の曲げ終局強度の算定は，次の方針で行う．

(1) 鉄筋の降伏強度およびコンクリート強度は，8.3.2「材料強度」に従う．

(2) 梁に取り付くスラブ筋に関しては，スラブ筋に関する資料や図面がなかったため，スラブ筋は無視する．

(3) 平面形がほぼ左右対称であるので，保有水平耐力計算は地震方向を左→右の1方向のみの計算を行う．

(4) 本建物は被害調査で梁のせん断破壊が確認されている．そのため，本検討では，梁のせん断強度を求め，せん断破壊の有無についても検討する．梁のせん断強度の算出は，以下の式（荒川 mean 式）による．

$$Q_{su}=\left\{\frac{0.068p_t^{0.23}(F_c+18)}{M/Qd+0.12}+0.85\sqrt{p_w\sigma_{wy}}\right\}bj$$

ここで，

p_t：引張鉄筋比（％）

p_w：せん断補強筋比

σ_B：コンクリート圧縮強度（N/mm^2）

σ_{wy}：せん断補強筋の降伏点強度（N/mm^2）

σ_0：柱軸方向応力度（N/mm^2）

b：梁幅（mm）

d：梁有効せい（mm）

M/Q：せん断スパン長さ

j：応力中心間距離（mm）

(5) 梁の降伏位置は，取り付く柱面とする．

(6) 梁のせん断力に対する鉛直荷重の影響は考慮しない．

Ultimate shear strength of beam was calculated with the following conditions.
(1) The strengths shown in the section 8.3.2 were applied for strengths of steel and concrete.
(2) The contribution of slab was ignored (No information about slab was available).
(3) The loading direction was X-direction from left to right.
(4) The shear strength was calculated with the following function.

$$Q_{su} = \left\{ \frac{0.068 p_t^{0.23}(F_c + 18)}{M/Qd + 0.12} + 0.85\sqrt{p_w \sigma_{wy}} \right\} bj$$

Where;

p_t: Tensile main bar area ratio (%)

p_w: hear reinforcement ratio

σ_B: Concrete strength (N/mm^2)

σ_{wy}: Yield strength of shear reinforcement (N/mm^2)

σ_0: Axial stress (N/mm^2)

b: Beam width (mm)

d: Effective depth (mm)

M/Q: hear span ratio

j: Distance between compression and tensile forces(mm)

(5) Beams yield at the face of columns.
(6) The effect of vertical load was ignored for calculating shear force.

8.3.3.2 梁の曲げ終局強度/ Ultimate Bending Strength of Beams

梁の曲げ終局強度 M_u は，次式によって計算した．

$$M_u = 0.9 \cdot \sum a_t \cdot \sigma_y \cdot d$$

ここで，

Σa_t：梁の引張鉄筋全断面積 (mm^2)

σ_y：梁主筋の降伏応力度 (N/mm^2)

d：梁の有効せい (mm)

Ultimate bending strength of beam M_u was calculated with the following function;

$$M_u = 0.9 \cdot \sum a_t \cdot \sigma_y \cdot d$$

Where;

Σa_t: Total area of tensile main bars (mm^2)

σ_y: Yield strength of main bars (N/mm^2)

d: Effective depth of the beam (mm)

8.3.3.3 柱の曲げ終局強度/ Ultimate Bending Strength of Columns

柱の曲げ終局強度は，次式によって計算する．

($0.4b \cdot D \cdot \sigma_B < N \leq N_{max}$ のとき)

$$M_u = 0.8 \cdot a_t \cdot \sigma_y \cdot D + 0.12 \cdot b \cdot D^2 \frac{N_{max} - N}{N_{max} - b \cdot D \cdot \sigma_B}$$

（$0 < N \leq 0.4 b \cdot D \cdot \sigma_B$ のとき）

$$M_u = 0.8 \cdot a_t \cdot \sigma_y \cdot D + 0.5 \cdot N \cdot D \left(1 - \frac{N}{b \cdot D \cdot \sigma_B}\right)$$

（$N_{min} \leq N < 0$ のとき）

$$M_u = 0.8 \cdot a_t \cdot \sigma_y \cdot D + 0.4 \cdot N \cdot D$$

ここで，　σ_y：柱主筋の降伏応力度（N/mm²）
　　　　　　a_t：柱の引張主筋の全断面積（mm²）
　　　　　　b：柱幅（mm）
　　　　　　D：柱せい（mm）
　　　　　　N：軸力（N）
　　　　　　σ_B：コンクリートの圧縮強度（N/mm²）

柱の曲げ終局強度の算定は，次の方針で行う．
(1) 鉄筋の降伏強度およびコンクリート強度は，8.3.2「材料強度」に従う．
(2) 建物の重量は，単位重量を 12kN/m² と仮定して算出する．また，柱の曲げ耐力の計算に用いる軸力 N は，長期荷重時軸力に対して，水平荷重による変動軸力分として梁の曲げ終局強度時せん断力による付加軸力を加減した値を用いる．
(3) 被害調査で柱のせん断破壊は見られなかったので，柱のせん断破壊は考慮しない．

Ultimate bending strength of column was calculated with the following functions.

(when $0.4b \cdot D \cdot \sigma_B < N \leq N_{max}$)
$$M_u = 0.8 \cdot a_t \cdot \sigma_y \cdot D + 0.12 \cdot b \cdot D^2 \frac{N_{max} - N}{N_{max} - b \cdot D \cdot \sigma_B}$$

(when $0 < N \leq 0.4 b \cdot D \cdot \sigma_B$)
$$M_u = 0.8 \cdot a_t \cdot \sigma_y \cdot D + 0.5 \cdot N \cdot D \left(1 - \frac{N}{b \cdot D \cdot \sigma_B}\right)$$

(when $N_{min} \leq N < 0$)
$$M_u = 0.8 \cdot a_t \cdot \sigma_y \cdot D + 0.4 \cdot N \cdot D$$

Where;
　　　　σ_y: Yield strength of main bar (N/mm²)
　　　　a_t: Total area of tensile main bars (mm²)
　　　　b: Column width (mm)
　　　　D: Column width (mm)
　　　　N: Column width (N)
　　　　σ_B: Concrete strength (N/mm²)

Ultimate bending strength of columns were calculated with the following conditions.
(1) The strengths shown in the section 8.4.2 were applied for strengths of steel and concrete.
(2) The unit weight was assumed as 12 kN/m². The varied axial force due to lateral force, which was calculated from the flexural strength of beams, was taken into account.

(3) Shear failure mechanism was ignored since shear damage was not observed.

8.3.3.4 壁の曲げ終局強度／Ultimate Bending Strength of Walls

壁の曲げ終局強度の算定は，次の方針で行う．
(1) 鉄筋の降伏強度およびコンクリート強度は，8.3.2「材料強度」に従う．
(2) 壁の曲げ耐力の計算に用いる軸力は壁の図心に作用すると仮定し，柱と同様に長期荷重時軸力に，水平荷重時の変動軸力分として，接続する梁の曲げ終局強度時せん断力による付加軸力を加減した値を用いる．
(3) 地震方向に対して壁の長手方向が直交する独立壁および地震方向と壁の長手方向が一致するが壁せいがおよそ 900mm を下回る部材については，8.3.3.2 に従って曲げ終局強度を算出する．その他の鉛直部材については，壁の曲げ終局強度の計算式を用いて，曲げ終局強度を計算する（Figure 8.3-3）．

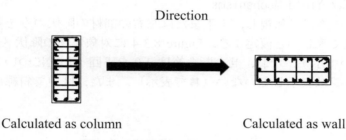

Figure 8.3-3 Walls and columns

壁の曲げ終局強度は，文献 8.3)に従って，次式により計算する．

$$M_u = \sum (a_t \cdot \sigma_y) l' + 0.5 \sum (a_w \cdot \sigma_{wy}) l' + 0.5 N \cdot l'$$

ここで，
Σa_t： 引張鉄筋の断面積（mm²）で，降伏曲げモーメントに有効な直交壁内の縦補強筋を含む．
ここで，降伏曲げモーメントに有効な直交壁の範囲は，片側につき直交壁厚さの 6 倍，または隣り合う耐力壁までの内法スパン長さの 1/4 および開口部端部までの長さのうち最小の数値とする．
σ_y： 同上鉄筋の規格降伏点（N/mm²）
l'： 両端に直交壁がある場合はその中心間距離．その他は耐力壁の長さ l の 0.9 倍の数（mm）
Σa_w： 耐力壁の中間部にある縦筋の断面積の和で，中間部に直交壁がある場合は，降伏曲げモーメントに有効な範囲内の直交壁内の縦補強筋を含む．
σ_{wy}： 同上鉄筋の規格降伏点（N/mm²）
N： 耐力壁に作用する軸力（N）

Ultimate bending strength of walls were calculated with the following conditions.
(1) The strengths shown in the section 8.4.2 were applied for strengths of steel and concrete.
(2) Axial force was assumed to be acted at the center of the section. The varied axial force due to lateral force, which was calculated from the flexural strength of beams, was taken into account.
(3) The ultimate bending strength of the walls of which depth is less than 900mm was calculated as column. (Figure 8.3-3).

The ultimate bending strength of walls was calculated with the function in the AIJ guidelines for wall type structures.

$$M_u = \sum(a_t \cdot \sigma_t)l' + 0.5\sum(a_w \cdot \sigma_{wy})l' + 0.5N \cdot l'$$

Where;
- Σa_t: Total area of tensile bars, which includes bars in the effective area of the transverse walls, where the area in the minimum width of the six times of the wall thickness, 1/4 of the transverse span length, and the distance to the opening.
- σ_y: Yield strength of the tensile bars (N/mm^2)
- l': The distance between the center of the transverse walls at both ends. If there is no transverse wall, 0.9 of the wall length (mm).
- Σa_w: Total area of the vertical bars
- σ_{wy}: Yield strength of the vertical bars (N/mm^2)
- N: Axial force (N)

8.3.4 降伏メカニズム/ Yield Mechanisms

3ヒンジ状態の部材の降伏は無視し，上下または左右の部材の降伏のみを考慮し，建物全体の塑性ヒンジ回転角は全て等しいと仮定する．Figure 8.3-4 に対象建物の降伏メカニズムを1-1構面～10-10構面について示す．なお，せん断余裕度1.0を下回った梁については，仕事をしないものと仮定して，ヒンジは表示していない（✖で表示）．また，図中で斜線部は壁であることを示している．

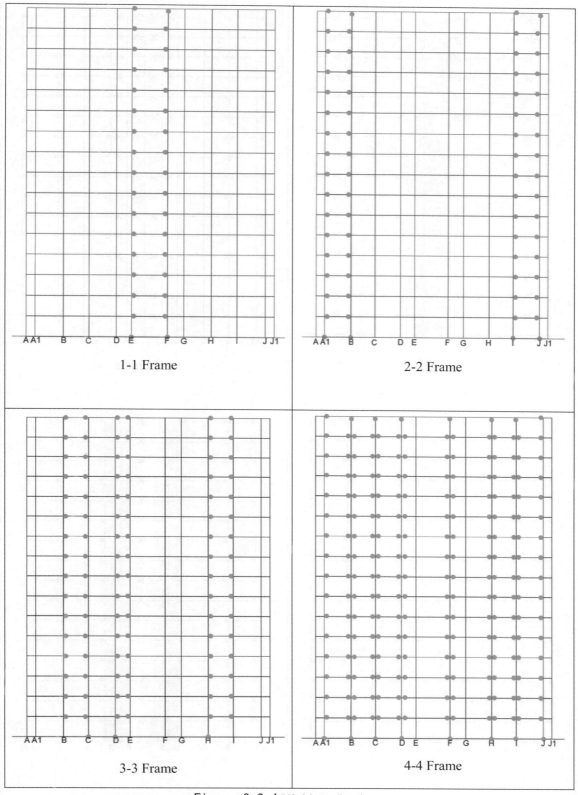

Figure 8.3-4 Yield mechanisms

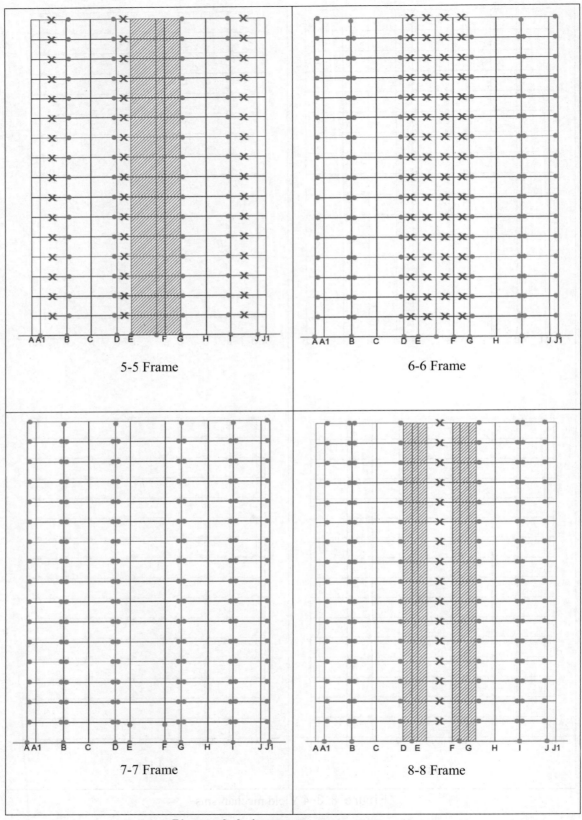

Figure 8.3-4 Yield mechanisms (Contd.)

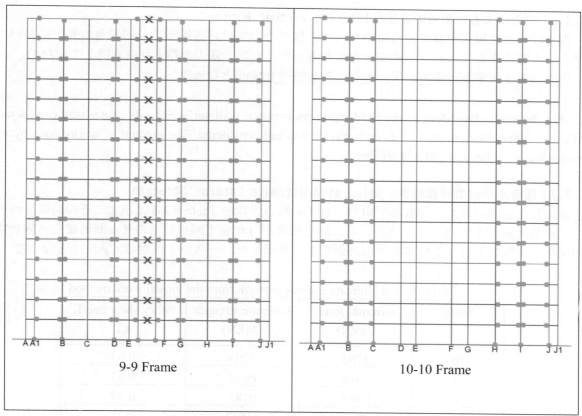

Figure 8.3-4 Yield mechanisms (Contd.)

If more than two yield hinges formed, the third hinge was ignored. Yield hinge rotational angle was assumed to be the same for all hinges. The yield mechanisms of the frame 1-1 to 10-10 are shown in Figure 8.3.4-1. The yield hinges of the beams of which shear margin was calculated less than 1.0 were ignored and shown as ✖ in the figure. Hatched area shows wall.

8.3.5 外力による仕事量の算定/ Virtual Work Due to External Force

外力は Ai 分布に従うとして，外力が行う仕事量を Table 8.3-7 に従って計算した結果，合計 4,718,640 $p \cdot \theta$ (kN·m) となった．ここで，p は基準荷重(kN)，θ はヒンジの回転角である．

Table 8.3-7 Conditions for external work

Floor area (m²)	8.4.5
W (per 1 floor) (kN)	10025
W_r (roof top) (kN)	5013
ΣW (kN)	155388
h (m)	44.7
T (s)	1.04

External lateral force distribution shape was calculated according to the demand story shear distribution shape of Ai that is defined in the Japanese Building Code. The amount of works due to external force was calculated as 4,718,640·$p·\theta$ (kN·m) with the condition shown in Table 8.3-7, where p; unit force and θ; rotational angle of the hinges.

8.3.6 内力による仕事量の算定/ Interior Virtual Work

内力による仕事量を算定するにあたって，壁については，塑性ヒンジ回転角の算出において，図心から壁表面までの長さを剛域として考慮した．なお，基礎の浮上りは考慮していない．

内力による仕事量の算定結果，合計 794891·θ (kN·m)となった．

For the walls, the effect of the rigid members between wall surfaces to its center was considered to calculate hinge rotation angle. Lift-up behavior was not considered. The amount of works done by yield hinges was calculated as 794,891·θ (kN·m).

8.3.7 保有水平耐力計算結果/ Calculated Ultimate Lateral Strength

算出した各階の外力，保有水平耐力，層せん断力係数を Table 8.3-8 に示す．その結果，ベースシア係数 C_B=0.17 となった．また，せん断余裕度が 1.0 を下回った梁のせん断破壊を考慮せず，曲げ終局強度に見合った仕事をすると仮定して算出したベースシア係数は C_B=0.23 となった．

Table 8.3-8 Ultimate Lateral strength from the virtual work method

Story	External force P_i(kN)	Ultimate strength Q_i(kN)	Story shear coeff. C_i
16	3203	3203	0.64
15	3315	6518	0.43
14	2664	9182	0.37
13	2331	11513	0.33
12	2089	13603	0.30
11	1890	15493	0.28
10	1714	17207	0.26
9	1554	18761	0.25
8	1403	20163	0.24
7	1259	21422	0.22
6	1120	22542	0.21
5	985	23527	0.20
4	854	24381	0.19
3	725	25106	0.19
2	598	25704	0.18
1	473	26176	0.17

The calculated external forces, ultimate strengths, and story shear coefficients are shown in Table 8.3-8. The base-shear coefficient was calculated as 0.17. The base-shear coefficient without considering the shear failure of beams was 0.23.

8.3.8 まとめ/ Summaries

本建物では，被害調査でいくつかの梁でせん断破壊が確認された．それらの梁の曲げ耐力，せん断耐力の計算耐力を比較すると，いずれもせん断余裕度 1.0 を下回った．せん断余裕度 1.0 を下回る梁は仕事をしないと仮定して内力の仕事量を算出し，外力は Ai 分布に従うとして，仮想仕事法によりベースシア係数 C_B を算出した結果，C_B=0.17 となった．せん断余裕度が 1.0 を下回る梁のせん断破壊を考慮せず，終局曲げ強度分の仕事をすると仮定して計算した場合は，ベースシア係数 C_B=0.23 となった．

The calculated shear margin of the beams, where shear failure was observed, was less than 1.0. The base shear coefficient of the building was calculated with the virtual work method as 0.17. If the shear failure was ignored, the base shear coefficient was calculated as 0.23.

8.4 参考文献/ References

8-1) 壁谷澤寿海，小谷俊介，青山博之：耐震壁を有する鉄筋コンクリート構造物の非線形地震応答解析，コンクリート工学年次講演会講演論文集，pp.213-216，1983

8-2) 株式会社構造システム：SNAP ver.6 テクニカルマニュアル，2012.2

8-3) 日本建築学会：鉄筋コンクリート構造計算基準・同解説，1999

8-4) T. Takeda, M. A. Sozen, N. N. Nielsen: Reinforced Concrete Response to Simulated Earthquakes, Journal of the Structural Division Proceedings of the American Society of Civil Engineers, 1970.12

8-5) 真田靖士，タンジュン ジャフリル，崔琥：途上国建築に普及した非構造レンガ壁の耐震性能の実験的評価 －2007 年スマトラ島南部沖地震による実被害建築を対象として－，住宅総合研究財団研究論文集 No.36, pp.329-338, 2009

8-1) Toshimi Kabeyasawa, Shunsuke Otani, Hiroyuki Aoyama: Nonlinear Dynamic Analyses of R/C Wall-Frame Structures, Proceedings of the Japan Concrete Institute, pp.213-216, 1983 (in Japanese)

8-2) Kozo system Ltd.: SNAP ver.6 Technical Manual, 2012.2

8-3) Architectural Institute of Japan: Standard for structural calculation of reinforced concrete structures, 1999 (in Japanese).

8-4) T. Takeda, M. A. Sozen, N. N. Nielsen: Reinforced Concrete Response to Simulated Earthquakes, Journal of the Structural Division Proceedings of the American Society of Civil Engineers, 1970.12

8-5) Yasushi Sanada, Jafril Tanjung, Ho Choi: "EXPERIMENTAL EVALUATION OF THE SEISMIC PERFORMANCE OF NONSTRUCTURAL BRICK WALLS USED IN DEVELOPING COUNTRIES - Findings from Damaged Buildings Due to the 2007 Sumatra, Indonesia Earthquakes -", Journal of Housing Research Foundation, No.36, pp.329-338, 2009 (in Japanese)

9 まとめ/ Concluding Remarks

本調査で得られた結論を以下に示す．

The concluding remarks obtained through the reconnaissance are listed below;

【2 地震の概要/ Outline of the Earthquake】
- 本震における，岩盤上の観測点で得られた強震記録の最大加速度は，既往の経験的な距離減衰式に比べて非常に小さい．
- 本震における，堆積層上の観測点で得られた強震記録の加速度応答値は，過去に観測された強震記録のそれと比較して，1~2秒では小さいが，3~5秒では非常に大きい．
- 最大余震では，1~2秒の加速度応答値において，本震時と同程度の値を記録した地点もあり，場所によっては被害が拡大した可能性もある．

- The largest peak ground acceleration recorded at the rock site KTP was very low.
- The acceleration responses of time period 1 to 2s were low but were very high in 3 to 5s.
- The intensity of the largest aftershock was same level as mainshock at one sedimentary site. The largest aftershock might have effect on building damage.

【3 地形・地質/ Characteristics of Surface Layers】
- 既往の文献と今回の調査で得られた地盤調査資料によると，カトマンズ盆地内の表層地盤について，地層が深くなるほど，シルト質が支配的になり，そのN値は平均で10~20程度となっている．また，GL-30mまでにN値50以上の堅固な地盤がほとんど確認できず，表層地盤は厚い．

- The characteristics of the surface layer of the Kathmandu basin is described in this investigation by referring to the previous reports. The major findings obtained from this study are summarized as follows; the silty strata become dominant with increasing deeper and SPT N value of silty stratum are about 10-20 according to borehole data in the Kathmandu basin, the surface layer is thick and the N value of more than 50 of the stratum is observed hardly.

【4 基礎構造/ Foundation of Buildings in Nepal】
- 近年建設数が増加している中高層集合住宅の基礎形式には，直接基礎とパイルド・ラフト基礎の事例が見られた．
- 地震後の中高層集合住宅を目視踏査した結果，基礎周りの埋土の沈下がしばしば見られた．また，人工地盤が設けられている例が多く見られたが，その中には，人工地盤の梁に長期荷重によると思われるひび割れや，地下外壁のひび割れによる地下水の漏水が見られた．

- High- and midium-rise buildings which was built in recent years have spread and piled raft foundations.
- The settlement of backfill soil around the foundations is often observed, the most high-rise buildings in Nepal have the artificial ground and the crack was observed near the middle of the beam caused by the vertical load, and the shear cracks and groundwater leakage in the basement wall were observed.

【5 建物の被害/ Building Damage】

- カトマンズ市北西に位置するGongabu地区において，鉄筋コンクリート造建物（全961棟）ではその約15%に，組積造建物（全323棟）では，その約25%に被害が生じていた．
- Gongabu地区の環状道路（リングロード）南側の地域において，鉄筋コンクリート造建物の被害率が突出して高く，組積造の被害率が低い結果となった．その他の地域では組積造の被害率が高かった．
- 鉄筋コンクリート造建物は階数が4階以上の中層の建物ほど被害率が高く，増築により上層の重量が増加したことが被害の原因の1つとして推察される．
- 詳細調査した建物1棟（鉄筋コンクリート造，6階建て）について，被災度区分判定を行った結果，桁行方向の耐震性能残存率は両方向ともに大破と判定され，被害状況と一致した．また，レンガ壁を無視して推定したベースシア係数は桁行方向で0.29，梁間方向で0.25であった．
- 全半壊した組積造の学校建物の壁率は2%から27%であり，なかでも10%程度のものが多かった．
- 層崩壊が生じた鉄筋コンクリート造3階建て校舎のベースシア係数は，桁行方向で0.21，梁間方向で0.22であった．隣接する崩壊した組積造3階建て校舎の壁に生じた最大せん断応力度を推定すると，$0.08N/mm^2$であった．
- 学校校舎および学校周辺建物の被災度の判定結果より，組積構造が鉄筋コンクリート造よりも総じて被害率は高いが，鉄筋コンクリート造についても少なからず全壊した建物が見られた．
- 鉄筋コンクリート造中高層建物（地上10～18階程度）の外壁や間仕切壁にはレンガ壁が用いられており，それらは構造要素としては考慮されていない．
- 一部の建物において，梁の曲げ・せん断による損傷，圧縮柱の損傷，コア壁のせん断による損傷，柱梁接合部の損傷が見られたが，それらを除けば，構造体の損傷は軽微であった．
- レンガ壁（外壁および内壁）の被害は大きく，調査した全ての鉄筋コンクリート造中高層建物でせん断破壊・ひび割れが見られ，一部崩落も見られた．落下したレンガにより死傷者が出ている．
- 構造被害が多く見られた鉄筋コンクリート造中高層建物の被災度区分判定を実施した結果，軽微や小破と判定された．軽微と判定された1棟について非線形荷重増分解析を行った結果，耐力はベースシア係数で約0.3程度であった．

- Number of damaged reinforced concrete buildings (961 buildings) and masonry buildings (323 buildings) in Gongabu area, which is in the northwestern part of Kathmandu, reached to about 15 % and 25 % of all buildings, respectively.
- Damage ratio of reinforced concrete buildings in the south part of Gongabu area was higher than that of masonry buildings but vice versa in other area.
- Damage ratio of reinforced concrete buildings which number of stories is larger than four was high, which was assumed to be due to increasing of weight of extended higher stories.
- Post-Earthquake Damage Evaluation was carried out for a six-story reinforced concrete building and the results, severe damage in both directions, agreed with observed damage. Assumed base shear coefficient without considering brick walls became to be 0.29 and 0.25 in the longitudinal and transverse directions, respectively.
- Wall ratios of completely and partially collapsed masonry school buildings were 2% to 27%, and most of the wall ratio were approximately 10%.

- Base shear coefficients of a three-story RC building with soft first story collapse were 0.21 and 0.22 in the longitudinal and transverse directions, respectively. And the maximum shear stress estimated for an adjacent collapsed three-story masonry building was 0.08 N/mm^2.
- Damage ratio of masonry school buildings was higher than that of reinforced concrete school buildings; however, collapsed reinforced concrete buildings were also observed.
- Brick masonry walls are used for partition walls and external walls, which are not considered as structural elements in reinforced concrete middle- to high-rise buildings, which have 10 to 18 stories.
- Generally, structure itself did not suffer severe damage, while a limited numbers of buildings suffered flexural and/or shear damages in beams, damages in the columns, shear damages in core walls, and damages in beam-column joints.
- Brick masonry walls suffered severe damages. That damage was very common and observed in most of all reinforced concrete middle- to high-rise buildings. Some walls fell down and killed passengers.
- The Japanese damage classification method was applied for reinforced concrete middle- to high-rise buildings and the buildings were classified as slight damage or minor damage. Base shear coefficient obtained by 3D non-linear dynamic response analysis of slightly damaged buildings was about 0.3.

【6 歴史都市の被害状況/ Damage to Historical Cities】

- 世界文化遺産のカトマンズ王宮広場，パタン王宮広場の歴史的建物の被害は深刻で（それぞれ全半壊率43%，25%），とくにNewar-Tower構造で顕著であった．周辺地盤における常時微動計測では，1Hz以下の周期帯のH/Vスペクトル比が卓越していた．
- 世界文化遺産のBhaktapur Durbar Square, Swayambhunath Templeの歴史的建物の被害も顕著であり，組積構造の被害が相対的に大きかった．Swayambhunath Templeの周辺地盤における常時微動計測で得られたH/Vスペクトル比の卓越周波数は3.6Hzであった．
- 世界文化遺産のBoudhanath Stupa, Pashupatinath Hindu Templeの歴史的建物の被害は総じて小さかった．
- 世界文化遺産のカトマンズおよびパタン歴史的市街地においては，数々の文化遺産建造物が倒壊した核となる王宮広場（カトマンズ王宮広場：全半壊率は43%でNewar-Tower構造の建物の全半壊率は52%，パタン王宮広場：全半壊25%ですべてNewar-Tower構造）と比較すれば，これを取り巻く伝統的住居建築に関する倒壊被害は少なかった（調査したパタン地区内のジャタプル住居地区の全壊建物はゼロ）．
- バクタプール王宮広場では，組積造の建物の全半壊率は83%であり，被害は深刻であった．周辺の伝統的住居群の被害も甚大であったが，同時代の歴史的地域であっても被害特性が大きく異なっていた．

- Historic buildings in the world heritage site, Kathmandu Durbar Square and Patan Durbar Square, were severely damaged: 43% and 25% of buildings, respectively. Especially, damage of Newar-Tower structure was remarkable. Dominant frequency in the near filed assumed by H/V spectral ratio with microtremor measurement was equal to or less than 1Hz.
- Masonry historic buildings in the world heritage site, Bhaktapur Durbar Square, Swayambhunath Temple, were severely damaged. Dominant frequency assumed by H/V spectral ratio measured in the near filed of Swayambhunath Temple was 3.6Hz.
- Historic buildings in the world heritage site of Boudhanath Stupa and Pashupatinath Hindu Temple were relatively small.
- Damage of historic residential houses in Kathumandu and the old city of Patan was smaller than historic buildings in Kathumandu Durbar Square and Patan Durbar Square.

- Eighty-three percentage of masonry buildings in Bhaktapur Durbar Square was totally or partially collapsed, and damage of surrounding historic residential houses were remarkable but the damage characteristics were different with their construction quality and maintenance.

【7 人的被害/ Human Damage】
- 郡別被害統計によれば，家屋全壊率は山岳地帯のラスワ（Rasuwa）郡から ヌワコット（Nuwakot）郡，シンドパルチョーク（Sindhupalchok）郡，ドラカ（Dolakha）郡まで東西 150km 以上にわたって 50%を超え，激甚な被害となった．カトマンズ盆地内 3 市の被害統計によれば，被害が集中している区が，カトマンズ市の場合は北西部と北東部，バクタプール市の場合，南東部に多く見られた．
- 死者数は 8,700 人を越え，北部山岳地帯の Sindhupalchok 郡と Rasuwa 郡の東西 100km で死亡率 1%を越え，同じく山岳地帯の Nuwakot 郡も死亡率が高い．カトマンズ盆地のバクタプール郡，カトマンズ郡，ラリトプール郡で死亡率は 0.12%未満となっている．ラリトプール市の人的被害が他の 2 都市と比べると全体的に少ない．ネパール人口住宅統計調査では，泥モルタル壁の割合の高い地域で死亡率が高い傾向が見られた．
- 死者数最大の Sindhupalchok 郡では，市町村別死亡率を GIS に示すと北西部の町村で高く，人口住宅統計でセメントモルタルの組積造割合が低い地域と重なる．
- 死者数は乳幼児から 9 歳までの子ども，70 歳以上の高齢者に多く，死亡率も高齢者が著しく高い．男女合わせた平均死亡率に対して 0〜4 歳は 2.1 倍，70〜74 歳は 4.2 倍，75 歳以上は 5.9 倍の死亡率になっている．また，多くの郡で女性の方が男性より死者数が多い傾向にあり，土曜正午前の在宅率の影響が考えられる．
- カトマンズ盆地におけるカトマンズ・バクタプール・ラリトプールの 3 市について，自治体から区別の被害統計データの提供を受け，家屋全壊数と全壊率，死者数と死亡率，家屋の重大被害 100 棟あたりの死者数を地図に示した．3 つの市ではバクタプールの全壊率，死亡率が共に高い．この 3 都市では，人口に対する死者の割合がいずれの区でも 1%以下であり，バクタプール以外の 2 都市の多くの区は 0.1%以下であった．

- According to the district damage statistics, rates of heavily damaged houses exceeded 50% spreading 150km EW in Rasuwa, Nuwakot, and Sindhupalchok mountain districts along the earthquake fault zone. According to the damage statistics of the three cities in Kathmandu Valley, higher housing damages were observed in northwest and northeast of Kathmandu city, and southeast of Bhaktapur city.
- Total number of human loss in Nepal exceeded 8,700 and human loss rates exceeded 1% spreading 100km EW in Sindhupalchok and Rasuwa districts in northern mountain region. It was also high in mountainous Nuwakot district. Human loss rates are less than 0.12% in Bhaktapur, Kathmandu and Lalitpur districts in Kathmandu Valley. Human loss in Lalitpur city was less than those in the other two cities. Human loss rates tended to be higher in the districts with higher percentage of mud mortar wall in the Nepal population and housing census.
- In the most heavily devastated Sindhupalchok district, human loss rates were higher in the north western towns and villages than eastern areas, corresponding to the lower percentage of houses with cement bonded brick or stone wall materials in the Nepal population and housing census.
- As for age distribution of human casualties, number of human loss was higher for infants and children under 9 years old and elderly over 70 years old. Human loss rate for infants (0-4 years old) was 2.1 times higher, that for elderly (70-74 year old) was 4.2 times, that for elderly over 75 year old was 5.9 times more than the average. In most districts, number of human loss was higher for females than for

males, suggesting that female population were more located at home at the time of the earthquake before noon on Saturday, Nepali holiday and were hit by the collapsed houses.
- In the Kathmandu valley, ward-wise damage statistics data were collected from 3 municipalities of Kathmandu, Bhaktapur, and Lalitpur. Damage distribution maps are indicated for the rates of heavily damaged houses, rates of human loss, ratio of human loss per 100 heavily damaged houses in 3 cities. Human loss percentageas are less than 1%, and most of wards in Kthmandu and Lalitpur cities have less thna 0.1 % ratio of casualties.

【8 詳細調査建物の解析/ Numerical Analysis】

- 詳細調査を行った建物の地震応答解析を行った．その結果，レンガ壁が建物の耐震性能に大きく寄与していることがわかった．
- 本建物では，被害調査でいくつかの梁でせん断破壊が確認された．それらの梁の曲げ耐力，せん断耐力の計算耐力を比較すると，いずれもせん断余裕度 1.0 を下回った．せん断余裕度 1.0 を下回る梁は仕事をしないと仮定して内力の仕事量を算出し，外力は Ai 分布に従うとして仮想仕事法によりベースシア係数 C_B を算出した結果，C_B=0.17 となった．せん断余裕度が 1.0 を下回る梁のせん断破壊を考慮せず，終局曲げ強度分の仕事をすると仮定して計算した場合は，ベースシア係数 C_B=0.23 となった．

- The nonlinear time history analysis of building that investigated the damage was carried out. As a result, the masonry wall contributes to the seismic performance of buildings.
- The calculated shear margin of the beams, where shear failure was observed, was less than 1.0. The base shear coefficient of the building was calculated with the virtual work method as 0.17. If the shear failure was ignored, the base shear coefficient was calculated as 0.23.

10 教訓/ Lessons

本調査から導かれた教訓を以下に示す．

- 構造物によっては非常に深刻な影響を及ぼす3～5秒の長周期成分が卓越する強震記録も含まれ，日本の耐震設計の高度化の観点からもその成分の生成要因の解明が必要である．
- カトマンズ市内に建てられる中層鉄筋コンクリート造建物において，増築が被害を増大させた要因の1つに考えられることから，何らかの対策が望まれる．
- 建物が隣接して建てられている地域においては，大破した建物に隣接する建物が被災する例が見られ，隣接する建物の建築方法を改善するなどの対策が必要である．
- カトマンズ市外にある被害が大きかった鉄筋コンクリート造建物では，補強鉄筋の不足や不十分な定着などの配筋に起因すると判断される被害事例も見られたため，新築建築に対しては設計，施工に関わるより適切な管理が，既存建築に対しては耐震診断，耐震補強により同様の被害を繰り返さない努力が必要である．
- 組積構造では建物の全半壊などの大きな被害が，組積造壁の面外方向への転倒に起因した被害事例が数多く観察された．面外方向の地震力に対する脆弱性の克服は喫緊の課題である．
- 本調査では調査期間の制限から壁率を評価できた校舎の数が限られたが，引き続きのデータ収集により壁率と被害率の関係を整理することで，将来の地震に対して脆弱（あるいは安全）な建物の合理的な判定に寄与できる．
- 地域ごとの気象条件による要求性能の違い，材料や施工技術の入手しやすさ等により用いられる構造形式は異なっており，被災地の中でも特に運搬が制限される山間部では，現地で入手できる石や日干しレンガが用いられており，熟練した施工技術を得ることの難しさがある．
- 外壁を構成する非構造レンガ壁の落下防止策は，緊急の課題である．
- 高層集合住宅では，非構造レンガ壁の損傷により，住宅としての機能が失われており，ネパールで施工可能な補修・補強方法の提案が必要である．
- レンガ壁は耐震壁に比べて小さな変形量で被害が大きくなる．
- 世界文化遺産の歴史的建物の被害傾向は，地域により異なる傾向が得られた．地盤（地震動）の卓越周期と建物の振動特性の関係について，より詳細な分析が望まれる．とくに被害を受けた建物と免れた建物の本質的な違いについて，慎重に分析する必要がある．
- とくに被害が大きかったNewar-Tower構造と組積構造の歴史的建物については，再建に際して，構造的に特別な配慮を行わないと（例えば，強度補強による短周期化や免震補強による長周期化など），将来の地震により同様の被害を繰り返すおそれを指摘できる．
- 倒壊しなかった伝統的な住居建築群についても，ひび割れが入ったり，全体が傾斜するなど，余震等でさらに被害が拡大する可能性を伴う深刻な状況にあった．復興に向けて文化的価値を維持しつつ将来の安全が確保できるレベルにまで，すべての伝統的住居群の補修を行うためには，多くの時間と費用を要することが懸念される．
- 伝統的で文化的なコミュニティ活動の核となってきた歴史ある広場空間（コートヤード）と水場空間（ヒッティや井戸）とが，震災時にもコミュニティの安全と生活を支える重要な要素として機能し続けていることが確認され，これら歴史的要素を保全することは災害安全にも通じることが明らかとなった．
- 地震発生の以前からメンテナンスが行き届いている場合は，古い建物であっても被害が少ない例が多い．文化財関係者によれば，それにもかかわらず風評被害によって歴史ある建物が見捨てられる社会的な傾向も生じているとのことであり，歴史的地域の復興のためには慎重な対応が求められる．
- 地震発生が夜間であれば，被災地の市町村で死者数がさらに増大したおそれがあり，組積造住宅の泥モルタルからセメントモルタルへの転換など，Build Back Betterの復興が重要である．

- 地震発生が夜間であれば，被災地の市町村で死者数がさらに増大したおそれがあり，組積造住宅の泥モルタルからセメントモルタルへの転換など，Build Back Better の復興が重要である．
- 非補強のレンガやアドベの組積造住宅において，妻壁の上部から破壊し，屋根や上階部分が崩壊していく被害パターンが多いこと，ネパールの住宅では上の階に台所や食事スペースを配置する間取りが多いことが，女性の死者割合の高さに影響した可能性があり，今後の調査研究が望まれる．

The lessons learnt from the reconnaissance are listed below;
- The strong ground motions including high responses of 3-5 s are very serious for high rise or base isolated buildings. It will be important to know the cause of these characteristics for consideration of construction requirement in Japan.
- Improvement of structural design considering extension of stories is required because the cause of damage of medium rise reinforced concrete buildings in Kathmandu was assumed to be due to increase of weight with added stories.
- In the area where buildings laying side-by-side, building lie adjacent to severely damaged building was damaged, which damage should be avoided by improving construction method.
- Since severely damaged reinforced concrete buildings outside of Kathmandu due to lack of reinforcements and poor anchorage were observed, adequate construction management for new buildings is needed to prevent similar damage along with seismic screening method and retrofitting for existing buildings.
- Since totally and partially collapse of masonry buildings due to out-of-plane deformation were observed, it is urgent issue to strengthen masonry walls in the out of direction.
- In this study, investigated wall ratio was limited but to collect and discuss relationship between wall ratio and damage is important to be able to give rational decision for seismic screening of buildings against future earthquake.
- Structural system was different with area in accordance with weather, required performance, available materials and technique. In the mountain area where transfer was limited, stone and adobe were used for construction, which made difficulty to acquire expert technique for construction.
- It is the urgent and critical issue to prevent damage and falling down of non-structural brick walls.
- Especially for high-rise apartment buildings, the rooms were not able to be used continuously due to the damage of brick walls. A retrofitting technique for Nepalese brick walls is required.
- It was observed that brick walls were severely damaged with smaller deformation than RC shear walls.
- Damage of historic buildings in the world heritage site was different with area, therefore more detailed investigation for relationship between dominant frequency of ground and characteristics of vibration of buildings are required. Especially, essential difference between damaged and non-damaged buildings is needed to be investigated carefully.
- Special consideration, e.g. shortening of fundamental period by strengthening of buildings and extending of fundamental period with base isolating, for reconstruction of historic buildings with Newar-Tower structure and masonry structure which suffered heavy damage is needed to prevent similar damage in future earthquake.
- Cracks and inclination on survived traditional residential houses were observed and which might be increased with aftershocks. More time and cost are required to repair all the traditional residential houses so that their seismic performances are upgraded to assure safety in future with keeping their cultural value.

- It was observed that historic courtyard and water place as the important core elements for traditional community activities were also utilized as important resources for saving peoples' life even after the disaster.
- There were less damaged old and historic buildings because of adequate maintenance regardless that all the historic buildings had vulnerabilities. But some heritage managers said that most of people believed the wrong information that old buildings were dangerous and only new buildings could survive because of careless journalism, hence carefully treatment is needed for reconstruction of historic area.
- If the earthquake should have occurred during night time when most people were at home, number of human loss might have increased more in many cities, towns and villages affected. It is very important to promote build back better policies for reconstruction using cement mortar for brick or stone masonry houses in Nepal.
- In Nepal, brick masonry houses tend to be destroyed from top part of end walls and roofs, while kitchens and living rooms are often located on top floors. Those conditions may have affected higher female fatalities, so that further study is important to clarify such causes and to reduce human casualties.

2015年ネパール・ゴルカ地震災害調査報告書
Reconnaissance Report on the 2015 Nepal Gorkha Earthquake

2016年12月15日　第1版第1刷

編　集　著作人　一般社団法人　日本建築学会
印　刷　所　昭和情報プロセス株式会社
発　行　所　一般社団法人　日本建築学会
　　　　　108-8414　東京都港区芝 5-26-20
　　　　　電　話・(03) 3456-2051
　　　　　Ｆ Ａ Ｘ・(03) 3456-2058
　　　　　http://www.aij.or.jp/

発　売　所　丸善出版株式会社
　　　　　101-0051　東京都千代田区神田神保町 2-17
　　　　　神田神保町ビル
　　　　　電　話・(03) 3512-3256

© 日本建築学会 2016

ISBN978-4-8189-2049-1　C3052